Drawing the Line on Natural Gas Regulation

Recent Titles from Quorum Books

Marketing and the Quality-of-Life Interface
A. Coskun Samli, editor

Energy Resources Development: Politics and Policies
Richard L. Ender and John Choon Kim, editors

International Law of Take-Overs and Mergers: Southern Europe, Africa, and the Middle East
H. Leigh Ffrench

Law, Policy, and Optimizing Analysis
Stuart S. Nagel

Six Roundtable Discussions of Corporate Finance with Joel Stern
Donald H. Chew, Jr., editor

Trading Energy Futures: A Manual for Energy Industry Professionals
Stewart L. Brown and Steven Errera

Selecting and Installing Software Packages: New Methodology for Corporate Implementation
Jud Breslin

Creative Problem Solving: A Guide for Trainers and Management
Arthur B. VanGundy

The Business Systems Development Process: A Management Perspective
Roger E. Walters

Quantitative Models in Accounting: A Procedural Guide for Professionals
Ahmed Belkaoui

Frivolous Lawsuits and Frivolous Defenses: Unjustifiable Litigation
Warren Freedman

Successful Corporate Turnarounds: A Guide for Board Members, Financial Managers, Financial Institutions, and Other Creditors
Eugene F. Finkin

DRAWING THE LINE ON NATURAL GAS REGULATION

The Harvard Study on the Future of Natural Gas

EDITED BY
JOSEPH P. KALT
AND
FRANK C. SCHULLER

CONTRIBUTORS: COLIN C. BLAYDON
HARRY G. BROADMAN
GEORGE R. HALL
WILLIAM W. HOGAN
HENRY LEE
CARMEN D. LEGATO
JOHN C. SAWHILL

Prepared under the auspices of the Energy and Environmental Policy Center, Harvard University

Q QUORUM BOOKS
NEW YORK • WESTPORT, CONNECTICUT • LONDON

Library of Congress Cataloging-in-Publication Data

Drawing the line on natural gas regulation.

"Prepared under the auspices of the Energy and Environmental Policy Center, Harvard University."
Includes bibliographies and index.
1. Gas industry—Government policy—United States—Congresses. I. Kalt, Joseph P. II. Schuller, Frank C. III. Blaydon, Colin C. IV. John F. Kennedy School of Government. Energy and Environmental Policy Center.
HD9581.U5D73 1987 338.2'7285'0973 86-25769
ISBN 0-89930-174-6 (lib. bdg. : alk. paper)

Library of Congress Catalog Card Number: 86-25769
ISBN: 0-89930-174-6

First published in 1987 by Quorum Books

Greenwood Press, Inc.
88 Post Road West, Westport, Connecticut 06881

Printed in the United States of America

The paper used in this book complies with the Permanent Paper Standard issued by the National Information Standards Organization (Z39.48-1984).

10 9 8 7 6 5 4 3 2 1

Contents

Figures and Tables

Figures

Tables

Preface

The Harvard Study on the Future of Natural Gas Policy reflects the ideas, discussions, and debates of nine authors and more than seventy experts from business, government, and academia. These study participants constituted the Executive Working Group, which met in three sessions during 1984–1985. The executive sessions provided forums for the authors to present versions of their chapters at progressive stages of development. The results were invaluable insights and perspectives from parties directly involved in the ongoing debates over the reform of natural gas policy. In addition, a number of participants have contributed written comments on the various chapters of this book. The participation of all members of the Executive Working Group is sincerely appreciated. Their names and affiliations follow this preface.

The desire to involve so many individuals in this study has meant unusual demands for organizational support. We particularly would like to express our gratitude to those organizations whose financial contributions underwrote the study:

Brooklyn Union Gas Company

Energy and Environmental Policy Center, Harvard University

Entex, Inc.

Northern Natural Gas Company

Ontario Ministry of Energy

Pacific Gas and Electric Company

Shell Oil Company

Southern California Gas Company

U.S. Department of Energy

Additionally, the Energy and Environmental Policy Center at Harvard University provided institutional support as well as meeting and research facilities.

Numerous individuals have made special contributions to this study and deserve our recognition and gratitude. Beyond their participation in the executive sessions, Joshua Bar-Lev, Robert B. Catell, Richard Landers, Thomas J. Lee, Charles Matthews, and Richard Nelson provided continuous advice on and discussion of the substance of the study.

Marcia Duvall was the organizational heart of this project. We deeply appreciate her kindness, enthusiasm, and cooperative spirit. Equally important were the editorial efforts, not to mention the tolerance, of Peter C. Heron. The staff of the Energy and Environmental Policy Center was also especially helpful, and we thank Joan Curhan, Maria Dellaripa, Ann Desmond, Laurie Doucette, Lynne Farnum, Nancy Kingston, and Barbara Westcott. The center's research assistants, too, made indispensable contributions of their time and effort: Richard Cooperstein, Anthony Hurtado, Peter Rossbach, and Jay Williams.

The chapter authors have relied on the help and advice of many other assistants and colleagues. Colin Blaydon wishes to thank Harry Broadman, Betty Mills, Audrey Brown, and Cathy Zoi. Harry Broadman has benefited from the comments of David Mead and Michael Toman. Marc Mozham and Jeffrey Petrash have provided capable research assistance to George Hall. William Hogan would like to acknowledge the assistance of Constance Burns. Joseph Kalt has been assisted by Joel Marcus, Eric Press, James Hamilton, and David Butler and has received especially helpful comments from Richard Caves. Henry Lee has benefited significantly from the comments of Douglas Haughey, Celeste Koeleveld, Bijan Mossaver-Rahmani, Linda Thomas, and Thomas Wander, as well as from Susan Bender and Stephen Pearlman, who provided him with research assistance. Carmen Legato greatly appreciates the comments of Joseph Swidler and the research assistance of Jeffrey Kehne. John C. Sawhill wishes to acknowledge the help of Michael Coda. Finally, Frank Schuller wishes to thank Robert Stobaugh for his continued support, Max Hall for his editorial advice, Muriel Drysdale for her valuable production assistance, and Katie and Clayton Schuller for their patience and understanding.

The views expressed in the chapters of this study reflect the opinions and findings of the individual authors. There is no implication that either the sponsors of the study or the participants in the Executive Working Group share these views. Any errors or omissions are solely the responsibility of the authors.

Participants

Catherine G. Abbott, Transwestern Pipeline Company

Jerry E. Akin, Northern Natural Gas Company

Scott Anderson, TIPRO

Manjit Bajwa, Northern Natural Gas Company

Joshua Bar-Lev, Pacific Gas and Electric Company

Arthur S. Berner, Inexco Oil Company

Colin C. Blaydon, The Amos Tuck School of Business Administration, Dartmouth College

John B. Boatwright, Exxon Company, U.S.A.

Harry G. Broadman, Department of Economics and Kennedy School of Government, Harvard University, and Resources for the Future

George Broussard, Panhandle Eastern Pipeline Company

Robert B. Catell, Brooklyn Union Gas Company

Dianne Caughey, Algonquin Gas Transmission Company

Michael Coda, McKinsey & Co.

Stephen J. Curran, Bay State Gas Company

William David Duran, U.S. Department of Energy

Charles Ellis, Bay State Gas Company

Charles Finnell, State Representative, Texas House of Representatives

John T. Fraser, Tennessee Gas Transmission Company

James R. Gattis, Shell Oil Company

Daniel E. Gibson, Pacific Gas and Electric Company

Ray G. Gibson, Jr., Carl H. Pforzheimer & Company

Julian M. Greene, Transcontinental Gas Pipe Line Corporation

Timothy Greening, First National Bank of Chicago

George R. Hall, Charles River Associates

David Harrison, Jr., Dun & Bradstreet Technical Economic Services

Gail Harrison, Wexler, Reynolds, Harrison & Schule

Thomas E. Hassen, Morgan Stanley and Company, Inc.

Donald C. Heppermann, Northern Natural Gas Company

William W. Hogan, Kennedy School of Government, Harvard University

Richard L. Hosto, Panhandle Eastern Pipeline Company

Frederick E. John, Southern California Gas Company

Wayne D. Johnson, Entex, Inc.

Robert Johnston, Arkansas Public Service Commission

Joseph P. Kalt, Department of Economics, Harvard University

Michael Kane, Bank of Boston

Stuart C. Kirk, ARCO Oil and Gas Company

Ronald Kitchens, Natural Gas Pipeline Company of America

Gary Kitts, Michigan Public Utilities Commission

Richard Landers, Venture Associates, Inc., Formerly of Southern California Gas Company

John A. Lauderdale, Jr., Houston Natural Gas Corporation, Enron Corporation

Henry Lee, Kennedy School of Government, Harvard University

Thomas J. Lee, Jr., Entex, Inc.

William L. Leffler, Shell Oil Company

Carmen D. Legato, Swidler & Berlin, Chtd.

Robert Loch, Southern California Gas Company

Vernell P. Ludwig, Texas Eastern Corporation

Cara McCue, Ontario Ministry of Energy

Thomas B. McDade, Texas Gas Transmission

Martin W. McGarry, Standard Oil Production Company

Matthew McLogan, Michigan Public Service Commission

Julian Martin, TIPRO

Craig G. Matthews, Brooklyn Union Gas Company

John Meyer, Kennedy School of Government, Harvard University

Stephen Minihan, U.S. Department of Energy

Richard D. Morel, Algonquin Gas Transmission Company

Bijan Mossavar-Rahmani, Kennedy School of Government, Harvard University

Richard Nelson, Shell Oil Company

James E. Nugent, Railroad Commission of Texas

Philip R. O'Connor, Palmer Bellevue Corporation, Formerly of the Illinois Commerce Commission, 1983–1985

John Donald Porter, The First Boston Corporation

Larry E. Powell, Southern Natural Gas Company

Joseph E. Ramsey, Tennessee Gas Transmission Company

Elliot D. Ranard, Combustion Engineering, Inc.

Oliver G. Richard III, Tenngasco Corporation

William L. Robey, Standard Oil Production Company

John M. Ryan, Exxon Corporation, U.S.A.

John C. Sawhill, McKinsey & Co.

Frank C. Schuller, Kennedy School of Government, Harvard University

Frank J. Setian, U.S. Natural Gas Clearinghouse

Thomas Sherman, Bay State Gas Company

Edward Sondey, Brooklyn Union Gas Company

Edson Spencer, Dyco Programs, Inc.

William B. Taylor, Office of Senator Bill Bradley, 1981–1985

Charles Teclaw, Federal Energy Regulatory Commission

Thomas Wander, Pacific Gas and Electric Company

Frank M. Weisser, Morgan Stanley and Company, Inc.

Nancy Williams, U.S. House of Representatives Energy Committee

Erving Wolf, Inexco Oil Company

Drawing the Line on Natural Gas Regulation

1

Introduction: Natural Gas Policy in Turmoil

JOSEPH P. KALT
AND FRANK C. SCHULLER

Regulation of natural gas markets in the United States historically has been memorable primarily for its poor performance. During the past half-century, natural gas markets have been the scene of acute shortages, prices perpetually out of step with market conditions, rancorous litigation, and intense political infighting. By the mid–1970s, as the so-called energy crisis drove the prices of all types of fuels to record heights, stiff federal price controls on natural gas sold in interstate markets artificially stimulated demand at the same time they discouraged supply. The results were what many feared the energy crises really meant—closed factories and cold homes.

The dramatic shortages of the 1970s provided the impetus for effecting fundamental change in the nation's natural gas policy. The country sensed that no market performs so poorly if left to its own devices; there must be improvements that could be made in the form and substance of natural gas industry regulation. In these perceptions lies an ongoing drive to overhaul and improve natural gas policy. Indeed, the nation is moving in the direction of a much more rational, responsive, and productive natural gas industry. The key to this development is an expansion of the realm of marketplace competition and a concomitant circumscription of the role of governmental regulation.

The Natural Gas Policy Act (NGPA) of 1978 was the first major step in reconstituting natural gas regulation. Its principal accomplishment was the gradual deregulation of producer ("wellhead") prices, which had been federally controlled for three decades. Adoption of the NGPA was motivated by the desire to avoid future natural gas shortages by allowing market prices to play a larger role in balancing supply and demand. Although this may appear to be an uncontestably positive, if not innocuous, direction for natural gas policy to take, the NGPA was passed only after protracted and contentious congressional debate.

Contemporaries may have viewed the result as the end of policy reform, but the NGPA proved to be only the beginning.

The NGPA slackened the regulatory leash on competition in the natural gas industry. For the first time in almost thirty years, interstate natural gas pipelines found themselves competing for producers' supplies primarily through price. Moreover, the presence of deregulated gas in the system meant that gas delivered by local distribution companies (LDCs) was priced at levels that reflected the prices of alternative fuels. Particularly since 1981, when worldwide energy prices began to soften, this end-market competition among natural gas and other fuels has dictated the economics of the gas industry.

Before this, the natural gas industry had become accustomed to perpetual excess demands. Available supplies virtually were guaranteed to find more than willing buyers, the concepts of aggressive marketing and strategic planning held little relevance, and pervasive regulation had ossified management and contracting practices into unchallenged routines. But the force of competition has shaken the legacy of balkanized traditions, practices, and precedents. The conduct of both business and regulation in natural gas markets now is being dramatically reshaped. An industry previously dominated by long-term, fixed-price, exclusive-dealing contracts is being forced to find pricing, contracting, marketing, and ownership arrangements that can respond quickly and economically to changing marketplace conditions.

The effects of change in natural gas markets extend beyond the industry to policymakers themselves. Regulators accustomed to worrying about the rationing of short supplies and policing the behavior of legally protected monopolies are now being charged with maintaining the position of natural gas in the overall fuels market and expanding the freedom and flexibility of market participants. The result is unprecedented turmoil in both natural gas policy and natural gas markets.

This volume represents an attempt to assess where the natural gas industry is going, how well it will perform, and what role government regulation can and should play. The work consists of the essays and comments produced by participants in the Harvard Study on the Future of Natural Gas Policy. The major components of this study were three conferences held during 1985–1986. They brought together a working group of business executives from various sectors of the natural gas industry, federal and state policymakers, and members of the academic community. The chapters that follow are intended to reflect the range of opinion, argument, and agreement expressed by the working group. In addition, selected participants have provided written commentaries on various chapters to provide further perspective on the diversity of views prevailing in current debates over the future of natural gas policy.

The economics and politics of natural gas policy are extremely complicated. Present conditions in the industry reflect the legacies of past regulation, the impacts of current policy measures, and developments in the volatile world energy market. Each of these potent factors periodically comes to the fore, dominates the price and supply performance of gas markets, and reshuffles the stakes that various interested industry participants have in natural gas policy. In addition, policy reform in the natural gas sector must remain cognizant of the fact that the industry is a *system*. A policy change at one end of the industry (e.g., wellhead decontrol) can affect the other stages of the industry in overt or subtle ways. In this context, assessing where the natural gas industry will or should go cannot not help but reflect each analyst's particular vantage point, experience, and expertise. The resulting diversity in analyses and recommendations is evident in this volume.

This study pulls several common themes from the variance of viewpoints on policy reform in the natural gas industry. These themes form the rudimentary premises for the nine chapters that follow.

1. *The key to improving the performance of the natural gas industry lies in increasing the flexibility and speed with which price and cost signals are transmitted up and down the supply chain.* ''Change'' is now the watchword of the world's energy markets, and the experience in the U.S. natural gas sector teaches that regulatory and market institutions that ignore this are nothing short of disastrous. If rising end-user demands, with their upward pressure on price, cannot be transmitted back up the natural gas supply chain, shortages arise. Conversely, if declining demands cannot be met with price reductions and volume cutbacks, surplusses and excessive cost burdens on captured customers are the result. Indeed, these shortage and surplus scenarios describe recent cycles in the nation's natural gas markets. Wellhead price ceilings produced shortages in the face of rising world oil prices, and long-term contracts have locked parties into excessively high-cost agreements in the current era of declining energy prices.

2. *The underlying structure and economics of pipeline transportation and local distribution of natural gas are such that an unregulated market would not be perfectly competitive.* This observation provides the principal justification, on economic grounds, for some form of public regulation in the natural gas sector. It implies that gas industry policy should be directed at and limited to offsetting the deleterious effects of elements of natural monopoly in pipelining and local gas distribution. As a corollary, it implies that there is no compelling defense for price ceilings on the production of gas.

Having noted the justification for and proper focus of governmental intervention into the natural gas industry, it is crucial to point out the distinction between regulation as a substitute for competition and regulation as protection from competition. At the natural gas wellhead, for example, a multitude of independent brokers, local distribution companies, and large end users potentially stand ready to compete for producers' supplies—provided that regulation is not used to protect this as the sole prerogative of pipelines. Similarly, competition from alternative fuels and the ability of large end users to arrange their own gas supplies potentially can provide some constraint upon the market power of LDCs in industrial gas sales. Under conditions such as these, the chief matter of public policy becomes the tradeoff between regulatory protection from monopolistic abuses, on the one hand, and excessive insulation from the discipline that unregulated competition brings to bear on prices, costs, and management practices, on the other hand. U.S. natural gas policy too often has tilted too far toward the latter. Hence:

3. *Policy reform in the natural gas industry should focus on delimiting the range of activities—including marketing, pricing, investment, and contracting—that is provided legal protection from competition.* As wellhead price regulation is phased out, the remaining core of natural gas regulation consists of legally granted monopolies (or at least oligopolies) in pipelining and local delivery. Defining the appropriate spheres and modes of operation for these entities and their potential competitors should be the principal task of regulatory reform in the natural gas sector. The authors of the chapters in this book generally share the view that the range over which regulation should direct and constrain competition in the gas industry should be reduced.

4. *Rising competition is fundamentally altering market institutions and familiar business practices in the natural gas industry.* This forces companies in the industry to reassess their corporate strategies, marketing techniques, pricing policies, and contracting practices. In all cases, premiums are placed on increasing flexibility and adaptability relative to the industry's balkanized past. The apparent ''chaos'' of fluctuating market shares, entry by new parties, and failures of established firms, institutions, and practices undoubtedly are threatening to some industry participants but are symptomatic of improvement in the operation of an industry that historically has failed to perform up to its potential.

Changes from Competition

The rise of competition in the natural gas industry has been exceptionally rapid. It began with the NGPA in 1978. In the face of the marked disparity between federal price ceilings that had been set before the energy-price shocks of the 1970s and the marketplace value of natural gas, the NGPA began to raise the overall level of gas prices. ''New'' natural gas fields brought into production after 1977, for example, were provided with eventual decontrol through a detailed schedule intended to bring ceiling prices up to market levels by 1985. Natural gas from ''deep'' wells was decontrolled even more rapidly. Prices of gas from fields developed before 1977 were provided with a partial adjustment toward market levels, although ''old'' gas was to remain permanently subject to price controls. Eventually, as old gas fields are exhausted, all gas would sell in an uncontrolled market.

The NGPA triumphed as a short-term success. Intended to eliminate recurring shortages of gas sold in interstate commerce and to stem the decline of supply reserves, the NGPA actually promoted a surplus of gas soon after its passage. This happened for two reasons.

First, the NGPA ended the distinction between gas sold to interstate and intrastate pipelines. Before the legislation, intrastate gas was not subject to federal price ceilings. As a result, intrastate pipelines began to dominate gas acquisitions by paying prices higher than the controlled wellhead prices that could be paid by interstate pipelines. The NGPA ended this imbalance by bringing intrastate and interstate gas under the same pricing rules.

Second, the NGPA's escalation of ''new'' gas prices was aimed at bringing parity with the oil prices that Congress, acting in 1978, expected to prevail by 1985. But parity with oil came much faster than anticipated. By 1980 world oil prices had begun to tumble. From 1980 to 1982 oil prices declined from about $40 to $25 a barrel. Meanwhile, beginning in 1978 the prices of controlled natural gas escalated monthly in accordance with the provisions of the NGPA, and some decontrolled categories of gas swiftly topped $10 per thousand cubic feet (Mcf). This translated into an oil-equivalent price of roughly $60 a barrel. Such ''above-market'' levels were reached as pipelines faced with declining reserve commitments competed heatedly for decontrolled gas. They could sustain above-market prices for uncontrolled gas as long as the ''rolled-in'' average price of gas delivered to their customers did not exceed parity with oil, that is, as long as extra-high prices of decontrolled gas could be offset with a cushion of low-priced, permanently controlled gas. By 1982–1983, however, the steady decline of oil prices left many pipelines with even rolled-in average costs of delivered gas that were beginning to exceed oil-equivalent prices.

Both pipelines and their LDC customers responded to the previously unheard-of phenomenon of *above-market* prices of gas by attempting to pass their gas costs on to end users. This was possible, to some extent, with residential and small commercial customers who had no significant ability to switch from gas to petroleum fuels and who could respond to high gas prices only by cutting back some of their use. Many large industrial users, however, responded to above-market gas prices by switching completely from natural gas to fuel oil.

As high prices began to drive customers away from natural gas, producers found their sales shrinking and were forced to shut in production. In numerous instances, it was producers with low-cost gas, rather than expensive above-market gas, that found themselves without buyers. Indeed, the anomaly of a natural gas market producing gas at $10.00 per Mcf while shutting in $1.50 gas has been more responsible than any other factor for the current upheaval in public policy. There certainly were willing buyers of gas to be matched to willing producers at $1.50 per Mcf. Why was the natural gas industry unable to perform the task of bringing such parties together?

The answer lies in a very complicated combination of regulatory and marketplace factors. In the second half of the 1970s, pipelines that were fearful of future shortages had coupled aggressive price offerings with generous contract terms in order to secure long-term supplies from producers. These contract terms included, for example, ''take-or-pay'' provisions that obligated a pipeline to pay for specified quantities of gas even if such quantities were not actually ''taken.'' As end-use prices began to soften in the 1980s under the competition from oil, pipelines might have preferred to drop their supplies of high-cost gas. But many pipelines found it more economical to eschew their low-cost gas and to take the high-cost gas for which they had contracted, since the latter had to be paid for anyway. This mismatch between the actions dictated by inflexible contractual obligations and the response that prevailing market conditions would have implied came to be known as "the contracts problem."

The reasonableness of pipelines' response to the combination of their take-or-pay obligations and weakening demand was of little consolation to low-cost gas producers and ultimate customers. The existence of willing, but unserved, buyers and sellers created pressure for innovations in both market and regulatory institutions. Specifically, the contracts problem gave impetus to the issue of "transportation" and regulatory change in the carrier status of pipelines.

Interstate natural gas pipelines traditionally have operated as private carriers. They purchase and take title to natural gas provided by producers and resell natural gas to LDCs and some large end users (such as electric utilities). In this manner, pipelines operate as both brokers and transporters of gas. Significantly, interstate pipelines are not common, or mandatory contract, carriers, whereby they would be required to transport natural gas owned and brokered by other parties. Not surprisingly, however, producers and pipeline customers that have been adversely affected by the pipelines' high-cost and high take-or-pay contractual obligations have sought to bypass such obligations by striking their own agreements with each other, seeking only transportation services from pipelines. Beginning in 1980, for example, a group of producers known as Equal Access began advocating that pipelines transport producers' shut-in gas to end users. From 1980 through 1983, however, pipelines strongly resisted such movements.

By 1983 continuing declines in alternative fuel prices and weakening demand had imposed substantial economic burdens on many pipelines. This created pressure for pipelines to attempt to renegotiate their supply contracts and to reconsider their opposition to transporting natural gas for other parties. For example, as a means of satisfying its contractual obligations, Transcontinental Gas Pipe Line Corporation (Transco) initiated a special marketing program (SMP) that allowed producers to sell gas to specific industrial customers that were threatening to switch to fuel oil. In exchange, Transco's take-or-pay obligations to participating producers were alleviated. Other pipelines soon followed with their own versions of the SMP.

Many LDCs and industrial users that did not qualify for SMPs (because, for example, they were unable to switch to alternative fuels) viewed the programs as discriminatory. On this ground, a group representing natural gas end users and known as the Maryland People's Council challenged the SMPs in federal district court. The result was a ruling in 1985 that required SMPs offered by a pipeline to be available to all customers on a nondiscriminatory basis. The immediate impact of this ruling was to reduce the pipelines' willingness to launch programs designed to promote transportation of natural gas for other parties. Pipelines feared that nondiscriminatory SMPs would encourage the loss of "core" customers for the pipelines' contracted gas supplies, thereby reducing the base from which the costs of such supplies could be recovered.

The Federal Energy Regulatory Commission (FERC) has primary responsibility for administering federal natural gas policy. In 1984 the FERC initiated its own movements toward heightened competition and institutional flexibility in the natural gas industry. Analogous to the pipelines' take-or-pay obligations to producers, LDCs traditionally have entered into minimum-bill agreements with pipelines. These agreements obligate LDCs to either take or pay for contracted volumes made available by pipelines. In the 1980s these minimum-bill agreements locked many LDCs into above-market natural gas costs. In response, the FERC issued Order 380. This rule effectively eliminated minimum bills and freed LDCs to purchase their supplies from the lowest cost suppliers they could find. It turned out to be only the beginning of the movement toward reducing federal restrictions and regulations in the pipeline industry.

The FERC issued Order 436 in October 1985. This allowed individual pipelines to choose between providing nondiscriminatory transportation for all interested customers or remaining a private carrier. By early 1986 twenty-eight filings for contract carriage programs had been made by interstate pipelines. At present, increasing competition among pipelines seeking to keep their capacities filled as well as the continuing competition from the oil market are mounting pressure on pipelines to expand their offerings of contracted transportation services.

Further impetus to the "unbundling" of the pipelines' transportation and brokerage functions came in 1986 from the FERC Order 451. This order proposes to "devintage" categories of controlled natural gas and effectively to move remaining wellhead price ceilings toward (or past) market levels. The consequence likely will be to weaken further the pipelines' abilities to satisfy above-market contracts for high-cost gas. In so doing, contractual impediments on the pipelines' willingness to engage in transportation for other owners of natural gas will be reduced.

Ongoing regulatory reform at the federal level, from wellhead price decontrol and "devintaging" the categories of the NGPA gas to the elimination of the pipelines' minimum-bill agreements with LDCs, is moving the locus of natural gas regulation downstream toward state Public Utility Commissions (PUCs). These commissions are charged with regulating intrastate pipelines and LDCs. Historically, their primary focus has been on the determination of "just and reasonable" pricing by the legal monopolies under their jurisdiction.

The revolution in natural gas markets and policy is quickly broadening the effective range of regulatory issues faced by PUCs. Previously routine and moribund regulations have become major topics of debate. For example, the new flexibility in the LDCs' natural gas contracts and supply portfolios that has been made possible by wellhead decontrol and contract carriage by pipelines has brought issues of LDC contracting practices and the status of LDC service obligations to the fore: What are the prudent limits to distribution-company reliance on short-term, variable-price, and even spot-market-supply contracts? What is the appropriate allocation of contracting costs and risk among LDCs and their various classes of customers? What obligations to provide service should

LDCs have vis-à-vis the fuel-switchable customers who go on and off the distribution system with the waxing and waning of gas-on-oil competition? In answering these types of questions, state PUCs have the de facto power either to promote or to block the objectives of policy reforms that are taking place at the upstream stages of the natural gas industry.

Policy Issues and Interest Groups

Policy reform in the natural gas industry during the last decade has been predominantly reactive. Changes in underlying market conditions are filtered through the layers of incentives and constraints that constitute natural gas regulation and propel industry participants into the search for new modes of management, marketing, and contracting. This process repeatedly has laid bare the shortcomings of the country's policy regimes. Shortages of supply, above-market prices for gas, discriminatory access to transportation networks, mismatches between willing buyers and willing sellers—these types of phenomena have been met as quickly as possible with accommodating redesign of state and federal policy. But regulatory reforms directed at the perceived problems of the moment have been continuously superseded by further market developments or by the unintended side effects of the reforms themselves.

Despite the appearance that current natural gas policy is a frantic and directionless game of leapfrog being played by policymakers and industry institutions, recent history has brought into focus the generic issues that remain to be resolved. These issues are raised explicitly and implicitly throughout this volume:

- The carrier status of natural gas pipelines
- Governmental constraints on the length, flexibility, and nonprice terms of private companies' natural gas supply and purchase contracts
- Regulatory restrictions on entry into and exit from pipeline and local distribution markets
- The design of pipeline and LDC rate (price) structures that efficiently and equitably provide for cost recovery and risk allocation
- PUC exercise of prudency review
- Regulatory limits on mergers, acquisitions, and vertical integration in the gas industry
- The persistence of historical contracts with above-market price terms or nonprice terms that restrain competitive trade
- The continuation of price controls on "old" gas

At least one lesson from recent attempts to deal with these matters is clear: Any move to change natural gas policy draws affected interest groups quickly and forcefully into the fray. Indeed, the Harvard study itself has provided a look at these interest groups. Throughout the study, participants have held different and, at times, diametrically opposed views on the major policy questions. No pretense can be made that the working group emerged with consensus positions on any significant issue. Participants differed among themselves and with the authors contributing to this volume.

As might be expected, any tendency toward agreement on the future direction of natural gas policy tends to be stronger within, rather than across, the various sectors that make up the gas industry. Natural gas producers, for example, fairly consistently favor deregulated wellhead prices for gas and support more open and nondiscriminatory access to the transportation systems of pipelines and LDCs. At the same time, many producers have been the beneficiaries of above-market-price contracts with pipelines, and these producers naturally are resistant to moves that would abrogate high-cost contracts or otherwise improve the relative bargaining positions of their pipeline counterparts in renegotiation proceedings.

The natural gas pipelines tend to hold the most united, if not the most adamant, views on policy reform. With almost complete uniformity, interstate pipelines have opposed measures that would alter their status as private carriers and brokers of natural gas. Contract or common carriage in any form is seen as destructive to their ability to manage the acquisition and allocation of available gas supplies. Moreover, pipelines argue that alterations in their carrier status are unnecessary in view of the existing extent of voluntary carriage by pipelines, interpipeline rivalry, and competition from alternative fuels. Beyond the question of the status of transportation access, pipelines consistently have sought relief from their high-cost contracts and protection of their core markets from competition. Overall, pipelines tend to favor a traditional system of regulated transportation rates and pipeline-controlled access to markets.

The policy positions of the nation's LDCs are probably the most complicated to decipher. The pure economics of policy impacts might suggest that LDCs stand to benefit from more open access to pipeline transportation and related increases in the flexibility of market institutions. More open access to transportation and more flexible contracting and trading arrangements could enhance the LDCs' abilities to pursue their own least-cost and least-risk strategies for acquiring natural gas supplies. The LDCs, however, are particularly sensitive to the political and regulatory repercussions that can emanate from major regulatory change. Many LDCs clearly fear that, in a more competitive environment in which they must assume increased responsibility for their own operations, PUCs will exercise oversight and prudency authority to shift excessively burdensome risks and costs onto the LDCs. Many LDCs are concerned, for example, that their obligations to serve any customer that requests natural gas supply are becoming one-way streets on which the LDC must stand ready to guarantee deliveries while certain customers can enter and exit the distribution system as they please (e.g., as the price of alternative fuels rises and falls).

State and federal regulators have shown at least as much zeal in articulating their viewpoints as have members of the private sector. In fact, much of the leadership in the debate over policy reform has come from the regulatory agencies themselves. The FERC, for example, has proven to be a primary force in favor of deregulation and competition. Recent FERC decisions, rules, and proposals have aggressively promoted more open access to transportation, effectively higher prices for old gas, easier entry by new competitors, and removal of regulatory support for high-cost contracts. In fact, the FERC has come under attack on the grounds that it has overstepped its authority in reforming natural gas policy without legislative approval.

State PUCs have ranged widely in their responses to the current upheaval in the natural gas sector. In some states, such as California and Illinois, PUCs are primary initiators of regulatory change. This takes forms such as urging LDCs to take aggressive advantage of new opportunities and strategies for acquiring gas supplies, pressuring pipelines to provide transportation for LDC-owned gas, and effectively deregulating LDCs where they compete for fuel-switchable customers. On the other hand, many LDCs appear to be overwhelmed by the choices confronting them and respond with measured conservatism. Most state PUCs depend on small staffs to analyze the issues of the natural gas sector and are understandably stretched thin by the pace of current change.

In general, state PUCs have opposed decontrol and supported measures to alter remaining above-market, high-cost supply contracts. Both positions are perceived as consistent with holding down consumers' gas costs. Opposition, or at least lack of support, for alterations in pipeline carriage policy, easier entry and exit of market participants, and more flexible contracting practices, meanwhile, seems to reflect the desire of many PUCs to maintain the scope of their institutional and geographic control. Increasing the extent to which LDCs are expected to compete against one another for gas supplies and transportation services may reduce the sphere of activities over which PUCs can delimit LDC actions. While the desire to maintain the role of the PUC may in part stem from bureaucratic impulses, it also reflects sincere concern and uncertainty over the ability of new marketplace institutions (at least in the U.S. natural gas industry) to deliver least-cost supplies reliably to the ultimate consumer.

Overview

Part I of this volume lays the groundwork for analysis of the major public policy issues under debate in the natural gas industry. In Chapter 2, John C. Sawhill examines the underlying conditions of domestic natural gas use and production. He concludes that gas use will be held in check by the level of demand and competing fuel prices, rather than by the availability of supply, well into the 1990s. This analysis of supply and demand conditions is complemented by Henry Lee's examination in Chapter 3 of imported natural gas. Lee finds that Canadian gas supplies will play significant roles in at least some regions of the country over the coming years. Chapter 4, by William W. Hogan, completes Part I by providing the criteria by which policy choices should be judged. Sound regulation of an industry should be both efficient and fair. But these prescriptions are too broad to be of much practical use; thus Hogan investigates their specific applications to today's natural gas markets.

Part II turns to the major policy issues under debate in the U.S. natural gas industry. It is a basic tenet of policy design that arguments for or against governmental intervention into a marketplace hinge most fundamentally upon the potency of unregulated competition: The more effective is the discipline of competition, the less compelling is the case for regulation. In Chapter 5, Joseph P. Kalt investigates the determinants of competition in each of the major segments of the U.S. natural gas industry. He concludes that the producer stage of the industry is naturally extremely competitive but that the pipeline and LDC stages are less so. In Chapter 6, Harry G. Broadman examines the implications of pipeline industry structure and competitiveness for policy design and argues for a system of pipeline regulation that would substantially deregulate entry and access into transportation and wholesaling. Chapter 7, by Colin C. Blaydon, takes up the issue of LDC regulation and urges PUCs to adapt to and promote, rather than block, movements toward more flexible contracts and trading arrangements.

The marked changes in natural gas markets and regulation in recent years have dramatically altered traditional ways of doing business and making policy. Part III assesses the problems of designing business and regulatory strategies applicable to the nation's evolving natural gas industry. In Chapter 8, Frank C. Schuller considers the implications of increased market competition and flexibility for the conduct of business strategy at the various stages of the gas industry. Schuller argues that industry planners now must focus more on the demand side of their markets, seeking out new ways to differentiate themselves through their marketing and contracting practices. The vexing problem of designing contracts that are appropriate for today's economic environment and that provide for efficient allocations of risk across market participants is taken up by Carmen D. Legato in Chapter 9. Legato argues forcefully for reduced reliance on long-term, fixed-price contracts and for expanded roles for spot markets and risk-bearing independent brokers and wholesalers.

The problem of designing a regulatory strategy for moving the natural gas industry toward more efficient and competitive behavior is discussed by George R. Hall in Chapter 10. It is easy to recommend sweeping changes in natural gas policy. It is another matter actually to implement policy redesigns that take the gas industry in desirable directions with minimal disruptions and transition costs. Hall provides a blueprint for "getting from here to there."

PART I

THE SETTING: MARKETS AND POLICY

Two main elements provide the context in which U.S. natural gas policy is being redesigned. One is the supply and demand setting of natural gas markets. The other is the conceptual framework that the principles of policy analysis provide to public decision makers. The chapters in this part analyze these components of the setting for natural gas policy reform.

In Chapter 2 John C. Sawhill examines conditions underlying domestic natural gas use and production. Natural gas demand fundamentally is determined by: price competition with alternative fuels; the composition of gas use among residential, commercial, electric utility, and industrial customers; and the overall growth of the nation's economy. On the supply side, the gas industry must find and develop new reserves as well as exploit the production capacity of existing gas fields.

The natural gas industry finds itself driven by market forces now more than at any time in the last four decades. Sawhill concludes that ongoing competition with petroleum products will continue to regulate natural gas demand and prices. Significantly, increases in gas demand that otherwise might tend to drive gas prices upward will tend to spill over and create demand for oil products, as increases in gas prices relative to oil prices cause fuel switching. Meanwhile years of price suppression have left the nation with a relatively large backlog of gas resources, and Sawhill anticipates that gas use will continue to be held in check by the level of demand rather than the availability of supply well into the 1990s.

It is perhaps natural to think of the natural gas industry as a network of pipelines radiating out from production fields located in Texas, Oklahoma, and Louisiana. This image, however, overlooks the international linkages of the U.S. gas industry. In Chapter 3 Henry Lee examines the role of imported natural gas. He concludes that while Mexican and ocean-borne gas from the Middle East or elsewhere will remain economically insignificant into the foreseeable future, Canadian natural gas is likely to play an important role in at least some regions of the country. Canadian imports can serve as "swing" supply sources that may be of sufficient volume to compete with and effectively discipline domestic production and pipeline markets.

The chapters by Sawhill and Lee describe the underlying supply and demand setting within which natural gas policy is being made. In Chapter 4 William W. Hogan provides the criteria by which policy choices should be judged. In general terms these criteria are efficiency and fairness. Sound policy should attempt to: (1) maximize the net value of the nation's scarce resources; and (2) allocate the costs and benefits of resource use and development equitably across sectors and individuals. Hogan then investigates the implications of this more general prescription within the specific context of U.S. natural gas policy reform.

2

The Outlook for Domestic Supply and Demand

JOHN C. SAWHILL

Until 1978 the U.S. government played a preeminent role in shaping the character and structure of the natural gas industry. By keeping prices below market-clearing levels, it helped create a growing demand for natural gas. With the passage of the Natural Gas Policy Act (NGPA) in 1978, a transition began from a government-controlled environment to one in which market forces dominated. That transition is largely complete. Now, although the government may regulate particular transactions, free-market competition will largely determine the average price at which natural gas is sold.

But government policy has not lost its importance for the natural gas industry. Both Congress and federal and state regulators will continue to influence the efficiency with which the gas market operates, its structure, and which firms will prosper or suffer in the new market environment. By action or inaction, they will determine whether consumers receive the full benefits of increased competition.

The Evolution of Natural Gas Policy

The natural gas industry is composed of three segments: (1) production, (2) transport from producing areas to consuming markets, and (3) distribution to residential, commercial, and industrial end users. From the time that natural gas was first sold until 1954, regulation expanded from covering only local distribution to the entire industry, including producers. Since 1978, this process has begun to reverse, as controls on production have been loosened and regulation of transport from producing areas to consuming markets has given companies more room to maneuver.

State and local regulators have exercised varying degrees of regulation over local distribution companies (LDCs) since the distribution of manufactured gas began in the 1800s. Significant federal regulation of natural gas began in 1938, when the Natural Gas Act granted to the federal government the authority to regulate the interstate transportation and sale-for-resale of natural gas. In 1954 this authority was expanded to the production of natural gas by a Supreme Court ruling that forced the Federal Trade Commission to exercise its statutory authority over the prices that natural gas producers charged to interstate pipelines.[1] The regulatory structure that developed was designed to set prices at the cost of service.

At the pipeline level, this led to rates that allowed companies to recover costs and earn a "reasonable" rate of return. Determining these costs (mostly of exploration and production) was so difficult that regulators simply set a price that would rise with exploration and production costs.

The most important effect of this blanket regulation was that prices were held below market-clearing levels. These low prices created a substantial boost to demand and a disincentive to search for new sources of natural gas, and this led eventually to supply shortages that forced Congress to respond.

The increases in demand were particularly impressive after 1950: In the following two decades, gas consumption more than tripled, growing by an average of 6.7 percent annually. Its proportion of total energy consumption grew from 18.0 percent in 1950 to 32.8 percent in 1970.[2]

When consumption peaked in 1972 and began to fall, it was due less to a leveling off of demand than to a shortage of supply available at prevailing (regulated) prices. At the time of the Supreme Court ruling in 1954, a large proportion of gas reserves lay in associated wells and were sufficient to accommodate a substantial increase in demand. But because regulation had reduced significantly the incentives to drill for nonassociated gas, a steep decline in the reserves-to-production ratio began to take place. By 1978 reserves were sufficient to supply only ten years of production, down from twenty-six years in 1954; from 1966 to 1978 nonassociated gas reserves fell by 30 percent.[3]

These conflicting supply and demand trends contributed to the natural gas shortages during the severe winter of 1976–1977. The shortages were exacerbated further by a regulatory structure that allowed gas produced and sold within a state to be sold without the price controls that applied to gas transported across state lines. In 1978 wellhead gas sold to interstate pipelines was about $0.86 per thousand cubic feet (Mcf), well below the $1.39 per Mcf paid in intrastate markets.[4] The resulting shortages increased pressure on Congress to change the fundamental nature of natural gas market regulation. In response, in 1978 Congress passed the NGPA.

The most crucial aspect of the NGPA was that it allowed some types of natural gas (principally gas from very deep wells) to be sold free from price controls. On January 1, 1985, controls on gas from certain other wells were also lifted: most importantly, gas discovered from wells drilled before 1977, commonly called "old" gas. By definition, however, this gas would decline over time in proportion to total (i.e., "old" plus "new") gas reserves.

This removal of price controls on the production sector had an important impact on the pipeline and LDC sectors. Deregulation took place at a time when the prices of petroleum products, the most attractive alternative fuels for many natural gas consumers, were rising rapidly. Due to interfuel competition, deregulation meant that natural gas prices also would rise. From 1978 to 1984 the average wellhead price of natural gas rose from $0.91 to $2.60 per Mcf. Adjusted for inflation, it doubled. Combined with the recession that began in 1981, this price increase had a dramatic impact on gas consumption: It fell from 19.6 trillion cubic feet (Tcf) in 1978 to 17.5 Tcf in 1984.[5] This combination of circumstances left pipelines and LDCs with spare capacity, and pressure increased for them to cut costs and prices.

With implementation of the NGPA, federal regulation began to change in ways designed to increase competition, while concurrently permitting pipelines to take steps to increase the utilization of their assets. Initially, the most important action was to allow sales to certain types of customers to take place under a "blanket certificate," meaning that the Federal Energy Regulatory Commission (FERC) did not have to grant case-by-case approval for certain sales. This encouraged short-term spot deals that would have been impossible if delayed by lengthy hearings. In addition, the FERC allowed producers and pipelines to sponsor their own spot programs in which buyers and sellers could be matched.

Late in 1985 the FERC issued a rule (Order 436) that instituted even more sweeping changes in the regulatory treatment of gas transportation and rates. (See Chapter 6 for a detailed discussion.) In general, through provisions providing incentives for increased carriage of gas by pipelines and an easing of regulatory restrictions on constructing pipelines to new markets, the rule reflects the view that competitive forces are increasingly important in the marketplace and are powerful enough in many areas to prevent pipelines from engaging in monopolistic behavior.

There is little question that regulation of pipelines will continue to change as the gas market tests the efficiency and effectiveness of new regulations (and as courts test their legality). Thus the likely shape of gas regulation in the next few years remains uncertain. However, one thing is clear: The natural gas market has changed fundamentally in the last ten years and natural gas policy has been forced to change with it.

Today's Natural Gas Market

The post-NGPA changes in the natural gas industry have effectively wrested control of the market from government policymakers. The mechanisms by which prices are likely to be set in the future are complex and based on demand, supply, and alternative fuel-pricing trends.

Demand

Table 2.1 illustrates how the decline in natural gas consumption was distributed among primary consuming sectors for the peak years of 1979 and 1984.

Table 2.1
Natural Gas Consumption by Sector for 1979 and 1984 (Tcf)

Sector	1979	1984	Change (%)
Industrial	8.40	7.16	– 14.8
Residential	4.97	4.33	– 12.9
Electric utilities	3.49	3.11	– 10.9
Commercial	2.79	2.37	– 15.1
Transportation	0.60	0.51	– 15.0
Total	20.24	17.48	– 13.6

Source: U.S. Department of Energy, *Annual Energy Review, 1984*, U.S. Government Printing Office, Washington, D.C., p. 137.

The most serious erosion in consumption took place in the industrial and residential sectors. Between 1979 and 1984 industrial consumption declined about 15 percent. Surprisingly, this cannot be attributed solely to the economic recession in those years, as shown by the fact that industrial production increased by 7 percent during this period.[6] Thus the amount of gas consumed per unit of industrial output—a useful measure of the efficiency of gas use—fell by more than 20 percent. Similarly, the 13 percent drop in residential consumption between 1979 and 1984 cannot be entirely attributed to economic slowdown, for during this period the number of households increased by about 4 percent, and personal income also rose.[7]

Accepting that the recession was not the primary reason for the fall in consumption, it is logical to assume that rising prices caused users to conserve gas and, in some cases, drove them away from gas to oil, coal, or electricity. The key question is whether these effects will continue in the future.

Several factors argue that conservation and fuel switching will keep gas demand close to 1985 levels. First, even if the price of gas continues to fall in the second half of the decade, some improvements in the efficiency of energy use can still be expected. Evidence suggests that the response to price changes is long term and heavily influenced by capital expenditures for industrial equipment, utility boilers, new homes, and so forth. Thus lower gas prices will have little short-term positive impact on consumption.

Second, there appear to be significant opportunities for further conservation. Advances in technology and efficiency in many modern industries are decreasing the demand for gas. For instance, in the paper industry, displacement bleaching technology uses about 50 percent less fuel per unit of output than does conventional bleaching technology.[8] In homes, gas-furnace efficiency is expected to show continued improvements. A comparison of energy-use indicators among the United States and other industrialized countries further suggests just how much room for conservation remains. For example, Japan uses about 45 percent less energy per unit of gross domestic product than does the United States.[9]

Third, the economics of fuel switching still are appealing. In industry, coal-burning boilers may become more common as industry takes advantage of coal that generally is priced lower on a Btu basis than gas. In addition, as industrial technology advances and new processes are introduced, electricity's share of industry's slowly growing energy consumption continues to increase. In the residential sector, the penetration of electricity into the home heating market poses a significant threat to natural gas. In 1983, the last year for which data are available, 63 percent of single-family homes used natural gas for heating, but only 43 percent of new homes used natural gas. Forty-nine percent of new homes used electricity (primarily heat pumps) for heating, substantially above the 15 percent in existing homes.[10] Much of this competition reflects the enormous reserve margins of many electric utilities, which have recently completed substantial new building programs. To use this surplus power, many utilities are instituting aggressive marketing programs. Oil products could also erode the market share of gas in all these sectors, particularly if gas prices do not react quickly to falling oil prices. The completion of nuclear and coal-fired electric utility plants will also reduce demand for gas.

Finally, a shift in the composition of industrial output could also reduce demand for gas. Gas-intensive industries such as steel are expected to improve far less than the economy as a whole. In industries such as chemicals, which have followed the economy closely in recent years, new factors such as the planned shutdown of ammonia production facilities or increases in imports will also drive down demand.

However, it should be acknowledged that the fundamentals of gas and, indeed, of demand for all energy sources are less than perfectly understood. Despite considerable research, it is difficult to quantify convincingly the relationship between prices and demand and their response to economic growth. The sharp decline in gas demand in the early 1980s generally was not anticipated, and a parallel increase conceivably could surprise industry participants in the future. Such an increase would imply at least a partial reversal of the trends toward conservation and fuel switching. It would indicate that demand was extremely sensitive to short-term price movements and contradict those who believe that the impact of the earlier price increases has yet to be completely felt by the economy. None of this is impossible. But it is more likely that the trends toward conservation and fuel switching will not reverse so rapidly. If this is true, natural gas consumption in the next ten years may not regain the 22 Tcf level reached in 1973. Instead, consumption is expected to be relatively steady as moderate growth in the economy is offset by improvements in energy efficiency and fuel switching.

Supply

The post–1979 drop in natural gas consumption helped contribute to what is referred to as the natural gas ''bubble''—a surplus of deliverability (the amount of gas that producers physically are able to deliver) relative to consumption.

It is difficult to be precise about deliverability, but several sources estimate that, at the beginning of 1986, U.S. producers could deliver 19.0 to 20.0 Tcf annually, while surplus Canadian export capacity stood at approximately 0.6 Tcf.[11] Surplus deliverability has increased somewhat in recent years, largely due to the decline in consumption and to new reserve additions that accompanied the increased drilling activity of the late 1970s and early 1980s. With deliverability to U.S. markets standing at 20.0 to 21.0 Tcf, the size of the deliverability surplus at the beginning of 1986 was 2.5 to 3.5 Tcf, a substantial check on future price increases.

How long this surplus lasts depends on several factors, including consumption, prices, the level and success of drilling efforts, future deliverability from current reserves, and the magnitude of imports (primarily from Canada but potentially from Mexico as well; see Chapter 3). Since 1983 some forecasters have predicted an imminent end to the deliverability surplus, usually based on the perception that there are insufficient price incentives for exploration and production.[12] However, the surplus has proven to be extremely durable and could continue for several years.

Two primary factors support this view. First, despite the relatively weak market outlook, drilling activity is expected to continue at a level high enough to provide substantial reserve additions. Second, Canadian gas exports should increase significantly, providing an additional source of relatively low-cost supply.

Turning first to drilling, note that despite the decline in gas prices and the radically changed consensus on the direction of future prices, drilling activity in 1984 and 1985 remained relatively high by historic standards (even though it represented a sharp drop-off from the levels achieved in 1980 and 1981). This apparently allowed substantial additions to reserves. Onshore and offshore, almost every measure of drilling activity—the number of wells completed, the number of operating drilling rigs, and the total amount of feet drilled—was about equal to levels in the latter half of the 1970s. At the same time, the efficiency of drilling increased substantially as operators sought and found ways to cut costs. The number of wells completed for each active drilling rig rose nearly 40 percent between 1981 and 1984.[13] In 1984 approximately 16,000 exploratory and development gas wells were completed, adding 14 Tcf to reserves in the lower forty-eight states.[14] This was only slightly below production levels of about 17 Tcf.

Another key factor is the decline in drilling costs. In 1980 and 1981, these costs rose dramatically. Combined with tax increases, this rise reduced the profits that producers could expect from higher prices. But since then, costs have fallen more quickly than prices. In fact, according to the American Petroleum Institute's

(API's) *Joint Association Survey of Drilling Costs*, the 1984 drilling costs were almost equal to 1977 costs and approximately 50 percent below 1982 costs.[15] Other surveys also show continuing price declines.[16] But wellhead gas prices were higher in early 1986 than in 1979, suggesting that the economics of drilling had improved. Although further declines of this magnitude cannot be expected, the relationship between gas prices and drilling costs is unlikely to be considerably worse during the rest of the decade than it was in the late 1970s and early 1980s.

Examples of dramatic cost reductions are abundant. The average bid for an acre of federal land in the Gulf of Mexico declined from $4,380 in 1980 to $484 in 1984.[17] At the same time the daily rates charged for the use of jackup rigs (rig rental is typically 30 percent of the costs of drilling and equipping a well) declined by about 66 percent in real terms.[18] Onshore, the costs of payments to drilling contractors, suppliers of tubular goods, and other oil-field service and equipment companies dropped by 30 to 50 percent during the 1981–1984 period.[19]

Another factor that will prolong the gas deliverability surplus is the increasing availability of reasonably priced natural gas imports from Canada (see Chapter 3 for a more complete discussion). Before 1984 Canadian gas exports to the United States were restricted by a price floor administered by the Canadian government. As a result, when gas demand began to slump in the United States and high-cost imports became less desirable, Canadian producers were unable to lower prices in response. In 1984 Canada exported about 0.8 Tcf to the United States, well below the government-authorized levels of 1.9 Tcf.[20] However, toward the end of 1984, the Canadian government changed its pricing policy, allowing producers to reduce prices in order to increase sales. Canadian exports immediately increased; U.S. imports in the first ten months of 1985 were 13 percent above those in the same period in 1984. Most forecasters predict that Canadian imports will continue to increase throughout the decade; by 1990 levels of 1.5 Tcf annually could easily be attained.

Ultimately, however, the likelihood of a supply shortfall will depend on the level of new reserve additions in the United States. Already-discovered gas will be of decreasing importance into the late 1980s and early 1990s. It is unlikely that proved reserves will provide more than 4.0 Tcf of annual production by 1995. All other production—11.0 to 12.0 Tcf domestically, assuming 1985 consumption levels, and 1.5 Tcf from Canadian imports—must come from additions to reserves or imports. Making simplifying assumptions about production rates, reserve additions must average about 10.0 to 11.0 Tcf annually to maintain a surplus market into the 1990s.

How likely is this? Admittedly, no analyst is comfortable projecting something as uncertain as the level and success of future oil and gas drilling. Indeed, the congressional Office of Technology Assessment (OTA) was so persuaded of the difficulty of this task that it forecast that reserve additions could range from 7–8 to 16–17 Tcf annually until 2000, a range so wide as to provide little basis for planning.

However, some observations are relevant. First, assuming consumption at the 18 Tcf level, a shortage in this decade would require reserve additions at the lower end of or below the OTA estimate. Second, if indicators of drilling success improve as a result of efficiency gains, reserve additions will not fall as rapidly as drilling activity. Third, improvements in drilling and production technology would reduce costs or make possible the development of reserves previously seen as uneconomic. Fourth, new import sources could expand supply capacity.

The more important issues concern how supply responds to changes in prices. When oil and gas prices fell precipitously in early 1986, drilling activity collapsed. In addition, the mix of drilling has undoubtedly shifted toward less risky development wells, with a resulting decline in the magnitude of reserve additions per well drilled. The financial troubles of independent producers, who perform a disproportionately high share of drilling, could also lead to a sharper-than-expected drop-off in reserve additions.

Thus it would be unwise to design natural gas policies that would succeed only in a glutted market. But the apparent magnitude and durability of the current surplus, as well as the continuing incentives to drill in the United States, suggest it would be even more foolish to tailor a policy appropriate only for a market characterized by shortage.

Pricing

To argue that gas prices are likely to rise significantly in the near future, one must believe either that oil prices are also going to rise or that gas and oil prices are basically unrelated. Most observers of energy markets believe that oil prices will remain well below the levels of the early 1980s, due to the excess capacity held by members of the Organization of Petroleum Exporting Countries (OPEC). Accepting this view, a long-term rise in gas prices would imply that gas and oil prices were moving in opposite directions. But this is unlikely, given the significant competition between gas and oil for end-use markets. On the contrary, gas prices are likely to compete with alternative fuels, particularly with residual fuel oil.

To appreciate the importance of interfuel competition, one must evaluate the capability of current gas customers to switch to alternate fuels. One by-product of the gas shortages of the 1970s was that many industrial and electric utility consumers made investments in equipment that enabled them to switch to other fuels if gas were not available and vice versa. As a result, approximately two-thirds of gas demand from these sectors now comes from customers who have fuel-switching capability. Approximately 50 percent of industrial natural gas demand could be lost to residual fuel oil virtually overnight.

The demand curve in Figure 2.1 illustrates the importance of customers capable of switching. The height of the bars represents the price at which consumers would switch to alternate fuels. (In the case of residential customers, this price includes the amortized costs of installing a new heating unit.) The width of the

Figure 2.1
Estimated Natural Gas Demand Curve, 1983

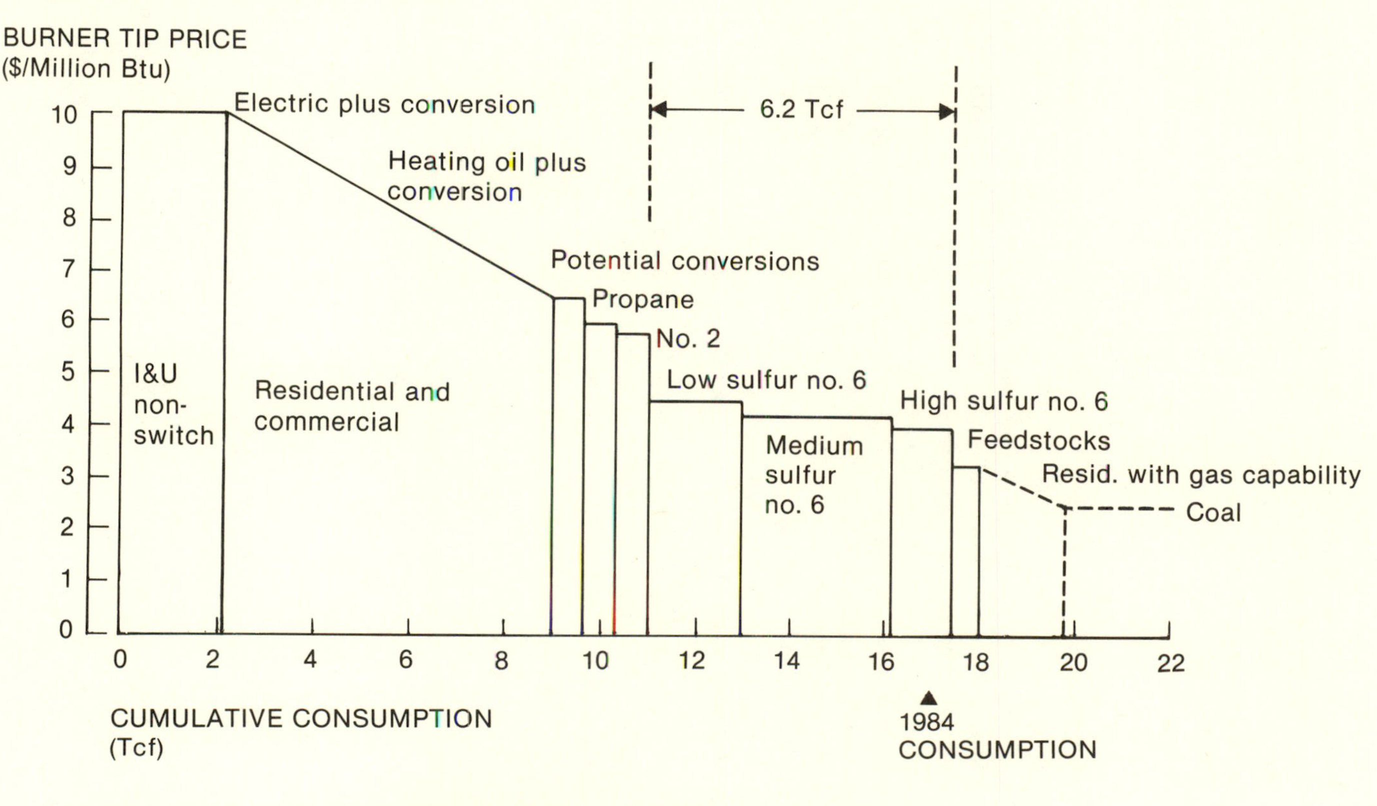

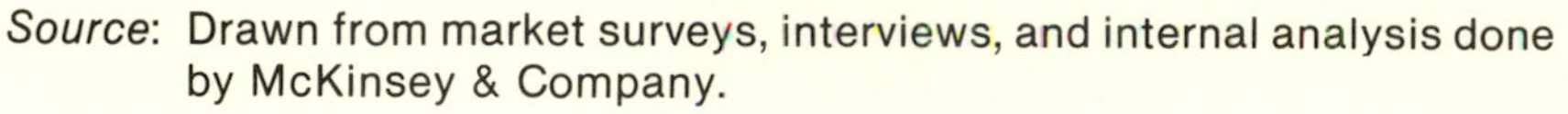

Source: Drawn from market surveys, interviews, and internal analysis done by McKinsey & Company.

bars corresponds to the amount of capacity that could be switched. The three blocks capable of converting to residual fuel oil, at the tail end of the demand curve, are clearly critical. A relatively small increase in the price of gas could lead to the loss of these customers, who together account for almost one-third of total demand.

If there is any question that such a loss would be critical, consider the effects on the pipeline industry. A rise in gas prices that led to customers switching to residual fuel oil could trigger a death spiral for some pipelines. Following such radical loss in demand, fixed costs would be allocated among fewer customers; this would lead to another price rise and still further loss of demand. Eventually, a pipeline could be forced into bankruptcy.

Therefore, residual oil prices are an important factor influencing natural gas prices. Movements in the prices of residual oil can best be understood by examining the economics of petroleum refineries.

The upper bound for residual oil prices (relative to crude oil) is that point where refiners shut down "upgrading" units designed to process residual oil into higher-valued "light" products, such as gasoline and heating oil. Decisions by several large refiners to shut down such units would flood the market with residual oil and eventually drive its price downward. The lower bound is defined by that level at which residual oil prices are so low that new investment in "upgrading" units is undertaken, thereby raising demand for residual oil and causing prices to rise.

Ultimately, then, natural gas prices will be linked to crude oil through competition with residual fuel oil. For the gas industry, the result is "netback" pricing, in which end-use prices are determined by competition with residual fuel oil and the costs of distribution and transmission are subtracted to derive a price.

The importance of alternative fuels is supported by examining wellhead prices of natural gas during the last five years (see Figure 2.2). Estimating the cost of gas transportation and assuming that residual oil prices range between 75 and 85 percent of crude oil prices, wellhead natural gas prices will range between 50 and 65 percent of crude oil (on a Btu basis). As price controls were lifted, gas prices rose quickly toward this barrier. However, since that time, wellhead gas prices have fluctuated within the 50 to 65 percent barrier.

Ignoring the importance of netback pricing in gas markets led many analysts falsely to predict a price "fly-up" after price controls were lifted from many categories of gas at the beginning of 1985. Such a fly-up, without a simultaneous increase in oil prices, would lead to an unacceptable loss of markets. But instead of a fly-up, there was a "fly-down," as falling oil prices and a continuing gas surplus forced gas prices downward. In the future, those looking to forecast gas prices would do well to keep a close eye on supply, demand, and the prices of alternative fuels and pay less attention to the wording of contracts and the timing of government policy changes.

Figure 2.2
Wholesale Interstate Natural Gas Prices

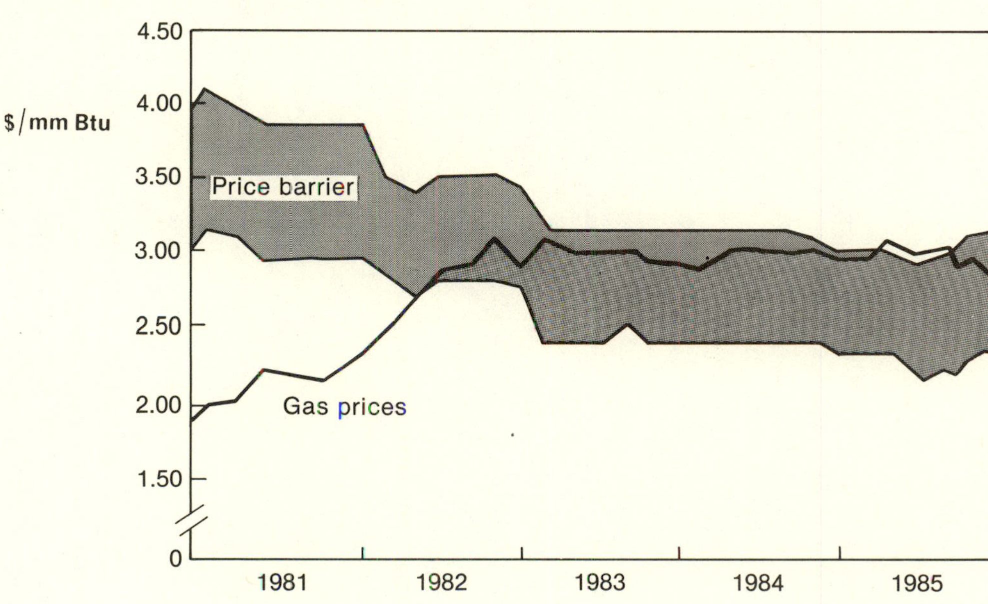

Source: Natural gas prices taken from interstate natural gas price series in U.S. Department of Labor, Bureau of Labor Statistics, *Producer Prices and Price Indexes*, U.S. Government Printing Office, Washington, D.C., table six, various issues; price barrier represents 50-65 percent of crude oil price. Crude oil price series from composite refiner acquisition cost of crude oil in U.S. Department of Energy, Energy Information Administration, *Monthly Energy Review*, various issues.

Government Policy in a New Natural Gas Market

The natural gas market has come full circle. Throughout most of the twentieth century, the gas industry shaped its behavior to accommodate government regulation. Now with gas prices driven by market forces, this is no longer the case. In fact, in some ways it is the market that is forcing government to respond. As gas companies do what they must to compete effectively, policy will continue to change—both to allow competition in new areas and to prevent anticompetitive behavior that frustrates market forces. The likely changes (many of them already underway) and the challenges they pose will be felt at all levels of the natural gas industry.

The production sector has been the most severely affected by changes in regulation. Before 1954, most producers were not regulated, although pricing restrictions did apply to production companies owned by interstate pipelines. These companies were at an important disadvantage. When gas production for sale to interstate pipelines was placed under price controls, producer strategy was directed toward maximizing sales to unregulated intrastate markets.

The NGPA's complicated wellhead pricing provisions further distorted production markets. Drilling for deep gas, which commanded an above-market price, surged. But deep gas was far more costly to find than gas in shallower fields, which was less desirable to producers, due to price controls. The regulatory system thus encouraged the production of high-cost resources over low-cost resources. After 1983, as the prices of other categories of gas reached market-clearing levels, deep gas drilling fell sharply (the number of deep wells drilled fell by 40 percent from 1981 to 1983[21]).

The onset of the gas surplus and the removal of controls from most new gas once again have forced producers to formulate new strategies. Exploration and production profits will suffer if producers cannot sell new gas quickly and if buyers do not consistently purchase the full amount for which they have contracted. Thus marketing and negotiating skills have become extremely important as a stabilizing tool. Producers will try to ensure that pipeline buyers are serving reliable, growing markets, trading flexibility on pricing for the assurance of steady purchases. They will be striving increasingly to make direct and spot sales to large end users and LDCs.

Another strategy that may become more common is downstream integration. By purchasing pipelines that are connected to their gas fields, producers would be in a better position to ensure that their gas has an outlet in a glutted market. Historically, the major oil companies, which are the largest gas producers, have held little or no equity in the pipeline industry. If they were to begin purchasing downstream assets, interstate pipeline regulators could feel an increased political pressure to regulate the resulting prices.

That aside, the pressures for producers to behave competitively raise questions about the wisdom of continuing price controls on old gas. These controls do little to lower overall prices while they distort incentives to prolong the life of old gas fields.

Lower prices can have a negative impact on gas production from proved reserves in several ways. First, and most important, these wells will be abandoned more quickly. The cost of maintaining sufficient reservoir pressure increases as the well is depleted, and producers will abandon wells when costs equal revenue. In addition, fewer "infill" wells, which are intended to increase recovery from known reservoirs, will be drilled if producers receive only the NGPA-mandated "old" gas price. Finally, various techniques to stimulate production, such as workovers, fracturing, and acidizing, will become uneconomic at lower prices.

Several studies have attempted to measure disincentives to production. C. S. Matthews estimated that 52 Tcf of reserves (the total remaining U.S. natural gas resources were estimated to be 774 Tcf by the U.S. Geological Survey in 1981) could be added if price controls were lifted on old gas. The Department of Energy (27 to 48 Tcf) and the Office of Technology Assessment (23 to 30 Tcf) estimated that lifting of price controls on old gas would have a smaller but still significant impact.[22]

At the same time, old gas price controls have complicated the task of downstream regulation. Pipelines with access to substantial quantities of gas controlled at prices far below market levels enjoy a potential advantage over competitors that is unrelated to the efficiency of their operations. To prevent pipelines from using this advantage to raid others' markets, regulators have been forced to design complicated pricing schemes that attempt to segregate old gas supplies from other gas. There simply is no easy way to accomplish this.

To some observers, these difficulties might be justified if price controls brought lower prices to consumers. But old gas controls, on the average, do little to limit gas prices because new gas prices rise to create an equilibrium in the market. The continuation of this policy stems from Congress' reluctance to readdress a politically explosive issue. In addition, support for price controls has been buttressed by the media attention given to figures indicating that a disproportionate amount of old gas reserves are owned by the major oil companies.[23] The implication is that if decontrol of old gas brought down the price of new gas, this would benefit the major oil companies to the detriment of the smaller independents. Thus, because of its own reluctance and lack of public support, Congress has put off passage of any decontrol bill, instead choosing to continue the inefficiencies of the present system. Fortunately, as the size of old gas reserves declines, these inefficiencies will become smaller over time. By 1990 old gas will account for less than 40 percent of total production and by 1994, only 25 percent.

More complex issues will surface as pipelines try to adjust to new market realities. In the past, transmission was a relatively risk-free business, with regulation governing prices and returns and virtually ensuring that all gas purchased would be sold. Now, with competition for markets rigorous and likely to remain so, pipelines are exploring strategies both to increase the amount of gas they transport and to reduce costs. Several of these strategies will force policymakers to confront a number of difficult issues.

One example is the growing spot market. Many pipelines are using spot sales programs to remain competitive in industrial markets or to expand into new geographic areas. The incidence of spot sales is likely to increase as downstream markets become more competitive.

The U.S. pipeline system offers customers widespread opportunities to select service from multiple pipelines. Even in New York, which lies far from major gas fields, LDCs may choose from among several major pipelines (see Figure 2.3). As a result, absent regulatory restrictions, downstream interchange points are likely to develop. Regulatory policy will be crucial to how such a system develops.

In 1983 and 1984, under special programs allowed by the FERC, pipelines ran their own spot programs, typically offering producers a price based on bids by potential purchasers or on alternative fuel prices. These programs grew quickly and some pipelines used them either to gain a foothold in new industrial markets or to retain customers who were threatening to switch to oil. But to protect pipelines with higher prices, the FERC originally restricted customer eligibility, forced prices to stay above a certain level, and made certain gas reserves ineligible for inclusion in these spot programs. Inevitably, market pressures rendered these restrictions untenable, and pressures mounted to allow uniform access to spot markets. Partially as a result, the FERC undertook a broad review of downstream pipeline regulation, which led to its issuing of Order 436, which substantially increased pressure on pipelines to offer end users and producers access to transportation. It remains to be seen whether Order 436 offers a durable foundation for future price regulation.

A related issue is pipeline transport of gas owned by others. Pipelines have shown an interest in using contract carriage to reduce their risks by avoiding taking ownership of gas. The volume of gas transported for LDCs and end users has increased significantly, and is likely to be greater than 1.5 Tcf in 1985 (see Figure 2.4). However, some pipelines are not eager to take on this new role, especially if it entails a reduction in their own sales volumes and gives competitors access to their markets. Pipelines have used their position as sole purchaser in many gas fields and as sole supplier in many markets to frustrate attempts by producers and consumers to arrange transactions at lower prices. The FERC's proposal in late 1985 to require pipelines to transport gas for others under certain circumstances was a response to this practice. Again, it is unlikely to be the final solution.

The recent changes in gas markets also have given pipeline companies an incentive to consolidate operations and to integrate both horizontally and vertically. Purchasing other pipelines provided them greater access to a number of different gas fields and led to a series of major pipeline mergers in 1984 and 1985. In addition, with ironclad long-term contracts no longer feasible in a

Figure 2.3
Natural Gas Suppliers in New York Area, 1984 (Percentage of Bcf)

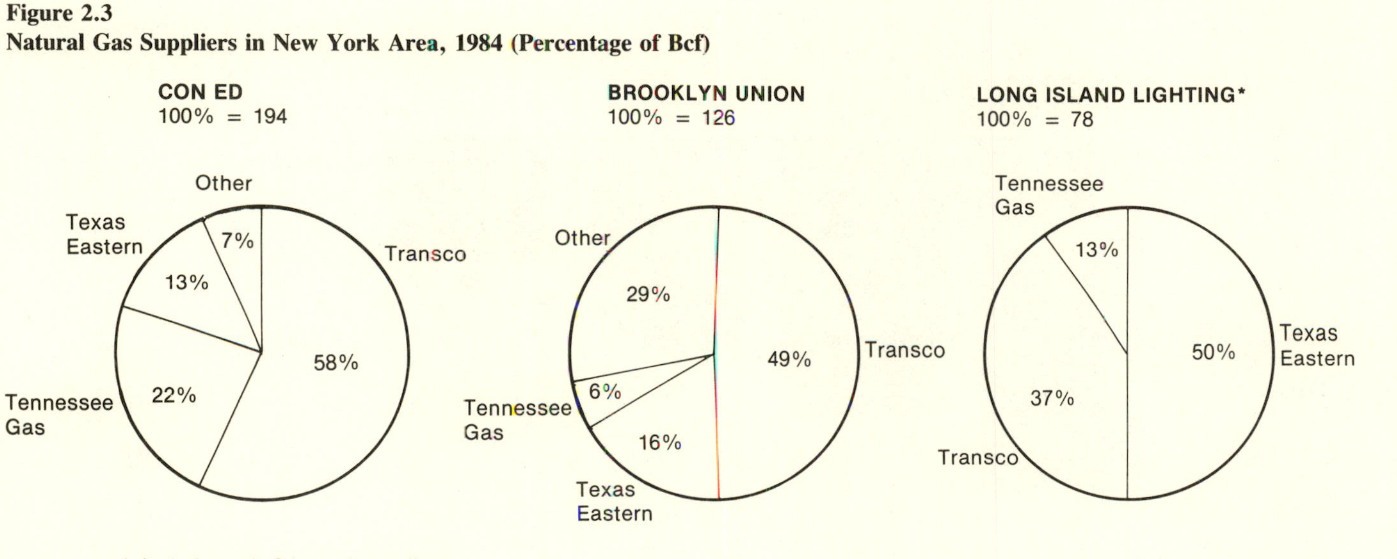

* Includes only 3 largest suppliers.

Source: Consolidated Edison Company of New York, "Uniform Statistical Report—Year Ended December 31, 1984," New York, April 29, 1985, p. G-15; Brooklyn Union Gas Company, "Uniform Statistical Report—Year Ended September 30, 1984," Brooklyn, April 18, 1985; Long Island Lighting Information based on phone conversation with gas purchasing department.

Figure 2.4
Carriage for Distributors and End Users by Interstate Pipelines (Bcf)

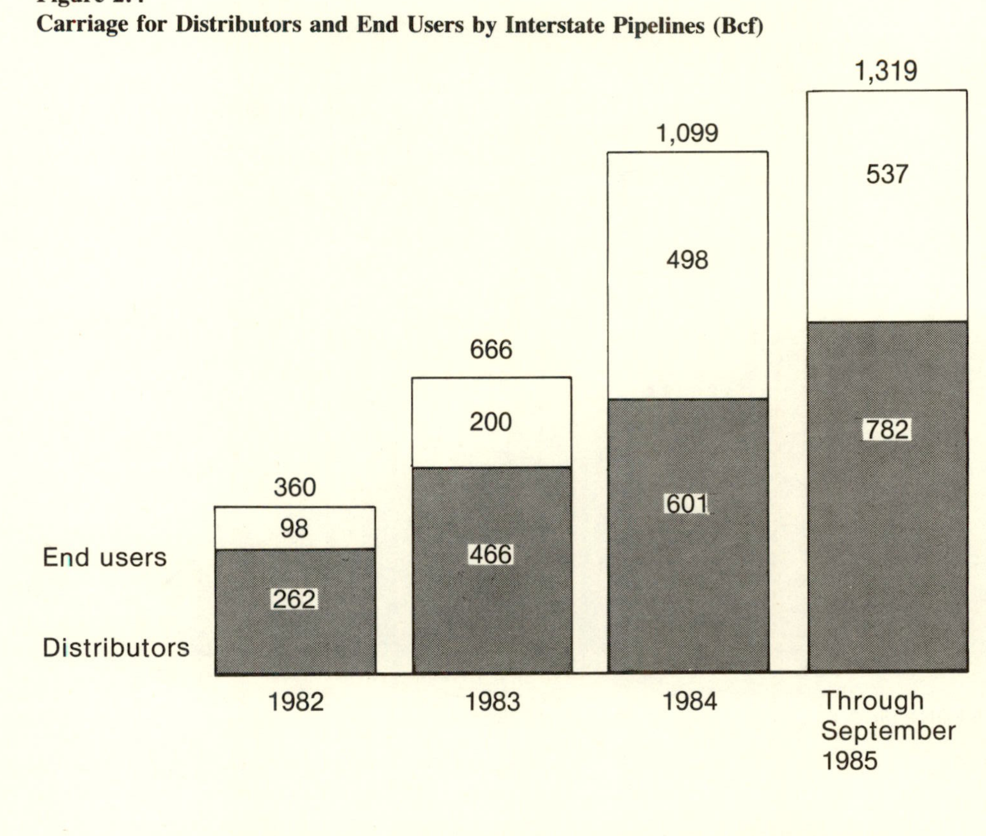

Source: Interstate Natural Gas Association of America, "Voluntary Carriage Third Quarter 1985," Washington, D.C., January 1986.

volatile gas market, pipelines may be tempted to move more heavily into production to eliminate the uncertainty of their purchased gas costs.

New strategies being used by LDCs also pose new challenges to policymakers. In an effort to retain customers capable of fuel switching, LDCs have turned to offering more attractive rate schedules. A 1984 survey found that 49 percent of all LDCs offered industrial rates pegged to alternative fuel prices, and many were considering rate structures that would take into account both the cost-of-service and alternative fuel capabilities. In addition, the never-ending debate over how fixed costs should be divided between the commodity charge (based on annual use levels) and the demand charge (based on peak use levels) has assumed new importance. By placing a greater proportion of fixed costs in the demand charge, LDCs (as well as pipelines) generally can reduce costs to industrial customers, who tend to have lower peak demands relative to their average demand levels. Undoubtedly, LDCs will attempt to do so.

LDCs and pipelines also will consider developing rate structures that allow an "unbundling of services," with separate charges for storage, transportation, and perhaps for "supplier-of-last-resort" services. Thus future rate hearings will likely focus more on rate *structures* than on rate *levels*.

Finally, efforts by large industrial end users to build connections directly to interstate pipelines, thereby bypassing LDCs, will create challenges for both the FERC and state Public Utility Commissions (PUCs). In the past, regulators have opposed such connections on the grounds that the loss of large industrial customers would shift the affected LDC's fixed costs to its remaining customers. In many cases, however, this impact is negligible. LDCs simply could cut back purchases of high-cost gas, thus lowering average prices for remaining customers. To the extent that fixed costs are reallocated, much of the reallocation simply will reduce preexisting subsidies from large industrial customers to residential users. Thus the damage to residential customers may not be severe. In addition, if industrial customers wish to retain the right to switch back to an LDC, a standby charge would be levied to cover a portion of fixed costs. The costs and benefits of large industrial customers hooking up directly to a pipeline should be assessed carefully by state PUCs.

The task of overseeing a natural gas industry that is partially regulated and partially free of regulation has made both the federal and state governments' task more difficult than ever before. When the natural gas industry was completely regulated by the government, the questions were narrow and technical: How much did this service cost? How should this transaction be categorized? Today, the questions are broad and conceptual. Industry initiatives, particularly by pipelines and LDCs, raise thorny questions that go directly to the heart of the issue of what role the government should play in regulating an industry that shows many of the characteristics of a monopoly. How these questions are answered are vital to determining the size and nature of the natural gas industry's future contribution to the American economy.

Notes

1. *Phillips Petroleum Company v. Wisconsin*, 347 U.S. 672 (1954).

2. U.S. Department of Energy, Energy Information Administration, *Annual Energy Review, 1984*, U.S. Government Printing Office, Washington, D.C., April 1985, p. 9.

3. U.S. Department of Energy, Energy Information Administration, *U.S. Crude Oil, Natural Gas, and Natural Gas Liquids Reserves, 1978 Annual Report*, U.S. Government Printing Office, Washington, D.C., 1979, p. 11; American Gas Association, Arlington, Va.; American Petroleum Institute, Washington, D.C.; Canadian Petroleum Association, Calgary, Alberta, Canada, *Reserves of Crude Oil, Natural Gas Liquids, and Natural Gas in the United States and Canada as of December 31, 1979*, 34, June 1980.

4. U.S. Department of Energy, Energy Information Administration, *Intrastate and Interstate Supply Markets under the Natural Gas Policy Act*, U.S. Government Printing Office, Washington, D.C., October 1981, p. 40.

5. U.S. Department of Energy, Energy Information Administration, *Annual Energy Review, 1984*, p. 135.

6. Board of Governors of the Federal Reserve System, *Federal Reserve Bulletin*, U.S. Government Printing Office, Washington, D.C., various issues.

7. Data Resources, ''U.S. Central Data Base,'' Lexington, Mass., Autumn 1985, On-Line Computer Data Base.

8. U.S. Department of Energy, Assistant Secretary, Conservation and Renewable Energy, *Industrial Energy Productivity Project—Final Report: The Pulp and Paper Industry*, U.S. Government Printing Office, Washington, D.C., February 1983, pp. A–48–A–57.

9. International Energy Agency, *Energy Policies and Programmes of the IEA Countries, 1984 Review*, Paris, 1985, pp. 328, 527.

10. U.S. Department of Energy, Energy Information Administration, *Energy Conservation Indicators, 1984 Annual Report*, U.S. Government Printing Office, Washington, D.C., December 1985, p. 71.

11. American Gas Association, ''1986 Outlook,'' *Gas Energy Review*, Arlington, Va., January 1986, supplement; U.S. Department of Energy, Energy Information Administration, *Natural Gas Monthly*, August 1985, p. 14; Foster Associates, ''Natural Gas Supply/Demand Outlook in the United States and Canada, 1985–2000,'' Report Prepared for Polar Gas Limited, Washington, D.C., February 1985, II, p. III–9.

12. ''Merrill Lynch Sees U.S. Gas Rebound,'' *Oil and Gas Journal*, February 1983, p. 67; ''Deliverability Surplus Keeps U.S. Natural Gas Industry in Quandary,'' *Oil and Gas Journal*, June 1983, p. 25.

13. American Petroleum Institute, ''Basic Petroleum Data Book,'' Washington, D.C., May 1985; American Petroleum Institute, ''Quarterly Completion Report,'' Washington, D.C., November 1985, p. 9.

14. U.S. Department of Energy, *U.S. Crude Oil, Natural Gas, and Natural Gas Liquids Reserves*, p. 26.

15. American Petroleum Institute, *Joint Association Survey of Drilling Costs*, Washington, D.C., various issues.

16. Independent Producers Association of America, ''Report of the Cost Study Committee,'' San Francisco, May 29–31, 1985.

17. U.S. Department of Interior, Minerals Management Service, *Federal Offshore*

Statistics, U.S. Government Printing Office, Washington, D.C., September 1985, pp. 14–15

18. Offshore Data Services, *Offshore Rig Locator*, Houston, Texas, various issues.

19. Independent Producers Association of America, "Report."

20. U.S. Department of Energy, Energy Information Administration, *Natural Gas Monthly*, May 1985, p. 58.

21. American Petroleum Institute, "Basic Petroleum Data Book."

22. C. S. Matthews, "Increase in United States 'Old Gas' Reserves Due to Deregulation," Report Prepared for Shell Oil Company, Washington, D.C., April 1985; U.S. Department of Energy, Office of the Assistant Secretary for Policy, Safety, and Environment, *Increasing Competition in the Natural Gas Market: The Second Report Required by Section 123 of the Natural Gas Policy Act of 1978*, U.S. Government Printing Office, Washington, D.C., January 1985; Office of Technology Assessment, *U.S. Natural Gas Availability*, U.S. Government Printing Office, Washington, D.C., February 1985.

23. Milton Benjamin, "Gas Decontrol Would Fatten Big Oil Firms," *The Washington Post*, July 20, 1983, p. 1.

Selected Bibliography

American Gas Association. "1986 Outlook." *Gas Energy Review*. Arlington, Va., January 1986, supplement.

American Petroleum Institute. *Joint Association Survey of Drilling Costs*. Washington, D.C.

———. "Quarterly Completion Report." Washington, D.C., November 1985.

Independent Producers Association of America. "Report of the Cost Study Committee." San Francisco, May 29–31, 1985.

International Energy Agency. *Energy Policies and Programmes of the IEA Countries, 1984 Review*. Paris, 1985.

Matthews, C. S. "Increase in United States 'Old Gas' Reserves Due to Deregulation." Report Prepared for Shell Oil Company. Washington, D.C., April 1985.

Office of Technology Assessment. *U.S. Natural Gas Availability*. U.S. Government Printing Office, Washington, D.C., February 1985.

Offshore Data Services. *Offshore Rig Locator*. Houston, Texas, various issues.

U.S. Department of Energy. *Energy Conservation Indicators, 1984 Annual Report*. U.S. Government Printing Office, Washington, D.C., December 1985.

———. *Industrial Energy Productivity Project—Final Report: The Pulp and Paper Industry*. U.S. Government Printing Office, Washington, D.C., February 1983.

———. *Intrastate and Interstate Supply Markets under the Natural Gas Policy Act*. U.S. Government Printing Office, Washington, D.C., October 1981.

U.S. Department of Energy, Energy Information Administration. *Annual Energy Review, 1984*. U.S. Government Printing Office, Washington, D.C., April 1985.

———. *U.S. Crude Oil, Natural Gas, and Natural Gas Liquids Reserves, 1984 Annual Report*. U.S. Government Printing Office, Washington, D.C., September 1985.

U.S. Department of Energy, Office of the Assistant Secretary for Policy, Safety, and Environment. *Increasing Competition in the Natural Gas Market: The Second Report Required by Section 123 of the Natural Gas Policy Act of 1978*. U.S. Government Printing Office, Washington, D.C., January 1985.

U.S. Department of Interior, Minerals Management Service. *Federal Offshore Statistics*. U.S. Government Printing Office, Washington, D.C., September 1985.

Comments

JAMES R. GATTIS
Manager, Natural Gas Planning
Shell Oil Company

John Sawhill's description of how market and regulatory forces produce major impacts on various segments of the natural gas industry is outstanding. Since natural gas must now compete directly with alternative fuels and since the efficiency of the entire industry is highly dependent on "economies of scale," full utilization of capacity in each segment—producers, pipelines, LDCs, and consumers—is critical to the vitality of the natural gas industry. Thus to make enlightened decisions, one must try to understand the perspectives and needs of all segments. The following comments are offered to complement Sawhill's work.

We fully agree that reactive government regulations have historically distorted natural gas markets. Sawhill's projection of steady consumption seems reasonable; however, actual gas demand will be highly dependent on the gas industry's ability to compete with alternate fuels. This, in turn, will depend both on the willingness of each segment to compete effectively and efficiently and on the willingness of regulators to support such competition.

Sawhill implied that improvements in drilling efficiency will allow producers to continue making substantial reserve additions at current low wellhead prices. However, this assessment is based on a misinterpretation of the data. The fact that the number of wells completed by each active drilling rig rose between 1981 and 1984 indeed reflects significant improvements in drilling efficiency, but it is also partially the result of a major drop in deep-well drilling (which takes orders of magnitude more time). Since active rotary rigs had dropped from an average of 1,976 in 1985 to 1,248 by March 1986, future completions and reserve additions should drop markedly, since further increases in drilling efficiency are unlikely.

While drilling costs per foot have declined, opportunities for finding significant new reserves have been mainly limited to remote, expensive areas such as the deep-water Gulf of Mexico. Producers now face high platform and transportation costs, greater market risks, oil and gas price uncertainties, potential revisions in taxation policy, and unpredictable regulatory responses, in addition to the traditional risks associated with exploration and well productivity.

Sawhill suggested that the economics of gas drilling have improved dramatically since 1979, citing as evidence the fact that wellhead prices are 60 percent higher in real terms in early 1986 than they were in 1979. He obviously was referring to average wellhead prices, but they have no impact on the economics of drilling. Drilling investment decisions are driven by expectations about future gas prices. In December 1979 most producers expected prices for gas from new wells to grow at 3.5 percent real through April 1981 and 4.0 percent real until gas decontrol on January 1, 1985. It was also expected that the price of oil would be higher than the price of this gas in December 1984 and that decontrol would exert upward pressures on gas prices. In contrast to these expectations, spot gas prices in 1986 are between $1.50 and $2.25 per million Btu, lower in nominal terms than 1979 prices, and they are now expected to remain depressed for several years due to the gas bubble and current low crude oil prices. In addition, the new market risk and proposed changes in tax laws will severely impact the economics of drilling, particularly the ability of independents to finance drilling programs. Consequently, we believe that the outlook for gas-drilling investments has been significantly reduced.

The assumption of a reserves-to-production (R/P) ratio of 8.0 is unrealistic. It understates the need for future gas additions. It is very unlikely that the gas R/P ratio will drop as low as 8.0, due to low production rates from associated gas caps and the seasonality of demand that precludes producing at capacity except in one or two winter months each year.

To prevent a significant decline in U.S. reserves and production capacity, several disincentives to drilling and production need to be removed. Prices will be limited by burner-tip prices less transportation and distribution costs. The following will be required to maximize efficiency (maintain supplies and throughout) and minimize consumer costs and risks:

1. Opportunities to enhance production from old fields (i.e., decontrol)
2. Credible regulatory policies (i.e., no reneges in government policy, assurance of contract sanctity)
3. Equitable regulatory policies between the various industry segments to ensure that adequate capital is invested to find, develop, and produce economical supplies, rather than encourage excessive spending reliance on rate-base projects
4. Efficient distribution based solely on actual costs
5. Predictability of competitive transportation
6. Predictability and efficiency of *free* wellhead prices and market flexibility (blanket abandonments)

These regulatory policies and economic systems will benefit the American public by maximizing the development of economical/competitive reserves, by maximizing "economies of scale," and by maximizing contributions to our domestic economy.

As regards Sawhill's very credible policy discussion, several additional points are in order. Rate-base regulations have outlived their original purpose to stimulate investment and new construction. Rate-base regulations allow investment risks to be passed on to customers and allow costs from bad operating decisions to be recovered. Transporters and distributors need to be held responsible and accountable for their investment and operating decisions, just as they need incentives to reduce operating costs, to maximize capacity utilization, and to better manage risk. As pipelines phase out their resale function, LDCs must work with producers to secure their gas supplies, both for the short and long term.

To minimize the detrimental effects of uncertainty, the transition to new regulatory policies should be accomplished swiftly and thoughtfully.

JAMES E. NUGENT

Chairman, Railroad Commission of Texas

John Sawhill provided a good overview of the changing role of goverment in the evolving natural gas industry. However, from my perspective as chairman of the state agency that regulates the production of one-third of the nation's natural gas, I must take issue with his supply and deliverability outlook.

An accurate assessment of long-term supply prospects is crucial if we are to understand today's natural gas market and predict future trends. Sawhill cited American Gas Association studies, which claim an annual deliverability to U.S. markets of around 20–21 trillion cubic feet (Tcf) (including Canadian supplies). He also said that deliverability has increased somewhat in recent years, as a result of a decline in consumption coupled with increased drilling activity in the late 1970s and early 1980s.

"With deliverability to U.S. markets at 20–21 Tcf, the size of the deliverability surplus at the beginning of 1986 was 2.5 to 3.5 Tcf, a substantial check on future price increases," he said. Although he acknowledged dissenting opinions by other forecasters, he nevertheless concluded that the surplus has been "extremely durable" and may continue for several years.

Unfortunately, this conclusion is based on two questionable assumptions: that drilling activity will be high enough to provide substantial reserve additions and that increasing Canadian imports will be available at relatively low cost. Neither assumption appears realistic when examined in the cold light of today's natural gas situation.

Those who believe in the myths surrounding the infamous "gas bubble" take comfort in noting that available natural gas supplies exceed demand, especially when imported gas is taken into account. This rosy view, however, ignores a crucial factor: deliverability—the industry's ability to supply gas to meet essential human needs. Of particular importance is deliverability during peak winter demand periods.

During the past several years, deliverability has been studied extensively, first in Texas, then in other producing states. The evidence warns us that deliverability in Texas, the nation's largest producing state, is declining. The same is true elsewhere, leading to the grim conclusion that neither Texas nor the nation may be able to deliver enough gas to meet peak winter demand.

This harsh reality was brought home to Texas in mid-December 1983, when the state suffered extremely cold weather. Although well-test reports on file with the Railroad Commission showed potential deliverability of 24.0 billion cubic feet (Bcf) per day, the state's wells actually were able to deliver only 13.5 Bcf per day. Texas could meet a demand approaching 17.0 Bcf per day only by withdrawing more than 3.0 Bcf per day from storage reservoirs. Had the cold spell continued, storage reservoirs would have been exhausted and pipelines would have faced shutdowns because of pressure drops.

Seeking more comprehensive information on this situation, the Interstate Oil Compact Commission (IOCC) studied deliverability to determine whether or not a gas surplus really existed and how much gas was available to meet peak demand. Using actual production figures and considering gas that could not be delivered due to frozen-off or shut-in wells, the IOCC calculated an average nationwide deliverability of 50.961 Bcf per day during the winter of 1983–1984, with an available surplus of 1.198 Bcf per day. During that same period, peak demand consumption rose as high as 73.015 Bcf per day. Average consumption was 46.12 and 47.91 Bcf per day in 1983 and 1984.

Aside from the dramatic contrast between average- and peak-day demand figures, the IOCC study makes two other telling points. First, we cannot count on delivery of a significant amount of gas during winter demand peaks because of frozen-off wells. Second, none of the producing states believes that its reported gas deliverability would be equal to the challenge of sustained periods of peak demand that a cold winter might bring about.

Financial forces at work in world energy markets point to continuing declines in the ability to deliver natural gas. The IOCC study, as well as testimony at the Railroad Commission's recent state-of-the-industry conference, challenge the notion that drilling, exploration, and reserve additions are continuing at healthy levels. As one industry veteran commented, "We are depleting our gas reserves faster than they are being replaced—in some cases for prices not only below replacement cost but below actual operating cost. The consequence could be bankruptcies and premature abandonments, with loss of recoverable reserves and delivery capacity that consumers will desperately need in the future."

In 1984, the latest year for which complete natural gas reserve data are available, proven reserves of natural gas were at their lowest level since 1976, the year the Department of Energy first began estimating reserves. Since then, new discoveries have replaced only about 80 percent of the gas we have produced.

Texas dramatically illustrates what appears to be taking place in the nation's other producing regions. In Texas, 51 percent of the natural gas produced last year came from wells drilled within the past five years. One-third of 1985 production came from wells drilled in the past three years. Plunging drilling and exploration today are precursors to steepening declines in future production and deliverability.

When one compares finding costs with the wellhead price, it is easy to see why many operators believe it is no longer worthwhile to explore for and develop new gas supplies. The average U.S. wellhead price is $2.28 per thousand cubic feet (Mcf), with spot gas in some cases as low as $1.29 per Mcf. With finding costs about $2.17 per Mcf, the economics are definitely against the business of gas exploration.

Given these fiscal realities, it is not surprising that several studies of planned industry expenditures spotlight the decreasing emphasis on exploration in general and on natural gas exploration in particular.

One study of 20 major companies and 127 independents completed in late 1985 indicated that they planned to cut exploration funds 6 to 7 percent in 1986 with an overwhelming shift from gas to oil exploration. Since then, falling prices have deepened the cuts. We recently have been told that many companies are cutting back their 1986 exploration budgets 20 to 30 percent. A comprehensive study conducted by the American Petroleum Institute bears this out and predicts that domestic natural gas production will fall below 14 Tcf per year in the early 1990s if oil prices stay at current levels.

This gloomy picture for exploration is being confirmed by drilling statistics. The domestic active rig count declined 50 percent between 1981 and 1985. Since January 1986, it has declined another 50 percent. Although gas well drilling constituted about 30 percent of all drilling at the beginning of the decade, it now is only 15 percent. Wildcat drilling for gas has dropped almost 50 percent in the past five years.

Should we depend on imported gas (primarily from Canada) for reliable, low-cost supplies to replace our own declining production? Many domestic producers would say that, as increasing gas imports displace domestic supplies, they further savage an already unhealthy domestic industry and hasten the production decline. The costs of such competition by imports must be weighed carefully against the benefits, whether the commodity is natural gas, farm products, or shoes.

Some Texas producers also would challenge the notion that Canadian supplies are either low cost or reliable. They claim that the Canadian producers' replacing of a flat import price with a two-part demand/commmodity rate acts as a subterfuge to compel purchases, despite the availability of cheaper domestic production.

They also question the reliability of these gas supplies, which are subject to a foreign government's changing policies. Even the present, looser Canadian gas policy includes a restriction on exports if prices are below the price charged in adjacent provinces—a prohibition recently invoked by the Canadian government in sales to U.S. markets by certain producers.

As Sawhill's chapter indicates, wise government energy policy must operate well in times of surplus as well as of shortage. Unfortunately, we suffer from the *lack* of a national energy policy. Policymakers must not be lulled to inaction by a phantom gas glut but instead must plan for the future based on a firm understanding of the realities of today's natural gas industry and markets.

3

U.S. Links to North American Supply Markets

HENRY LEE

Although natural gas imports constitute only a small fraction of U.S. energy consumption, they are the focus of intense interest. Major natural gas producing and consuming states, producers, pipelines, and distribution companies all view imported gas as an important factor, and their individual perspectives collectively have a strong voice in the formation of U.S. natural gas policy. To those nations who export gas to the United States, natural gas is not only significant politically, but it plays a crucial role in their balance of trade and economic health.

This chapter explores factors that will shape the future level of gas exports to the United States from Canada and Mexico. The first section analyzes both geological and economic factors shaping U.S. natural gas imports from Canada for the period 1985–2000. The second section assesses the political and institutional factors that will influence Canada's export and import decisions. The third and final section reviews the potential of gas imports to the United States from Mexico.

Factors Affecting the Availability of Exportable Gas

There are several issues governing the supply of exportable gas. First, are potentially importable gas resources constrained by either geological or economic circumstances? Only a limited amount of gas can be produced from any individual field. As production declines with diminishing supply, the cost of extraction accelerates. Taking an entire country as a whole, however, there are questions about the efficacy of the geological approach to forecasting. Past experience shows that oil- or gas-price increases spur the discovery and development of additional resources. For example, in 1972 and again in 1977 there was widespread concern that Canadian reserves were declining.[1] The 1974 and 1979 price hikes erased that concern, and today the outlook for future Canadian gas supplies is much more optimistic. This suggests that gas availability is more a function of economics than geology. At some price incremental supplies will always become available.

The second issue concerns the relationship between crude oil and gas prices. Most marginal gas is used in industrial or utility boilers. In these markets, gas competes directly with residual oil for both existing and new customers.[2] In the future, gas will receive increasingly vigorous competition from electricity. In the short term, residual oil prices will continue to serve as a ceiling above which gas prices cannot rise without risking significant loss of market share.

This relationship is essential to understanding the economics of gas production. If oil prices remain stable in real terms, so too will gas prices. If gas prices do not rise, the incentive to invest in additional gas production will decrease. Furthermore, in a country such as Mexico where gas reserves are often found associated with oil, decisions about which fields to develop are directly related to the comparative market price of the two fuels. If gas prices increase, Mexico will have a stronger incentive to increase production from fields in which the gas-to-oil ratio is high.

The third issue concerns the relationship between domestic gas demand and the market for exports. Specifically, increases in domestic gas consumption within an exporting country may substantially curtail the amount of gas available for export. This factor is significant in determining the future level of exports from Canada and Mexico, both of which are discussed below.

Canada

Since as early as 1958, the United States has been a net importer of natural gas from Canada. During the past ten years Canadian exports have comprised 4 to 5 percent of total U.S. gas demand (see Table 3.1), consumed principally in three markets: the Northwest, California, and the Midwest. These regions originally turned to Canada to meet rapidly growing demand at the same time that Canada needed additional revenues to expand its domestic delivery service eastward. The relationship was mutually advantageous and still is.

Economics of Canadian Gas

Natural gas production in Canada is concentrated in one province—Alberta. Although there is some production in Saskatchewan and British Columbia and reserves have been discovered on the East Coast off Newfoundland and Nova Scotia and in the Canadian Arctic, Alberta accounts for fully 61 percent of all known reserves. Table 3.2 presents a breakdown of the latest estimates of Canada's natural gas resources.

At what *price* will Canada's considerable reserves become available for export? Although marginal cost data are scarce, and existing estimates are open to debate, a recent study suggests that at a price under $11 per thousand cubic feet (Mcf),

Table 3.1
Canadian Gas Exports (Tcf)

	U.S. Demand[a]	Canadian Gas Exports to U.S.[b]	Canadian Share (%)	Authorized Export Volumes[c]	Rate of Take (%)
1976	19.946	0.953	4.8	1.045	91
1977	19.521	0.996	5.1	1.045	95
1978	19.627	0.881	4.5	1.045	84
1979	20.241	1.001	5.0	1.055	95
1980	19.877	0.796	4.0	1.159	69
1981	19.404	0.762	3.9	1.454	53
1982	18.001	0.783	4.4	1.625	48
1983	16.835	0.711	4.2	1.625	44
1984	17.645	0.755	4.3	1.625	47

[a]1976-1983, U.S. Department of Energy, Energy Information Administration, *Natural Gas Monthly*, May 1985, p. lx; 1984, U.S. Department of Energy, Energy Information Administration, *Monthly Energy Review*, July 1985, p. 58.

[b]*Natural Gas Monthly*, May 1985, p. lxiii.

[c]National Energy Board of Canada, "Reasons for Decisions in the Matter of Phase II—The License Phase, and Phase III—The Surplus of the Gas Omnibus Hearing, 1982," Ottawa, Ontario, Canada, January 1983.

approximately 270 trillion cubic feet (Tcf) would be available (see Table 3.3).[3] Extrapolating from this study suggests that 150 Tcf would be available from conventional sources if gas prices reached $6.45 per Mcf (delivered in Chicago).[4] More than 73 Tcf would be available at $3.53 or less.[5] In any event, the marginal cost of developing new reserves in Canada is significantly lower than that in the United States, thus demonstrating Canada's long-term capacity to produce ample supplies at prices equal to or below competitive prices in the United States.[6]

Price and Supply

Are gas prices likely to reach the levels necessary to develop these reserves? The gas available for export is a function of *total* availability, and therefore of oil prices. As prices increase, more gas becomes available, not only because of increased investments in production but also due to decreases in domestic demand. Either extreme—rapidly increasing or decreasing oil prices—will dampen gas exports. If oil prices skyrocket, they are likely to ratchet upward in discrete

Table 3.2
Canadian Gas Resources, December 1982 (Tcf)

Established Reserves[a]		**Amount Remaining**
Conventional Areas		
British Columbia	7.8	
Alberta	61.0	
Saskatchewan	1.0	
Ontario	0.3	
Subtotal	70.1	
Frontier Areas		
Mainland Territories	0.4	
MacKenzie Delta/Beaufort Sea	7.5	
Eastern OCS[b]	5.4	
Arctic Islands	13.4	
Subtotal	26.9	
TOTAL		97.0
Undiscovered and Unproven Conventional Resources[b]		
Eastern Canada	16.6	
British Columbia	5.9	
Alberta	36.0	
Saskatchewan	0.4	
TOTAL		58.9
Deep Tight Natural Gas[c]		77.0
TOTAL RESOURCES		232.9

[a] Canadian Petroleum Association, *CPA Statistical Handbook*, 1982, Section II, Table 3.

[b] National Energy Board of Canada, "Reasons for Decisions in the Matter of Phase II —The License Phase, and Phase III—The Surplus of the Gas Omnibus Hearing, 1982," Ottawa, Ontario, Canada, January 1983, p. 21. The Eastern Canadian estimates are from the Geological Survey of Canada, October 1984.

[c] ICF, *North American Gas Study: The Benefits of Increased Trade*. Washington, D.C., February 1984, p. A-10.

increments, stimulated by some type of supply disruption. Such increases would provide incentives for additional exploration and production, but these incentives would be offset by worldwide decreases in economic growth and oil and gas consumption. Furthermore, investors are not likely to expect high oil prices to

Table 3.3
Gas Resource Cost and Availability (1984 U.S. Dollars)

	Cost/Mcf	Field to Border	Border to U.S. Market[a]	Total Cost	Amount (Tcf)[b]
Western conventional	0.57	0.43	0.65	1.65	23
Western conventional high	2.46	0.43	0.65	3.53	50
Western deep	5.38	0.43	0.65	6.45	77
Northwestern Arctic	3.53	5.10	0.65	9.28	58
Northwestern Arctic high	4.35	5.10	0.65	10.10	41
Eastern offshore	4.01	2.55	0.84	7.40	13
Eastern offshore high	6.55	2.55	0.84	9.10	9

[a] All the gas except Eastern gas is assumed to move into Chicago through existing systems. The cost of a pipeline from the Maine border to Massachusetts is assumed to be $333 million and incorporated into the per mcf cost.

[b] The difference between this forecast and that of the Canadian Petroleum Association (Table 3.2) is due to different estimates of Arctic gas.

Source: For cost/mcf and amount: S. L. Schwartz, J. D. Fuller, and W. T. Ziemba, "Long Run Effects of the Canadian National Energy Agreements," *Energy Journal*, April 1985, p. 66. (The figures were converted to 1984 dollars using Department of Commerce GNP inflators.) For field to border price: ICF, *North American Gas Study: The Benefits of Increased Trade*, Washington, D.C., February 1984.

hold steady for long periods and therefore may delay additional investments until the dust settles.

If oil prices decline to the vicinity of $15 per barrel or lower, incentives for investment in gas exploration and production would decline as well, unless the Canadian government were to adopt offsetting tax reductions for the industry. In 1981–1984 Canadian gas drilling declined from 4,333 to 1,927 completed wells.[7] In 1984 there were 7,631 oil and gas completions in western Canada, of which only 25 percent were gas wells.[8] Furthermore, a large portion of the gas drilling occurred in Saskatchewan, which is striving to become self-sufficient in gas and is providing its gas industry with substantial investment incentives. Recently announced changes in Canadian federal and provincial tax structures will help reverse this downward trend, but a rapid reduction in oil prices will more than offset these tax changes and further dampen incentives to invest.

If oil and gas prices somehow could be decoupled, gas exports might not be reduced by extreme movements in oil prices. For example, to stimulate interfuel substitution, Canadian price regulation kept gas prices below those of oil. If

Canada allows gas prices to remain low in the face of oil price hikes, exports could theoretically increase. Yet this theory is unlikely to survive the realities of domestic politics. Canada has not been willing to export gas at prices below those paid by its citizens for *either* oil or gas products. It would be hard to decouple domestic pricing policies from export policy, especially in a tight market when distributional issues and concern for the consumer would be of paramount political importance.

Domestic Gas Demand

Gas-export availability also depends on domestic demand. Canada's official policy is to export only gas in excess of domestic needs. In recent years gas demand has grown rapidly, first due to the lower price of gas relative to that of oil and second due to a series of government incentives to induce interfuel substitution. However, falling world oil prices, a continued surplus of relatively cheap electricity, and changes in government policy should moderate this growth. Moreover, the Canadian National Energy Board (NEB) has forecast relatively low economic and population growth, further supporting lower rather than higher domestic demand projections.

Canadian domestic demand in 1984 was approximately 1.74 Tcf.[9] If gas demand grows annually at 2.5 percent, Canadians will use another 38.0 Tcf between 1985 and the year 2000—barely one-sixth of their currently predicted resource base. Whatever the scenario, Canada should have an abundance of gas available for export.

Transportation

Even given ample supplies, is there sufficient pipeline capacity in place to transport the gas to U.S. markets?

Present pipeline capacity is in the vicinity of 1.7 Tcf.[10] Pipeline expansions are currently proposed that could move Alberta gas and East Coast offshore gas into New England and additional western gas across the border at Emerson and Monchy. These expansions would increase capacity to some 2.35 Tcf.[11]

To some extent the figure of 2.35 Tcf is misleading. First, it is an annual averaged figure and thus ignores seasonal surges in demand. Bottlenecks could occur during the coldest winter day, when gas demand in the Midwest and Northeast is at its highest level. Although peak utilization varies from one pipeline to the next, there is generally spare capacity in the system during peak demand.[12] If Canadian exports increase to the 1.5–2.0 Tcf level, and if this increase is predominantly in winter sales to the Midwest, bottlenecks could occur unless new facilities were constructed.

Yet even under these circumstances, several remedial options are available. First, utilization of existing storage in the United States could be increased and new storage facilities could be built in Canada. Second, pipelines could move gas from one region to another by displacement (i.e., gas bound for California could be diverted into the Midwest, while more Canadian gas could flow through to California). There are physical barriers to the amount of gas that can be rerouted through displacement, but they are not insurmountable and could be overcome if the economic incentives are sufficiently attractive.

One transportation constraint is that almost three-quarters of Canadian exports enter the United States at three points: Kingsgate, Monchy, and Emerson. The first two contain excess capacity. There is limited capability to transport Canadian gas into the North Central, Northeast, and Mid-Atlantic regions. Although proposals to increase pipeline availability to these regions are now under active scrutiny by both the United States and Canada, this additional capacity will not be in place until the early 1990s.

Summary

Ample supplies of Canadian gas are available. If oil prices remain stable or increase slowly, there will be sufficient *economic* incentives for Canada to increase gas exports. Over the long term, rapid change in oil prices (in either direction) will reduce export levels in proportion to the magnitude of these price fluctuations. Finally, there may be short-term, region-specific transportation constraints, but in the long term pipeline capacity will not be a limiting factor on Canada's ability to export gas.

Institutional Factors in Canadian-U.S. Gas Trade

The trade of natural resources across national boundaries does not depend exclusively on economic factors. Internal politics, nationalism, and popular perceptions are often more influential than economics in shaping a country's international trade. The previous section noted the relationship between inceases in domestic gas prices and levels of gas available for export. Therefore, this section focuses on two variables: the willingness of Canada to export gas and the willingness of the United States to receive it.

The United States and Canada share a 5,524-mile border, and 80 percent of the Canadian population lives within 100 miles of the United States. Trade between the two nations totaled $113 billion in 1984, 35 percent greater than trade with Japan, the United States' second largest trading partner.[13] Canadian exports to the United States account for more than 15 percent of Canadian GNP, and approximately 3 million Canadian jobs depend on trade with the United States.[14] Seventy-five percent of all foreign investment in Canada is controlled by Americans.[15]

Relations between the two countries have vacillated from cooperation to contention. One observer noted that Canadian sentiment traditionally swings between nationalism and continentalism.[16] At present, the pendulum is swinging back from a long stretch of nationalism, as the Mulroney government attempts to change those policies of the mid- and late–1970s that it believes discouraged foreign investment and inhibited trade. Such historical fluctuations are inevitable.

However, the difference in the size of the two countries alone (the U.S. population is ten times as large) ensures Canada's ongoing apprehension of U.S. "paternalism." Pierre Trudeau once remarked that "living next to the United States is in some ways like sleeping with an elephant. No matter how friendly or even-tempered is the beast . . . one is affected by every twitch and grunt."[17]

Interprovincial Energy Politics

A major factor shaping the political economy of Canada's natural gas industry is the relationship between her provincial and federal governments. No factor is more difficult for Americans to appreciate or more important. Located within Canada's 3.8 million square miles are ten provinces and two territories. Each has its own identity, traditions, economic base, and—in some instances—language. There is a much greater difference between Alberta and Quebec than between Maryland and Oklahoma. The energy crisis and the discovery of the large oil and gas fields in western Canada exacerbated the economic disparities among the provinces. The result has been a continuing effort by petroleum-poor provinces to persuade the federal government to correct economic imbalances created by nature and an equally fervent effort by petroleum-rich provinces to evade this reallocation.

The constitutional powers of Canada's federal parliament and the provincial legislatures relating to the management of natural resources were established by the British North America Act of 1867.[18] This legislated that ownership and control of natural resources lying within a province fall within the jurisdiction of that province. This principle was reaffirmed in 1981 when the new Canadian Constitution was adopted by Parliament. Alberta, the major oil- and gas-producing province, has the authority to establish the volume and price of all gas leaving its borders, as well as retaining a percentage of royalties on its gas. In many respects Alberta is in the position of a monopolistic seller.

Until the Arab oil embargo of 1973–1974, the Canadian federal government took a hands-off position toward oil and natural gas. This changed dramatically in the following twelve years. With the National Energy Program (NEP), the federal government established regulations that governed pricing, taxation, production, transportation, and export. The major goal was to reallocate the benefits of oil and gas production from Alberta to the energy-poor provinces, which contained a majority of the electorate. Much of the NEP, especially its tax provisions, reflects the long-standing interprovincial economic struggle and the resultant commitment by the federal government to acquire greater control over the distribution of benefits derived from the sale of natural resources—control traditionally granted to the provinces.

When the federal government in the United States enacted a national energy program, the producing states had little choice but to live with it. The reaction in Canada was very different. The producing provinces had had total authority to manage oil and gas resources. Almost as soon as the NEP was announced, Alberta commenced negotiations with the federal government to "persuade" Ottawa to amend the tax package. To enhance its negotiating position, Alberta cut back its oil production, reminding Ottawa who had the constitutional capacity to control supply. The Federal/Alberta Memorandum of Agreement (signed in September 1981) gave victory to Alberta on the tax issues, but more importantly it reestablished the principle that the provinces had equal stature at the bargaining table.

One of the Mulroney government's first acts was to enter into negotiations with Alberta, Saskatchewan, and British Columbia on the issue of petroleum prices and taxation. In early 1985 the parties agreed to several measures, including gradual repeal of the Petroleum and Gas Revenue Tax (PGRT), a major fiscal provision of the old NEP anathema to the industry. The federal government agreed despite the prospect of budgetary deficits far in excess of those confronting the United States. To an American, this position might seem illogical, but to the Mulroney government, it was more important to return to the provinces what was constitutionally their property.

Although the Mulroney government has restored a substantial amount of power and control to the provinces and has begun to deregulate certain energy markets, it would be a mistake to interpret these actions as ideologically synonymous with the laissez-faire policies espoused in the United States. Canadians are more pragmatic than ideological, and there is a strong tradition of government intervention. Because of the unequal distribution of economic wealth among the provinces, Canadians throughout their history have been receptive to a level of government intervention that would be labeled "interference" in the United States. For example, 86 percent of economic activity in the Maritime Provinces is generated by government spending; in Ontario it is more than 45 percent.[19]

The present move toward a deregulated market for oil and gas stems from a perception that all Canadians—producers and consumers alike—will benefit. But in announcing the deregulation of oil, Minister of Energy, Mines, and Resources Pat Carney stated that "Canadian consumers will be protected from the volatility of the international markets. If world price escalates rapidly . . . the federal government, in consultation with the producing provinces, would take appropriate measures to protect Canadian interests."[20] Carney's remarks make it clear that, under certain circumstances, government intervention remains an option. If this position is expressed by a Conservative government, it is apt to be embraced with even more vigor by a Liberal government.

In summary, three broad political factors have in the past and will in the future affect Canadian petroleum policy: (1) Canada's relationship with the United States, which is characterized by cycles of nationalism followed by periods of cooperation; (2) reliance on negotiations between the provinces and the federal government to set national oil and gas policies; and (3) a national willingness to rely on government intervention to "protect" its consumers.

Canadian Export Policy

To decontextualize drastically the words of the southern preacher of American myth, Canadian gas-export policy "ain't what it should be; it ain't what it will be; but it sure ain't what it was." Understanding where that policy is today and where it is heading provides a barometer by which to measure the potential for increasing gas exports to the United States.

Three aspects of gas-export policy transcend all others: (1) pricing, (2) the requirement that all gas be priced identically at the border, and (3) the surplus test for calculating exportable volumes.

Pricing

On October 31, 1985, Minister Pat Carney announced that the federal government and the gas-producing provinces of Alberta, British Columbia, and Saskatchewan had reached an agreement (the Natural Gas Agreement) to deregulate domestic gas prices by November 1, 1986. This decision continued a four-year trend toward lower gas prices. Gas-export prices dropped from $4.94 in the early 1980s to $4.40 in 1983, to the $3.40 incentive price in 1984, to prices as low as $3.10 by early 1985. Under the Natural Gas Agreement prices will drop still further. To understand both the dynamics of Canadian pricing policy and the proposed deregulation, it is necessary to understand the perspectives of the three key participants: the federal government, the provincial governments (specifically Alberta), and the producers.

The Federal Perspective

The Conservative Mulroney government has three goals on its agenda:

1. Protect the consumer. Like the Liberals before them, the Conservatives understand that they must protect the interests of consumers, particularly those in Ontario and Quebec, who constitute the largest regional voting bloc. These two consuming provinces have exerted continuing pressure on Ottawa to lower gas prices to improve the competitive position of their manufacturing industries vis-à-vis U.S. competitors. The Conservatives realize that politically, Canadian gas cannot be sold at lower prices to factories in Detroit than to those located across the river in Windsor, Ontario.

2. Restore the constitutional right to control natural resources to the provinces, with the expectation that this right will be exercised in a manner benefitting all Canadians.

3. Move Canada to a more market-oriented regime for natural gas and oil by removing unnecessary government intervention.

Alberta's Perspective

Alberta shares the federal government's interest in streamlining provincial control of natural resources as well as the belief that a more market-oriented regime will serve Canada's long-term interests. But it also has several additional concerns.

First, Alberta relies heavily on oil and gas revenues. Ninety percent of gas production is from provincially owned land. Royalties accruing to Alberta from gas production vary from 25 to 40 percent. If gas prices decline and volumes sold do not increase, Alberta loses revenue that must be either foregone or made up by increasing other taxes.

Second, because of peculiarities in the regulatory system, Alberta's industrial users have had access to discounted gas, often at prices 50 percent below those paid by competitors. Loss of that competitive advantage will have negative intra-Albertan political repercussions.

Third, Alberta is blessed with large volumes of gas, for which there are presently no markets. Removal of regulatory restrictions that prevent access to these markets is perceived by Alberta as essential to long-term industrial stability. Alberta is willing to allow gas prices to fall, if in return its producers are given freer access to markets, especially those in the United States.

The Producers' Perspective

Since gas producers are major actors in the Alberta political scene, it is not surprising that they echo many of the positions of the province. Yet there is a subtle, but important, division within the industry. The smaller- and mid-sized independents believe that their inherent flexibility and entrepreneurial zeal will provide them with a competitive advantage in a deregulated market—not only in absolute terms but also relative to the larger companies. The independents are eager to make the price-volume tradeoff. Many of the majors, however, are less enthusiastic about deregulation, believing it will force them to confront a world of lower prices and declining market share.

Others

Three other actors also play an important role: the TransCanadian PipeLine, local distribution companies (LDCs), and the provincial government of Ontario. Their role historically has been secondary, but as issues such as pricing of transportation services, access to the distribution system, and renegotiation of existing producer pipeline contracts become more important, this situation is likely to change. Furthermore, Ontario no longer perceives the federal government as its surrogate at the negotiating table and will invariably take a more active position.

The Natural Gas Agreement

The Natural Gas Agreement (NGA) of October 1985 attempted to resolve the conflicting concerns of all parties. Although complex and not definitive, it was as important a step toward a market-oriented regime as Trudeau's NEP was a step toward an interventionist regime. Both policies were sensitive to the political pendulum. In 1978–1981 Canada was buffeted by escalating energy prices and an economic recession that released pressures for increasingly nationalistic policies. By 1985 the pendulum had reversed direction: Energy prices were falling, economic recovery was progressing, and sentiment was growing for increasing economic cooperation with the United States. Both the NGA and the NEP were attempts to formulate a delicate consensus to meet short-term political needs. Each was born of the belief that it would result in greater benefits for Canadian consumers and increased revenues for government coffers. In the case of the NEP, the weakness of this premise lay in the assumption that world oil and gas prices were heading in one direction—up. For the NGA it lay in the assumption that gas markets—both domestic and U.S.—would grow rapidly in response to lower prices.

The NGA contained three key pricing provisions:

1. After a one-year transition period, the Toronto city-gate reference price and the regulated Alberta border price would be replaced by an open market in which gas customers would be able to negotiate with gas producers over both price and volume. Existing contracts would be renegotiated during this transition period.
2. Volume restrictions would be removed on short-term (twenty-four months or less) natural gas exports.
3. The single Toronto city-gate price would be replaced with a series of regional price tests to determine the floor for export prices to the United States.

The NGA did not provide Albertan producers unlimited access to U.S. markets, nor did it provide a guarantee that U.S. consumers would pay more for Canadian gas than Ontario consumers.

Before assessing the implications of the NGA and taking a closer look at the future prospects for exports, it is important to explore the implications of changing two Canadian policies: border prices and present federal and provincial methods of determining the availability of gas for export.

Border Pricing

In 1980 U.S. Secretary of Energy Charles Duncan and Canadian Minister of Energy, Mines, and Resources Marc Lalonde met to establish an agreement on how gas exports to the United States would be priced. Duncan sought and received an agreement by Canada to price gas at the same level regardless of where it crossed into the United States. Previously, Canadian gas was attractive to U.S. markets that were close to Canada and distant from U.S. fields. The uniform border price undermined this logic. Pricing gas that cost $1.10 to transport to Niagara Falls at the identical price as gas sent to the Northwest that cost only $0.20 to transport was inefficient.

The NGA replaced the uniform border price with a regional reference (or adjacent zone) price. This met Ontario's minimum criteria that gas to their industrial users be priced equal or lower than gas exported across the border to Midwest manufacturers. It concurrently responded to the concern of Albertan producers whose gas was becoming uncompetitive in certain markets.

Uniform border prices discriminated in favor of gas exported to distant markets, such as the Northeast. Adjacent-zone pricing eliminated this bias. For example, in November 1985 the uniform border price would have been $2.96 per Mcf, while under adjacent-zone pricing, gas crossing into the United States at Kingsgate would be priced at $2.16, and gas at Niagara Falls would remain at $2.96.[21] There remain certain definitional problems such as which adjacent price (firm residential versus interruptible industrial) will determine the export price, but they should be worked out over time.

Surplus Requirement

In Canada the word *surplus* has two connotations. The first refers to the requirement that proved reserves must equal twenty-five years of anticipated Canadian domestic demand, and only gas in surplus to that level can be exported. The second definition refers to the amount of gas contracted for by Canadian pipelines, either to meet domestic or export demand, but not taken due to a decline in consumption. For example, in 1980–1983 TransCanada did not take approximately 30 percent of the gas for which it had contracted. That gas is then defined as surplus. Perhaps it would be useful to differentiate the two definitions by labeling the NEB-required surplus as "wanted surplus" and the excess deliverability as "unwanted surplus."

Although the *unwanted* surplus provides an incentive for spot sales, the *wanted* surplus has had a more significant impact on future Canadian gas-export policy. By requiring that twenty-five years of domestic production as well as all previously committed export volumes be reserved before any exports can be approved, the federal government exerted downward pressure on prices. This requirement forced Canadian producers to incur incremental capital costs that would be considered superfluous in a purely competitive market and to assume carrying costs external to "normal" business practices. In fact, by building up the reserves the producers were forced to undercut their own negotiating position, because domestic buyers knew that producers had a surplus of gas that could only be sold within Canada.

From a Canadian consumer's perspective this policy was almost as successful at keeping gas prices low as any of the NEB's direct pricing provisions. The program also appealed to Canadian nationalism by guaranteeing that conventional gas supplies would be available to meet Canadian demand for the forseeable future. Domestic consumers received low-priced gas and a supply insurance policy, all paid for by producers. Naturally, consumers favored this policy while producers did not. The wisdom of a supply insurance policy depends on the probability of a future supply shortage. Given the estimates of reserves and resources discussed earlier, this probability is low.

Producers have made it clear that any move toward gas deregulation has to be concomitant with a relaxation of the twenty-five-year surplus requirement. As one producer recently pointed out: "it is extremely hypocritical of the federal government to impose stringent price controls during periods of tight markets, force us to build up our reserves way above market requirements, and then in a soft market turn around and propose removing all price regulation."

The NEB commenced hearings in late 1985 to review its surplus determination procedure as the first phase of a new Gas Export Omnibus Hearing. In April 1986 the board announced a new formula that moves away from a calculation based on the current year's domestic demand plus existing exports to a system based on production to reserve ratios. The new formula requires a 15:1 ratio and allows for periodic readjustment. Alberta has initiated a similar review process, stating that it will "review its surplus test requirements and anticipates that this review will result in significantly freer access for producers to domestic and export markets."[22]

Changes in the surplus requirement will have a significant impact on the level of gas exports. Whereas the NGA focused on short-term sales, changing the surplus requirement addresses *all* gas sales. The ongoing debate between consuming and producing provinces over this issue is understandable. Ontario is concerned that any reduction in the surplus requirement will result in the sale of cheap gas to the United States, forcing Ontario consumers to pay much higher prices in the 1990s. Its position is based on the premise that there exists a limited supply of inexpensive gas and a larger supply of significantly more expensive gas and that sometime in the future, the former will be depleted, forcing Canadian consumers to rely on high-priced supplies. Allowing producers to increase exports of cheap gas only accelerates the rate of depletion and brings the day of higher prices that much closer.

There is still some question about whether a twenty-five-year surplus test is in Canada's long-term interest. Exports to the United States generate revenue, some of which goes directly to Alberta and other producing provinces and some of which goes to consuming provinces in the form of dividends to shareholders in gas production and transportation companies. The money that ends up in Alberta will be either spent, saved, or taxed by the provincial or federal government. In either event, some of these funds will contribute economic benefits to consuming provinces. For example, Albertans will purchase more goods and services, many of which are manufactured or located in Ontario and Quebec. Funds that are saved will be invested, and many of these investments, especially those by banks and pension funds, will be in enterprises located outside Alberta. Finally, federal tax money is distributed throughout all of Canada.

Rigid surplus requirements would be in the long-term interest of the consuming provinces if the discounted flow of savings accruing to those provinces from the retention of additional inexpensive gas for future domestic consumption is equal to or greater than the discounted flow of economic benefits from increased exports plus the long-term benefits of removing the efficiency losses in the form of disincentives to future gas exploration and production.

From the perspective of large consuming provinces such as Ontario and Quebec, the answer to the twenty-five-year surplus test was uncertain. From the perspective of Canada as a whole, trade and efficiency benefits forced the federal government to consider adopting a more flexible policy. Like energy tax issues, the surplus test is basically an income distribution issue with significant interprovincial repercussions and as such is politically sensitive. The NEB decision is a compromise that attempts to meet the concerns of all of the parties but in so doing may make neither side happy. Because of the changes in the formula, the actual drop in the surplus requirement is much smaller than the move from twenty-five to fifteen years would indicate. Finally, by establishing an ongoing review process, the NEB has ensured that this issue will be a permanent fixture on Canada's political horizon.

Implications of the Natural Gas Agreement

The success of the NGA is premised on the emergence of additional gas markets. There is presently a deliverability surplus of gas in Canada equal to at least three years of domestic consumption. Under these circumstances gas prices in a deregulated market will fall. Duncan Allan, deputy minister of energy for Ontario, predicted that gas prices will fall by at least $1 if the old system of regulated prices is replaced by genuine, market-sensitive negotiation.[23] This would constitute a 35 percent decrease in price. To maintain revenues there would have to be an offsetting 35 percent increase in volume. Reductions in oil and gas taxes will offset some of these losses, but to stay even Canada will have to sell between 400 and 550 billion cubic feet (Bcf) of additional gas. Is this probable, in light of rapidly falling oil prices?

The U.S. Market

The United States is the major outlet for Canada's incremental surplus gas. In 1984 Canada exported 750 Bcf to the United States, receiving slightly more than $3 billion in return. In 1985 regulatory changes resulted in a price close to $3.10 per Mcf, which would require Canada to export at least 950 Bcf to stay even. (Actual annual export levels for 1985 were in the vicinity of 905 Bcf.)

What would happen if the Canadian price dropped still further, perhaps to $2.50 per Mcf? Then the issue gets more complicated. In the short term, one Mcf of Canadian gas sold in the United States translates into one Mcf of surplus U.S. gas that will not be sold. This would spur U.S. producers to lower their prices and thereby prevent Canadians from making inroads into their markets. In the long term, lower prices will attract some additional consumption by providing an incentive for users of other fuels to substitute toward gas. This situation, however, is not conducive to short-term revenue maximization. Furthermore, Canadian government officials believe that the U.S. surplus will evaporate by the early 1990s, providing Canadian producers an opportunity to realize much higher prices.

These factors explain Canada's reluctance to allow its producers and pipelines to underprice U.S. markets to obtain incremental business. In early 1985, the NEB rejected several export contracts on the grounds that their prices were too low.[24] Former NEB chairman Geoffrey Edge repeatedly stated that Canada has no intention of engaging in a price war and would abide by the principle of achieving "full commodity value" for its gas, which means that Canadian gas would not sell below the price of either competing fuels or U.S. gas.[25]

The NGA amended these policies. The Canadian government has removed all volume restrictions on short-term sales, but it has not relinquished its interest in policing prices, nor has it removed regulatory limits on longer-term sales. The retention of the former has significantly inhibited the ability of Canadian producers to sell their gas in the growing U.S. spot market.

What are the implications of these changes for Canadian exports? Will producer and government revenues rise or fall? If prices are falling, the only way to increase revenues is to sell more gas. Unfortunately, the markets in which Canadian gas must compete are relatively flat and characterized by declining prices and intensive interfuel competition. Success in achieving incremental sales will not be easy.

The U.S. market for Canadian gas can be divided into three parts: California and the Pacific Northwest, the Midwest, and the Northeast. Each region has different characteristics.

California and the Pacific Northwest

California and the Pacific Northwest are geographically neighbors to Canada, and with the adoption of adjacent-zone pricing Canadian producers will be able to compete aggressively in these markets. However, there are several notable constraints. First, gas consumption in California is expected to remain relatively flat for the next several years, guaranteeing intense competition for market shares. Second, the recent decision by the California Public Utility Commission to deregulate the "noncore" sectors (i.e., all but residential and small commercial users) will only intensify this competition as LDCs scramble for low-cost gas to remain competitive with direct sales opportunities. The key issue confronting Canadian producers is how far they want to go in following falling gas prices, especially if the gains are temporary, potentially destabilizing, and result in lower total revenues. In the longer term, California will remain a strong market for Canadian gas, primarily because of the predicted growth in gas consumption by the electricity sector, pushed in part by environmental concerns over air quality and nuclear power.

Midwest

Since 1982 the Midwest market has experienced overcapacity. The recession in the smokestack industries, combined with aggressive investments to reduce consumption, ensures that demand will recover slowly. Short-term Canadian sales will compete either with existing Canadian or U.S. pipeline gas. Displacement of these entrenched sources is possible but not likely. The long-term picture is brighter—transportation and storage facilities are already in place, and the Midwest will be a gas-intensive region for the remainder of the century.

Northeast

There is a growing consensus on both sides of the border that the Northeast offers the best market for Canadian gas exports. This forecast is based on the observation that a large share of residential and commercial users who now burn oil could convert to gas, although it is not logical that thousands of New Englanders would suddenly rip out their oil furnaces and invest $2,000 to $3,000 in gas-burning equipment. With heating oil prices falling, and with gas prices tied either formally or informally to oil prices, widespread conversions are improbable, at least through the end of the decade. Only if electric utilities and industrial users in the Northeast increase their demand for gas will these optimistic scenarios be confirmed. In fact, the best short-term potential for Canadian exports may be the utility sector, especially in New York, Pennsylvania, and southern New England.

In the longer term (i.e., post–1990), the prospects for growth in the Northeast market may improve. If only a small percentage of the new transportation projects connecting the Northeast to the TransCanadian system are completed, the total market options for Northeast gas users will increase dramatically. On the one hand, the Northeast will have access to large supplies of gas; on the other hand, they will be in a position consistently to purchase the lowest priced supply. Therefore, there will be opportunities for increased market penetration by Canadian gas, but such gas will have to be priced competitively not only with oil but also with U.S. gas.

The Reality of Doing Business in a Soft Market

All three U.S. markets will provide varying opportunities for Canadian gas exports. Aggressive and imaginative producers and pipelines will take advantage of these opportunities. In the near term, however, the total volume of Canadian gas will not offset price reductions, and therefore total revenues realized from exports will decline.

The reason is the simple law of supply and demand. By holding on to the old NEP regime after it became clear that its provisions were untenable in a soft market, Canada built up a large surplus. Simultaneously, gas demand in both Canada and the United States flattened, so there was no outlet for the surplus. No policy will magically change these market realities.

To expect the NGA to result in immediate growth in exports ignores reality. Bitter as it may be, Canadians must accept a painful transition period and use it to create optimal regulatory regimes for the late 1980s and early 1990s. Canada should construct a foundation for the future rather than seek immediate relief, especially if that relief is presently unattainable.

Is there a possibility that the new agreement may unravel due to interprovincial squabbling? The crux of the debate is the distribution of income between producing and consuming provinces, an issue that has always had the capacity to bring the political process to a standstill. When the additional income to be distributed is either small or negative, the discord between Alberta and Ontario does not necessarily moderate. In fact, when the stakes are lowest the intensity of the combat is sometimes paradoxically at its height.

Just as Canada must accept the inevitability of short-term revenue reductions, so must it accept gradual rather than dynamic evolution in gas-pricing policy. In the near term this situation will retard export growth. Absent a major shift in either Canada's institutional outlook, U.S. demand patterns, or oil prices, gas exports will increase only moderately to 1.2 to 1.4 Tcf by 1989.

The situation in the 1990s depends on oil prices, trade policy, and the political environment. Unforeseen events could spark a renewed infusion of Canadian nationalism, which might restrict gas trade. Yet Canadian gas is a commodity characterized by large sunk costs, low exploration and development costs, limited sales options, and ample long-term supplies. These factors argue for expansion rather than restriction of trade, the scope of which depends heavily on the growth in U.S. demand. Export levels as high as 2.0 Tcf are possible, but only if governments on both sides of the border limit their intervention.

Interaction with U.S. Regulatory Policy

Historically, the predominant political concern in the United States has been to protect consumers from high-priced imports, but overall there has been more rhetoric than action. Despite complaints about high Canadian prices in the late 1970s, the U.S. government agreed to a pricing formula that guaranteed those high prices. From 1981 to 1983 there were numerous threats of retaliatory action—on the floor of Congress and elsewhere—unless the Canadians lowered their border price; yet neither the Department of Energy nor Congress acted precipitously. Subsequent Canadian actions were largely due to market realities, not to political arm twisting.

Instead, U.S. political activity has focused on protecting U.S. producers and pipelines from foreign competition. This concern varies from region to region. In the Midwest, for example, U.S. pipelines have an advantage in terms of low transportation costs; therefore, pleas for protection in this region are not apt to gain much credence. On the other hand, in the Pacific market Canadian producers enjoy some logistical advantages, and U.S. pipelines and distributors will seek political intervention if they feel threatened. Yet it is difficult to construct a scenario in which the U.S. Congress would adopt trade barriers to Canadian gas imports.

However, the Federal Energy Regulatory Commission (FERC) has signaled that it is prepared to protect U.S. pipelines from what it perceives to be unfair competitive practices. One example is the FERC's intervention on behalf of U.S. pipelines over how Canadian exporters allocate demand-commodity charges.

Theoretically, the demand charge covers the fixed costs of the infrastructure used to deliver gas, and the commodity charge covers the cost of gas itself. U.S. pipelines have accused the Canadians of loading commodity-related costs onto the demand charge and then unfairly reducing the price of incremental gas. From the perspective of the Canadian NEB, the method of allocating demand-commodity charges is critical in distributing fixed costs—and therefore investment risk—equitably between Canadian citizens and U.S. importers. The FERC's concern is that all players in the U.S. market should be subject to the same rules. Eventually, a compromise will be found, but in the meantime each country will be under pressure to support the concerns of the industries they regulate.

Both the FERC and the Canadian NEB have used these issues to indicate that they will continue to police the trade of gas. Their involvement will act as a brake on the rate of change in export volumes.

Changes in the FERC regulation of the U.S. gas industry could have a dramatic impact. If the FERC is able to force a restructuring of the U.S. gas industry by creating two businesses—transportation and resale—the volume of gas sold directly from producers to consumers will increase. To the extent that this restructuring creates an active market for short-term spot transactions, it will complement the provisions of the NGA in promoting an aggressive Canadian position.

Two-block tariff schemes—in which all old U.S. gas is placed in one block and all new U.S. gas and imports in a second block—would reduce the role of Canadian gas in the U.S. market. By lumping price-competitive Canadian gas with other U.S. sources, this tariff scheme would indirectly increase the price of this gas block, thus offsetting many of the benefits of the NGA. Canadian exports would act as a cushion for certain categories of otherwise unmarketable U.S. gas. Gas in the second block would invariably become the marginal supply, both for new sales and for seasonal peaks. Canada has traditionally sought to avoid the financial instability of being such a supplier. Furthermore, if demand changes are separated from transportation rates—rates that would be related only to volume—the allocation of financial risk between Canadian investors and U.S. consumers would be altered.

The winds of regulatory change are reaching storm proportions. Which of the proposed changes will be enacted, how Canadian officials—both public and private—will respond, and what further amendments will be made in the years ahead are questions that remain to be answered. Yet one theme is clear: If there is a regulatory revolution in the United States, Canada's federal and provincial regulators will not escape its reach. If Canada is affected when the ''elephant'' to the south twitches, it certainly must react when the elephant somersaults.

Mexico

Petroleos Mexicanos (PEMEX) estimates that its proven natural gas reserves are in the vicinity of 75 Tcf.[26] This figure might be high since there is controversy over the potential of the Chicontepec field, but even discounting this field, Mexico's proved reserves are still at least 55 Tcf. They should be sufficient to meet all of its domestic needs through 1995. This scenario assumes that natural gas reserve additions will be negligible, a highly unlikely circumstance given that Mexico is estimated to have explored less than 20 percent of its potential petroleum-bearing structures.[27]

If the geology of Mexican natural gas reserves is promising, what about the economics? First, 75 to 80 percent of Mexico's gas production is associated with oil. Therefore, decisions on gas production are directly related to decisions on oil production. An ICF model of Mexican production potential through the year 2000 shows that additions to gas reserves are dependent on Mexico's ability and willingness to increase oil production.[28] In addition, the model assumes a continuation of the historical trend in which a disproportionately large percentage of Mexico's gas supplies is found in association with oil. If oil markets remain flat, there will be little incentive to invest in major new oil exploration and production projects. Furthermore, Mexico's fiscal problems pose uncertainty about her ability to attract the capital needed to fund an aggressive exploration and production program. The present soft oil market has prompted Mexico to reduce investments in exploration dramatically and turn its attention to developing an improved domestic infrastructure to handle and use petroleum products. Although these changes will have a limited effect on Mexico's ability to meet its own domestic demand, they will certainly affect the availability of surplus gas for export.

Domestic consumption also plays an important role. Here Mexico confronts a grave dilemma, because historically it has kept gas prices very low, both for residential and industrial users. Industries in the Monterrey area paid $1.60 per Mcf in May 1985, or approximately 0.5 percent of the average industrial price in the United States.[29] Until recently, operators of PEMEX facilities (which consume approximately one-third of the nation's gas) have considered gas to be virtually a free good. By pricing gas substantially below market-clearing levels, Mexico has created a situation in which a substantial amount of gas is used inefficiently. As a result, domestic gas demand sometimes exceeds supply, necessitating the imposition of allocation programs. A large segment of the industrial sector, however, has the capability to use either residual oil or gas, and thus allocation simply means requiring certain large industrial users to switch fuels.

Mexico could increase its domestic gas prices and thereby eliminate these demand uncertainties. In fact, residential and commerical gas prices have been gradually allowed to increase.[30] However, Mexico is a poor country with serious economic and social problems. There are economic and political costs to letting domestic gas prices rise to market-clearing levels. Future industrial gas prices, albeit higher, will probably remain below the level that would mirror the commodity's true economic value. The combination of low gas prices and substantial population increases—Mexico's population will increase from 70 to 110 million by the year 2000[31]—makes it unlikely that Mexico will have substantial amounts of gas available for export any time in the near future.

In the past several years, Mexico has been forced by depressed market conditions to reduce crude oil (and therefore associated gas) production below earlier projected levels. As a result, all gas and most residual oil produced has been used to meet domestic demand.[32] If oil and gas production increases in the future, additional gas could become available to free residual oil for sale on the international market.[33] Historically Mexico has sold its residual oil in its domestic industrial market at prices below world levels. Additional export sales would be profitable, but until domestic demand is brought under control or total oil production increases, Mexico will not be able to take advantage of these opportunities. If the country is successful in rationalizing its domestic consumption, it likely will adopt policies to substitute gas for oil to meet environmental standards and sell the additional oil on the international market.

Mexico is caught on the horns of a fiscal dilemma. Every $1 reduction in oil prices reduces its annual revenue by $550 million; on the other hand, every 1 percent increase in the interest rates increases Mexico's debt by $800 million. Interest rates and oil prices tend to move in the same direction, each partially cancelling the effect of the other. Nonetheless, oil prices and interest rates are both highly unpredictable, leaving Mexico to cope with tremendous fiscal uncertainty.

There is no easy answer to this dilemma. Mexico is not likely to be in a position to embark on an aggressive exploration program within the next five to ten years, especially given expectations of continuing soft oil markets. It is more probable that Mexico will maintain a moderate investment program that allows reserve additions to equal annual production levels. This would avoid the prospect of lasting domestic supply shortages, but it would not create the surplus conditions necessary for Mexico to export substantial volumes to the United States or any other country.

For these reasons Mexico will not have a significant influence on U.S. natural gas markets in the foreseeable future.

Conclusions

What wisdom can we extract from this discussion of Canadian and Mexican gas exports? Perhaps the most important lesson is that the rhetoric on all sides of the border usually exceeds the reality. Dynamic change seems always to be on the horizon; yet moderation seems to rule. Part of the reason why this is true is that the world is not governed by economics alone; political and institutional factors are often more significant. Economics determines the direction but politics the rate of momentum.

Canada will continue to be a major supplier of gas to the United States. The politics of gas trade will often be volatile on both sides of the border, but this volatility will not erase the long-term potential for growth. Mexican gas exports will be a possibility but, unfortunately, an unlikely reality.

Appendix: Imported Liquefied Natural Gas

The United States has imported gas from only one country in the Organization of Petroleum Exporting Countries (OPEC), Algeria. (Negotiations with Indonesia never bore fruit.) With the cancellation of the Trunkline and El Paso projects and the recent bankruptcy of the Distrigas project in Massachusetts, no imported liquefied natural gas (LNG) was entering the United States as of the late fall of 1985.

Table 3.4
Illustrative Cost Calculations of a 640 Bcf per Year OPEC Liquefied Natural Gas Project (1984 U.S. Dollars per Thousand Cubic Feet)

	Algeria-U.S.	Iran-U.S.
Wellhead price[a]	2.00	2.00
Production and gathering	0.30	0.30
Pipeline transportation to liquefaction plant	0.30	0.30
Liquefaction[b]	2.10	2.10
Transportation[c]	1.75	2.62
Regassification[d]	0.44	0.44
East Coast cost, insurance, and freight price	6.89	7.76
U.S. transportation via displacement[e]	0.60	0.60
Midwest city-gate price	7.49	8.36

Calculations based on gas of 1000 Btu per cubic foot. Average Btu content of Algerian and Iranian natural gas may actually be higher.

[a] Assumed netback.

[b] Assumes an interest rate of 12 percent and a loan repayment period of twenty years with no interest payment during construction. Also includes the cost of natural gas for fuel and losses.

[c] Based on 130,000 cubic meter LNG carriers. Eight percent of natural gas used for ship fuel and losses.

[d] Includes receiving terminal and jetties. Also includes use of 2.2 percent of natural gas as fuel.

[e] Transportation cost from East Coast to Midwest.

Source: Estimates based on calculations in Bijan Mossavar-Rahmani and Sharmin Mossavar-Rahmani, *The OPEC Natural Gas Dilemma*, Westview Press, Westview, Conn., January 1986.

Reserves in Indonesia and Algeria, as well as in Iran and the Arab Gulf States, are substantial. Economics and security concerns, not geology, will prove to be the stumbling block to any future LNG projects. Table 3.4 estimates the cost of moving gas from Algeria and from Iran to the Chicago market. It is assumed that both countries will demand a producer netback of at least $2.00 per Mcf and that the transportation cost reflects the cost of displacing gas bound for the East Coast and rerouting it to Chicago (approximately $0.60 per Mcf). LNG from Algeria can be delivered to Chicago for slightly less than $7.50 per Mcf, and gas from Iran would cost approximately $8.36 per Mcf. These prices are substantially higher than the 1984 average Chicago city-gate prices (approximately $4.00–4.30 per Mcf). But it is worth noting that they are significantly below those projected for Alaskan gas delivered through the Alaska Natural Gas Transportation System ($10.00–12.00 per Mcf) or Canadian Arctic gas ($9.10–10.10 per Mcf).

A second obstacle to LNG sales from OPEC nations to the United States is simple logistics. Western Europe and Japan are closer to OPEC gas reserves, and therefore it is less expensive to transport gas to these regions than to the United States. Furthermore, the Europeans and Japanese have been more flexible in contract negotiations than have U.S. pipelines. Barter arrangements, price premiums, and even partial equity ownership are becoming more common.

Notes

1. ICF, *North American Gas Study: The Benefits of Increased Trade*, Washington, D.C., February 1984, p. II–3/4.

2. There are exceptions to this rule. In certain regions in which oil use is limited for environmental reasons or which are served by more than one pipeline, gas from one carrier may compete with gas from another.

3. S. L. Schwartz, J. D. Fuller, and W. T. Ziemba, "Long Run Effects of the Canadian National Energy Agreement," *Energy Journal*, April 1985, p. 66.

4. Unless otherwise specified, all price figures in this chapter are in 1984 U.S. dollars.

5. For example, substantial conventional gas reserves in Alberta are probably available at prices between $0.57 Mcf at the wellhead and $2.46 Mcf. The supply curve for Alberta may be fairly flat until producers begin to develop the deep tight gas formations. This conclusion is supported by a recent ICF study, which courageously attempted to draw a supply curve for Canadian resources. The ICF study projects the availability of 140 Tcf at a price slightly above $5 Mcf at the wellhead. Adding transportation costs and converting to 1984 rather than 1983 dollars, the ICF result mirrors those in the Schwartz, Fuller, and Ziemba study (see note 3).

6. M. A. Adelman and Michael C. Lynch, "Supply Aspects of North American Gas Trade," in *Final Report on the Canadian-U.S. Natural Gas Trade*, MIT Energy Laboratory, International Gas Trade Project, Cambridge, Mass., October 1985, Working Paper MIT-EL 85–013 WP, pp. 15–26.

7. Interview with Steven Rodriguez, Canadian Petroleum Association, Calgary, February 1985.

8. Ibid.

9. Interview with Richard McVean, internal documents, National Energy Board of Canada, Ottawa, September 1985.

10. Figures represent preliminary calculations by the National Energy Board of Canada. Interview with Ross Wright, National Energy Board of Canada, Ottawa, July 30, 1985.

11. Ibid.

12. Peak utilization rates in 1981–1984 averaged 70 to 80 percent of capacity.

13. Bruce Stokes, "The Economic Ties That Bind the United States and Canada May Be Broadened," *National Journal*, March 9, 1985, p. 529.

14. Ibid., p. 530.

15. Andrew Malcolm, *The Canadians*, New York Times Books, New York, 1985, p. 165.

16. Stokes, "Economic Ties," p. 530.

17. Malcolm, *The Canadians*, p. 10.

18. Royal Bank of Canada, Global Energy and Minerals Group, "The North American Natural Gas Industry," Calgary, 1984, p. 110.

19. Malcolm, *The Canadians*, p. 28.

20. Canadian Department of Energy, Mines, and Resources, Press Release #85/37, Ottawa, March 28, 1985.

21. *Crossborder Report*, Washington, D.C., November 27, 1985, p. 15.

22. Canadian Department of Energy, Mines, and Resources, "Natural Gas Act Outlined" [Communique 85/162], Backgrounder attachment, Ottawa, p. 3.

23. Duncan Allen, "Life after the Natural Gas Act," Speech before the Financial Post Conference, Toronto, November 14, 1985, page 5.

24. The National Energy Board rejected the proposed sale of gas from TransCanandian Pipeline to Great Lakes Pipeline and from Czar Resources to Weyerhauser Co. on the grounds that both sales were at prices below those of competing fuels.

25. C. Geoffrey Edge, *A Progress Report on the Export of Canadian Natural Gas to the United States*, Speech to Conference on the New Realities of Natural Gas, Sponsored by the Energy Bureau, Arlington, Va., May 6, 1985.

26. ICF, "North American Gas Study," p. I–15.

27. Royal Bank of Canada, "The North American Natural Gas Industry," p. 94.

28. ICF, "North American Gas Study," p. I–25.

29. *Energy Detente*, 6, no. 12, June 26, 1985.

30. On December 6, 1985, Mexico announced that natural gas and residual oil prices would rise 3.5 percent per month from January through June 1986. The recent agreement between Mexico and the International Monetary Fund will accelerate this process of rationalization.

31. Royal Bank of Canada, "The North American Natural Gas Industry," p. 100.

32. In 1984 petroleum product exports were limited to 16.0 percent of Mexican production, and those to the United States accounted for less than 7.5 percent of product sales. These figures were developed from PEMEX's "Annual Report 1984" and from the Department of Energy, Energy Information Agency, *Petroleum Supply Monthly*. Figures for the last half of 1985 were substantially lower, but this is probably a short-run anomaly.

33. In addition to the economic arguments for substituting gas for oil, air pollution concerns, especially in Mexico City and Monterrey, are growing and will invariably result in public support for greater use of gas in place of dirtier fuels.

Comments

ROBERT B. CATELL
Executive Vice President
Brooklyn Union Gas Company

Henry Lee's chapter provides an excellent overview of a very complex subject. The facts that will shape the future level of gas exports from the OPEC nations, Mexico, and Canada to the United States are correctly stated to be much more than those of geology and economics.

We agree that gas availability is more a function of economics than of geology, that marginal gas markets are susceptible to lower residual fuel prices, and that in the short-term, residual oil prices will act as a ceiling on gas prices.

In the longer term, however, we believe that there will be an increased demand for natural gas in certain U.S. markets, particularly in the Northeast, where there remains a significant potential for conversions of older equipment that use No. 2 fuel oil or very low-sulfur residual fuel oil, as well as development of new markets due to factors such as cogeneration, combined cycle electric generation, gas-fueled air conditioners, and compressed natural gas used to fuel vehicles. This increased demand, coupled with an eventual decline in domestic gas, undoubtedly will provide a potential for increased imports, particularly from Canada. We agree with Lee that Canada will be the major source of gas imports into the United States for at least the next ten years and, we believe, even longer.

It is in this context that we offer the following comments to complement Lee's chapter.

Lee painted a somewhat pessimistic picture of the role that imported gas will play in the energy future of the United States. According to him, imported LNG carries too high a transportation price tag to compete in U.S. markets. Structural, political, and social problems in Mexico make any substantial increase in Mexican imports, at least in the short run, highly unlikely. As for Canada, he concluded that "gas exports will increase only moderately to 1.2 to 1.4 Tcf by 1989." Accepting the larger number, *in arguendo*, would approximately double the current level of Canadian gas actually being exported to the United States to a total that is approximately 80 percent of the level of currently authorized exportable volumes. This would increase Canada's share of the U.S. gas market to about 8 percent.

Is this correct? Only time will tell. We agree that Mexican gas is not likely to be a factor in U.S. markets for the remainder of this decade. We also agree that large capital requirements and distances from U.S. markets make imported LNG unattractive, particularly in light of the recent $15 to $20 per barrel (bbl) oil price range. We do not agree, however, with Lee's assessment that actual

Canadian exports will not increase even to the current level of authorized export volumes.

Our evaluation of Lee's conclusions about the future of Canadian gas is made in the context of the New Jersey, New York, and New England markets with which we are most familiar. (I will take geographic license to call this region the Northeast.) In this region Canadian gas provides attractive operational opportunities, and it provides an attractive market to the Canadians. If we couple this marriage with what we see to be a healthy and realistic attitude on the part of the Canadians to export gas to the Northeast, Canadian gas exports to the U.S. Northeast should boom.

Markets

Lee downgraded the market for gas in the Northeast by concluding that "it is not logical that thousands of New Englanders would suddenly rip out their oil furnaces and invest $2,000 to $3,000 in gas-burning equipment." We agree, but Lee missed the point. We never have been very successful in convincing home owners to rip out perfectly good equipment. We continue to be very successful, however, in convincing the tens of thousands of customers in the Northeast whose oil equipment is near or at the end of its fifteen-year life cycle to convert to gas.

The point is that the oil-replacement market in the Northeast is huge, where gas saturations are typically only in the 25 to 50 percent range. In addition to having our traditional residential and commercial markets, we have unique opportunities for newer gas markets in the Northeast, such as combined-cycle power generation, cogeneration, and the redevelopment of recovering areas. As indicated below, Canada is ideally located to serve these markets.

Operational Opportunities

The Northeast, which lies at the furthest end of the U.S. pipeline system, has always been supply constrained. New capacity, if available at all, has been available only at great cost. The result of this pipeline bottleneck was often the loss of market opportunities or the construction of expensive "self-help" supply projects. Gas from Canada offers an opportunity to correct these accidents of geography. Canadian gas can backfeed our distribution systems from the north with the bonus of freeing up existing capacity from the south, creating a result not unlike the capacity benefit we all received by converting from manufactured to natural gas. The proposed Iroquois Pipeline is an example of this phenomenon, where the New York City area will be served directly by Canadian gas and the New Jersey area to the south served by displacement. Additionally, Canadian gas will provide many of us with the opportunity to retire aging facilities, such as LNG and propane facilities, to the benefit of our rate payers. These are opportunities that in large part are dependent upon receiving incremental Canadian supplies into our markets.

The Canadian Scene

Lee is correct in observing that a host of complex issues on both sides of the Canadian border need to be considered when projecting what role that Canadian gas will play in the U.S. energy future. He has covered these complex and interrelated issues well, and they need not be repeated here. It is safe to state, however, that the two key elements involved in a significant increase in Canadian exports to the Northeast (and, I expect, to any region) are, first, that Canadian gas be priced to clear the U.S. market and, second, that it be committed contractually to the United States on a long-term basis.

On both of these issues we are encouraged. The supply contracts underlying the Boundary contract and the Iroquois project both are long-term and have market-sensitive pricing formulas. We additionally are encouraged by the April 1986 decision of the National Energy Board entitled "Phase I: The Surplus Determination Phase of the Gas Export Omnibus Hearing, 1985." This decision, issued after Lee's chapter was completed, will replace the so-called twenty-five-year exportable surplus test with a new test based upon maintaining a fifteen-year reserves-to-production ratio. We have been advised that the new procedures will greatly increase the amount of gas available for export from Canada and are more appropriate to a market-sensitive pricing regime in the export market.

On balance, we envision a greater role for Canadian gas than does Lee. Diversification of our supply sources to include a greater percentage of Canadian gas is part of our long-term supply strategy and, we believe, of other LDCs' as well. If for no other reason, a comparison of the reserve life indexes of our domestic suppliers vis-à-vis those of Canada makes Canadian gas a good bet.

JOSEPH E. RAMSEY
Vice President, Rates and Strategic Planning
Tennessee Gas Transmission Company

Henry Lee showed a thorough understanding of natural gas import trade, where political considerations are often as important, if not more important, than economic ones. Some very important conclusions stand out that were much less apparent (if not invisible) ten to fifteen years ago. First, incremental supplies of imported gas must meet the market test *on their own*. The days of rolling-in high-cost supplies into a low-cost base are gone, probably, one hopes, forever. Second, political risks are real, both as regards supply interruption and unimpeded price escalations in times of tight supply. Changes in the domestic economy or ruling political party of a gas-exporting country can totally upset existing or prospective gas trade patterns.

Mexico

The unfortunate situation described regarding Mexico's potential as an exporter of natural gas is unfortunately correct. I would point out one slight correction to the discussion concerning Mexico's high level of associated gas production (80 percent of total production). This results from a conscious decision by PEMEX to explore and drill for oil at the expense of gas exploration, a decision made at a time when oil was the fuel in demand worldwide. Mexico spent billions to pursue oil production. Vast areas of gas-rich territory remain untouched because of this decision. Mexico's approach was correct at the time because the market for gas (domestic or export) was not so clearly available.

Now, given Mexico's severe financial straits and the precipitous decline in U.S. gas market prices, aggressive gas exploration has been pushed much further into the future.

Thus Lee's conclusion—that Mexico will be unlikely to have substantial amounts of gas available for export in the near future—is certainly correct.

Canada

Lee's discussion of Canada is a solid presentation of the facts. He indicated that Canadian gas exports to the United States have been hampered more severely by political battles between Canada and the United States and between Ottawa and Alberta than they have by economics, supply, or demand issues. Now, however, the dictates of the free market are being heard more loudly. It is abundantly clear that Canadian energy policies, which are designed to protect Canadian consumers against free-market price swings, will also ensure that Canadian producers' ability to compete for U.S. markets will be hampered.

There is no doubt that huge amounts of Canada's proven gas reserves are "backed up," waiting for a market. Many Canadian producers are willing to accept the very low spot prices now prevalent in the United States, provided that they can get some meaningful level of takes and that the various governments involved do not impede their access to U.S. markets. I believe the estimated levels of future Canadian exports are accurate.

Gas Supply/Demand Outlook

Lee properly pointed out the important relationship between gas prices and the oil-product prices with which gas competes.

This oil-price competition, combined with current regulatory gas-pricing policy, bodes ill for long-term gas supply availability and security. This arises because gas competes with high-sulfur residual fuel oil at the margin and, during times of low oil prices, that price competition generates a very low wellhead netback. (A rough rule of thumb is the "10 percent rule": $15 per bbl of oil means gas must be available at $1.50 per Mcf at the wellhead to compete with resid made from that oil.) In other words, the lowest price-marginal competition is setting the netback price for all gas competition, resulting in wellhead price signals that are inadequate for sufficient gas exploration. Thus if current forecasts of a small increase in the price of oil from present levels over the next few years are correct, not only will the current gas deliverability "bubble" be worked off quickly, but little new exploration will occur to offset this decline.

The remedy is simple to state but nearly impossible to implement: Gas at the burner-tip must be priced on a value-of-service basis so that margins available against high-price competition (electricity, heating oil, propane) can somehow be flowed back to the producing industry. We need an *average* netback pricing structure, not a marginal netback pricing structure.

The opposition to such change is overwhelmingly the political pressure on LDCs and Public Utility Commissions (PUCs) to shield high-priority customers from higher gas prices. The argument that because the home owner has only higher-priced alternatives available he should pay significantly more for the gas-commodity portion of his bill than the industrial user is an extremely hard sell.

Lack of a solution to this problem will have severe impacts on domestic gas supply and, therefore, the need for and affordability of future gas imports to the United States.

LNG

Lee's general conclusions presented in the appendix to his chapter concerning the near-term outlook for LNG trade to the United States are irrefutable. Economics do not dictate such projects in times of U.S. gas surplus and very low spot prices. However, some of the specific cost categories shown in Table 3.4 need further clarification.

1. *Wellhead price*. Although the $2 price is assumed merely for purposes of calculation, the actual wellhead price has a hidden impact on project economics. Because fuel and losses through liquefaction, shipping, and regasification can approach 10–11 percent in an LNG project, the beginning value of the product sets the cost of the fuel and losses, with an attendant impact on total project economics.

2. *Liquefaction*. The $2.10 price is a good estimate for *new* construction, but liquefaction in existing plants, such as in Algeria, can be accomplished for considerably less.

3. *Shipping costs*. As the figures clearly show, shipping costs are highly variable with distance, since more ships are required to haul the same amount of daily plant output. Shipping costs can be drastically reduced if existing out-of-service tankers are used versus new construction.

4. *Regasification*. The $0.44 figure is reasonable for the existing receiving terminal at Cove Point, Maryland, and not far off for the Elba Island, Georgia, and Boston, Massachusetts, terminals. However, vaporization charges for the

Trunkline facility at Lake Charles, Louisiana, were at least three times that amount, as would be charges for any newly constructed plant.

Three final comments on LNG:

1. The appendix addresses only LNG from OPEC countries, but there are also non-OPEC countries (e.g., Trinidad, Norway) that have large gas reserves within reasonable shipping distance. They should not be ignored as future sources of LNG.

2. Because of the Algerian experience, financing for future projects will be much more difficult. Even if the economics of a project can be shown to be attractive, bankers will want solid protection against political interruption.

3. Even though at this time LNG economics appear poor, we should remember that the exporting country often is the owner of the gas reserves; sovereign states can make decisions or investments for political reasons to build an LNG project, just as they can to interrupt one. Employment, development, national pride, and other such considerations can be as strong an influence as economic considerations.

4

The Boundaries between Regulation and Competition

WILLIAM W. HOGAN

> In its oversight of the natural gas market, FERC confronts baffling problems. It must administer a pair of statutes that sometimes seem at cross purposes; it must seek out the elusive mix of competition and regulation; and whatever it does, it subjects itself to the slings and arrows of outraged producers or pipelines or [local distribution companies] or consumers.[1]

Recent dramatic changes in the natural gas market will test the ingenuity, gumption, and resiliency of the public process. There is little prospect and even less desire for a return to the heavily bureaucratic regulatory policies of years past. Marketplace incentives and industry initiatives are supplanting rules and reliability as the dominant themes of natural gas policy. But the sweeping changes that accompanied deregulation will still leave public oversight as a central fact of the natural gas industry.

Hence policymakers are confronted with difficult choices that must be made in an unfamiliar environment. One step in meeting this challenge is to clarify or redefine our public goals and set the framework for market transactions. This chapter establishes a springboard from which to review the major policy goals motivating arguments for and against public intervention in natural gas markets.

Regulatory policy has gyrated from the stagnancy of the 1970s through nearly a decade of turbulence keyed by the Natural Gas Policy Act (NGPA) of 1978.[2] The most tumultuous changes are yet to come. For example, the Federal Energy Regulatory Commission (FERC) is considering thousands of pages of comments received on its Notice of Proposed Rulemaking (NOPR) to alter the regulation of interstate natural gas transportation and pricing.[3] Although the details of the forthcoming FERC decisions are not yet known, we can be confident that Congress and the courts will have a decisive hand in crafting the new regime. The

FERC pronouncements will launch a new wave of legislation and litigation. During this period of turmoil and debate, America must refine her general criteria for organizing and evaluating the competing arguments about ends and means.

Competing Goals

One preeminent policy goal is the attainment of economic efficiency. Natural gas is a precious resource whose exploitation must be balanced with the many competing demands for it. Efficient producers must balance present markets, the technical constraints of prudent resource management, inevitable future scarcity, and the management of risk. Pipelines must facilitate the efficient delivery of gas and effectively transmit supply, demand, and price signals between producers and consumers. Local distribution companies (LDCs), regulated by state Public Utility Commissions (PUCs), must conserve natural gas for high-valued uses and withhold it from wasteful uses that distort the true cost of gas production and distribution.

Whatever the aspirations for improved economic efficiency, the history of regulation and institutional momentum in the natural gas industry guarantee a prominent place for the goal of social equity. Local public bodies will intervene in natural gas markets to achieve a redistribution of income, regardless of some accompanying losses in economic efficiency. Regulators can and rightly should intervene to ensure that the poor, the elderly, and other special groups have affordable and guaranteed access to natural gas. On a national level, attention turns to the pot of gold created by the low costs of production of a large portion of natural gas reserves. Just under 50 percent of all reserves are cheap "old" gas, sold at about half the market price.[4] The resulting scarcity rent—the difference between current market prices and costs of production—has been a constant target of policymakers, who maintain regulations that transfer these rents among producers and consumers. This transfer of income dominates many regulatory choices. Despite the turmoil in the industry, there has been little change in the political urge to share this new wealth. Hence social-equity concerns will continue to be a dominant factor in shaping regulatory policy. The challenge is to define equity goals with enough candor to allow public policy to operate in ways that minimize the costs and inefficiencies of sharing the pie.

The impacts of energy production and use on the environment raise an additional concern. Environmental impacts have inevitable effects on third parties who have no voice in current markets. To protect these interests, governments at various levels play a major role in controlling or influencing the fuel choices of major energy-consuming facilities. Because it is nonpolluting, natural gas is a focal point of environmental interest, an interest that will increase over time. For example, given the cumulative negative effects of sulfur emissions, increased natural gas consumption may be a desirable goal.

The exigencies of energy security, most notably the vulnerability of America's oil imports, further enhance the attractions of natural gas. Because it is a predominantly domestic resource, natural gas will play a significant role in reducing vulnerability to oil-supply interruptions.

These sometimes complementary and sometimes conflicting goals—promoting economic efficiency, striving for social equity, protecting the environment, and securing America's energy supply—motivate arguments for and against public intervention in natural gas markets. Policymakers must weigh the merits of these arguments as they design a new generation of crucial public policies.

The Limits of Public Policy

The current trend toward reduced government intervention lies in direct opposition to a long history of support for government intervention. In part, ideology motivates this trend, an ideology that seeks to reduce government involvement as a strategic move for the economy as a whole, without detailed analyses of the costs and benefits to the affected markets. This presents a challenge. Even under the heroic assumption that the costs and benefits of reregulating and deregulating the gas industry can be done calmly, rationally, and well, there remains the more difficult task of reconciling the particulars of natural gas policy with the broader, strategic view of public policy.

Both the dissatisfaction with past regulations and the reascendance of the conservative philosophy of limited government argue against government controls. In part, the argument is that public policy is limited in its ability to achieve otherwise worthy goals in complicated markets. For example, it now is widely accepted that whatever imperfections remain in the gas market, efficient management of wellhead production is beyond the capacity of government. Wellhead prices and supplies held by thousands of producers cannot be regulated without creating a bewildering array of self-defeating and economically costly constraints.

Hence any review of public policy in the natural gas industry must include an assessment of the management capacity of public processes. It is not enough to demonstrate that there is a particular problem in how a particular market operates. The proactive policy alternative should bear the burden of proof that intervention will provide demonstrable and substantial benefits. Establishing the practical boundaries of public policy remains a challenge for any assessment of the evolution of energy markets.

Economic Efficiency

The rationale for public intervention to promote economic efficiency centers on market imperfections. Concentration of markets in the hands of a few actors, significant barriers to new entrants, widespread neglect of societal costs, social-equity issues, tax distortions, and so forth all reveal imperfect market conditions where pursuit of private interest can thwart the public purpose. In a world without these imperfections, the forces of competition, allowed to operate freely, would seek out the efficient economic solution.

In the ideal market, natural gas would be produced according to cost-minimizing principles, with a clear recognition of the impacts of future supply scarcity. The familiar theoretical arguments supporting competition, which provide one foundation for the philosophy of limited government involvement, lie behind analyses of the potentially workable competitive nature of natural gas markets.

Recognizing the practical limits of government and bolstered by the ideology of free-market competition, society might accept a few imperfections as an ailment easier to endure than the remedy of public intervention. The second-best alternative to the unattainable goal of perfect economic efficiency, or so the argument goes, is found not in the bureaucratic struggles of regulatory hearings but in the aggressive pursuit of market niches by visionary entrepreneurs.

The contemporary political climate and the appeal of the entrepreneurial model both point to the attractions of reduced government participation. But any practical policy agenda for the natural gas industry must be responsive to important differences among its three principal components: production, transportation, and distribution. Each has different achievable goals and different standards of performance, and the meaning of competition varies considerably from one to another.

Competition in Production

The prevailing conventional wisdom and the clear judgment of the Congress that legislated the NGPA is that the natural gas production industry is workably competitive.[5] The relative ease of entry and the large number of producers are convincing evidence that, without the inhibitions of regulation and without distortions in the other sectors of the gas market, producers are competitive; that is, they may freely bid against each other in supplying natural gas. Through competition, producers provide low-cost supplies and drive the price of natural gas to the marginal cost of the least-efficient producer.

It is for this reason that the elimination of most wellhead price controls has been widely accepted. This was a major achievement of public policy, one that corrected a significant economic inefficiency created by previous regulation. From the economic efficiency perspective, there still is concern over continued controls on cheap old gas, but the belief is that, at least at the margin, and allowing for the unavoidable fog of future uncertainty and the limits of human knowledge, conditions in the producing sector will help foster the efficient allocation of natural gas.

Regulation of LDCs

At the opposite end of the market, there is a consensus that economies of scale in the LDC sector have eliminated idealized competition as a practical alternative to regulation of sales to end users.[6] Multiple and parallel LDC networks are not needed, and a single customer typically has access only to one

LDC. Hence LDCs enjoy a substantial degree of potential market power, and this justifies the need for public oversight. LDCs are regulated by a variety of elected and appointed commissions.[7] The details of the regulatory mechanisms differ from state to state, but the basic principles of cost-of-service rate making provide the general standard for the LDC sector.

LDCs play a dual role in the market: They supply natural gas to their consumers, and they purchase gas from both producers and pipelines. In this regard, their alleged market power is forestalled by the reality that pipelines have many alternative customers. Hence it is difficult for an LDC to orchestrate substantial market power in its role as a buyer. Therefore, the predominant justification for regulating LDCs rests with their role as buyers and focuses on issues of prudence in their purchasing practices. Their regulation is intended to ensure that they do not exploit their capacity to raise prices to captive consumers. But there has been relatively little regulatory concern with the possibility that LDCs, through their market power as buyers, might depress prices below competitive levels. There is little indication that these fundamental realities will change for LDCs. Hence they are competitive buyers but monopolistic sellers.

Regulated Competition for Pipelines

Between producers and LDCs lies the pipeline industry. It is difficult to generalize about this sector, and the analysis of market imperfections differs from pipeline to pipeline. Equally important, the analysis and the resulting policies differ substantially when deciding whether the pipeline is considered a seller or a buyer of natural gas.

Today and in the future, proponents of reduced pipeline regulation can point to cases of aggressive competition among pipelines in particular regional markets or market-share competition among natural gas and other fuels.[8] For example, among the nearly 30 percent of LDCs served by more than one pipeline, the average LDC enjoys 3.6 pipelines competing for a share of its purchases.[9] But the supporters of strict regulation can provide a list of examples where monopoly prevails or pipelines have engaged in uncompetitive practices.[10] Whatever the extreme cases—competition or monopoly—policy will hinge on the degree to which the industry is workably competitive or the absence of competition is worth the benefits of efficiency. For example, vertical integration of pipelines, from production through distribution, offers opportunities for efficiency gains and risk sharing that could benefit all participants in the market. However, this same aggregation of power raises the specter of pipelines exploiting their strength in one market to overcome the forces of competition in another.[11]

Deregulation of at least new gas is an accomplished fact. David Mead observed that there is no competition in the delivery of natural gas to 70 percent of LDCs served by only one pipeline.[12] Holding to the view that many producers are competitive sellers and many LDCs are competitive buyers, the balance of power then tilts in the direction of pipelines. Here public policy may continue to reverse the trend of political ideology and impose the burden of proof on those who would rely on competition among pipelines to achieve economic efficiency.[13] Our educated guess is that the pipeline industry will pose the most difficult challenge for policy design and management: regulation to promote competition.

Regulation for Competition

Although all disagreements on how best to meld competition and regulation cannot be resolved fully, we can make partial progress by clarifying the terminology that defines our view of competition. We already have mentioned the idealized view of perfect competition, where ease of entry and a large number of actors ensure vigorous price bidding, eliminate excess rents, and yield prices equal to marginal costs. In public debate about natural gas markets, however, an alternative and looser definition of competition often prevails. Its basis lies in the unarguable fact that alternative fuels can serve many of the same purposes of natural gas. Homeowners can heat with distillate fuel or electricity, and many large industrial consumers of natural gas can convert to residual fuel oil on short notice. This competition among fuel types is real, and with enough time to change the capital stock of energy-using equipment, natural gas can be replaced with other forms of energy.

By 1985 the marketplace was littered with casualties who ignored this interfuel competition. The flexibility of some consumers and the ready availability of alternative fuels established an effective ceiling on the price of natural gas. With prices rising dramatically after 1978, many analysts pointed to the self-evident fact that the price of natural gas, especially for industrial customers, had pierced the ceiling, causing many customers to switch to cheaper residual fuel oil. This led to a wide range of responses that allowed high-cost pipelines to compete in this residual fuel oil market. For example, the FERC authorized a number of Special Marketing Programs (SMPs) that would allow price discrimination among consumers. Under the SMPs, pipelines could sell gas at low prices to fuel-switchable customers, covering their costs by charging higher prices to captive customers. Such programs illustrated the importance of price and revealed the market power of pipelines over captive customers.

The natural gas industry learned the fundamental lesson of the law of demand. When prices rise, consumers seek alternative supplies. While recognizing the importance of interfuel competition, we nonetheless distinguish between this *element* of competition and the theoretical ideal, which ensures that a free market will achieve economic efficiency. An example illustrates these distinctions.

First, assume a market in which a single pipeline serves a mix of industrial and residential consumers. Ignoring for a moment the issues of rate setting at the LDC level, turn instead to the issues that would arise if alternative sources of fuel oil were available but alternative sources of natural gas were not. In this example, a pipeline may face increasing costs to purchase gas supplies, and eventually it will bump into a ceiling set by prices in the alternative fuel oil markets. Faced with rising costs of supply and customers shifting to oil, the pipeline naturally would see itself as being pressured by enormous competition.

But this is far from the theoretical ideal of competition achieving economic efficiency. For example, the pipeline may have access to a mix of cheap old gas and expensive new gas, a typical circumstance, and average the costs of both forms of gas to provide a rolled-in cost that is competitive with residual fuel oil at the LDC level.

In contrast to the single pipeline with a single owner, consider an example with the same physical arrangement—a single pipeline connecting many producers to many consumers—but now assume that the pipeline has been divided into the ''condominium'' arrangement proposed by Allen Jacobs.[14] In this instance, the producers of the cheap old gas would rent a small portion of the pipeline, as would the producers of the expensive gas. In this condominium pipeline, producers would be free to compete with each other to provide larger volumes at lower prices. Consumers, or their agents in LDCs, would be free to choose among those producers to purchase the least expensive gas.

This condominium arrangement would produce a very different competitive environment than that of the single pipeline owner using rolled-in prices. It is conceivable that the price of gas could be driven below that of residual fuel oil, and a majority of fuel-switchable customers then would convert to natural gas. Producers of the most expensive gas, at least those unwilling to lower their prices, would be left with no sales. But producers willing to lower their prices would enjoy substantial increases in their sales volumes. The pipeline would provide transportation services, but it would no longer obstruct deals between producers and consumers. Without rolled-in pricing, both consumers and producers would receive more realistic market signals. The condominium arrangement moves closer to idealized competition.

Although often confused, these two visions of competition are not the same. It is not enough to state that there is some effective constraint on price in order to conclude that competition reigns supreme. After all, every market has some limit on the price that can be charged. If economic efficiency is to serve as the rationale for limiting government's role in natural gas markets, the proponents of competition should meet a more exacting standard than simply demonstrating that an entity is not free to increase its price without limit. The standard rather should be to demonstrate that substantial and workable gas-on-gas competition is available to all participants in the market.

Social Equity

The fundamental argument over social equity concerns ownership of natural gas rents. Given the decisions embodied in the NGPA, this argument translates into a dispute over the rights to scarcity rents for old gas, which were developed during a long-standing regulatory regime that effectively transferred rents from producers to consumers. From the economic-efficiency perspective, it is difficult to justify price controls on old gas. From the social-equity perspective, however, if rents are to be transferred from producers to consumers, there is no practical alternative to continuing price controls on old gas.

The magnitude of the potential rents ensures that any proposal to decontrol old gas will receive keen attention. Decontrol would eliminate constraints on production and increase overall supply. Were it not for rent-transfer issues, the removal of all wellhead controls would be politically an easy choice.

Even accepting the merits of the rent-transfer argument, the question for public policy is whether or not price controls are effective. No one yet has established how to decontrol part of the producing market, promote competition at the margin, maintain average-cost pricing for pipelines, and still transfer rents to consumers. To the extent that average-cost pricing succeeds in rolling in higher-cost with lower-cost gas to produce lower prices for consumers, the direction of the rent transfer is from producers of low-cost gas to producers of high-cost gas, with relatively little benefit accruing to consumers.[15] The challenge is to find alternative ways to regulate pipelines so that the rent benefits of old gas are transferred to the intended recipients, consumers.

Recognizing this central problem in its proposals for regulatory reform, the FERC originally proposed using a two-part block structure to price pipeline sales. The first block would cover the old, low-cost gas, which woud be allocated according to historical consumption patterns. The second block would cover all other gas, which would be priced at market rates. If adopted, this proposal would meet the necessary conditions of transferring rents and promoting competition. But by itself it was insufficient. For example, it would move the focus of concern downstream to PUCs and LDCs. If an LDC averaged the costs of the two blocks, the high-cost gas producers would still be the beneficiaries. Whether the two-block system succeeds will depend in part on instituting local rate designs that pass the benefits of low-cost old gas to consumers without distorting the prices that determine marginal consumption choices. Thus the debate over rent transfer should shift from the FERC to the PUCs.

Another often misunderstood issue of social equity concerns the effects of the regional transfer of rents from producng to consuming states. Battle lines were drawn under the assumption that producing states would be big winners from deregulation, as they captured more of the scarcity rents, and consuming states, especially in the Northeast, would be big losers, as a result of major increases in wellhead prices.

But this characterization is a substantial oversimplification. A more reasonable characterization, which accounts for the second- and third-round rent transfers, changes in federal taxation, and higher consumer prices, suggests that the regional disparity plays a substantially smaller role than appeared at first glance. Henry Lee, Susan Bender, and Joseph Kalt undertook a detailed analysis of (1) the patterns of natural gas ownership, (2) the distribution of federal taxation and federal aid, and (3) the incidence of higher prices for natural gas.[16] Their results showed a slight overall gain for the Northeast as a result of natural gas price decontrol, a slight gain for producing states, a roughly breakeven position in the Northwest, and losses in the central states (where a higher per capita consumption of natural gas at extremely favorable prices imposed the greatest relative costs of decontrol).

Hence the real issue of natural gas pricing and social equity is not so much regional competition as a dispute across income classes. As a result of higher gas prices, the more affluent citizens of the Northeast, who benefited from direct ownership of gas-producing fields or from indirect ownership through pension funds and income tax reductions, enjoyed an increase in wealth. Less affluent consumers, on the other hand, paid higher prices but reaped little of the benefits of ownership. Hence the social-equity issue is really a question of rent distribution across income classes.

This social-equity problem might be tackled in a number of ways. One traditional argument for most efficiently achieving social equity is to focus on direct income transfers, rather than on commodity price and distribution regulation. It is more economically effective to transfer wealth directly to the poor than it is to hold down the price of gas for all. Despite the compelling logic of this argument, PUCs will continue to face pressure to provide special benefits to the poor, especially for those who are eligible for lifeline rates. Social obligation and social policy extend well beyond the goals of promoting economic efficiency.

A more interesting dimension of the social-equity issue arises when regulatory agencies assume responsibility for protecting various segments of the natural gas industry. Following the intent and directives of Congress, the FERC in recent years has shown an interest in promoting competition to achieve the benefits of economic efficiency. At the same time, it has shown an interest in protecting existing pipelines. Inflexible, long-term, and high-cost contracts threatened pipelines with such significant losses that some of them would go bankrupt. The FERC responded with SMPs, which sacrificed competition to protect the balance sheets of the pipelines. The problem is that the FERC failed to confront squarely the inescapable fact that competition inherently entails the risks of failure as well as the rewards of success.

A review of 1985 bankruptcy records in Louisiana, Oklahoma, and Texas reveals many examples of natural gas producers who went out of business due to cash-flow problems related to the excess supply of natural gas. Apparently, no regulatory agency felt compelled to protect these producers from the forces of competition. Unfortunately, there is no practical mechanism for protecting producers and simultaneously enhancing competition in the producing market.

In contrast, the FERC developed a large number of experimental programs allowing pipelines to discriminate among consumers, to recapture markets lost to oil, and to protect their existing "core" markets from competition by other pipelines. Here the FERC transparently promoted noncompetitive practices in order to protect the pipelines from severe financial penalties for misreading the market. At the same time, the FERC dampened and in some cases wholly eliminated the effective transmission of price signals to producers.[17]

Recent regulatory reforms proposed by the FERC represent a radical departure from this protective approach to the pipeline industry. For example, new proposals requiring pipelines to transport gas for all interested customers will dramatically reduce the subsidy of inefficient pipelines. If these proposals survive legislative and court challenges, the FERC will strengthen its support of competition by weakening its capacity to modify the play of market forces.

But pressures to assist pipelines will play a major role in determining whether the new regulatory policies succeed. The desire for social equity and the obligation for fair play have motivated the FERC to preserve a measure of intertemporal equity for pipelines. Any regulatory scheme inevitably creates implicit contracts among the affected parties. Just as consumers can argue that they have a legitimate claim to rents from low-cost old gas, so too can pipelines argue that they have an implicit right to protection from absorbing the full force of a swing in market conditions.

Social equity cannot be achieved by an instantaneous balancing of costs and benefits, nor does the nation gain by imposing a regulatory standard based on perfect hindsight. Surely, producers and pipelines made prudent investments based on a reasonable presumption that regulatory policy would permit a reasonable return on investment. The government shares an obligation to mitigate some of the losses incurred due to changes it imposed. This does not mean that every investment must be protected, but good public policy can hardly incorporate an assumption that investors should absorb all of the risks of abrupt changes in that same policy.

Unfortunately, regulatory agencies cannot simultaneously achieve the benefits of competition and protect all major participants from financial loss. The challenge is to find an equitable balance between these two goals. Once again, recent FERC regulatory reform proposals reveal an explicit awareness of its obligations to treat producers and pipelines fairly. For instance, one FERC proposal focused on resolving pipelines' "take-or-pay" obligations embedded in contracts signed during the regulated regime but no longer viable in the competitive market. Although some details of the proposal are open to debate, its overall attempt to settle these contract claims and to apportion some of the resulting costs to consumers represents a quid pro quo for producers and pipelines. It demonstrates the FERC's partial recognition of its implicit obligations created by the history of regulation.[18]

The challenge for the future is to develop alternative institutional mechanisms that more closely approximate competition and that moderate the disruptions caused by market corrections and the possible failure of some firms. Should the FERC intervene to prevent the bankruptcy of a major pipeline? This is an unresolved but important question for public policy, whose answer in part requires a balancing of economic-efficiency and social-equity goals.

Environmental Protection and Energy Security

The problems of environmental protection and energy security are secondary to achieving economic efficiency and social equity. If we could solve the problems of social equity or achieve the benefits of economic efficiency, we then might turn to environmental and energy-security issues. But a thorough examination reveals that these latter issues would not have a great deal of practical impact on the professed goals or policies with respect to natural gas markets.

The Environmental Protection Agency allows electric utilities to burn natural gas in order to avoid sulfur emissions from burning oil, but this has little effect on broader policies. Or planners in the Department of Energy concerned with efficient use of the oil stockpile may count on a limited ability to convert to natural gas, but this contingency plan also will have no appreciable effect on larger natural gas policy issues.

Probably the only existing legislation that has a significant impact on the natural gas market and that was motivated by concerns other than economic efficiency or social equity is the now-infamous Fuel Use Act of 1978.[19] This rule, which prohibited the use of natural gas in power plants, was motivated by a misguided interpretation of the problems of energy security and the need to conserve a putatively dwindling natural gas resource. A responsible review of long-term public policy goals should address the foundations of the Fuel Use Act. Perhaps the next major natural gas legislation will include a repeal of this constraint on the efficient use of natural gas.

Other than this, however, there presently are no policies concerning environmental or energy-security issues that are of major concern in the design of public policy for natural gas markets. More to the point, policymakers should be attentive to misusing environmental or energy-security arguments to thwart or confuse economic-efficiency or social-equity goals.

The Design of Public Policy

The absence of perfect competition and the lack of preconditions for achieving economic efficiency alone do not justify public intervention. If anything, the lessons of the regulations spawned by the Natural Gas Act of 1938 and the Phillips decision of 1954 and the gross inefficiencies created by other governmental intervention shift the burden of proof to proponents of regulation to demonstrate that the gains from a given policy justify the costs.[20]

In pursuing regulatory policy, we can choose broadly between an emphasis on direct control of the market or an indirect reliance on private incentives.[21] Under direct control, regulatory agencies would assume responsibility for determining the prices and conditions under which gas would be produced, delivered, and sold. This was the dominant regulatory approach of the past, and we have witnessed the failures of regulators and legislators to anticipate correctly shifts in supply and demand. Legislated prices and the resulting artificial shortages and gluts all produced great losses in a world of uncertainty and changing market conditions.[22] The alternative is to use regulation to create incentives that achieve public purposes, recognizing its inability to dictate the particulars of private contracts. Fortunately, the United States enjoys a confluence of practical experience, ideology, and theory that points heavily in the direction of less government intervention and greater emphasis on the use of incentives to achieve economic efficiency and social-equity goals.

These new realities provide ample opportunity for managers of production, pipeline, and LDC companies to develop creative alternatives to regulatory control. A significant unbundling of services in the pipeline industry, for instance, would go a long way toward eliminating the obstacles to competition, thereby reducing the need for federal intervention. The FERC proposal to move toward an open transportation policy will counter incentives that in the past occasionally led pipelines to refuse to provide transportation services. Pipelines could continue to provide full-line purchasing and delivery services, but customers would have the option to purchase gas directly at the wellhead and to use the pipeline only to transport it. The resulting increase in competition would have a dramatic effect on the operation of the market. With transportation available to all, the forces of competition among producers at the wellhead and among LDCs at the city gate will provide conditions favorable to competitive bidding, which in turn will move natural gas toward its high-valued uses. Thus it will no longer be necessary for the FERC to dictate the price of each transaction. Incentives will replace price controls, and regulation of transportation will promote competition.

Perhaps a segmentation of the market would provide avenues for achieving the otherwise conflicting goals of social equity and economic efficiency, by giving customers access to a portfolio of secure long-run contracts coupled with more volatile short-run supplies. If, as the FERC has proposed, consumers could purchase old gas directly, and separate rights to old gas from access to incremental supplies, thereby eliminating the perverse effects of rolled-in average-cost pricing, the intended transfer of scarcity rents might be achieved without sacrificing incentives for efficient production and consumption. The expansion of spot markets and enhanced roles for gas brokers would transmit price signals faster and more efficiently. The proliferation of transportation alternatives to open the pipeline bottleneck would enhance competition in the producing market. This task will test the mettle of the FERC and the PUCs.

During the transition period, however, the various regulatory agencies must wrestle with the problems created by past regulation. For example, while promoting a spot market or a mixed portfolio of gas contracts, the obligation to provide gas to all customers cannot be left untouched. Rate-making practices must continue to evolve in recognition of the distinction between capacity obligations, reliability services, and the commodity costs of various sources of gas supply.

Perhaps the most perplexing problem for PUCs will be how to balance the transition to more competition with obligations created by past implicit promises in rates and access. The old rules created powerful interest groups, who have valid claims on future supplies of gas. Whatever the attractions of efficiency at the margin, PUCs will not abandon these groups.

PUCs face similar challenges when establishing rates for LDCs. Here the objective of approximating marginal-cost pricing should continue to provide the competitive guide in regulating LDC rates. At the same time, local PUCs can use the competitive market at the wellhead, facilitated by open transportation, to establish a benchmark for evaluating the prudence of LDC gas-purchasing practices. PUCs should ensure that the incentives motivating LDCs reflect both the forces of competition and long-term social-equity goals.

The conflict between social-equity and incentive issues will deepen when, inevitably, we return to an era of constrained supplies and higher prices. During a period of supply surplus, responding to incentives means buying gas at lower prices. Consumers and PUCs have little objection to lowering prices, shutting-in expensive supplies, and reducing the transfer of rents to producers. All of these steps are essential to using competitive forces to provide incentives for future investments and meaningful consumption decisions. However, the arguments for marginal-cost pricing and the free pursuit of market equilibrium will apply with equal force when events lead to a return to market deficits and rising prices. No one knows for sure when the gas "bubble" will burst. But any commodity so closely tied to the volatile world oil market inevitably must experience cycles in aggregate supply and demand. When demand grows or supply contracts, competition will drive out inefficient users, raise prices, and increase the transfer of rents to producers. The incentives thereby created will expand supply and reduce demand to bring the system in balance and to achieve the most efficient aggregate outcome. These incentives and market adjustments will be substantially less appealing to consumers than the present adjustments to a surplus. Political pressures will arise to protect national security, to meet environmental concerns, to stop wealth transfers, or to respond to any number of secondary arguments that frustrate market adjustments.

How will regulatory bodies, especially the politically sensitive PUCs, respond to the pressures brought about by tighter markets? The proponents of competition should anticipate these circumstances. Policies should be designed to be responsive and responsible in the face of both shortages and surpluses. When prices are falling, the proponents of competition should anticipate the problems that will arise when prices begin to rise, as inevitably they must.

The policy implications of relying on incentives and the symmetry of the forces of competitive markets color social-equity issues. For example, PUCs must balance a desire to achieve lower costs with the implicit obligations faced by LDCs. Consider the issues of "bypass" and obligations to serve. Many large consumers, especially those with easy access to interstate pipelines, would like to bypass their LDCs or even use them to transport gas purchased elsewhere. In periods of abundant supply, a large customer has no difficulty in arranging for adequate purchases of gas and is attracted to the low cost of distress sales. The LDC, eager to preserve its markets, fears both the loss of revenue and the problems to be faced later when market conditions change.

What measures can be taken to relieve LDCs of their obligation to serve in future tight markets? At a minimum, PUCs should recognize the obligations faced by LDCs and establish compensation to cover costs incurred during a supply shortage. We might go even further and suggest that for many high-priority customers, it is implausible to expect that LDCs should be relieved of their obligation to serve. After all, current PUCs cannot tie the hands of their successors, and a change in the political climate combined with a shift in the market might leave LDCs with the short end of the deal—required to supply customers when markets are tight and costs are high but losing their cash flows during periods of surplus. Such a policy would raise costs for everyone. It would be plausible for PUCs to oppose bypass of LDCs. At a minimum, the use of incentives and the promotion of competition must adjust to such implicit obligations.

These examples illustrate some of the compromises that are essential to balance the conflicting goals of economic efficiency and social equity. No single standard, including the powerful appeal of the competitive model, will suffice as the sole measure of public policy design. In negotiating these compromises, the natural gas industry and its regulators must balance the advantages of competition against the claims on scarcity rents and the myriad problems involved in providing reliable service.

Conclusions

Fundamental market realities influencing the natural gas industry will continue to require public oversight. Hence the regulatory regime will continue to provide an arena for politically oriented interest groups operating in conjunction with market-oriented entrepreneurs. A greater reliance on incentives should improve regulation's effectiveness in using the market to achieve social-equity goals.

America can agree on the need for more competition while still responding fairly to the needs of producers, transporters, distributors, and consumers of natural gas. In all public matters, the design of particular policies depends critically on the larger framework of values and goals. Too often, competing frameworks give little weight to opposing points of view, so opportunities for mutual gain are lost, to the detriment of all. A clarification of goals will enhance the benefits of compromise. The natural gas industry needs a better balance of regulation to achieve competition.

Notes

1. *Maryland People's Counsel v. Federal Energy Regulatory Commission*, Docket No. 84–1090, U.S. Court of Appeals, Washington, D.C., Circuit Court (May 10, 1985), p. 19.

2. *The Natural Gas Policy Act*, Public Law No. 95–621, 92 Stat. 335 (Washington, D.C., 1978), legislated prices for numerous classes of natural gas and set a schedule for decontrol of some gas prices in 1985.

3. Federal Energy Regulatory Commission, Notice of Proposed Rulemaking, "Regulation of Natural Gas Pipelines after Partial Wellhead Decontrol," Docket No. 2M85–1–000 (Washington, D.C., May 30, 1985).

4. In 1984, 47.5 percent of all reported interstate sales were classified as old gas, with an average price of $1.45 per Mcf. With rolled-in pricing, the average price of all sales, $2.77 per Mcf, is the best proxy for the "market" price. See U.S. Department of Energy, Energy Information Agency, *Natural Gas Monthly*, Report No. DOE-EIA–0130(85/06), U.S. Government Printing Office, Washington, D.C., June 1985, pp. 11–13.

5. For wellhead producer concentration ratios, see U.S. Department of Energy, Energy Information Administration, Office of Oil and Gas, *Producer Revenues, Prices, and Concentration in the Natural Gas Market*, Report No. DOE-EIA–0404, U.S. Government Printing Office, Washington, D.C., 1983. This and earlier studies were reviewed in Harry G. Broadman, "Elements of Market Power in the Natural Gas Pipeline Industry," *The Energy Journal*, 7, no. 1, January 1986, pp. 119–138. Broadman found the producer markets either to be competitive or to have a balance of power between buyers and sellers.

6. Regulation of LDCs began in the 1800s when they sought government assistance through eminent domain, first to lay pipe and then to be protected from competition once investments were in place. For an interesting summary of the evolution of natural gas regulation, see Arlon R. Tussing and C. C Barlow, *The Natural Gas Industry: Evolution, Structure, and Economics*, Ballinger Publishing Company, Cambridge, Mass., 1984.

7. Ibid., pp. 22–23.

8. Data on pipeline market share are presented in David Mead, *Concentration in the Natural Gas Pipeline Industry*, Report Prepared for the Federal Energy Regulatory Commission, U.S. Government Printing Office, Washington, D.C., August 1981.

9. Ibid., p. 26.

10. The Department of Energy has produced a series of reports that cite the now familiar examples of pipelines attempting to reduce sales of inexpensive gas, refusing requests to transport gas for end users, and then using the FERC regulations to develop discriminatory-pricing rules to segment the market. For example, see U.S. Department of Energy, Energy Information Administration, *Recent Market Activities of Major Interstate Pipeline Companies*, Report No. DOE-EIA–0440, U.S. Government Printing Office, Washington, D.C., January 1984.

11. See R. J. Pierce, "Reconsidering the Roles of Regulation and Competition in the Natural Gas Industry," *Harvard Law Review*, 97, no. 2, December 1983, pp. 345–385.

12. Mead, *Concentration in the Natural Gas Pipeline Industry*, p. 25.

13. This burden of proof would not be impossible. For instance, Tussing and Barlow, *The Natural Gas Industry*, pp. 236–237, make the case that the limits of government's ability to regulate are so great that the failures of imperfect competition among pipelines will not be half as detrimental as the costs of further attempting to fine-tune regulation.

14. See E. Allen Jacobs, "Competitive Ownership Rules for Natural Monopolies," Unpublished paper, University of Texas at Austin, Department of Finance, March 1984.

15. See Tussing and Barlow, *The Natural Gas Industry*, p. 118.

16. See Henry Lee, Susan Bender, and Joseph Kalt, "Natural Gas Decontrol: A Northwest Industrial Perspective," Energy and Environmental Policy Center, John F. Kennedy School of Government, Harvard University, Cambridge, Mass., November 1983; Joseph Kalt, Henry Lee, and Robert Leone, "Natural Gas Decontrol: A Northeast Industrial Perspective," Energy and Environmental Policy Center, John F. Kennedy School of Government, Harvard University, Cambridge, Mass., October 1982.

17. See *Maryland People's Counsel v. Federal Energy Regulatory Commission*, which

summarizes the Washington D.C. Circuit Court's review of these pipeline practices as sanctioned by the FERC.

18. See Maryland People's Counsel, "Regulation of Natural Gas Pipelines after Partial Wellhead Decontrol," Docket No. RM85–1–000, Testimony before the Federal Energy Regulatory Commission (Washington, D.C., July 15, 1985), for a "take-or-pay" alternative to the FERC proposal from a group representing consumers but offering a system for sharing the losses among producers, pipelines, and consumers.

19. *The Powerplant and Industrial Fuel Use Act*, Public Law 95–620, 92 Stat. 3289 (Washington, D.C., 1978), prohibited new utility plants from burning oil or natural gas. There is a process of exceptions for environmental reasons.

20. *The Natural Gas Act*, Public Law 75–688, 52 Stat. 821 (Washington, D.C., 1938), laid the legislative foundation later articulated in the *Phillips Petroleum Company v. Wisconsin* decision, which ordered the Federal Power Commission to regulate the price of natural gas purchased by interstate pipelines.

21. Many examples of the use of private incentives to achieve public goals are provided in Charles L. Schultze, *The Public Use of Private Interest*, The Brookings Institution, Washington, D.C., 1977.

22. For one analysis of the hubris in past policy design and a call for more competitive conditions in transportation, see P. R. Carpenter and A. W. Wright, "The Natural-Gas Policy Drama: An Unfinished Tragicomedy in Three Acts," MIT Center for Energy Policy Research, Report No. MIT-EL 84–012WP, Cambridge, Mass., July 1984. For a review of the role of transportation in improving competitiveness, see U.S. Department of Energy, Office of the Assistant Secretary for Policy, Safety, and Environment, *Increasing Competition in the Natural Gas Market: The Second Report Required by Section 123 of the Natural Gas Policy Act of 1978*, U.S. Government Printing Office, Washington, D.C., January 1985, Chapter 7.

Selected Bibliography

Broadman, Harry G. "Elements of Market Power in the Natural Gas Pipeline Industry." *The Energy Journal*, 7, no. 1, January 1986.

Carpenter, P. R. and A. W. Wright. "The Natural Gas Policy Drama: An Unfinished Tragicomedy in Three Acts." MIT Center for Energy Policy Research. Report No. MIT-EL 84–012WP. Cambridge, Mass., July 1984.

Federal Energy Regulatory Commission. Notice of Proposed Rulemaking. "Regulation of Natural Gas Pipelines after Partial Wellhead Decontrol." Docket No. 2M85–1–000 (Washington, D.C., May 30, 1985).

———. Order #436. Final Rule and Notice Requesting Supplemental Comments. "Regulation of Natural Gas Pipelines after Partial Wellhead Decontrol." Docket No. RM85–1–000 (Washington, D.C., October 9, 1985).

Jacobs, E. Allen. "Competitive Ownership Rules for Natural Monopolies." Unpublished Paper. University of Texas at Austin, Department of Finance, March 1984.

Kalt, Joseph, Henry Lee, and Robert Leone. "Natural Gas Decontrol: A Northeast Industrial Perspective." Energy and Environmental Policy Center, John F. Kennedy School of Government, Harvard University, Cambridge, Mass., October 1982.

Lee, Henry, Susan Bender, and Joseph Kalt. "Natural Gas Decontrol: A Northwest Industrial Perspective." Energy and Environmental Policy Center, John F. Kennedy School of Government, Harvard University, Cambridge, Mass., November 1983.

Maryland People's Counsel. "Regulation of Natural Gas Pipelines after Partial Wellhead Decontrol." Docket No. RM85–1–000. Testimony before the Federal Energy Regulatory Commission, Washington, D.C., July 15, 1985.

Maryland People's Counsel v. Federal Energy Regulatory Commission. Docket No. 84–1090. U.S. Court of Appeals, Washington, D.C., Circuit Court (May 10, 1985).

Mead, David. *Concentration in the Natural Gas Pipeline Industry*. Report Prepared for the Federal Energy Regulatory Commission. U.S. Government Printing Office, Washington, D.C., August 1981.

The Natural Gas Act. Public Law 75–688, 52 Stat. 821 (Washington, D.C., 1938).

The Natural Gas Policy Act. Public Law No. 95–621, 92 Stat. 335 (Washington, D.C., 1978).

Pierce, R. J. "Reconsidering the Roles of Regulation and Competition in the Natural Gas Industry." *Harvard Law Review*, 97, no. 2, December 1983, pp. 345–385.

The Powerplant and Industrial Fuel Use Act. Public Law 95–620, 92 Stat. 3289 (Washington, D.C., 1978).

Schultze, Charles L. *The Public Use of Private Interest*. The Brookings Institution, Washington, D.C., 1977.

Tussing, Arlon R., and C. C. Barlow. *The Natural Gas Industry: Evolution, Structure, and Economics*. Ballinger Publishing Company, Cambridge, Mass., 1984.

U.S. Department of Energy, Energy Information Administration. *Natural Gas Monthly*. Report No. DOE-EIA–0130(85/06). U.S. Government Printing Office, Washington, D.C., June 1985.

———. *Producer Revenues, Prices, and Concentration in the Natural Gas Market*. Report No. DOE-EIA–0404. U.S. Government Printing Office, Washington, D.C., 1983.

———. *Recent Market Activities of Major Interstate Pipeline Companies*. Report No. DOE-EIA–0440. U.S. Government Printing Office, Washington, D.C., January 1984.

U.S. Department of Energy, Office of the Assistant Secretary for Policy, Safety, and Environment. *Increasing Competition in the Natural Gas Market: The Second Report Required by Section 123 of the Natural Gas Policy Act of 1978*. U.S. Government Printing Office, Washington, D.C., January 1985.

PART II

THE REDESIGN OF REGULATORY POLICY

Arguments for and against governmental intervention into an industry turn, in large part, on assessments of economic performance. In particular, the less potent is competition, the more compelling is the case for regulation. Of course, even if competition in an unregulated market is imperfect, it is not always possible to implement successful remedial policies. The challenge for the policymaker is to devise regulations that induce or mimic competition but avoid introducing distortions or excessive administrative burdens of their own.

In Chapter 5 Joseph P. Kalt concludes that the salient features of the natural gas industry are (1) economies of large-scale operations in pipelining and distribution, and (2) largely irreversible investments that lock parties into one-on-one relationships at each stage of the industry. The first conclusion provides sufficient rationale for continuing regulation of the industry: pipelines and local distribution companies (LDCs), but not producers, are naturally monopolistic (or at least oligopolistic). The second observation means that parties often must resort to long-term contracts that guarantee performance in accordance with expectations, but that subsequently can turn out to restrain trading opportunities and flexibility. Regulatory oversight of gas industry contracts and trading practices must be tempered by recognition of their role in allowing investments to be committed.

Harry G. Broadman argues in Chapter 6 that, although regulation of natural gas pipelines may be justified on the basis of natural monopoly (or oligopoly) in transportation services, past regulation has provided pipelines with excessive protection from competition. In particular, the combining of transportation and gas resale functions under the sanctioned status of private carriage has inhibited parties other than pipelines from competing for natural gas at the wellhead and has allowed pipelines to deny access to the transportation of gas brokered by others. Broadman recommends a policy that would provide open access to transportation facilities by requiring pipelines to make capacity available to non-pipeline-owned gas, coupled with reform of pipeline rates to ensure that prices reflect costs borne for services provided. In addition, Broadman urges that restrictions on entry be eliminated and that service obligations and related guarantees be matters of voluntary contract to the extent politically feasible.

The state Public Utility Commissions (PUCs) have the capacity substantially to promote or thwart natural gas regulatory reform. In Chapter 7 Colin C. Blaydon argues that the central problem now faced by the PUCs is the need to adapt to increased competition and flexibility in the merchandising and transportation of gas. In particular, the traditional reliance on long-term, fixed-price contracts with pipelines as the exclusive guarantors of supply reliability is becoming outmoded, as is simple cost-of-service rate making. The evolving gas market now is shifting considerable risk to the LDCs, which are being challenged to find innovative portfolios of supply contracts and to design rates and transportation policies that respond to end-market competition. This shifting of risk requires PUCs to avoid excessively conservative oversight and to allow rates that not only force LDCs to bear the burden of their mistakes, but also reward successful risk bearing.

5

Market Power and the Possibilities for Competition

JOSEPH P. KALT

The regulation of the natural gas industry arose from allegations that certain parts of the industry were engaging in monopolistic practices. The Public Utilities Holding Company Act of 1935 and the Natural Gas Act of 1938 were crafted to respond to these alleged anticompetitive abuses. Two arguments were used to justify this original federal intervention. One was the assertion that vertically integrated pipeline companies could collude to establish exclusive geographic supply and delivery markets. The second claimed that integrated firms systematically engaged in restraints of trade by denying independent producers and users access to the market.

Are these concerns still warranted? Since certain segments of the industry still are structured in a way that could diminish the economic benefits of competition, the answer is, at least theoretically, yes. Although the 1930s are distant and gas markets have grown larger and more established, the underlying economics of the industry fundamentally are unchanged. Significant economies of scale in transmission and distribution and the need for natural gas to respond efficiently to demand still are foundations of the industry. Yet in the 1980s new questions have arisen about the gas industry's competitiveness now that partial wellhead decontrol and a plethora of state and federal regulatory reforms have taken place.

This chapter examines how the evolving structure of the natural gas industry will influence its economic efficiency and competitive performance, with an ultimate eye to determining the type and degree of regulation that best satisfies criteria of sound economic performance. Accordingly, this chapter undertakes two tasks: (1) It first outlines the economic and regulatory factors that will drive the industry in the future, and (2) it assesses the likely performance of that restructured industry.

Performance Criteria: How to Decide Whether Gas Markets Are Working Well

The gradual deregulation of natural gas wellhead prices that began with passage of the Natural Gas Policy Act (NGPA) in 1978 saw an industry, once molded by government regulation, suddenly thrust into an era where its new shape would be determined by the forces of the marketplace. To gauge the performance of the resulting industry structure, one can employ six basic economic criteria.

Competition

For an industry to function well, it must be structured either to operate competitively or to mimic competition through some combination of competitive structure and regulation. The value of competition derives from ensuring that prices and costs determine production and allocation with maximum benefit to the economy. Competition drives up supply until incremental costs are no less than the incremental benefits delivered to consumers—as these benefits are reflected in the prices they are willing to pay.

Cost Minimization

Past regulation failed to induce buyers and suppliers to purchase the least expensive gas. The economy gains if gas can be delivered to end users from sources that minimize operating and resource-depletion costs. Horizontally, cost minimization requires taking advantage of economies of scale and optimally combining inputs to produce output. Vertically, it entails integrated management and planning that does not overtax managerial resources; it allocates risk among producers, pipelines, distributors, speculators, and consumers, so choices among alternative gas and nongas energy sources reflect realistic risk-return tradeoffs; and it requires that transfers of gas between and within firms reflect true resource costs.

Flexibility and Reliability

The natural gas industry is subject to considerable risk from both the supply and demand sides. A well-functioning industry should be flexible enough to minimize supply/demand imbalances that leave buyers with unfilled demand or suppliers with unsold output.

Historically, much of this risk has been channeled to end users in the form of supply shortages. Producers, pipelines, and local distribution companies (LDCs) effectively were assured, through regulation and take-or-pay contracts, that they could sell all available gas at determinable prices. As wellhead deregulation proceeds, excess demands are cleared increasingly by price adjustments, and supply and demand risks are being distributed away from end users and back upstream. One of the crucial functions of upstream vertical relationships—contracts and integration—will be to allocate these risks across firms. If vertical relationships are excessively rigid, supply shortfalls and gluts will not be avoided. The implication is that the structuring of vertically integrated firms, long-term contracts, and spot and futures markets all will affect risk allocation and market flexibility.

Efficient Allocation

Efficient allocation requires that natural gas be distributed across consumers, regions, seasons, and years such that it goes to all uses that have value in excess of (minimized) costs and that it has equal value at the margin across its various uses. The second of these criteria would be violated to the extent that the horizontal or vertical structure of the gas industry promoted anticompetitive price discrimination. If horizontal or vertical relationships do not minimize the cost of gas or prices are kept artificially high, the first criterion would be violated as gas use is reduced and gas loses its market share to other fuels. The result of excessively high prices even could be the gradual loss of customers that appear, in the short run, to be unable to switch to alternative fuels: As successively larger shares of pipeline/LDC distribution costs are loaded onto such customers, their long-term decisions on installation of gas-using capital may be adversely affected.

Optimal Level and Timing of Investments

The gas industry needs to be able to make capital investments whenever and wherever the present value of benefits exceeds the present value of costs. Because most investment in the gas industry is physically "sunk" once it is made (i.e., cannot readily be withdrawn from the industry), there is a particular premium placed on holding down the risk that sunk investments could go unused or underused. The industry's responses to this have included long-term contracts and horizontal and vertical integration. Once in force, these responses limit the options available to industry participants and may result in ex post conflicts with the other criteria of good performance. Producers' needs for assured customer links, for example, result in take-or-pay contract clauses that lock parties into trading relationships and may hamper cost minimization or competitiveness. Yet without such clauses, ex ante investment opportunities and funds may be inadequate. The implied tradeoff between ex ante incentives and ex post performance requires the careful weighing of offsetting factors.

Fairness in the Distribution of Income

Policies that improve the allocation of the country's scarce economic resources may not benefit every individual or firm. The national economic pie clearly would be increased, for example, by bringing old gas prices up to market levels.

The decontrol of old gas, however, would transfer income from one segment of the gas industry (especially high-cost gas producers) to the producers of old gas.[1] Some theories of social equity hold that such transfers are unfair, particularly if the would-be beneficiaries are relatively high on the income scale, or if the prospective transfers are windfalls, or if above-market prices for high-cost gas were agreed to in good-faith contracts. Alternatively, some theories of social equity hold that such transfers are just, based on old gas producers' justifiable property rights to the revenues generated by their actions.

These competing notions of fairness are forever open to debate. However, it is clear that to the extent that concerns over fairness in the distribution of income are regarded as legitimate, regulation of particular markets is a second-best approach, because it can be inordinately distortive and administratively costly. When alternative, more direct means of achieving distributional fairness are available (i.e., through state and federal income-assistance programs), regulatory intervention should be resisted.

The Importance of Market Structure

The six criteria listed above provide a convenient checklist with which to evaluate the economic performance of the natural gas industry and of the regulations that shape it. However, whether these criteria can be met depends in large part upon how natural gas firms and markets are structured, that is, their degree of horizontal or vertical integration. Horizontal and vertical structure can influence both the vitality of competition and how efficiently an industry responds to the distortions caused by a regulated marketplace. In addition, the performance of the gas industry depends on its behavior, specifically its ability to negotiate its way around the distortions that may accompany an industry structure that is less than perfectly competitive.

This last point is worth emphasizing: It is commonly argued that economic distortion caused by monopoly and market power are directly due to industry structure, but this is overly simplistic. In a fundamental sense, the true source of a monopoly problem is "transaction costs"—the costs of negotiating and enforcing deals. The inefficiencies of monopoly/monopsony arise from gaps between price and cost, and it is always in the buyers' and sellers' interests to capture the net benefits that this gap represents. If there are no costs to bargaining and contracting, buyers facing a monopolist, for example, can and will "bribe" that monopolist to expand output to the point where incremental additions to value will equal incremental additions to cost. Such a negotiated solution to the distortions of monopoly will involve some form of high payment on before-the-margin purchases (e.g., a hookup fee for access to the first thousand cubic feet [Mcf] of gas), coupled with marginal cost pricing.[2] To be sure, such nonmarginal considerations affect a buyer's willingness to enter into trade. But as long as incremental prices reflect incremental costs, buyers who do agree to trade are induced to buy until their incremental valuation of gas is equal to the incremental cost they pay.[3]

An example illustrates. Multipart pricing is prevalent in the natural gas industry. For example, pipeline rates almost always are stated in two parts, a "demand" and a "commodity" charge. A "demand" charge bills customers for access to service (under the banner of recovering fixed costs), independent of volume. A "commodity" charge, in turn, varies with the volume of gas provided. The Federal Energy Regulatory Commission (FERC) has moved toward placing fixed costs in the demand charge and leaving variable costs in the commodity charge. In October 1983, for example, a rate structure that left a return to stockholders' equity and fixed production/gathering costs as the only fixed components of the commodity charge was approved for the Natural Gas Pipeline Company of America.[4] Take-or-pay and minimum-bill provisions similarly provide one party with valuable consideration that is independent of marginal prices and rates. The role of such contract terms is examined more closely below.

The norm in monopolized markets involves a small number of sellers facing a very large number of buyers differing in size and access to substitutes. In such a setting, negotiations between sellers and buyers are inordinately expensive, and discriminatory before-the-margin pricing is hard to implement. In the gas industry, however, direct negotiations between relatively small numbers of buyers and sellers are not infeasible, at least at some important stages of the industry. This fact plays an important role in determining the horizontal and vertical structure of gas companies, contracts between companies, and economic performance.

Horizontal Structure

The horizontal structure of the natural gas industry concerns the size of companies' operations, relative to overall market size. There are a number of economic justifications for relatively large firms.

Technological Economies of Scale

The pipeline and LDC segments of the natural gas industry are subject to classic technological economies of scale. Specifically, large pipelines have lower unit operating costs than do a combination of many small pipelines. Any expansion in the carrying capacity of a pipeline requires less than a proportionate increase in the line's surface area (i.e., its material inputs). Thus the amount of gas carried can be expanded more rapidly than material inputs, and unit costs decrease as the scale of operations grows. Even a market that starts out populated by many small firms is likely to evolve toward very high concentration, because competition favors the survival of only the largest—that is, least-cost—companies. This tendency toward natural monopoly is the most common justification for public utility-style rate-of-return regulation, which restricts firms to earning no more than the normal profits needed to cover their costs of capital.

Economies of Scope

Each segment of the natural gas industry provides a unique service: Producers extract gas, pipelines transport it, and LDCs deliver it to myriad end users. In reality, however, firms "bundle" together a number of distinct services at any given stage: Producers may explore, drill, and manage a gas field; pipelines may provide storage, brokerage, and transportation services; and LDCs may provide storage, gas-using equipment or advice, and delivery service. This bundling is justified by economies of scope—cost savings that result from combining services.

Economies of scope play a major role in debates over the regulatory status of pipelines. Historically, pipelines operated by purchasing, transporting, and brokering gas. This bundling of the transportation and brokerage functions has been criticized as anticompetitive: Monopoly may prevail naturally in transportation, but the acquisition and brokering of gas are susceptible to competition. It is argued that officially sanctioned and protected private carriage stifles competition and allows pipelines to prevent independent parties from acting as brokers by competing for gas at the wellhead and competing for customers downstream.[5]

There is a strong case to be made that the regulatory policies that effectively granted pipelines monopoly status in their brokerage functions have had anticompetitive consequences. Experience in other industries, however, suggests that genuine cost-based economies of scope may underlie pipelines' bundling of brokerage and transportation functions.

The bundling of transportation, storage, and brokerage is encouraged in industries characterized by: (1) a product that is interchangeable across customers, (2) demand fluctuations that are unpredictable across customers (or geographic regions), (3) *relatively* limited storage capacity among customers, and (4) substantial costs to market transactions (i.e., spot brokerage transactions) that might balance unanticipated shifts in short-run supply or demand.[6]

When these conditions prevail, unanticipated short-term fluctuations in demand and supply typically are not met by market transactions (i.e., through brokers or spot transactions). Rather, they are handled by managers within firms who allocate supplies. In the gas industry, for example, a rise in demand at one point in the distribution system on a given day (e.g., due to weather conditions) typically is met with a reallocation of supplies directed from within the firm, rather than from a market-directed change in prices or a renegotiation of contracts. This does not mean that a system of spot markets and brokers could not achieve the same reallocations; the point is that reallocations by managers are likely to be cheaper.[7]

To the extent that there are natural economies of scope associated with pipelines' bundling of transportation and brokerage, the forced divestiture of these functions is inadvisable. The flip side of this—protecting pipelines from the competition of independent brokers or even from self-brokering—is equally unwise. If there are cost savings associated with bundling, such bundling will survive competition. Concomitantly, economies of scope in pipelines are likely to limit the extent of contract carriage and the growth of spot and futures markets under regulatory regimes designed to foster the independent sale of pipelines' transportation services (e.g., mandatory contract carriage).

Recent moves by some pipelines to unbundle themselves voluntarily and become more exclusively *transportation* specialists suggest that the limits of economies of scope may have been reached. In fact, recent years have witnessed significant expansions of both spot-market sales and voluntary contract carriage. The former are estimated to have reached as high as 12 percent of all natural gas sales by the end of 1984.[8] Approximately 6 percent of all 1985 pipeline volume for LDCs and end users is estimated to have been by contract carriage (more than double the 1982 volume), and total carriage for other sectors (including carriage by pipelines for other pipelines) may now be as high as 40 percent.[9]

Although significant, the economic functions of spot markets and contract carriage are bounded by pipelines' economies of scope. That is, the presence of such economies of scope suggest that spot and contract carriage will serve primarily as a procompetitive brake on pipelines' purchasing and brokering practices, arising where independent parties outbid pipelines. Pipelines likely will remain the principal storage managers and guarantors of service reliability, provided rate structures generate sufficient remuneration for such functions.

System Economies

The stereotypical interstate pipeline is a single large trunkline fed by several gas fields and delivering gas to multiple consuming areas. A number of recent mergers, however, have begun to change this stereotype. The combinations of Transwestern, Houston Natural, Northern Natural, and Florida Interstate, as well as the mergers of United with Mid-Con and Coastal with American Natural Resources, all share the common characteristic of creating a pipeline system that is notable for its considerable geographic scope at both ends of the pipeline.

The origin and fate of these ventures lie in their system economies. Such economies are likely to result from the combination of economies of scope and more competitive wellhead and LDC markets. With premiums increasingly placed on the ability of pipelines to meet gas-on-gas competition and to respond to changes in alternative fuel prices, integrated systems offer pipelines both expanded portfolios of suppliers and purchasers and an increased ability to shift supplies to and from various markets according to seasonal and irregular demand patterns. Although such shifts could be accomplished through independently brokered transactions in the open marketplace, pipelines are banking on the expectation that within-firm management by fiat will be both cheaper and more rapid.

The Tension between Firm Size and Competition

The presence of significant scale, scope, or system economies implies that there are pressures to create firms that are large relative to the size of the markets in which they operate. The objection to large firms is that they may exercise market power over prices, output, and contract terms.

Highly concentrated seller markets are likely to result in both monopolistic restrictions of output and higher prices. In highly concentrated buyer markets, the results are a monopsonistic depression of the prices paid for upstream inputs, lower supply from upstream producers, and higher ultimate prices for end users. In all cases, the economic objection is that supply that could have been available at costs less than the value generated is not. In the natural gas industry, the monopoly/monopsony (seller/buyer) distinction is important because significant interfuel competition at the burner tip acts to limit horizontal monopoly power flowing out of the industry's horizontal structure. Thus problems of imperfect competition are particularly likely to show up as upstream monopsony.

This should not imply that seller market power is of no concern. In defense of the pipeline industry's competiveness, for example, it is frequently but incorrectly argued that interfuel competition eliminates the effects of seller market power.[10] Interfuel competition makes demand more elastic (i.e., sales more responsive to price), but it does not completely eliminate the range over which gas sellers can raise prices and still maintain sales. Absent regulatory restrictions, firms will take advantage of this range by raising prices above competitive levels (i.e., above the incremental costs of output).

A monopolistic or highly concentrated market does not guarantee that anticompetitive pricing and practices will occur. If entry is not blocked and the capital plants and equipment of existing firms are mobile, even a market in which a single large firm has naturally lower costs than any combination of smaller firms will be competitive—because incumbents face the threat of entry if their prices diverge from costs.

Even if entry is difficult, monopolistic and monopsonistic distortions can be checked by direct bargaining between buyers and sellers. Buyers facing a monopolist, for example, may acquiesce to a discriminating pricing or bonus structure that gives the monopolist its profit but be offered incremental purchases at cost. In fact, the outlines of such a structure are evident in pipelines' frequently used practice of setting a lump-sum demand charge that does not vary with the level of purchases, coupled with a commodity charge tied to variable (especially gas) costs. Nonprice contract terms, such as take-or-pay provisions in pipeline/producer contracts and minimum-bill terms in buyer/pipeline agreements, also can ensure above-competitive returns that leave marginal sales prices undistorted. Although these kinds of pricing schemes are subject to regulatory oversight, they illustrate the opportunities that contracts provide for designing sales terms different from uniform pricing.[11]

The feasibility of nonuniform pricing is likely to improve if, under regulation, buyers are unable to resell gas to other customers of the monopolist seller. Resale would provide certain buyers with the opportunity to sidestep the monopolist's demand charges. In the gas industry, where multiple LDCs typically are located along a pipeline's system but lack any direct transportation links among themselves, resale is difficult and nonuniform pricing is feasible. However, nonuniform pricing of gas, even when practiced between pipelines and LDCs, can overcome the distortions of pipeline (or LDC) monopoly if similar pricing schemes are allowed by LDCs. Simple, uniform, average-cost pricing by LDCs now purchasing gas under nonuniform pricing structures will necessarily raise consumer costs above competitive levels.[12]

Evidence on Horizontal Structure

The economy has an interest in promoting horizontal integration at each stage of the natural gas industry *if* it minimizes the cost of delivering gas from field to burner tip. It is economically appropriate for firms to take advantage of available economies of scale. But as large firms proliferate, it is reasonable to become more concerned about anticompetitive pricing. That is, the rationale for regulation gathers force as any horizontal structure moves toward natural monopoly/monopsony. Accordingly, it is appropriate that the natural horizontal structure of each segment of the gas industry be assessed.

Producers

An examination of data on natural gas producers indicates that cost-effective firms are not particularly large relative to the market. As Table 5.1 indicates, natural gas production is not highly concentrated at the national level. The top four firms control less than one-fifth of the market, and the top twenty firms control only one-half of the market. By comparison, the average four-firm concentration ratio in all United States manufacturing industries is slightly more than 30 percent.

As Table 5.2 illustrates, producer submarkets also are generally unconcentrated. Only Alaska appears concentrated enough to warrant concern about substantial market power. Otherwise, the gas-producing industry is structured such that it is workably competitive. This is reinforced by the fact that entry is relatively easy, with relatively low capital costs and few regulatory barriers. One indication of this is the fact that there were 105 separate new bidders for Gulf Coast leases (where capital costs tend to be relatively high) from 1960–1974. Of them, more than half were successful.[13]

Pipelines

As regards horizontal market structure, the gas industry is marked by buyer (pipeline) concentration. The implied problem is not wellhead producer monop-

Table 5.1
U.S. Natural Gas Production, 1980 (Mcf)

	Production	Share of Total (%)
Top 4 producers	3,718,985	19.2
Top 8 producers	5,926,217	30.6
Top 15 producers	8,541,076	44.1
Top 20 producers	9,778,302	50.5
Top 30 producers	10,930,474	56.5
Top 40 producers	11,550,779	59.7
Total	19,348,000	100.0

Source: Robert Portman, *Competition Issues for Integrated Natural Gas Pipelines*, Staff Report of U.S. Department of Energy, Office of Policy, Planning, and Analysis, Division of Energy Deregulation, U.S. Government Printing Office, Washington, D.C., 1982.

oly but wellhead pipeline monopsony. Table 5.3 breaks down pipeline buyer concentration along geographic supply areas. Although few areas are characterized by one-firm monopsony, four- and eight-firm concentration is extremely high. Even where there is a fairly large number of pipelines buying in a supply area, concentration is also high. This is not likely to be offset by a significant threat of potential entry. New pipeline entry is discouraged by the sunk and unsalvageable costs of incumbent pipelines, which are unlikely to withdraw from the market if their dominance is contested. Moreover, any proposed addition to or entry of a major trunkline is likely to face substantial land-use and environmental regulatory barriers—even absent current FERC regulations requiring demonstration of "public convenience and necessity." Additional small lines that might link geographically distinct supply areas provide an avenue for entry. However, insofar as such lines are purely a response to the presence of monopsony rather than to underlying transportation economies, they are an excessively costly mechanism for enforcing competition.

The horizontal structure of the pipeline industry is not conducive to competition in the buying of gas by pipelines. This assessment must be tempered, however, by a recognition that the buying of natural gas typically involves repeated, ongoing transactions with a relatively small number of producers. The importance of this is that monopsonistic distortions to efficient incremental resource development—but not enrichment of monopsonistic pipelines—may be overcome through direct pipeline/producer bargaining. In an unregulated setting, this would require some form of nonuniform pricing in which producers are shown their pipeline's incremental value as the price they receive for gas, while the pipeline makes its monopsonistic profit on before-the-margin extractions from producers.

Table 5.2
Concentration of Natural Gas Reserves Ownership, 1981

Area	Area Share U.S. Reserves	Herfindahl Index of Concentration[a]				
		Major Producers	*Interstate Pipelines*	*Independent Producers*	*Total Market*	*Equivalent Number of Equal-Sized Producers*[b]
Appalachia-Illinois	3.0	0.012	0.011	0.006	0.029	34
Other South	7.1	0.013	0.000 +	0.009	0.022	45
South Louisiana	21.5	0.039	0.002	0.002	0.043	23
Texas Gulf Coast	12.2	0.050	0.001	0.002	0.053	19
Permian Basin	8.8	0.032	0.000 +	0.001	0.033	30
Hugoton-Andarko	15.6	0.018	0.003	0.002	0.023	43
Rocky Mountain	13.2	0.021	0.036	0.005	0.062	16
California	2.7	0.045	0.007	0.001	0.053	19
Alaska and misc.	15.9	0.238	0.000 +	0.000 +	0.238	4
Total	100.0	0.027	0.001	0.000 +	0.028	36

[a]The Herfindahl Index is the sum of the squared market shares of the individual firms. The index rises as the number of firms declines and as market output is concentrated in larger firms. The reciprocal of the Herfindahl Index indicates the number of equivalent-sized firms that would yield the indicated Herfindahl value.

[b]If all firms have the same market share, say 1/*N*, of the market (where *N* is the number of firms), the Herfindahl Index equals this share. The reciprocal of the Herfindahl index then equals *N*—the number of equal-sized firms in the market.

Source: U.S. Department of Energy, Energy Information Administration, Office of Oil and Gas, *Producer Revenues, Prices, and Concentration in the Natural Gas Market*, U.S. Government Printing Office, Washington, D.C., 1983.

The latter might include excessively low take-or-pay levels, a rising block structure to prices, or producer hook-up charges.

Having stressed the monopsonistic nature of the wellhead sector, it is important to contrast the implications for performance when pipelines are (hypothetically) unregulated. Whereas the unregulated pipeline effectively can maximize its profits through monopsonistic price depression or multipart pricing, the regulated pipeline monopsonist faces a different set of payoffs. In general, effective rate-of-return regulation completely can remove the incentive to behave as a monopsonist. For example, if any depression of price or extraction of nonmarginal payments from producers simply must be passed through in the form of lower prices upon resale, no profit is possible. In fact, under such regulation standard monopsony price depression could result in shortages, as lower resale prices stimulate demand while lower wellhead prices discourage production. If actual regulation is short of perfect and allows, for example, a slight markup of resale

Table 5.3
Buyer Concentration Ratios for Dedicated Natural Gas Reserves (1983 Year-End)

Supply Area	1 Firm	4 Firm	8 Firm	Number of Firms
Alabama	0.357	1.000	1.000	4
Arkansas	0.873	0.976	0.998	10
Colorado	0.398	0.855	0.983	10
Florida	0.728	1.000	1.000	2
Illinois	0.656	1.000	1.000	5
Indiana	0.781	1.000	1.000	2
Kansas	0.359	0.900	0.999	13
Kentucky	0.513	0.998	1.000	5
Northern Louisiana	0.223	0.626	0.845	21
Southern Louisiana onshore	0.276	0.709	0.923	16
Southern Louisiana warranty	0.905	1.000	1.000	2
Southern Louisiana offshore	0.238	0.580	0.854	19
Maryland	0.995	1.000	1.000	2
Michigan	0.885	1.000	1.000	2
Mississippi	0.491	0.910	0.992	12
Montana	0.713	1.000	1.000	3
Nebraska	1.000	1.000	1.000	1
New Mexico-San Juan	0.843	1.000	1.000	5
New Mexico-Permian	0.518	0.993	1.000	11
New York	0.390	0.963	1.000	5
North Dakota	1.000	1.000	1.000	1
Ohio	0.659	0.960	1.000	5
Oklahoma	0.202	0.614	0.872	25
Pennsylvania	0.265	0.896	1.000	10
South Dakota	1.000	1.000	1.000	1
Tennessee	0.909	1.000	1.000	2
Texas offshore	0.394	0.636	0.829	16
Texas RR District 1N	1.000	1.000	1.000	1
Texas RR District 1S	0.503	1.000	1.000	4
Texas RR District 2	0.302	0.451	0.899	12
Texas RR District 3	0.406	0.773	0.922	14
Texas RR District 4	0.447	0.854	0.979	11
Texas RR District 5	0.892	1.000	1.000	2
Texas RR District 6	0.296	0.870	0.996	9
Texas RR District 7B	0.670	1.000	1.000	2
Texas RR District 7C	0.729	0.996	1.000	6
Texas RR District 8	0.454	0.972	1.000	10
Texas RR District 8A	0.891	1.000	1.000	3
Texas RR District 9	0.887	0.999	1.000	5
Texas RR District 10	0.194	0.611	0.931	20
Utah	0.337	0.981	1.000	7
Virginia	0.561	1.000	1.000	4
Washington	1.000	1.000	1.000	1
West Virginia	0.501	0.966	1.000	8
Wyoming	0.358	0.695	0.908	16

Source: U.S. Department of Energy, Energy Information Administration, Office of Oil and Gas, *A Study of Contracts Between Interstate Pipelines and Their Customers*, U.S. Government Printing Office, Washington, D.C., 1984.

Table 5.4
Pipeline–Local Distribution Company (LDC) Relationships, 1979–1980

All LDCs	
Total number of LDCs	1,443
Total number of separate pipeline–LDC relationships	2,544
Average number of pipelines serving each LDC	1.8
Number of LDCs served by only one pipeline	1,012
LDCs Supplied by More than One Pipeline	
Number of LDCs	431
Number of separate pipeline–LDC relationships	1,532
Average number of pipelines serving each LDC	3.6

Source: David E. Mead, "Concentration in the Natural Gas Pipeline Industry," U.S. Federal Energy Regulatory Commission, Office of Regulatory Analysis, Staff Working Paper, Washington, D.C., August 1984.

price above the input cost of gas, pipelines have incentives to maximize their throughput. When some gas is available at below-market prices (e.g., due to price controls), the result may be that pipelines bid more than the market price for available uncontrolled gas. This is the antithesis of monopsony.

In short, even under current regulation, potential monopsony at the wellhead is likely to be an insignificant problem. This conclusion holds despite the observation that the industry may not be competitively structured.

Distribution

After a pipeline purchases gas from a producer, it then sells that gas to an LDC (or a direct end user). This pipeline/LDC market is even more concentrated than the pipeline/producer market. More than one thousand of the roughly twenty-five hundred LDCs in the United States are served by only 1.0 pipeline; the average LDC is served by only 1.8 pipelines (see Table 5.4).[14] An inspection of pipeline system maps indicates that a considerable number of LDCs could be served by more pipelines, for example, when two or more pipelines run through a corridor but an LDC is connected to only one. This, however, would require costly—and duplicative—investment. Note also that even if pipelines were not in the business of (re)selling gas but merely offered transportation services, the possibility of monopolistic power would not be fundamentally altered—natural monopoly in the pipeline industry is due to the economics of transportation, not of reselling.

In the end-user market, measurement of horizontal structure requires special attention to the definition of the relevant market. Almost without exception, LDCs are franchise monopolies, traditionally justified on the grounds that they are natural monopolies. This view, however, obscures the importance of interfuel competition. To the extent that end users can switch quickly and cheaply to other fuels whenever gas prices rise above the prices of other fuels, the monopoly power of the LDC is eliminated. The patterns of consumption and prices in the early 1980s revealed that LDC monopolies face severe competition from oil and coal in the industrial end-user market.[15] Significant monopoly power tends to be found consistently in only the residential and commercial sectors. The large number of these residential and commercial customers, and their heterogeneity of size and responsiveness to price, make it unlikely that an unregulated monopoly could implement nondistortive, nonuniform pricing.

Summary

This examination of the horizontal structure of the natural gas industry indicates that the producing sector is not characterized by an overconcentration of firms, while the pipeline and LDC sectors tend much more toward natural monopoly and highly concentrated markets. This is exemplified by buyer (pipeline) concentration at the wellhead. The potential for monopsony is real, although the inefficiency costs are likely to be limited by the ability of pipelines and producers to negotiate directly with each other. Pipeline monopsony is mirrored by monopoly in the pipeline/LDC market, although again it is limited by the relatively low costs of bargaining between pipelines and LDCs. Natural monopoly in LDCs is pervasive but is particularly worrisome in the residential and commercial sectors. In these sectors, interfuel competition is less potent and the design of nondistortive price structures is limited by the costs of setting them up in a complicated retail market.

Vertical Structure

The vertical structure of an industry can range from complete financial and managerial control under fully integrated firms to one-shot, arm's-length transactions between unrelated parties. Long-term contracts lie somewhere between the extremes. The organization of an industry over this spectrum is dictated by the interaction of its technology, its economic setting, and its policy environment. The incentive to transact via the marketplace or to bring transactions out of the market and into the firm is governed by the relative costs of market and within-firm transactions.

Vertically integrated firms (and long-term contracts) become more economically viable when the following exist.

System Economies

As with horizontal integration, so are there potential economies associated with vertical integration, that is, bringing producers and pipelines or pipelines and LDCs under the management of a single firm. Economies from vertical integration are particularly likely when, for example, short-term supply disruptions are costly and rapid access to open-market supplies is inhibited. Under these circumstances, a pipeline facing a short-term shortage would prefer to have access to supplies from its own producers, which it can command by managerial directive. Similarly, a pipeline with a temporary oversupply of gas might prefer to reduce volume takes from its affiliated producers, rather than incurring the take-or-pay obligations demanded by unaffiliated producers.

Investment Risk

Inputs that are specialized to an industry may require direct supervision to guarantee their proper integration into the sector's production flow. This may be accomplished most easily through centralized management of vertically linked processes, rather than through market transactions. Importantly, when such processes have large fixed costs and (especially) when they are immobile and linked to a specific physical production chain, they are likely to be targets of opportunistic or ''hold-up'' behavior. ''Hold-up'' refers to unilateral changes in output demand or input supply by a downstream or upstream party in a trading relationship. By such changes, an opportunistic party can take advantage of the fact that the trading partner's sunk fixed costs can be used to extract concessions from the partner before it will exit the trading relationship.

The investment risk associated with hold-up behavior is the risk of contract nonperformance. If contracts are well specified this nonperformance is limited legally. But litigation can be expensive, and full specification of all contingencies is costly to include in contracts. As a result, the party with opportunities for taking advantage of a trading partner's commitment to a physical investment in the production chain may continually do the ''little things'' that strain interfirm relations: delaying performance, delaying payment, resisting renegotiation when public policy changes, asking for ''favors'' in unstable times, and so on.[16]

The hold-up problem can be addressed in a number of ways. For example, in an industry where news of opportunistic behavior travels fast, firms must be cognizant of their reputations and the future willingness of suppliers or buyers to deal with them. The hold-up problem can be policed further by writing contracts that induce parties to share an interest in good performance (e.g., by sharing certain fixed costs or by invoking automatic penalties for nonperformance).[17] However, when contracts are expensive to write and enforce and the effects of reputation are limited, the only solution may be explicitly to give both sides of a vertical relationship the same objective—to share in the profits of a single, vertically integrated firm.

The role of long-term performance contracts is important. In the gas industry, these contracts typically specify a fairly long term (10 to 20 years) over which a pipeline agrees to purchase gas from a producer. The quantities to be delivered are specified, with take-or-pay provisions requiring payment for a minimum percentage of stipulated deliveries, regardless of actual deliveries. Prices are set according to expected market conditions, with provisions for periodic or automatic adjustments. These provisions include: most-favored-nation clauses, which link prices to those prevailing in like markets; ''market-out'' options, which allow buyers to reopen price negotiations when market conditions warrant; and market-indexed prices, which are linked to market reference points (such as competing oil prices).

Pricing structures in pipeline/LDC contracts typically split payments into fixed demand charges and variable cost-based commodity charges. Contracts also specify certain nonprice terms, such as payment schedules and methods. Exclusivity provisions often are included, as are *force majeure* terms by which parties may abrogate contractual terms in response to unforeseeable events such as labor strikes or natural disasters.

Take-or-pay and minimum-bill clauses provide insurance against hold-up by locking buyers into specified quantities. Most-favored-nation provisions, price-renegotiation terms, and automatic price-adjustment mechanisms, in turn, discourage opportunistic behavior by making supply perfectly elastic at some independent, market-determined level. Exclusivity provisions limit the threat that purchasers will turn to alternative suppliers or buyers as an opportunistic ploy. In these ways, long-term contracts induce both parties to make investments where the hold-up problem otherwise might prevent exchange. This is a benefit to both buyer and seller, as well as to the economy as a whole.[18]

The essential feature of long-term contracts is their ability to induce parties to commit capital to a risky business and to potentially risky trading relationships. They do this ex ante by imposing ex post restrictions on parties' options. By design, such restrictions are ex post anticompetitive. They restrain parties' full abilities to respond to particular future supply, demand, and price developments. For example, a pipeline, bound to a producer by a long-term contract that includes price clauses and take-or-pay obligations, might encounter an alternative supplier offering better terms of price, location, or supply security. Its existing contract, however, may cause it to refuse to deal with this newly discovered producer.[19]

The same reasoning applies with equal force to minimum bills. Consequently, recent moves by the FERC to regulate the structure of minimum-bill obligations (specifically, disallowing the recovery of variable costs by a pipeline if those costs have not, in fact, been incurred) must be viewed with some skepticism.[20] Ex ante, penalties invoked under minimum bills serve to punish opportunistic behavior and, by implication, are insurance payments for guaranteed service. Tying them to particular costs incurred or services provided fails to recognize these purposes.

Rigorous analyses by economists tend to confirm that contract terms are, indeed, procompetitive responses to ex ante investment risks of hold-ups, rather than anticompetitive squeezing and pressuring by one side. If the latter were the case, it might be expected that take-or-pay levels would decline as the market power of producers wanes: Producers in weak bargaining positions might be less able to command high take-or-pay levels from monopsonistic or oligopsonistic pipelines. Similarly, take-or-pay levels, if they are primarily monopolization devices, would be expected to rise as the market power of pipelines wanes: Less monopsonistic pipelines might be less able to counteract producers' demands for high take-or-pay levels.

Both of these hypotheses appear to be contradicted by the facts. Measuring market power on both sides of the wellhead market by, for example, the numbers of producers and pipelines, Scott Masten and Keith Crocker and J. Harold Mulherin found that take-or-pay levels are highest in markets where the number of producers is highest and where the number of pipelines is lowest.[21] In other words, take-or-pay levels granted to producers are highest precisely where producers are least likely to be monopolistic but where a pipeline's opportunistic threat to take gas from another producer would be most potent but for take-or-pay obligations. With more producers in a field, a pipeline not bound by take-or-pay terms could credibly engage in the ex post hold-up of any particular producer by threatening to take gas from other nearby suppliers. Take-or-pay levels granted to producers are also highest precisely where pipelines are most likely to be monopsonistic—but also where the threat that a producer could be completely shut off from a market would be most potent but for take-or-pay obligations. With fewer pipelines to compete against, an opportunistic pipeline not bound by take-or-pay terms could credibly hold up a producer by impeding access to transportation facilities.

Price Risk

Uncertainty about supply or demand, and hence price uncertainty, can provide parties with incentives to allocate risk through their contracts. Guaranteed takes at guaranteed prices, for example, can ensure reliable cash flows for gas producers. As contracts become more expensive to write and enforce, however, vertical integration may become the preferred alternative. Having noted this, it is important to point out that price risk is not likely to be a significant force behind vertical integration or long-term contracts in the gas industry.

For price risk to play an important role in determining the design of vertical contracts and integration, investors involved in the separate stages of a vertical relationship must have different preferences for bearing risk; that is, one side of the relationship must be more willing to live with risk than the other. Moreover, shareholders must be unable effectively to diversify risks in their personal portfolios. Much of the price risk in the gas industry, however, is pegged to the risk of world energy-price fluctuations and thus is easily diversifiable (e.g., by holding stock in both energy-extracting and energy-using industries). In addition, there are no obvious differences in risk preferences across the various stages of the gas industry, and available research fails to turn up price risk as a significant source of vertical integration or long-term contract design.[22]

Noncompetitive Pricing

Monopoly or monopsony pricing at a given stage of an industry leads inputs purchased for use in subsequent stages to be valued at other than their resource cost. In the case of an upstream monopoly, for example, above-cost pricing tends to shrink the size of downstream buyers, as they cut back on a range of input use that has value in excess of (the monopolist's) costs. Integration of the upstream and downstream firms into a single unit can overcome this type of distorted input valuation. That is, vertical integration can be a cure for, rather than a cause of, an anticompetitive marketplace. As noted above, there are also contractual bargaining solutions to the problems of monopoly and monopsony. The choice between vertical integration and a contractual approach depends on the costs of contracting relative to any diseconomies from integration.

Regulatory Incentives

The degree and appeal of vertical integration can be influenced substantially by taxation and regulatory policies. Thus preferential tax treatment of independent producers can yield a producing sector that is (relatively) disintegrated. Similarly, downstream regulation of, for example, the rate of return can blunt both the exercise of monopoly power vis-à-vis buyers further downstream and the wielding of monopsony power vis-à-vis upstream suppliers. Other things being equal, this would have the effect of reducing incentives for vertical integration.

Limits to Vertical Integration

Vertical integration becomes less viable when the following exist:

Loss of Managerial Control

The efficiency of managerial monitoring, control, and planning decreases as the scope of the firm expands vertically or horizontally. This is most likely to happen when the activities of the vertically linked operations differ markedly. For example, retail marketing and load management on a pipeline involve fundamentally different tasks, so top management is likely to have difficulty in melding and balancing the operations of an integrated pipeline/LDC. This consideration acts as a limitation to vertical integration.

Absence of Market Discipline

Reliance on within-firm transactions insulates the integrated firm from exposure to marketplace realities such as information on price trends, cost trends, viable marketing strategies, technological developments, and so forth. Within-firm transactions also insulate the firm from tests of its own pricing, production, managerial, and investment policies.

Viability of Long-Term Contracts

Long-term contracts become less viable when there is loss of responsiveness to market signals. It is in the nature of long-term contracts designed to overcome problems of opportunistic hold-ups that ex ante they lock parties into binding behavior that, as market conditions change ex post, reduce the flexibility that firms have to respond to market supply and demand conditions. In addition to carrying the appearance of anticompetitive restraints of trade, these ex post restrictions impose opportunity costs on firms. Such potential losses in ex post opportunities limit the attractiveness of long-term binding contracts. The tradeoff between ex post inflexibility and ex ante assurances of performance determines the length, breadth, and malleability of contract terms that parties are willing to adopt.

Policy Concerns

From a policy perspective, the limits to vertical integration and long-term contracting are determined by how they affect the performance of the marketplace—according to the criteria noted above. It is commonly believed that vertical integration can be used to extend monopoly power in one stage of an industry to other stages. In general, however, such a strategy does not pay unless the acquired stage already is subject to monopoly/monopsony power or unless there are true natural monopoly advantages (i.e., cost savings). The amount of profit that a monopolist receives for the sale of gas depends upon the amount final customers are willing to pay for delivered gas, and if a monopolist already controls one stage of the industry, controlling another stage does not increase the amount that can be extracted from ultimate customers.[23]

This is not to dismiss the potential problems of vertical integration. There are two areas with particular relevance for the natural gas industry.

Price Discrimination

A monopolist could discriminate profitably by charging relatively low prices to buyers who can turn to substitutes while charging higher prices to captive customers. Similarly, the monopsonist would prefer to pay lower prices for inelastic supplies and higher prices for supplies that might otherwise be withdrawn from the market. Thus, for example, a monopsonistic pipeline governed by a most-favored-nation clause may have an incentive to integrate into production where supply is fairly responsive to price, paying at least implicitly high

Table 5.5
INGAA Survey of All Gas Volumes by Producer Category

	1982		1983	
	Share of Total (%)	*Price ($/Mcf)*	*Share of Total (%)*	*Price ($/Mcf)*
Affiliated and pipeline-owned	11.4	2.54	11.6	2.61
Nonaffiliated	88.6	2.66	88.4	2.88

Source: Interstate Natural Gas Association of America, Policy Analysis Department, "Pipeline Purchasing Practices: The INGAA Affiliated Production Survey," Washington, D.C., 1983.

prices on its own production while depressing the price of outside purchases. In practice, this is severely limited by taxation and regulatory oversight.

Evasion of Regulation

Rate-of-return regulation is designed to restrict naturally monopolistic industries to recovering no more than their costs of doing business. A regulated firm might circumvent this restriction by vertically integrating backward into an unregulated supplier. By paying its affiliated supplier an artificially high price, the costs reported to the regulator are raised artificially, and consequently regulated output prices rise. By hiding profits in the upstream affiliate, the natural monopolist thus evades regulatory intent. A number of pipeline-industry analysts have alleged precisely this.[24]

For this practice to serve the pipeline's interest, the pipeline either must be in a position to price discriminate or to deny access to other, nonaffiliated producers. Absent price discrimination, an artificially high price for gas from *all* producers will induce even nonaffiliates to expand production, and an increase in total gas deliveries eventually will drive down end-use prices, thus thwarting the pipeline's purposes. When access can be denied, however, a pipeline can gain from charging artificially high prices for its purchased gas if the gains on payments to affiliates are not outweighed by the higher prices paid to nonaffiliates. Furthermore, if access to nonaffiliates can be denied, these discriminating pipelines necessarily will become more vertically integrated.

Available evidence thus far does not suggest that such discrimination is systematic, although it may exist. Tables 5.5 and 5.6 show data on affiliated and nonaffiliated producer sales to and prices paid by the Interstate Natural Gas Association of America (INGAA) pipelines for regulated and deregulated natural gas. The data are restricted to areas where deregulation might allow discriminatory pricing. Table 5.7 shows similar data reported by the Department of Energy.

If pipeline discrimination were systematic, we would expect these tables to

Table 5.6
INGAA Survey of Price and Purchases of Deregulated Gas

1982 Supplier Type	Share of Total Supplies (%)	Average Price ($/Mcf)
Affiliated	5.4	7.92
Pipeline-owned	2.6	6.29
Nonaffiliated	92.0	8.08
Total	100.0	8.07

1983 Supplier Type	Share of Total Supplies (%)	Average Price ($/Mcf)
Affiliated	5.2	5.66
Pipeline-owned	2.5	4.22
Nonaffiliated	92.3	6.37
Total	100.0	6.32

Source: Interstate Natural Gas Association of America, Policy Analysis Department, "Pipeline Purchasing Practices: The INGAA Affiliated Production Survey," Washington, D.C., 1983.

show both higher prices paid to affiliates and a trend toward vertical integration. But the INGAA data indicate that affiliates are paid less on average for both all gas and deregulated gas. Furthermore, pipelines show no trend toward increased vertical integration over the (admittedly short) period covered by the data. Even more significantly, pipelines are less vertically integrated into the production of deregulated gas than regulated gas. Notably, the Department of Energy data of Table 5.7 are consistent with the INGAA data. Pipelines also appear to be considerably less integrated into high-cost gas than into most other categories of gas. However, note that pipelines have been relatively heavily integrated into new gas, which is now deregulated—a development that pipelines reasonably might have anticipated. Moreover, there is no systematic evidence on the possibility that integrated pipelines could benefit by paying all producers, including nonaffiliates, high prices. This suggests that profits on pipelines' own production would outweigh losses on purchases from nonaffiliates.[25]

The issue of pipeline discrimination for purposes of monopsony or regulatory evasion also is controversial and unresolved. Although evidence does not suggest a systematic problem, more subtle forms of discrimination may take place. Solutions are problematical.[26] On the one hand, if vertical integration in the pipeline market allows regulatory evasion and monopoly distortions, it is tempt-

Table 5.7
Interstate Wellhead Sales by Producer Category and Type of Gas, 1982–1983

Producer Category	Old Gas		New Gas		High-Cost Gas		Miscellaneous Gas		Total Gas	
	Share of Total (%)	*Average Price ($/Mcf)*	*Share of Total (%)*	*Average Price ($/Mcf)*	*Share of Total (%)*	*Average Price ($/Mcf)*	*Share of Total (%)*	*Average Price ($/Mcf)*	*Share of Total (%)*	*Average Price ($/Mcf)*
Major integrated producing company	61.0	1.32	37.3	3.27	30.1	7.75	22.0	3.22	48.4	2.28
Major interstate pipelines and affiliated producers	12.7	1.46	13.0	3.33	9.0	6.90	8.8	2.60	12.4	2.60
Independent producers	26.3	1.48	49.7	3.33	60.9	7.00	69.2	3.25	39.2	3.22
Total	100.0	1.38	100.0	3.31	100.0	7.22	100.0	3.19	100.0	2.69
Total Quantity (Bcf)	5,136		4,087		907		91		10,221	

Source: U.S. Department of Energy, Energy Information Administration, Office of Oil and Gas, *Producer Revenues, Prices, and Concentration in the Natural Gas Market*, U.S. Government Printing Office, Washington, D.C., 1983.

ing to exercise some prohibition. However, this would obviate the positive benefits of integration, including the economies of system planning and avoidance of hold-up problems. An antievasion policy designed to preserve the investment benefits suggests that pipelines be made common or mandatory contract carriers, with their transportation prices, but not their gas resales, subject to regulation. Another alternative would be to value affiliated gas (re)sold by pipelines at its netback value, rather than to use the present practice of valuing affiliated gas at some price paid to comparable nonaffiliated producers.

Evidence on Vertical Structure

Producer/Pipeline

The natural gas industry is probably more naturally vertically integrated, particularly in the pipeline/producer link, than the current structure borne of regulation would indicate. That is, in the absence of regulatory intervention, there would be strong incentives for pipelines to become more vertically integrated.

Before regulation, pipelines were integrated heavily into production. Under the Natural Gas Act, however, the Federal Power Commission (FPC) allowed pipeline sales of gas by affiliated producers to recover only actual expenses on a cost-of-service basis. This understated production costs for an exhaustible resource, which include a depletion burden in the form of less future supply as production is undertaken today. As a result, FPC policy essentially discouraged all interstate pipeline integration into production. With the passage of the NGPA and its "comparable sale" treatment of affiliated gas, integration incentives were rekindled and pipeline ownership of production generally has grown.

The historically unregulated intrastate natural gas market provides further evidence that a fully deregulated gas market would encourage more vertical integration. On average, interstate pipelines in 1982 bought approximately 12 percent of their supplies from affiliated sources (see Table 5.8). By comparison, more than 25 percent of first sales of gas in the intrastate market in 1982 was made by producers affiliated with pipelines.[27]

The sources of pressure for vertical integration between pipelines and producers are dominated by investment risk (i.e., hold-ups). Pipeline and producer investments are by nature immobile, have low salvage value (or high salvage cost), and are specific in their design and configuration to each linkage. This means that once investments are made by, for example, the producer, that producer is "stuck" and subject to hold-up in contractual relations. Similarly, a pipeline that has built a spur line is irreversibly committed and is subject increasingly to hold-up as the number of producers in a field declines. The clear implication is that vertical integration should tend to edge out contractual relations as the dominant form of relationship between producers and pipelines in smaller fields, where there are fewer producers and fewer pipelines. Moving in the opposite direction, contractual relations should be less subject to hold-up and

Table 5.8
Vertical Integration of Pipelines with Local Distribution Companies

Major Pipeline	Share of Purchases from Affiliated Producers (%)	Number of Distribution Affiliates
Cities Service	3.4	0
Colorado Interstate	10.1	0
Columbia	10.2	2
Consolidated Gas Supply	39.5	4
El Paso	20.3	0
Florida Gas	15.7	0
Kansas-Nebraska	20.3	4
Michigan-Wisconsin	3.8	1
Natural Gas P/L	4.2	2
Northern Natural Gas	6.3	1
Northwest	12.3	0
Panhandle	24.5	0
Southern Natural	7.7	0
Tennessee Gas P/L	32.6	NA
Texas Eastern Transmission	4.2	0
Texas Gas Transmission	9.6	0
Transcontinental	10.8	0
Transwestern	0.4	0
Trunkline Gas Co.	4.0	0
United Gas P/L	0.5	0
Total	12.3	

Source: Robert Portman, *Competition Issues for Integrated Natural Gas Pipelines*, Report prepared for the U.S. Department of Energy, Office of Policy, Planning, and Analysis, Division of Energy Deregulation, U.S. Government Printing Office, Washington, D.C., 1982.

more viable as producers can more credibly threaten to cease trading with an opportunistic pipeline and vice versa for a put-upon pipeline.

Pipeline/LDC and LDC/End-User Integration

Vertical integration is less prevalent in pipeline/LDC and LDC/end-user relationships. Very few major pipelines were affiliated with distributors as of 1982 (see Table 5.8). To some extent this may reflect the fact that some Public Utility Commissions (PUCs) actively have opposed LDC ownership of pipelines. A more fundamental reason, however, involves dissimilarities in the transmission and retailing businesses. These dissimilarities impart diseconomies of scope in planning and management.

The system planning and bargaining talents demanded by pipeline/producer and pipeline/LDC vertical relationships are particularly strained when the LDC turns to vertical integration with end users. Interestingly, the most common form of vertical integration involving end users appears to be end-user/pipeline and even end-user/pipeline/producer integration, as exemplified by large end users such as petrochemical and chemical manufacturers. The sunk and specific nature of these end users' investments, with the implied high costs of hold-up, provide strong incentives to integrate vertically.

Summary

The incentives to integrate vertically in the natural gas industry primarily arise from attempts to avoid the costs of opportunistic behavior. The problem of hold-up can be solved by designing appropriate contracts. When this is costly, vertical integration can solve the hold-up problem by giving both parties the same profit incentives.

Incentives to integrate vertically also stem from the naturally monopolistic character of natural gas pipelines, coupled with the relatively small numbers of producers and the sunk investments of both pipelines and producers. As the wellhead market is deregulated, vertical integration of producers and pipelines should follow. Pipelines and LDCs also have incentives to integrate vertically, although they are constrained by managerial diseconomies.

The potential negative consequences of vertical integration stem from the possibility that some pipelines could evade rate-of-return regulation by hiding monopolistic profits in prices paid to affiliated producers. Although there is little systematic evidence suggesting that this is a widespread problem, its possibility underscores the need to pay attention to how integrated pipelines report their costs. The least attractive approach is a wholesale prohibition on pipeline/producer integration. This would eliminate any potential economies of cost associated with vertically integrated management and might lead to less effective methods of controlling investment risk and hold-ups. The consequence would be reduced investment in the production and delivery of natural gas.

Implications for Regulatory Reform

A number of lessons for regulatory reform emerge from the foregoing analysis of the structure of the natural gas industry.

Regulatory Oversight on Nonprice Contract Terms

Sunk investments, capital immobility, economies of scale, and economies of scope all influence the design of contractual and vertical ownership relationships in the natural gas industry. The resulting relationships act to promote efficient investments. Long-term contracts and vertical integration, however, impose constraints on companies' opportunities. When future developments deviate from the economic expectations embodied in the concrete terms of contracts, for example, companies may find themselves facing economic distress. Situations may arise where take-or-pay contracts are detrimental from the point of view of a pipeline, or an LDC's minimum-bill obligation to a pipeline may inhibit its switching to another supplier. These constraints will appear, after the fact, as anticompetitive restraints of trade, particularly in contrast to newly negotiated contracts.

When the divergences between current market conditions and those expected at the time of contract negotiations are sufficiently drastic, firms on the losing end of long-term contracts will prefer to vacate those contracts. One source of such a drastic divergence is a dramatic change in public policy (such as wellhead decontrol); another is a sharp change in market conditions (such as the 40–50 percent decline in real oil prices between 1981 and 1985).

The economic result has been to widen the gap between potential and actual performance in the gas industry. The political result has been not only increased efforts to force more open carriage by pipelines but also pressures for increased regulatory oversight over the contract terms used in the industry. These pressures for reform arose in part from efforts to correct economic distortions brought on by the mismatch of contract obligations and ownership relations since the passage of the NGPA. The nation pays a price for these distortions—in terms of prices, supplies, and demands out of synchronization with competitive conditions. The pressures for reform, however, also grew from the private interests that various actors have in the abrogation of embedded contract terms.

Regulatory reform in the first half of the 1980s laudably has attempted to eliminate restraints on competition. Examples include the FERC's special marketing program (SMP), which allowed new sellers to move into markets previously reserved for existing pipelines, and the proposed easing of certification procedures governing entry into transportation and brokerage markets. Calls for expanding the regulation of practices and contractual/ownership relationships, on the other hand, are less salutary. Although certain of these relationships (e.g., take-or-pay and minimum bills) have recently been ex post restraints on flexible trade, regulatory restrictions are likely to worsen performance by precluding the development of new, economically optimal contracts and relationships.

The recommended policy for dealing with contractual restraints on competition or market inflexibility is to place the burden of proof on the complaining party. Thus, for example, rather than regulating ex ante minimum-bill terms or exclusive dealing agreements, it should be the burden of challenging parties to demonstrate: (1) that such provisions are, in fact, anticompetitive or otherwise distorting and (2) that tampering with them will improve market performance sufficiently to outweigh any negative precedents.

Pipeline Carrier Status

Traditionally, pipelines have been granted monopolistic transport and brokerage rights under public convenience and necessity (PCN) certification regulations. These regulations have proven to be anticompetitive barriers to entry in numerous transportation sectors, including the natural gas, airline, and surface freight industries.[28] Under PCN certification, incumbent certificate holders typically argue that public convenience does not require a new entrant into the market if the result would divert traffic away from the incumbent. But "traffic diversion" is the essence of competition and the weakest of reasons to block entry into an industry. In the gas industry, traffic-diversion arguments have been used to protect pipelines' and LDCs' "core" markets from load loss.[29]

Considerable improvements in market performance and competitiveness have resulted in industries (such as commercial aviation and surface-freight transportation) where entrants have been obligated only to demonstrate that they are "fit, willing, and able" (FWA) to serve, where FWA generally entails evidence of sufficient capitalization and insurance. In practice, the switch from PCN to FWA shifts the burden of proof in certification requests from the party seeking entry to the party seeking to block entry. This switch would be appropriate for the pipeline industry, leaving the question of exclusive territories to be worked out by, for example, voluntary contract between gas sellers and buyers.[30]

Were pipelines to lose protection against entry into their transportation or brokerage functions, to what extent should they be able to engage in exclusive dealings with producers and LDCs? As noted above, producer/pipeline exclusive arrangements can provide producers with needed assurances that theirs will be the gas that a pipeline takes. Pipeline/LDC exclusivity agreements can assure pipelines that LDCs will buy the gas pipelines have taken and that LDCs will not opportunistically hold up the pipeline by threatening to take gas from another supplier. From LDCs' (or other buyers') perspectives, pipeline exclusivity can ensure that, in periods of unanticipated peaks in demand, production and transport facilities will be available instantaneously. The implied restriction on pipelines' abilities to make short-term unanticipated sales to transient customers also inhibits their interest in opportunistic hold-ups of LDCs—particularly when they simultaneously are carrying take-or-pay obligations.

In general, all parties—producers, pipelines (or brokers), and LDCs (or other buyers)—have some ex ante interests in exclusive dealing arrangements. To date, regulatory barriers to entry have virtually guaranteed exclusivity in pipeline dealings. The easing of regulatory barriers to entry likely would be accompanied by more explicit exclusivity arrangements. LDCs, for example, in some ex ante circumstances may sign away their right to use other suppliers, and pipelines may agree with producers (or LDCs) to deny other producers (or LDCs) access to their facilities. The same results might be obtained through stringent take-or-pay or minimum-bill provisions. But resulting exclusivity arrangements can appear to portend ex post impediments to competition. As with other contract terms, however, it may be wise to adopt the rebuttable presumption that exclusivity arrangements are ex ante beneficial, thereby passing the burden of proof to those who would challenge them.

As regulatory policy in the mid–1980s moves toward a policy of more open carriage by pipelines, there are numerous reports of pipelines denying brokers and others access to transportation facilities. Under the FERC's special marketing program, for example, a number of pipelines refused to transport gas for independent parties when this would have displaced the pipeline's own sales.[31] The appropriate regulatory response is problematical. The inability to limit access to customers increases the risk of opportunistic buyer hold-ups and reduces the value to producers of pipeline purchase commitments. Moreover, a truly monopolistic denial of access would not be conditioned on the prospective impact on current sales, since the new customers who might have been captured but for an independent entrant are of as much interest to a monopolist pipeline as are existing customers.

Recognition of the potential ex ante value and role of long-term exclusivity arrangements carries implications for the appropriate carrier status of pipelines. To the extent that (1) producer, pipeline, and buyer investments are targets of opportunism and that (2) pipelines are subject to significant economies of scope in the linking of transportation and brokerage functions, such arrangements are beneficial and likely to arise on their own in an unregulated marketplace. Economies of scope and threats of opportunism place a premium on pipelines' fiat control both over transportation facilities and the physical allocation of gas. This argues against a regime of mandatory contract carriage, which effectively places the burden of proof of denying entry on the pipeline itself. The preferable alternative thus may be a regime of voluntary contract carriage under which (1) there are no regulatory barriers to entry that protect pipelines, (2) exclusivity arrangements are a matter of voluntary contract, and (3) the burden of proof regarding denial of access is shifted to the offended party.

The distinction between (unprotected) voluntary and mandatory contract carriage may simply be a shifting of the regulatory function away from the FERC and toward antitrust litigation.[32] The antitrust laws applicable to pipeline access issues are sufficiently clear to allow policing of anticompetitive practices.[33] Under the doctrine of "essential facilities," private (as opposed to common) carriers are not exempt from the antitrust laws, and a pipeline would have a duty to share its facilities "if duplication [of facilities] . . . would be economically infeasible" and "if no legitimate reason for denial of access exists."[34] "Legitimate reasons" for denial include recognition of ex ante contracting necessities (e.g., commitment and exclusivity), pipeline economies of scope, and the possibility of short-term supply/demand imbalances requiring fiat control over gas allocations.

Whether an antitrust or a mandatory contract carriage approach is preferred is ultimately an empirical question about which there is little hard evidence. Nevertheless, the choice between the two approaches depends on (1) the relative private and public costs of administering each approach, (2) the predicted effectiveness of each approach in reaching sound decisions and preventing anticompetitive outcomes, (3) the ability of continued rate-of-return regulation to police anticompetitive tendencies, and (4) the cost savings realized from the full exercise of pipeline economies of scope.

Regarding point 1, any system of public oversight, whether explicit regulation or antitrust policy, carries costs with it. They include the time and expense of the attorneys, managers, economists, and accountants who are involved. The cost of these resources is no small matter;[35] complicated regulatory systems can be extremely wasteful.

Point 2 concerns the performance of public officials. Neither system will function in accord with theoretical models of perfect policy. Point 3 suggests that total deregulation of naturally monopolistic pipelines and LDCs is quixotic. Rate-of-return regulation will continue to serve, in principle, as the most direct check on market power. To the extent that this regulation is effective at the pipeline level, an antitrust-policed, voluntary carriage system would be preferred to mandatory contract carriage. The former would permit fuller realization of pipeline economies of scope and more effectively would overcome problems of opportunism and investment disincentives. As point 4 suggests, the larger these payoffs are, the more desirable a voluntary approach to contract carriage becomes.

Conclusions

The natural gas producing industry is naturally competitive in most aspects and will remain so under most contemplated policy regimes. The appropriate regulatory approach in the producing sector is to leave the policing of price, entry, and investment to the marketplace. This conclusion does not hold so readily for the pipeline and LDC segments of the industry.

Pipelines and LDCs are subject to significant elements of natural monopoly. For some customers (i.e., those able to switch from gas to alternative fuels), interfuel competition at the margin acts as a viable impediment to monopolistic pricing. Significantly, the monopolistic aspect of the gas industry could show up as monopsony, particularly at the wellhead. The result would be underinvestment in production, unless monopsony were checked by market or regulatory forces.

Monopsony problems in the production sector tend to be checked by producer/pipeline contracts that provide producers with marginal prices reflecting pipeline marginal valuations of gas inputs. Monopsony problems also are checked by rate-of-return regulation that forces roughly dollar-for-dollar passthrough of input costs and prevents otherwise monopsonistic pipelines from profiting by driving a wedge between their gas-purchase costs and their gas-resale revenues.

The unregulated, vertical structure of the natural gas industry is driven by investment risk and the likelihood of noncompetitive pricing, rather than by price risk and companies' desires to stabilize cash flow. Regarding investment risk, the specialization and immobility of production wells, pipelines, and LDC systems imply strong incentives for opportunistic behavior. The noncompetitive structure of the industry, in turn, implies that some parties have more power than others in contract negotiations. Although spot and futures markets, as well as investors' portfolio diversifications, can alleviate the problem of price risk, vertical integration and long-term contracts better address the more pressing problems of investment risk and noncompetitive distortions. Past regulation of wellhead prices discouraged pipeline/producer vertical integration, but increased integration is likely as the wellhead market is decontrolled.

The pervasiveness of investment risk and the possibility of opportunism in vertical relationships leads to the ex ante design of contractual and ownership relationships that bind parties to ex post behavior that is relatively inflexible in the face of market conditions. Recognizing that these restraints provide the assurances firms need to sink investments into the gas industry should temper enthusiasm for regulatory intervention into voluntary contracting. Recognizing the role of these restraints, coupled with strong economies of scope in the integration of transportation and wholesaling by pipelines, should temper enthusiasm for mandatory contract carriage. Problems of anticompetitive denials of access by pipelines would be better handled by removing remaining FERC barriers to entry and by promoting voluntary contract carriage.

Notes

1. Joseph P. Kalt, *The Economics and Politics of Oil Price Regulation*, MIT Press, Cambridge, Mass., 1981.

2. In the case of monopsony, a reverse hookup fee structure achieves the same result.

3. A regulated distribution company facing the type of pipeline pricing structure implied here, and required to price on the basis of average gas costs, would still bring its customers' prices above incremental costs, and reduced sales would result. Under such circumstances, efficient pricing at the pipeline level could be offset by inefficiency at the LDC level.

4. See U.S. Department of Energy, Energy Information Administration, "Natural Gas Wellhead Markets: Structures and Trends," *Natural Gas Monthly*, September 1984, p. xx.

5. For this line of argument, see, for example, Chapter 6; Putnam, Hayes & Bartlett, "Mandatory Contract Carriage: An Essential Condition for Natural Gas Wellhead Competition and Least Consumer Cost," Cambridge, Mass., 1984; Broadman and Montgomery, *Natural Gas Markets after Deregulation*, Resources for the Future, Washington, D.C., 1983.

6. Interestingly, in coal transportation, railroads share many of the same structural characteristics of natural monopoly as natural gas pipelines. From buyers' perspectives, however, coal is not fungible, since individual power plants and boilers are designed to burn coal of specific types. Consequently, users place a premium on controlling supply, and railroads typically do not take title to and broker coal.

7. These forces are reinforced by producers' demands that pipelines commit to long-term performance.

8. See U.S. Department of Energy, Assistant Secretary for Policy, Safety, and Environment, *Increasing Competition in the Natural Gas Market: The Second Report Required by Section 123 of the Natural Gas Policy Act of 1978*, U.S. Government Printing Office, Washington, D.C., 1985, p. 80.

9. See Interstate Natural Gas Association of America, Policy Analysis Department, ''Pipeline Purchasing Practices: The INGAA Affiliated Production Survey,'' Washington, D.C., 1983.

10. See American Gas Association, ''Competition in the Natural Gas Industry,'' Arlington, Va., 1984.

11. These multipart pricing structures are variants of ''nonlinear'' pricing, which allows a monopolist to extract profits—or at least fixed costs—through above-cost prices on before-the-margin sales while setting charges for incremental purchases at incremental cost. Although this sort of pricing may enrich the monopolist, it can avoid the distorted pricing and underproduction normally associated with monopoly.

12. See note 3.

13. See J. Harold Mulherin, ''Vertical Integration and Long-Term Contracts in the Natural Gas Industry,'' Ph.D. diss., University of California at Los Angeles, 1984, p. 52.

14. See David E. Mead, ''Concentration in the Natural Gas Pipeline Industry,'' U.S. Federal Energy Regulatory Commission, Office of Regulatory Analysis, Staff Working Paper, Washington, D.C., August 1984.

15. See Chapter 2.

16. Indeed, the Department of Energy's *Increasing Competition in the Natural Gas Market* is replete with allusions to such behavior.

17. Note the possible role for take-or-pay, minimum-bill provisions and mutual exclusive-dealing agreements.

18. See Mulherin, ''Vertical Integration and Long-Term Contracts in the Natural Gas Industry''; Scott Masten and Keith Crocker, ''Efficient Adaptation in Long-Term Contracts: Take-or-Pay Provisions for Natural Gas,'' *American Economic Review*, December 1985, pp. 1083–1093.

19. See U.S. Department of Energy, Assistant Secretary for Policy, Safety, and Environment, *Increasing Competition in the Natural Gas Market*.

20. See U.S. Department of Energy, Energy Information Administration, Office of Oil and Gas, *A Study of Contracts between Interstate Pipelines and Their Customers*, U.S. Government Printing Office, Washington, D.C., 1984.

21. Masten and Crocker, ''Efficient Adaptation in Long-Term Contracts: Take-or-Pay Provisions for Natural Gas''; Mulherin, ''Vertical Integration and Long-Term Contracts in the Natural Gas Industry.''

22. See Mulherin, ''Vertical Integration and Long-Term Contracts in the Natural Gas Industry.''

23. This conclusion holds with particular force when outputs from the vertically linked stages of the industry (e.g., production and transportation) are used in roughly fixed proportions. For example, with one unit of gas requiring a given amount of transportation and distribution to move that gas to the ultimate customer, this is a reasonable approximation of the case in the gas industry. Also note that the conclusion regarding the lack of gains to ''extending'' monopoly applies as well to the ''extension'' of pipeline market power into wholesaling/brokerage services. In the gas industry these services tend to be supplied in approximately fixed proportions with gas itself.

24. See, for example, Mulherin, ''Vertical Integration and Long-Term Contracts in the Natural Gas Industry.''

25. Such behavior would appear inconsistent with the widespread use of end-market indexed and other price-adjustment clauses, which substantially remove price-setting power from pipelines.

26. Statistical analysis in Stephen Brown, ''Consumers May Not Benefit from Wellhead Price Controls for Natural Gas,'' *Economic Review of the Federal Reserve Bank of Dallas*, July 1985, pp. 3–8 provides no systematic evidence of evasive self-dealing.

27. See U.S. Department of Energy, Energy Information Administration, Office of Oil and Gas, *Producer Revenues, Prices, and Concentration in the Natural Gas Market*, Report No. DOE-EIA–0404, U.S. Government Printing Office, Washington, D.C., 1983.

28. See, for example, Paul MacAvoy and John Snow, eds., *Regulation of Passenger Fares and Competition among the Airlines*, American Enterprise Institute, Washington, D.C., 1977: Thomas Moore, ''The Beneficiaries of Trucking Regulation,'' *Journal of Law and Economics*, October 1978, pp. 327–344.

29. Regarding pipelines, see U.S. Department of Energy, Energy Information Administration, Office of Oil and Gas, *A Study of Contracts*, p. 36. At the LDC level, state PUCs continue to use traffic diversion as a justification for blocking entry. See *Pipeline and Gas Journal*, August 1983, p. 6, for the case of competition between Southern California Gas Company and Pacific Gas and Electric Company in California oil fields.

30. This provides support for easing certification procedures as recommended in the Federal Energy Regulatory Commission, Notice of Proposed Rulemaking, ''Regulation of Natural Gas Pipelines after Partial Wellhead Decontrol,'' Docket No. 2M85–1–000 (Washington, D.C., May 30, 1985).

31. U.S. Department of Energy, Assistant Secretary for Policy, Safety, and Environment, *Increasing Competition in the Natural Gas Market*, especially Appendix A.

32. Putnam, Hayes & Bartlett, ''Mandatory Contract Carriage.''

33. See J. Lambert and N. Gilfoyle, ''Reforming Natural Gas Markets: The Antitrust Alternative,'' *Public Utilities Fortnightly*, May 12, 1983.

34. Ibid., pp. 17–18.

35. Joseph P. Kalt, *The Economics and Politics of Oil Price Regulation*, MIT Press, Cambridge, Mass., 1981.

Selected Bibliography

American Gas Association. ''Competition in the Natural Gas Industry.'' Arlington, Va., March 1984.

Baumol, William, John Panzar, and Robert Willig. *Contestable Markets and the Theory of Industry Structure*. Harcourt-Brace, New York, 1982.

Bork, Robert. *The Antitrust Paradox*. Basic Books, New York, 1978.

Breyer, S., and Paul MacAvoy. ''The Natural Gas Shortage and the Regulation of Natural Gas Producers.'' *Harvard Law Review*, 86, 1973, pp. 941–987.

Brown, Stephen. ''Consumers May Not Benefit from Wellhead Price Controls for Natural Gas.'' *Economic Review of the Federal Reserve Bank of Dallas*, July 1985, Unpublished Manuscript, pp. 3–8.

Congressional Research Service. ''Natural Gas: On the Road to Deregulation.'' Report No. 85–1405. Washington, D.C., July 1985.

Interstate Natural Gas Association of America, Policy Analysis Department. ''Pipeline Purchasing Practices: The INGAA Affiliated Production Survey.'' Washington, D.C., 1983.

———. ''Voluntary Carriage through 1984.'' Washington, D.C., May 1985.

Kalt, Joseph P. *The Economics and Politics of Oil Price Regulation*. MIT Press. Cambridge, Mass., 1981.

———. "Old Gas Decontrol, FERC's Block Billing for Pipelines, and the Winners and Losers in Natural Gas Policy." Harvard University, Cambridge, Mass., December 1985.

Lambert, J., and N. Gilfoyle. "Reforming Natural Gas Markets: The Antitrust Alternative." *Public Utilities Fortnightly*, May 12, 1983.

MacAvoy, Paul, and John Snow, eds. *Regulation of Passenger Fares and Competition among the Airlines*. American Enterprise Institute, Washington, D.C., 1977.

Masten, Scott, and Keith Crocker. "Efficient Adaptation in Long-Term Contracts: Take-or-Pay Provisions for Natural Gas." *American Economic Review*, December 1985, pp. 1083–1093.

Mead, David E. "Concentration in the Natural Gas Pipeline Industry." Staff Working Paper. U.S. Federal Energy Regulatory Commission, Office of Regulatory Analysis, Washington, D.C., August 1984.

Moore, Thomas. "The Beneficiaries of Trucking Regulation." *Journal of Law and Economics*, October 1978, pp. 327–344.

Mulherin, J. Harold. "Economic Structure and Behavior in the Natural Gas Production Industry." Staff Report of the Bureau of Economics to the Federal Trade Commission. Washington, D.C., 1979.

———. "Vertical Integration and Long-Term Contracts in the Natural Gas Industry." Ph.D. diss., University of California at Los Angeles, 1984.

Portman, Robert. *Competition Issues for Integrated Natural Gas Pipelines*. Report prepared for the U.S. Department of Energy, Office of Policy, Planning, and Analysis, Division of Energy Deregulation. U.S. Government Printing Office, Washington, D.C., 1982.

Putnam, Hayes & Bartlett. "Mandatory Contract Carriage: An Essential Condition for Natural Gas Wellhead Competition and Least Consumer Cost." Cambridge, Mass., 1984.

U.S. Department of Energy, Assistant Secretary for Policy, Safety, and Environment. *Increasing Competition in the Natural Gas Market: The Second Report Required by Section 123 of the Natural Gas Policy Act of 1978*. U.S. Government Printing Office, Washington, D.C., 1985.

U.S. Department of Energy, Energy Information Administration, Office of Oil and Gas. *Gas Supplies of Interstate Natural Gas Pipeline Companies, 1983*. U.S. Government Printing Office, Washington, D.C., 1984.

———. "Natural Gas Wellhead Markets: Structures and Trends," *Natural Gas Monthly*. Washington, D.C., September 1984.

———. *Producer Revenues, Prices, and Concentration in the Natural Gas Market*. Report No. DOE-EIA-0404. U.S. Government Printing Office, Washington, D.C., 1983.

———. *A Study of Contracts between Interstate Pipelines and Their Customers*. U.S. Government Printing Office, Washington, D.C., 1984.

U.S. Federal Trade Commission. *Report of the FTC to the U.S. Senate*. S. Doc. 92. 70th U.S. Cong. Washington, D.C., 1936.

Comments

JOHN B. BOATWRIGHT
Coordinator of Economics
Corporate Planning Department
Exxon Company, U.S.A.

In general, Joseph Kalt's chapter is highly theoretical and thus significantly understates the practical role of regulations and regulatory changes on vertical integration (or the lack thereof) in the domestic natural gas industry.

Beginning in the 1930s, the FPC regulated the wellhead price of natural gas when the seller was affiliated with the buyer. In the *Hope* case (320 U.S. 591, 601, 1944), it was ruled that this regulation should be based on cost of service, using original cost to determine allowable prices. This ruling provided a powerful incentive for producers not to integrate into pipelines. The *Phillips* case (347 U.S. 672, 681–685, 1954) extended this regulation to independent producers. The only escape from cost-of-service regulation was intrastate sales. In the case of such sales vertical integration did not, at the time, pose a threat of wellhead regulation. The rest is history. The intrastate pipeline market grew rapidly and had a relatively high degree of vertical integration. The pervasive role of regulation—and industry efforts to avoid it—in shaping the industry's structure seems to have escaped Kalt's analysis.

In this connection, it would be constructive to compare interstate gas pipelines with intrastate gas pipelines and interstate petroleum pipelines. The obvious differences in vertical integration among various types of pipelines are explicable primarily in terms of regulation.

Kalt's conclusions regarding natural gas contract terms rely heavily on the type of data examined by Scott Masten and Keith Crocker. These data represent snapshots at a moment in time. Yet the industry is dynamic, with rapidly changing incentives and driving forces. In the mid–1970s pipelines perceived supply shortages and frantically tried to lock in supply regardless of the take-or-pay consequences. By the end of the decade, there was a surplus and these same pipelines were trying to get out from under contracts with take-or-pay clauses. It seems that little confidence should be placed in conclusions drawn from snapshots taken at a time when conditions were changing so rapidly.

Finally, there are problems with the voluntary carriage *cum* antitrust policing scenario. In pure theory, there is nothing wrong with voluntary carriage. In the real world, however, the regulated pipeline with its monopolistic markets has far more bargaining power than the unregulated, competitive producer, particularly during periods of surplus. This is suggested by the far greater number of producers that are facing insolvency in the current environment. Antitrust is not the answer to this imbalance of power. Regulatory agencies can provide fairly prompt relief to problems, but antitrust is a morass that seems to take forever to work out. Unless some way to expedite antitrust actions can be found, it is not an acceptable replacement for regulation that provides open, nondiscriminatory transportation.

FREDERICK E. JOHN

Vice President, Regulatory Affairs
Southern California Gas Company

Both Joseph Kalt in this chapter and Harry Broadman in Chapter 6 argued for relaxing regulatory constraints on entry into interstate natural gas markets. Kalt suggested that a pipeline project simply be " 'fit, willing, and able' (FWA) to serve, where FWA generally entails evidence of sufficient capitalization and insurance." Thus the project is presumed to be in the public interest if it becomes financially viable. By begging the question, this argument raises a broader issue: When is competition not in the public interest?

Proponents of an FWA approach argue that the PCN certification process requires that the proposed pipeline's sponsor(s) prove that the pipeline is in the public interest. The PCN process, Kalt stated, protects LDCs and existing interstate pipelines from bypass or load loss. An FWA approach would change the certification process by presuming that a pipeline project is in the public interest, unless opponents could prove otherwise.

However, the FERC's expedited certification process already adopts this burden-of-proof shift. Thus the burden is on FWA proponents to prove that the expedited certification process is too inflexible to meet the needs of future pipeline projects. This task will not be easy, especially since the expedited certification process for building a new pipeline has not yet been tested. If proposals to build an interstate pipeline into California are typical of future requests, it may never be tested. The sponsors of these competing interstate pipeline proposals all seem to prefer the security of the PCN process over the freedom of the expedited certification process. Thus further relaxing of the constraints on market entry does not appear to gain much but does potentially compromise the public interest.

Nonetheless, Kalt and others argue that the FERC must remove most, if not all, restrictions on market entry. For example, unlike the FERC's expedited certification option, an FWA policy would abandon traditional PCN guidelines for establishing whether or not a project was in the public interest. Consequently, "public interest" and "market efficiency" would become synonymous. However, the "public interest" cannot be defined simply as market efficiency. As William Hogan (Chapter 4) pointed out, energy security, environmental costs, and social-equity concerns all are aspects of the public interest. Although it may be convenient to ignore these issues, it certainly is not wise public policy to do so.

This is not to say that the "public interest" is incompatible with market efficiency. To the contrary, efficiency generally promotes the public interest. But short-term efficiency does not always promote the long-term public interest. For example, the gas industry still is coping with the significant changes brought about by new regulatory policies and increased competition. At the national level, interstate pipelines are balancing access to inexpensive gas supplies with take-or-pay obligations. At the state level, LDCs are coping with access to spot markets and changing regulatory policies. These transitional problems may make a proposed pipeline appear more efficient than the pipeline or LDC currently providing service to that market. However, once the transitional problems are solved, existing pipelines will become more efficient. If an interstate pipeline is built based on its ability to compete with transitional rates, the post-transition market will have substantial excess capacity. The cost of this excess capacity is borne by society, frequently by the ratepayers of both pipelines. This outcome is hardly in the long-term public interest.

Identifying the future impact of today's policy decisions is not merely an analytical exercise. Many problems facing the gas industry today are the result of short-term solutions in the past. In today's regulatory climate, where the watchword is *competition*, this point is often ignored.

6

Deregulating Entry and Access to Pipelines

HARRY G. BROADMAN

If the 1970s was the decade for debate over federal regulation of natural gas wellhead markets, the 1980s is the decade for debate over federal regulation of the pipeline segment of the industry.

This progression is natural: The removal of wellhead price controls initiated by the Natural Gas Policy Act (NGPA) of 1978 uncovered a host of distortions in downstream gas markets, particularly in the pipeline sector.[1] Some distortions—such as the gradual, staggered deregulation of "old" gas prices—will fade over time; others—such as rigidities in "take-or-pay" provisions—likely will be resolved through the process of contract renegotiation.[2]

This chapter is concerned with a set of less easily resolved distortions. The most troubling of these distortions concerns the difficulties experienced by buyers and sellers of natural gas. On the one hand, there are gas producers whose wells have been shut in even though they would be willing to accept prices equal to or lower than those that selling producers have received. Consequently, some local distribution companies (LDCs) and end users have been buying gas from pipelines at prices higher than what should have been paid. On the other hand, in an attempt to bypass the pipeline as a middleman, some gas producers and customers wishing to arrange gas sales and purchases directly with one another have been denied access to transmission facilities. These problems have been nationwide.[3]

The distortions in the gas industry have prompted changes in both the regulation and business practices of pipeline companies. For example, with government approval of "special market programs" (SMPs), pipelines have devised discount prices for "direct sales" to industrial end users. As a result, in many industrial markets the price of gas has retreated to the market-clearing level and in some cases has dropped significantly below that of alternative fuels. Similarly, changes in rules governing pipeline tariffs for transactions with LDCs have enhanced interpipeline competition in many "sales-for-resale" markets. Most recently, rules regarding access to transmission facilities by producers, LDCs, and industrial end users have been made ostensibly more equitable. Still, despite these various changes, pervasive distortions remain.

Against this backdrop, all major segments of the industry—producers, pipelines, and LDCs alike—have raised serious questions about whether traditional downstream gas-market institutions can perform satisfactorily as wellhead deregulation becomes complete. In particular, there is increasing concern that unless the basic structure of pipeline regulation is modified, these distortions will be long lived. In addition, there is growing uneasiness over the sizeable administrative costs associated with the process of gas pipeline regulation itself. A more efficient regulatory regime—whatever form it takes—is viewed as crucial to resolving the problems within the industry.

This chapter proposes some fundamental changes in natural gas pipeline regulation. The approach is first to appraise the efficiency of current federal regulation of gas pipelining and then to suggest how it can be reformed both to be more cost-effective and to foster pipeline business practices that can better respond to market uncertainty and risk.

It should be noted that underlying the analysis in this chapter is the assumption that, as a result of economic and technological features inherent to gas pipelining, there exist important and fundamental opportunities for gas pipeline companies to exercise market power, and therefore some form of regulatory oversight will continue to be necessary. The validity of this assumption turns on the extent of competition in gas pipelining, absent regulation. Space does not permit a detailed assessment of available evidence here; a brief summary must suffice.[4]

Gas pipelines are characterized by extensive economies of scale in their transmission activities, which results in a high degree of market concentration; they are protected by appreciable technical and economic barriers to entry and exit; and they do not face effective intermodal competition. These factors, taken together, suggest that the extent of competition in the setting of gas transmission rates is unlikely to be socially sufficient. Additionally, although pipeline companies may realize strong "economies of scope" by integrating gas purchase and resale activities with transmission, only to a modest extent are such economies technical. As a result, absent unrestricted access to transmission facilities, producers, LDCs, and wholesale end users wishing to buy and sell gas directly with one another may be subject to the market power that arises from pipelines excessively bundling the provision of gas supplies with the provision of transportation.

The Structure of Natural Gas Pipeline Regulation

Regulation of interstate gas pipelining is rooted in the Natural Gas Act (NGA) of 1938. The NGA grants pipeline companies "private carrier" status, allowing them to purchase in field markets and resell in city-gate markets the gas they ship. Thus, under private carriage, a gas pipeline company assumes the twin roles of gas merchandiser and broker as well as gas transporter.

However, the NGA does not prescribe that gas pipeline companies must operate exclusively as private carriers; it permits pipelines to transport voluntarily the gas owned by others as "contract carriers." When a pipeline obtains a certificate to offer contract carriage service from the Federal Energy Regulatory Commission (FERC)—the agency with jurisdiction over the interstate gas-pipeline industry—gas producers, LDCs, and wholesale end users can purchase from the pipeline its transmission service alone.

Equally important, the NGA also specifies that regardless of whether a pipeline offers a private or contract carriage arrangement, it must provide service on a nondiscriminatory basis. However, because under the NGA pipelines cannot be compelled to transport gas they do not own, they are not subject to a common-carrier obligation to provide transmission access to all comers, an exemption that was the clear intention of Congress in framing the NGA.

The general economic environment in which gas-pipeline companies have operated, particularly the extent to which field prices have been subject to government controls, has influenced directly their choices over the type of carrier service offered. It also has had a direct impact on how the FERC's regulation of carriage has evolved.

It should be clear that private and contract carriage arrangements generically confer different bundles of risks and incentives on pipeline companies.[5] Given that gas is a storable commodity and that pipelines own most of the storage capacity, under private carriage pipelines face strong incentives to broker gas to minimize the risk of buying supplies that cannot be sold. In contrast, the incentive for pipelines to match sellers and buyers of gas under a regime of contract carriage may be muted, and in the face of heightened uncertainty, other parties (including independent brokers) may have a comparative advantage in assuming that role—hence, the recent emergence of a number of gas brokerage firms.

In the years following the 1954 *Phillips* decision (which initiated wellhead regulation), private carriage exposed pipelines to relatively low risks in gas purchasing and reselling.[6] The purchase price was relatively stable, and most gas sales were (and still are) to regulated LDCs that (like their pipeline suppliers) did not have strong incentives to bargain down the price of their gas inputs.

With wellhead deregulation under the NGPA allowing the average price of gas to reach the market-clearing level, pipelines have become more exposed to fluctuations in field prices, and the end-use demand they face has become more sensitive to changes in prices of alternative fuels. Certain provisions of the NGPA reduced the need for pipelines to obtain regulatory approval for contract carriage on a case-by-case basis, and in 1983 the FERC developed an experimental "blanket" certification program through which a pipeline could obtain ongoing approval both to engage in contract carriage and to devise SMPs to regain customers who had switched away from gas to cheaper fuels.[7]

Not surprisingly, in the new deregulated environment many pipelines took advantage of these experimental certificates and engaged in a greater amount of contract carriage. For example, whereas 24 percent of interstate gas shipments in 1978 were arranged through contract carriage, in 1984 roughly 37 percent of interstate gas shipments moved under contract carriage. Still, it is important to note that of the contract carriage service that took place in 1984, only 16 percent was on behalf of downstream customers (up significantly from 6 percent in 1982), while the majority of the remaining 84 percent was on behalf of other pipelines.[8] Thus although contract carriage has grown considerably in recent years, private carriage arrangements predominate.

In October 1985 the FERC, in a major ruling, terminated the experimental blanket certificates for contract carriage and attendant SMPs and in their place developed a permanent set of rules specifying the conditions under which blanket certificates for such services could be issued.[9] In part, the impetus for and the nature of the new carriage rules were influenced directly by decisions in several court cases. The cases were brought on behalf of downstream private carriage customers who were unable to obtain contract carriage service from their pipeline suppliers to ship gas that could be purchased cheaper directly from producers. The courts found that the blanket contract carriage program and SMPs—which were applicable generally to large industrial end users (who usually possess fuel-switching capabilities) but not for LDCs serving "captive" residential and small commercial customers—violated the NGA's requirement that pipelines must serve on a nondiscriminatory basis. Accordingly, the FERC's new rules, which became effective on November 1, 1985, stipulate that a pipeline company that obtains a blanket certificate to provide contract carriage service must offer such service in the same manner to all of its customers. As a corollary to this new stipulation, if a pipeline opts for a blanket certificate, all of its customers can completely transfer their private carriage service to contract carriage service (although LDCs are required to phase in such transfers over several years).

It is important to emphasize that since the NGA precludes the FERC from compelling a pipeline to serve, under the new program pipelines continue to have discretion over whether or not they will apply for authorization to offer contract carriage service. As of this writing, most major pipeline companies have decided not to apply for new blanket certificates, and thus authorization for their SMPs has terminated. This has resulted in a general decrease in contract carriage transactions, and for former SMP customers who now must buy relatively expensive private carriage gas from their pipeline suppliers, higher gas costs have resulted.

Beyond determining carrier status, the NGA specifies that several other equally important aspects of pipeline company activities are subject to regulation by the FERC. Rates charged by pipelines to LDCs for "sales for resale" are regulated using a traditional public utility cost-of-service approach. "Direct sales" to industrial end users are not under the jurisdiction of the FERC, but they are still influenced by regulation because portions of a pipeline's costs are common to its ''jurisdictional'' and ''nonjurisdictional'' sales.

Rate regulation by the FERC affects not only the level of transmission rates—by limiting a pipeline's return on invested capital—but also the structure of transmission rates. Traditional utility regulation requires that revenues collected from a given customer class be proportional to the cost of providing service to that class. In this regard, both a pipeline's fixed costs (the costs of pipes, compressors, and other equipment, as well as taxes and interest payments on debt) and variable costs (gas acquisition costs and pipeline operation and maintenance costs) must be allocated among its customers. Generally, the gas-acquisition component of variable costs is the weighted average of all gas supplies purchased by the pipeline. Thus, importantly, gas-pipeline rate regulation entails average-cost rather than marginal-cost pricing.

A two-part rate structure is used to apportion a pipeline's costs. It is comprised of a ''demand charge,'' representing the maximum daily volume of gas that a pipeline customer is entitled to purchase at any time during the year, and a ''commodity charge,'' representing the actual volume of gas purchased.

Although all variable costs are incorporated into the commodity charge, a variety of rate-design methods may be used by the FERC to allocate fixed costs. At one extreme, the ''volumetric'' method, the commodity charge reflects 100 percent of fixed costs; at the other extreme, the ''fixed-variable'' method, all fixed costs are incorporated into the demand charge. Three rate designs lie between these extremes: (1) the *United* method, which apportions 25 percent of fixed costs to the demand charge and 75 percent to the commodity charge; (2) the *Seaboard* method, which allocates 50 percent of fixed costs to both demand and commodity charges; and (3) the ''modified fixed-variable'' method, which allows the pipeline to recover its return on equity and income taxes through the commodity charge and 100 percent of fixed costs (less return on equity and income taxes) through the demand charge.

In practice, the FERC has employed the United method for most major pipeline systems and, to a lesser extent, the Seaboard and modified fixed-variable methods (although in the last few years adoption of the last method has been growing rapidly). In its October 1985 ruling, the FERC stipulated that a pipeline providing contract carriage service under a blanket certificate is required to charge volumetric rates for such service, but it may also charge a ''standby fee,'' which reflects the fixed costs of the portion of transmission capacity that a contract carriage customer wants to reserve for future use.

The FERC's jurisdiction over rate setting also relates to how the prices a pipeline pays for self-produced gas are reflected in its tariff. Historically, prices paid to affiliated producers have been incorporated into pipeline rates on a cost-of-service basis. Since 1983, however, when the Supreme Court ruled that prices charged by affiliated producers are to be accorded the same treatment as those charged by independent producers, prices for affiliate gas have been incorporated into rates in accordance with whatever the NGPA specifies as the legal price for that gas. Thus if affiliate gas qualifies as deregulated gas under the NGPA, a pipeline can charge itself "whatever the market will bear" for those supplies.

Still, like other pipeline gas purchase costs, prices paid to affiliates are subject to review by the FERC to ensure that "fraud or abuse" is not involved. Moreover, to ensure that pipelines integrated into deregulated production will not deliberately inflate the costs of affiliate purchases above competitive levels (with the intention of passing them on to their customers), the NGPA specifically requires the FERC to use the prices such pipelines pay to independent producers as the criteria by which to judge whether or not fraud or abuse has occurred.[10]

Under the NGA, the FERC also has jurisdiction over the scope and nature of pipeline investment decisions. In general, before construction of any new trunk line or any related facility (including looping and spurs) is permitted, a pipeline must apply on a case-by-case basis to the FERC and obtain (usually after a set of complex hearings) a "certificate of public convenience and necessity." With the advent of the FERC's October 1985 transportation rules, an expedited certification procedure became available, but generally it applies only to pipeline companies that apply and receive blanket authorization for contract carriage service.

Among other things, the certificate of "public convenience and necessity" defines a set of statutory service obligations between the pipeline and its customers. These obligations amount to conferring on the pipeline a statutory right to sell gas and on its customers a statutory claim to both a portion of the reserves under contract to the pipeline and a portion of the pipeline's capacity. It should be noted that a pipeline also has contractual service obligations, which are defined through the contracts it negotiates with its customers. The typical pipeline has some customers for which its contractual obligation to serve is "firm" (usually LDCs) and others for which such service is obligated only on an "interruptible" basis (usually large industrial end users).

The FERC also has jurisdiction over "abandonment," the termination of a pipeline's statutory service obligations. In general, if a pipeline wishes to terminate service, it cannot do so until abandonment is approved by the FERC, even if the operative sales contract has expired. This means that, as a matter of course, pipelines cannot transfer sales rights, and pipeline customers cannot transfer reserves and transmission capacity rights among themselves without first obtaining approval from the FERC for abandonment of service and then its approval for initiation of service. The only exceptions to these rules are the following: (1) If a pipeline receives blanket authorization for contract carriage service under the FERC's October 1985 rules, in which case abandonment is automatically "pregranted" corresponding to any transfer from private to contract carriage service elected by the pipeline's customers; (2) "off-system sales," for which approval by the FERC currently is granted on a blanket basis as long as the parties demonstrate that such transactions are not permanent extensions of service, will be conducted on an interruptible basis, and will not harm in any way regular, on-system customers; and (3) "interpipeline contracts," which are longer term although not permanent transactions that are scrutinized in great detail by the FERC before it grants approval.

Taken together, these last two aspects of the FERC's authority imply that gas pipelines are subject to both entry and exit regulation. The legislative history suggests that one rationale for this has been to prevent the "wasteful duplication" of transmission facilities that would arise if (as a result of significant pipeline economies of scale) there were more investment than the market could support. A complementary rationale for such regulation is to ensure that LDC service franchises granted at the state level are respected. In fact, if a pipeline wishes to provide service by constructing a spur to a new industrial customer that is in close proximity to an LDC, the FERC is unlikely to grant approval. Finally, concern about preserving or enhancing competition also enters into the justification for entry and exit regulation, insofar as an insufficient amount of investment may produce opportunities for the exercise of market power by established pipeline suppliers. Accordingly, the FERC is supposed to consider antitrust principles in deciding to approve or deny entry and exit. In this regard, the NGA yields to the FERC the power to mandate construction of pipeline facilities.[11]

To complete this description of the regulatory institutions that govern pipeline business practices, it should be noted that the FERC has the authority to allocate pipeline gas supplies and transmission capacity in the event demand exceeds supply. Should there be excess demand, pipeline service is rationed according to curtailment rules, which generally accord LDCs serving residential users, schools, hospitals, and small, commercial customers "high-priority" status and large, industrial, direct end users (including electric utilities) "low-priority" status.

Appraisal of the Current System of Regulation and Goals for Reform

Allocative Costs

The prevailing system of regulation exacerbates rather than neutralizes the prospects for gas pipelines to exercise market power in three fundamental respects, giving rise to losses in allocative efficiency over and above those engendered by the imperfections endemic to pipeline market structure.

First, by conferring on pipelines complete discretion over whether or not contract carriage service is provided, the NGA effectively gives pipelines a franchise as the quasi-exclusive buyers and sellers of gas between the field and the city gate.[12] As a result, it creates an opportunity for excessive bundling of the provision of gas transmission with the provision of gas supplies. Under this regulatory regime, it is legal for pipelines to refuse service, even if they have excess transmission capacity. It is clearly in the best economic interests of pipeline companies to exercise discrimination in transporting private carriage gas and competing contract carriage supplies owned by others. The effect could well be to force ''captive'' customers (primarily LDCs) to purchase more expensive pipeline-owned gas. Clearly, such a franchise system fails to balance equitably the public and private interests.

The FERC's new transportation rule, which stipulates that if any (blanket authorized) contract carriage service is offered, it must be provided to all customers on a nondiscriminatory basis, ostensibly helps close this gap, particularly by allowing customers to transfer their private carriage service into contract carriage service. But consistent with the NGA, the decision of whether contract carriage service will be offered—and thus whether an opportunity actually will exist for customers to substitute contract carriage service for private carriage service—still resides with pipeline companies. Although the FERC hopes and it is conceivable that competition among pipelines will propel them to offer nondiscriminatory contract carriage, this outcome is not guaranteed. Indeed, as previously noted, most major pipeline companies have yet to embrace the new program and instead have relinquished their contract carriage blanket certificates. Ironically, this has worsened market inefficiencies—many contract carriage customers who were formerly purchasing discounted gas through SMPs now must obtain higher priced, private carriage supplies.

Second, the NGA's entry and exit requirements foster losses in allocative efficiency, mainly by posing institutional barriers to interpipeline competition. The usual rationale for entry and exit regulation—to ensure against ''wasteful duplication'' and corresponding ''ruinous competition''—may apply to nascent industries, but it is obsolete for a relatively mature industry such as gas pipelining. Interestingly, the oil-pipeline industry, which has never been governed by entry and exit regulation, has by all accounts never suffered from either wasteful duplication or ruinous competition.[13] Although the FERC's new transportation rule provides both for an expedited entry certification process and for a pregranted abandonment procedure to reduce this source of inefficiency, because only pipelines that obtain blanket authorization for nondiscriminatory contract carriage can use them, the actual gains in efficiency probably are limited.

Third, the NGA's service obligations, which impart a statutory exclusivity to pipeline transmission and gas-supply transactions that endures beyond exclusivity conferred by private contracts, also contribute to allocative costs. Together with entry and exit requirements, these service obligations prevent efficient transfers of rights to capacity and reserves among a pipeline's customers and prevent analogous supply and customer transfers among pipelines.

To be sure, contractual exclusivity serves a variety of valuable functions.[14] At the city gate, it ensures that LDCs can meet state-level statutory service obligations. Thus even in the absence of federal statutory service obligations for pipeline companies, exclusivity probably would remain a characteristic of the contracts pipelines sign with LDCs. The desirability of easing or eliminating statutory pipeline service obligations is in part contingent on the ability of LDCs to have unfettered, nondiscriminatory access to transmission facilities. With such guarantees, there is no more reason to subject pipelines to statutory service obligations than there is to subject producers to them.

In light of these three inefficiencies, it is clear that the existing system of pipeline regulation does not adequately meet present realities of the natural gas industry. Moreover, even where the system is currently serving the public interest, one cannot be certain it will continue to do so when wellhead markets are decontrolled completely. As suggested earlier, field-price deregulation under the NGPA and the take-or-pay problem have changed the risks and incentives associated with private carriage such that some degree of contract carriage is appealing to pipelines. Another reason for the present volume of contract carriage is excess transmission capacity, a surplus much greater than historic levels. As this surplus capacity disappears, the constraints engendered by the current regulatory system on independent shippers' access to transmission facilities will no doubt become more binding.[15]

Beyond these core inefficiencies, current gas-pipeline regulation generates allocative costs in three other important respects, although they relate less directly to regulation of gas pipelines per se and more to specific features of traditional utility regulation itself.[16]

The first concerns rate design. As noted above, the dominant practice by the FERC has been to apply the United method, which apportions 25 percent of fixed costs to the demand charge. This approach was instituted to reduce gas demand by industrial, high-load-factor customers (those with a high ratio of average to peak use) during the gas shortages of the 1970s in order to make supplies available for residential and commercial markets, which are dominated by low-load-factor customers (those with a low ratio of average to peak use). However, this type of rate structure encourages rather than discourages consumption in peak periods. Since peak usage causes greater capacity to be installed, an efficient peak-load pricing-rate design should result in peak customers bearing a high proportion of capacity costs. This would mean allocating a large rather than a small share of fixed costs to the demand charge.

Notwithstanding the incremental adoption of the modified fixed-variable method (which incorporates a relatively large percentage of fixed costs to the demand charge), and the recent stipulation that blanket contract carriage service can employ "standby fees," the FERC has been reluctant to institute rules that would allow pipelines the flexibility to set rates in line with economic efficiency (i.e., willingness to pay), presumably because of the distributive consequences that such a pricing regime would engender. Although the rate designs that have been proposed in the literature to accommodate both efficiency and equity concerns generally are too complicated to be employed "off the shelf," the peak load, reliability of service, and Ramsey pricing principles that they incorporate provide the right direction for rate restructuring.[17]

Another inefficiency relates to the regulatory oversight of the prices pipelines pay for deregulated supplies from affiliated producers. As described above, such prices are judged by the FERC to be free from "fraud and abuse" if they are no higher than those paid to independent producers. But given that regulation allows a pipeline to set its sales price according to average rather than marginal gas-acquisition costs, this criterion actually may promote the regulatory evasion it is designed to prevent.[18] Specifically, a pipeline integrated into deregulated production can charge itself above-market prices without regulatory retribution by simply paying similar prices to independent producers; it will do this as long as profits earned in affiliated purchases are greater than losses incurred in non-affiliated purchases. Whether this conduct actually is practiced is difficult to determine.[19]

In any event, there is no easy way to counteract the incentives for "self-dealing." More detailed scrutiny or more stringent standards for reviewing affiliated purchase costs, by stipulating a "netback" standard for example, are likely to invite a sizeable administrative burden and may be construed as re-regulation of wellhead prices.

Finally, costs arise from the method used to allocate pipeline gas supplies and capacity when there is excess demand. Very simply, although curtailments arranged according to high- versus low-priority uses may be justified on equity grounds, this kind of rationing, if unaccompanied by some system of price differentials, breeds inefficiency. The problem is related to rate design. Employing a system of peak-load pricing would choke off excess demand as well as create incentives to scale investments in capacity to the appropriate level.

Administrative Costs

The current system of regulation also imposes significant administrative costs. These costs stem from the time, talent, and resources that a pipeline company—and the FERC—must devote to satisfying an awesomely complex and labyrinthine system of regulatory requirements. A pipeline wishing to obtain a certificate to initiate service, for example, may—if a formal hearing is necessary—wait one year, and in some cases longer, before the process is completed. The recent institution of blanket certificate programs has helped reduce this burden, but even so, the administrative costs are substantial.[20]

Goals for Regulatory Reform

The foregoing discussion outlines some of the inefficiencies that regulation imposes on the natural gas pipeline system. Any base for reform must strive to achieve five fundamental goals:

1. To exploit the economies of scale and scope inherent in natural gas pipelining
2. To neutralize the market inequities caused by extensive pipeline concentration, excessive bundling of transmission and gas supplies, and lack of intermodel competition
3. To eliminate regulatory and institutional impediments to interpipeline competition

4. To permit market incentives to dictate industry response to risk regarding all aspects of transmission activities
5. To impose minimal administrative costs

Taken together, these five goals suggest that reform should include three general features:

1. Continued but more flexible regulation of transmission rates
2. Guaranteed nondiscriminatory access to transmission facilities, as well as the availability of private carriage service
3. The easing or elimination of pipeline entry and exit regulation (including statutory pipeline service obligations)

The following section assesses several options for reform currently in favor, using these features as standards for comparison. Each option has both costs and benefits, and none lives up to the goals outlined above. Consequently, the concluding section of the chapter synthesizes these goals and the currently proposed but imperfect options to devise an alternative scheme for reform.

Options for Regulatory Reform

Virtual Deregulation

As noted earlier, analysis of competition in gas pipelining does not support complete deregulation. Just short of that, however, are two models of virtual deregulation that, if nothing else, provide a useful benchmark from which to draw lessons about how far to one end of the spectrum reform might go.

The first example is provided by the Texas Railroad Commission's regulation of the Texas intrastate natural gas pipeline industry. Intrastate wellhead gas supplies in Texas have long been free of price controls (that is, until the passage of the NGPA in 1978), so examining that state's system of pipeline regulation provides insights for the national market as federal price controls are eliminated.

Nominally, rates for all Texas intrastate pipeline transmission and gas sales—intrastate gas pipelines in Texas have the discretion to operate either as private or contract carriers—must be filed with the Railroad Commission. However, only rates governing transactions with LDCs whose principal customers are residential and commercial end users are required to meet cost-of-service standards, which are roughly similar to federal standards for interstate city gate transactions.[21] Transactions with industrial end users, including electric utilities, and transactions between (intrastate) pipelines are not regulated. Because nearly 90 percent of gas consumption in Texas is by industrial users, this implies that, de facto, the vast majority of intrastate pipeline rates are unregulated.

The Railroad Commission also has jurisdiction over the regulation of (intrastate) pipeline entry and exit, but it does not exercise this authority. In general, potential entrants do not shoulder the burden of proof to show, for example, that adequate supplies and demand exist or that on-system customers will not bear greater economic costs as a result of a contemplated investment. Rather, the commission's principal concern is to ensure that investment, maintenance, and operation decisions do not jeopardize the safety of the public.

To be sure, there are market characteristics unique to Texas, such as a high proportion of sales to industrial end users and a considerably uniform spatial distribution of gas production and consumption. These factors are likely to mitigate economic inequities that would otherwise exist under a strongly deregulated system. However, it is important to emphasize that even with these unique market features, the Railroad Commission deems it important to regulate transactions between pipelines and LDCs. In some sense this is supporting evidence that generically, regulation of such transactions has substantial merit.

The Texas model suggests another lesson for federal policy. It is probably unnecessary to establish regulatory oversight over investment decisions in a mature industry that has pronounced economic and technological barriers to entry and exit. In short, the Texas experience suggests that maintaining entry and exit requirements for interstate gas pipelines is unlikely to be defensible national public policy.[22]

The second model for deregulation is a proposal by the Northern Natural Gas Pipeline Company.[23] Northern's proposal virtually eliminates all federal regulation of interstate gas pipeline business practices. To summarize, discretion would remain with pipeline companies regarding access to transmission facilities, and rates would be decontrolled. The FERC's role would be limited to mediating shipper protests regarding "rate discrimination," presumably in accordance with both the NGA and prevailing antitrust statutes.

For our purposes, one desirable feature in Northern's proposal is that it would allow existing statutory pipeline service obligations to expire with current contracts. As argued above, such institutions, along with the NGA's entry and exit requirements, inhibit competition among pipelines; by limiting transfers of rights to reserves and capacity, they prevent customers from playing off pipelines against one another. Insofar as private contracts can provide for adequate legal obligations to serve, statutory obligations that endure in perpetuity until cancelled with the FERC's approval are economically superfluous, if not deleterious.

Both the Texas model and Northern's proposal offer benefits relative to current regulation, chiefly concerning the elimination of institutional constraints on interpipeline competition. However, insofar as both schemes do not reform regulation of access to pipeline facilities in such a way that customers have discretion over the extent to which the purchase of gas supplies can be unbundled from the purchase of transmission services, they are likely to generate appreciable social costs.

Moreover, both examples implicitly ascribe to antitrust enforcement a greater role in ensuring competitive pipeline performance. Students and practitioners of antitrust policy have long recognized the applicability of antitrust law to a number of regulated industries, particularly the applicability of the ''essential facilities doctrine'' (which prohibits, as a corollary to the Sherman Act, the monopolization or otherwise unreasonable denial of access to a facility that provides a vital linkage between markets). The gas-pipeline industry is no exception.[24] Although deregulation of gas pipelining, coupled with strong antitrust enforcement, ultimately may yield the socially efficient outcome, the costs incurred in the enforcement process (particularly the time spent in litigation) can be sizeable. These costs need to be added to the losses in social efficiency generated by eliminating pipeline regulation in order to appraise accurately the total benefits and costs of such a policy, relative to the total benefits and costs of devising a regulatory regime that narrows the need to resort to antitrust action.[25]

Mandatory Contract Carriage

One option for reform that has been the focus of intense debate is to subject gas pipelines to so-called mandatory contract carriage regulation. Although several regimes have been proposed, each somewhat different, the common principal features can be summarized as follows.[26]

To the extent that a pipeline possesses excess transmission capacity, mandatory contract carriage would oblige it to provide transportation service to shippers, including existing private carriage customers, who wish to transport gas the pipeline does not own. The charge for this service would be set according to the currently applicable NGA ''just and reasonable'' criteria and would allow the pipeline to recover the full cost of providing that service. (Some mandatory contract carriage proposals actually specify a fixed fee.) Existing statutory service obligations would remain in force but would be segmented into a statutory service obligation for gas sales (hence rights to reserves) and a statutory service obligation for access to transmission capacity.

Moreover, the customer, rather than the pipeline, would be granted the discretion to decide how much of its claim on capacity would go to ship pipeline-owned gas and how much to ship gas it owned. In the event that total claims on capacity exceed the amount of available capacity, the pipeline would be obligated to serve contract carriage customers with ''high-priority'' status first, displacing as many private and contract carriage customers with ''low-priority'' status as necessary to equilibrate capacity demand and supply. In any event, the capacity allocated to high-priority private carriage customers would be undisturbed. Low-priority customers could contract for ''firm'' transportation service (for contract carriage use) only insofar as it did not preclude providing such service to high-priority customers. ''Interruptible'' transportation service would be available, which could be pre-empted in order to fulfill ''firm'' transportation service.

There is little question that this system produces socially desirable results. They arise because mandatory contract carriage would fundamentally alter the way access to pipeline facilities is regulated. As economic analysis increasingly recognizes, a necessary condition for achieving competitive performance in a transport industry such as gas pipelining, where there are facilities characterized by appreciable economies of scale and scope, large sunk costs, and lack of intermodal competition, is regulation that provides broad, unfettered access to those facilities. On the other hand, it can be argued that mandatory contract carriage does not go far enough in opening up competition among pipelines, insofar as it does not reduce or eliminate the NGA's entry and exit requirements and statutory service obligations.[27]

At a more specific level, mandatory contract carriage raises several issues that must be assessed before making a more complete cost-benefit accounting. One is which criteria would be used—by a pipeline company, its regulators, and its customers—to define how much capacity is available for transporting nonpipeline-owned gas. Most mandatory contract carriage proposals stipulate that a contract carriage claim on excess transmission capacity must be honored only to the point where high-priority, private carriage customers are not disturbed. Beyond this, however, the various proposals differ in how they define excess capacity. Some specify that a pipeline must ship contract carriage gas on the "rebuttable presumption" that excess capacity is always available unless the pipeline demonstrates otherwise (hence forcing the pipeline to bear the burden of proof); others specify that such gas must be shipped on a "best-efforts" basis.

The mandatory contract carriage bill introduced by Senator Bradley is an example of the former. Under its terms, a pipeline, after receiving a contract carriage request, would have ten days to petition the FERC for a determination on capacity, and the FERC would have forty-five days to issue a final decision on the petition. If the FERC finds that capacity is available, it could order the pipeline to provide the requested transportation. In addition, the FERC would play a role in defining interruptible contract carriage capacity. Upon enactment of the bill, capacity on an interruptible basis would be defined as the greater of either the difference between a pipeline's total capacity and the average of its actual throughput over the previous three years or the difference between its total capacity and the "reasonably foreseeable" requirements of existing customers. By the twelfth month after enactment, the FERC would be required either to select between these two definitions or to develop an alternative definition.

To be sure, with wellhead deregulation and market-clearing prices, excess demand is unlikely to be as chronic or widespread a problem as it was in the past. Still, regardless of which rule for defining capacity is used, it is reasonable to expect that a mandatory contract carriage regime would result in disputes before the FERC, or perhaps even in litigation, both of which would generate costs. Virtually any set of regulatory rules imparts costs on society. But these rules place the burden of proof on pipelines, and resolving the resulting tugs-of-war might be an especially costly question to resolve one way or the other.

A second issue concerns allocating transmission capacity when demand exceeds supply.[28] In general, under excess demand, capacity would be allocated according to curtailment priorities (as under current regulation). As pointed out earlier, this sort of rationing scheme generates inefficiency, but under most mandatory contract carriage proposals there is another effect as well. Because existing private carriage customers are to be left undisturbed, there is in effect a ceiling on how much capacity actually can be made available for contract carriage—regardless of whether the prospective contract carriage shipper is designated as a low- or high-priority customer. In essence, if the incremental (contract carriage) customer has needs that are greater than the amount of capacity available, it is faced with the choice of ''take it or leave it.''

Such first-arrival rules for allocating capacity are unlikely to yield an economically efficient outcome. It is doubtful that vintage of utilization corresponds closely with willingness to pay for the use of a scarce resource. On the other hand, it might be argued that allocation on a ''first-come, first-served'' basis has desirable equity attributes; in the present context, however, it is arguable whether such a scheme is more (or less) equitable than one where the burden of a capacity constraint is shared among all shippers, both established and prospective. Some of the proposed mandatory contract carriage schemes provide a solution in the event a shortage of capacity appears more long term. They stipulate that the FERC could order a pipeline to undertake ''minor'' construction of new transmission facilities (including pipe and storage units, gathering lines, and spur lines) where the requesting customer pays (or furnishes the security of payment) for such ventures. As noted earlier, the FERC is now authorized to require such construction to serve private carriage customers; this provision would give the FERC the authority to do the same for contract carriage customers.

A third problem posed by adopting mandatory contract carriage concerns the statutory service obligations the NGA imposes on pipeline companies. In the aggregate, they would be preserved. In part, this flows from a desire to maintain legal harmony with state-level obligations bestowed on LDCs, which are likely to continue. However, as argued above, private contracts alone provide sufficient legal assurance for rights to serve and be served, and the NGA's obligations tend to inhibit interpipeline competition.

Moreover, under mandatory contract carriage, allocative costs arise in the way these obligations are preserved. To be sure, it is desirable to permit customers the freedom to contract both for how much of their gas purchases is obtained from the pipelines that serve them and how much directly from producers, as well as for the degree of reliability of the transportation and sales services entailed in either case. However, codifying such choices into a new set of statutory service obligations may chill ex post competition among pipelines and prevent efficient trading of property rights among customers in the same way that the existing system of statutory service obligations does; the only difference is that new, relatively rigid patterns of buyer-seller relationships might be created.

A final issue concerns the possibility that, under a mandatory contract carriage regime, private carriage customers would be saddled with transmission rates higher than those paid by contract carriage customers, because they would bear a greater portion of fixed costs as a result of load loss. Those who believe such cost shifting would take place argue that "captive" residential or small commercial customers will suffer greatest in this regard, based on the assumption that industrial end users will use contract carriage more than LDCs.

However, this argument overlooks the fact that the FERC and state Public Utility Commissions (PUCs) establish rules that govern the structure of transmission and distribution rates, respectively, and thus can preserve or alter the present allocation of fixed costs among customer classes. In addition, the presumption that industrial end users are likely to use contract carriage more extensively than LDCs is contradicted by available data. LDCs have tended to dominate contract carriage service.[29] If anything, the recent ruling by the FERC prohibiting the inclusion of variable-cost payments and take-or-pay clauses in LDCs' minimum-bill contracts (FERC Order 380) should, all other things being equal, enhance their incentive and ability to use contract carriage. Furthermore, nothing prevents LDCs from forming "buyers' cooperatives," which would allow them to pool risk and to realize economies of scale in purchasing and brokering gas supplies.

Moreover, to mitigate the costs associated with load loss if an industrial end user arranging contract carriage bypasses the LDC, most mandatory contract carriage proposals specify that, under those circumstances, contract carriage would require approval by the PUC (unless the end user agrees to let the LDC deliver the gas, that is, to let the LDC serve as a contract carrier).[30] This scheme harmonizes pipeline regulation at the federal level with the franchise system governing LDCs at the state level. Finally, the probability is low that private carriage customers will face higher rates, because most mandatory contract carriage proposals stipulate that pipeline rates cannot discriminate between transportation for contract carriage and transportation for sales for resale.

Common Carriage

Most fixed-route interstate-transportation systems in the United States are subject to common carriage regulation. The origin and history of common carriage is traceable to British common law, wherein common carriers are expected to fulfill the following general conditions: (1) the carrier may not refuse to serve; (2) the carrier must serve at a reasonable price; (3) the carrier must serve in a nondiscriminatory fashion; and (4) the carrier is responsible for the safe delivery of the goods entrusted to its care.[31]

Common carriage regulation of the U.S. interstate oil-pipeline industry generally conforms to these conditions and serves as a useful model of how such a regulatory system might be applied to the gas pipeline industry.[32] The system of oil-pipeline common carriage regulation can be summarized as follows.[33]

An oil pipeline is obligated to provide transportation service to all shippers upon reasonable request, where *reasonable request* is defined as the shipper meeting the conditions of tariff schedules posted by the pipeline with the FERC. These schedules include not only the rates to be paid but also minimum volume requirements, compatibility requirements specifying the type of oil to be transported, and other more minor stipulations. Although the majority of pipelines specify a single rate for service from a receiving point to a delivery point, some post multiple rates specifying prices that vary with volume, product type, and the nature and extent of service rendered. In general, pipelines must post a rate change thirty days before it becomes effective, but by requesting special permission from the FERC, they can alter rates on five days' notice. This provision allows them to meet intermodal competition efficiently.

The FERC may review a tariff schedule at the time it is posted, although in practice reviews take place only if the tariff appears to be blatantly discriminatory (for instance, if it requires one class of shippers to meet stipulations not imposed on other classes) or when a protest is filed by a shipper. The criterion the FERC uses to judge the "reasonableness" of a rate is a return-on-valuation standard, where valuation is determined by a composite of the pipeline's original, reproduction, and depreciation costs. Rarely has a rate been suspended by the FERC.

Although an oil pipeline is obligated to arrange through-service with another, it cannot be required to construct trunk lines or spur lines or to expand existing facilities. In addition, it is not obligated to provide storage, a service paid for independent of shipping. Importantly, in oil pipelining the FERC's approval is not required to initiate construction or to offer service, nor is it required to terminate or modify service.

Finally, the most distinguishing characteristic of common carriage regulation of oil pipelines relates to how transmission capacity is allocated when there is excess demand. All customers—both established and prospective—are still accorded access to the pipeline, but on a pro rata basis, where capacity is allocated in proportion to the volume of each customer's shipment; thus to allow the incremental customer access to the pipeline, existing customers' shipments are reduced. Under this regime, the burden of excess demand is shared by all shippers.[34]

At a general level, this regulatory regime yields benefits similar to the stylized mandatory contract carriage proposal outlined earlier. This stems from how access is regulated. Specifically, it does not prohibit pipelines from shipping commodities in which they have an interest and from reselling them downstream, but it also provides nonpipeline owners the right to ship commodities to which they hold title, as long as they pay the posted rate and meet supplemental requirements. Thus, like mandatory contract carriage, the effect of this access rule is to provide downstream customers the freedom to choose between buying from a pipeline a bundled good (transportation and the commodity itself) or an unbundled good (transportation alone).

If applied to the gas industry, the oil pipeline common carriage system would generate an important benefit over the status quo. Because gas pipelines would not be required to obtain certificates of "public convenience and necessity" or approval for abandonment from the FERC (thus reducing regulatory barriers to entry and exit), threats from would-be rivals would be more effective and interpipeline competition would be enhanced. Gas pipelines probably would face stronger incentives to construct the socially optimal amount of transmission capacity.[35] To the extent this is true, it would reduce the need to vest the FERC with the authority to mandate pipeline investment in new facilities.

One apparent advantage of common carriage over most mandatory contract carriage proposals is that questions about availability of capacity are eliminated. Under common carriage, the burden of proof rests squarely with the pipeline and the presumption that capacity is available is not rebuttable. Such a regime would go a long way toward reducing the administrative costs that mandatory contract carriage entails. However, this benefit is illusory. It arises because common carriage uses a pro rata allocation scheme that, like the "first-come, first-served" rule incorporated in mandatory contract carriage, is not economically efficient; an allocation based on size of volume need not correspond to an allocation based on willingness to pay.

Moreover, because of key differences between oil and gas pipelining (and the nature of the oil and gas industries in general), pro rata allocation might be an ill-suited reform for gas pipelines. Granted, important similarities between the industries argue in favor of some form of common carriage obligation for gas pipelines. Both oil and gas pipelines exhibit sizeable economies of scale and appreciable sunk costs.[36] But the fact is that oil pipelines face intermodal competition, whereas gas pipelines do not.[37] This fact suggests that common carriage obligations might be even more applicable to gas than to oil pipelining.[38] Overriding this, a pro rata regime in gas pipelining generally would preclude the writing of contracts for "firm" pipeline service, which are essential to LDCs, which must satisfy legally mandated service obligations.

In short, a pro rata allocation scheme for gas pipelines would not foster a system of federal regulation that is harmonious with state-level regulation in the distribution sector of the gas industry.[39] The availability of storage as a hedge against pro rata interruption is unlikely to mitigate the problem. Under a pro rata cutback, there is no guarantee that sufficient transmission capacity will be available with which the desired amount of stored supplies could be delivered.

Overall, it appears that the costs of allocating capacity on a pro rata basis are potentially high enough to offset the benefits of regulating gas pipelines with the same common carriage system applied to oil pipelines. The logical next step is to consider how these costs may be reduced.

As argued earlier, the other methods used to allocate excess demand—by curtailment priority and by "first come, first served"—also yield inefficiencies. An alternative scheme might be to allow transmission rates to be negotiated between pipeline and shipper, presumably where a willingness to pay higher prices would reflect a demand for greater reliability of service and so on. In so doing, the pipeline would have strong incentives to provide sufficient capacity to meet anticipated demand. The problem with such a scheme is that rates would likely reflect pipeline market power, and thus there would be losses of economic welfare—precisely the outcome we are seeking to prevent.

A more satisfactory approach would be to require that the rates a gas pipeline posts with the FERC fall within a specified ''zone of reasonableness,'' reflect different degrees of reliability of providing access to capacity, and conform to established peak load and Ramsey pricing rules.[40] This approach would allow increased flexibility in gas-pipeline rates but need not add to the administrative burden of regulation. Moreover, inasmuch as differential rate postings along these lines have an established tradition in oil-pipeline regulation, the learning costs associated with instituting such a regime for gas pipelines are unlikely to be sizeable.

Conclusion: A Proposal for "Open Carriage" and an Agenda for Regulatory Reform

Since the partial decontrol of field prices under the Natural Gas Policy Act, both natural gas pipelines and the institutions that regulate them are struggling to adapt to the uncertainties and risks engendered by freer wellhead markets. This is reflected in the greater flexibility embodied in new (and renegotiated) pipeline-producer contracts; the development of special marketing programs and the associated increase in contract carriage; and the FERC's reformation of rules regarding: (1) blanket authorization for activities such as contract carriage and off-system sales, (2) use of minimum bills in pipeline-distributor contracts, and (3) entry and exit requirements.

But the response still is not sufficient, even accounting for the appreciable transition costs that have followed wellhead deregulation, the costs associated with wildly fluctuating world oil prices, and the impact on gas demand of unusual weather patterns. The reasons partially lie with the FERC's interpretation and execution of its statutory authority. The experience of other deregulated industries such as aviation, trucking, and railroads has demonstrated that regulatory agencies have considerable discretion to influence business behavior in socially desirable ways. Clearly, there are areas where the FERC can exercise greater discretion than it has in the past. However, not only has the FERC lacked motivation to initiate action autonomously (as exemplified by the fact that its new rules for contract carriage came only after court order), but there is substantive disagreement within the FERC about the precise path it should take, both philosophically and practically. But this insufficient response also results from constraints that federal legislation has placed on the FERC, suggesting that any truly comprehensive remedy will require fundamental legislative changes, not simply administrative reforms.

Without doubt, the core restraints on the FERC stem from the Natural Gas Act. It was legislated at a time when both the natural gas industry and the energy industries with which it competes were structured vastly differently and operated in an economic environment different from that of the present day. Although the deleterious effects of a gap between an obsolete law and marketplace realities are increasingly understood by Congress, gas industry participants, and both state and federal regulators, and although there is growing acceptance that the

NGA must be amended or drastically overhauled, establishing a consensus in Congress on precisely what changes should be made presents an even more formidable challenge than that posted by further administrative reform by the FERC.[41]

Each of the three regulatory regimes evaluated above represents a combination of individual reforms, some of which are desirable. But taken as a whole, none of the proposed regimes offers a comprehensive, cost-effective, long-run solution to current pipeline-related distortions in gas markets. By combining the desirable features of all three, and supplementing them with other reforms, a regulatory regime that better meets this objective can be composed.

In the remaining pages I sketch out an agenda for establishing such a regime, which I call ''open carriage.'' Some aspects of open carriage would require major legislative action that Congress may be unwilling to take; in these instances, a ''second-best'' alternative, requiring administrative reform by the FERC, is noted.

An Agenda for "Open Carriage"

1. While continuing present rate-of-return regulation, the FERC should develop and institute ''zone-of-reasonableness'' criteria. These criteria should be based on either the fixed-variable or modified fixed-variable cost-allocation approach and should permit posted transmission rates to vary more directly with reliability of service and seasonal demand.

This system would create both the incentives for pipelines to invest in building capacity sufficient to meet anticipated demand and for LDCs to design rates that levelize their own peak demands. The likelihood of excess demand and thus of ''allocation-of-capacity'' problems would be reduced. To the extent that it is necessary to ration ''firm'' customers, federal and state curtailment schedules would still be used.

2. Congress should enact legislation that eliminates pipeline companies from having exclusive discretion over access to transmission facilities, in other words, legislation that deregulates access. This would allow customers to choose the extent to which they purchase private carriage (bundled) service and the extent to which they purchase contract carriage (unbundled) service from pipeline companies. It would not preclude pipelines from engaging in private carriage. Indeed, inasmuch as pipeline companies have a comparative advantage in minimizing coordination and scheduling costs, LDCs would likely choose private carriage to meet their core service needs. Giving customers the ability to opt for contract carriage service would create a system of checks and balances that should ensure such costs would be minimized.

Second-best reforms include the following: (a) The FERC should devise a rule specifying a fixed ''incentive transportation rate'' to encourage voluntary contract carriage for gas that competes with private carriage supplies, or (b) the

FERC should exercise its antitrust authority to mandate contract carriage where such competition exists.

3. Congress should enact legislation eliminating the requirement that new pipeline investments and services must obtain certificates of public convenience and necessity. This reform would eliminate regulation of entry, including entry by spur, gathering, and trunk lines. Threats by pipeline rivals to lower prices, to provide access or supplies, and so on would gain credibility, thus enhancing interpipeline competition.

Second-best reforms (with statutory initiation requirements still in place) include the following: (a) The FERC should relax rules governing entry and streamline the certification process for *all* applicants, not just those who have obtained blanket authorization for contract carriage; (b) the FERC should further relax rules governing blanket authorization for off-system sales; and (c) the FERC should streamline the approval process and relax requirements for long-term, interpipeline contracts.

4. Congress should enact legislation that mandates existing statutory pipeline-service obligations to expire with current contracts and that eliminates the need for pipelines to obtain regulatory approval to abandon service. This reform would eliminate both exit regulation and statutory exclusivity in pipeline transactions, thus enhancing interpipeline competition. Together with the elimination of entry regulation, it would allow the development of a market for subcontracting or recontracting among pipelines and among customers, thus providing for efficient transfers of property rights to reserves and transmission capacity. Wholesale contract renegotiation, with its resulting confusion, is avoided by allowing service obligations to expire concurrent with, rather than prior to, contract expiration. Newly signed contracts would vary depending on private parties' risk-bearing preferences in three ways: (a) by degree of reliability of service—so LDCs could fulfill their own statutory service obligations; (b) by degree of exclusivity—in line with attitudes toward bearing opportunistic risk; and (c) by choice of carriage service. This reform would force LDCs to perform their gas-purchasing functions more efficiently, whether they purchased gas from pipelines, independent brokers, or directly from producers. Terminating pipeline-service obligations would eliminate the need for the FERC's involvement in the determination of transmission capacity (except for emergency curtailments). Thus the capacity-allocation problem would reside more squarely in private agents' hands. Priority for private versus contract carriage service would be determined by the configuration of contracts held by a particular customer, as well as by the price system (through the reformed rate structure described in point 1). Thus an LDC who desires a traditional private carriage arrangement would negotiate "firm" supply and transmission contracts with a pipeline, paying higher rates for each service than, perhaps, an industrial customer who purchased "interruptible" transmission and supply services. Any undue exposure to risk could be minimized by holding a diversified portfolio of contracts.

Second-best reforms (with statutory pipeline service obligations and abandonment requirements still in place) include the following: (a) The FERC should relax rules governing exit requirements and streamline the abandonment process for all pipelines, not just those that have obtained blanket authorization for contract carriage; and (b) the FERC should devise a rule allowing transitory transfers of rights to reserves and capacity, perhaps on a "use or lose" basis.

Implementing this open-carriage regime would promote greater flexibility, a more efficient allocation of risk, complement market signals, and ease the transition to complete wellhead deregulation. It would offer pipelines a way of doing business that is considerably less regulated than at present, while concurrently allowing a fully deregulated gas-supply market to develop separately from a regulated gas-transmission market. This, in turn, would promote the development of a broader spot market for gas sales and purchases and, perhaps, a futures market.

Notes

1. See, for example, Harry G. Broadman and W. David Montgomery, *Natural Gas Markets after Deregulation*, Resources for the Future/Johns Hopkins University Press, Washington, D.C., 1983; essays in Edward J. Mitchell, ed., *The Deregulation of Natural Gas*, American Enterprise Institute for Public Policy Research, Washington, D.C. 1983.

2. Two other transitory distortions are the following: (1) Regional differentials in delivered gas prices do not correspond directly to transport cost differences, and (2) pipelines with large "cushions" of "old" gas may have an incentive to pay above-market prices for decontrolled supplies. Immediate decontrol of "old" gas would effectively reduce these distortions. For further discussion, see Harry G. Broadman, "Natural Gas Deregulation: The Need for Further Reform," *Journal of Policy Analysis and Management*, 5, no. 3, May 1986, pp. 496–516; idem, "Competition in Natural Gas Pipeline Wellhead Supply Purchases," *RFF Discussion Paper EM–85–05*, Natural Gas Policy Series, Resources for the Future, Washington, D.C., November 1985.

3. See U.S. Congress, House of Representatives, *Hearings of the Committee on Energy and Commerce*, 97th Cong., U.S. Government Printing Office, Washington, D.C., May 10 and September 23, 1982; idem, *Hearings of the Subcommittee on Fossil and Synthetic Fuels of the Committee on Energy and Commerce*, 98th Cong., U.S. Government Printing Office, Washington, D.C., April 7, 12, and 14, 1983; idem, *Hearings of the Committee on Public Works and Transportation*, 98th Cong., U.S. Government Printing Office, Washington, D.C., November 9 and 19, 1983, and forthcoming in *The Energy Journal*.

4. A more detailed analysis of competition in the gas pipeline industry is contained in Harry G. Broadman, "Elements of Market Power in the Natural Gas Pipeline Industry." *The Energy Journal*, 7, no. 1, January 1986, pp. 119–137.

5. For further analysis on this score, see Harry G. Broadman, W. David Montgomery, and Milton Russell, "Field Price Deregulation and the Carrier Status of Natural Gas Pipelines." *The Energy Journal*, 6, no. 2, 1985, pp. 127–139.

6. *Phillips Petroleum Company v. Wisconsin et al.*, 347 U.S. 672, 681–685 (1954).

7. Under most SMPs a pipeline agrees to transport, as a contract carrier, gas that the producer releases from the pipeline's take-or-pay account and sells directly to the down-

stream customer (usually large industrial end users) at a price below what the pipeline would charge (as a private carrier).

8. See Interstate Natural Gas Association of America, "Voluntary Carriage through 1984," Issue Analysis, Interstate Natural Gas Association, Washington, D.C., May 1985.

9. See U.S. Federal Energy Regulatory Commission, *Order 436*, U.S. Government Printing Office, Washington, D.C., October 9, 1985.

10. The effectiveness of this constraint on "self-dealing" is questionable; see the discussion below.

11. Note that although the NGA does not impart to the FERC the power to mandate carriage, it does impart the power to mandate construction.

12. Strictly speaking, under the NGA pipelines are not granted an exclusive franchise for buying and selling gas.

13. See, for example, George S. Wolbert, Jr., *U.S. Oil Pipe Lines*, American Petroleum Institute, Washington, D.C., 1979.

14. See Harry G. Broadman and Michael A. Toman, "Non-Price Provisions in Long-Term Natural Gas Contracts," *Land Economics*, May 1986, pp. 111–118.

15. One way to ensure against insufficient capacity for contract carriage arrangements in a tighter market might be for the FERC to require pipelines to build new facilities for this purpose. However, this option is closed under current law: Although the FERC can order pipelines to build facilities to serve private carriage customers, it does not possess the authority to require construction for contract carriage customers.

16. A fourth aspect, that rate-of-return regulation may induce a pipeline to inflate its rate base, has been addressed adequately elsewhere and is not examined here; see Broadman and Montgomery, *Natural Gas Markets after Deregulation*.

17. See the discussion in Alfred E. Kahn, *The Economics of Regulation*, Wiley and Sons, New York, 1973; Broadman and Montgomery, *Natural Gas Markets after Deregulation*. "Reliability of service pricing" refers to pricing according to "firm" versus "interruptible" demand, and "Ramsey pricing" refers to pricing according to elasticities of demand.

18. See Richard J. Pierce, "Reconsidering the Roles of Regulation and Competition in the Natural Gas Industry," *Harvard Law Review*, 97, December 1983, pp. 348–385, for a detailed description of the problem. See also Putnam, Hayes, and Bartlett, "Mandatory Contract Carriage: An Essential Condition for Natural Gas Wellhead Competition and Least Consumer Cost," Cambridge, Mass., September 1984, for a numerical example, and Interstate Natural Gas Association of America, "An INGAA Review of 'Mandatory Contract Carriage.' "

19. Broadman, "Competition in Natural Gas Pipeline Wellhead Supply Purchases," for example, finds no evidence that such behavior took place in 1982 and 1984. However, a relatively small percentage of gas supplies was deregulated in those years and therefore, such a strategy may not (yet) have been profitable.

20. See Robert C. Means and R. Angyal, "The Regulation and Future Role of Direct Producer Sales," *The Energy Law Journal*, 1984, pp. 1–25.

21. See Energy Planning, "The Texas Natural Gas Transmission Industry during the 1970s," Houston, Texas, October 1983.

22. It should be noted that under the current system of federal entry regulation, once a gas pipeline's new construction has been approved in the certification process, the increase in the rate base that such construction engenders may not be reviewed in subsequent rate hearings. Thus elimination of the certification process may give greater

importance to rate hearings because they would become the forum for rate base approval of new construction.

23. See, for example, the testimony of Othol White in U.S. Congress, House of Representatives, *Hearings of the Subcommittee on Fossil and Synthetic Fuels of the Committee on Energy and Commerce*.

24. See, for example, Jeremiah D. Lambert and Nathalie P. Gilfoyle, "Reforming Natural Gas Markets: The Antitrust Alternative," *Public Utilities Fortnightly*, May 12, 1983.

25. As noted earlier, the FERC is supposed to consider implications for antitrust when rendering judgments in the entry and exit process. In this way, it indirectly enforces the antitrust laws. It is questionable, however, whether the commission can directly enforce these laws. Compare, for example, Lambert and Gilfoyle, "Reforming Natural Gas Markets"; Robert C. Means and Deborah A. Cohn, "Common Carriage of Natural Gas," *Tulane Law Review*, in press; and Stephen F. Williams, "How to Spur Competition in the Natural Gas Market: Remedies Available to the Federal Energy Regulatory Commission," Unpublished manuscript, University of Colorado at Boulder School of Law, Colorado, 1985.

26. The Reagan administration was an early advocate of mandatory contract carriage; for a comprehensive statement of the administration's position, see U.S. Department of Energy, *Increasing Competition in the Natural Gas Market*, U.S. Government Printing Office, Washington, D.C., January 1985. Several bills containing mandatory contract carriage provisions have been introduced in Congress. The most prominent is that introduced by Senator Bradley, which serves as the principal model for the description of mandatory contract carriage found in the text. Other mandatory contract carriage bills have been introduced by, among others, Representatives Dingell, Madigan, and Sharp. As always seems to be the case when Congress considers natural gas legislation, the various segments of the industry, its trade associations, its regulators, consumer groups, and consultants to all of these parties weigh heavily in the debate. The issue of mandatory contract carriage is no exception. For a spirited exchange of ideas from some of these groups see, for example, American Gas Association, "Operating Problems under Mandatory Carriage," *Gas Energy Review*, 12, no. 4, April 1984, pp. 1–3; Cambridge Energy Research Associates, "Mandatory Carriage: Consequences for the Natural Gas Industry and for Consumers," Cambridge, Mass., 1984; Illinois Commerce Commission, "Analysis of the Cambridge Energy Research Associates Study of Mandatory Contract Carriage," Illinois Commerce Commission, Springfield, Illinois, October 1984; Interstate Natural Gas Association of America, "An INGAA Review of 'Mandatory Contract Carriage: An Essential Condition for Natural Gas Wellhead Competition and Least Consumer Cost' by Putnam, Hayes, and Bartlett, Inc.," Background Memorandum, Interstate Natural Gas Association of America, Washington, D.C., November 1984; Putnam, Hayes, and Bartlett, "Mandatory Contract Carriage."

27. This is the result of choices made by the particular framers of mandatory contract carriage proposals; it does not mean that mandatory contract carriage inherently precludes elimination of these barriers.

28. That is, after all interruptible and low-priority customers are off the system.

29. Interstate Natural Gas Association of America, "Voluntary Carriage through 1984."

30. Contract carriage service by LDCs has been practiced for some time. See, for

example, ARTA Energy Insights, ''Carriage of Customer-Owned Gas,'' ARTA, Seattle, Washington, September 1984.

31. These conditions are defined, for example, in Theodore E. Keeler, *Railroads, Freight, and Public Policy*. The Brookings Institute, Washington, D.C., 1983.

32. At least one bill purporting to propose common carriage regulation of gas pipelines has been introduced in Congress (by former Representative Corcoran). The regulatory system proposed by Corcoran by and large does not possess the requisite characteristics, such as pro rata allocation of capacity, that are described below as unique to common carriage. Indeed, his system is more akin to the mandatory contract carriage proposals. The Association for Equal Access to Natural Gas Markets and Supplies has proposed common carriage regulation for gas pipelines. Paul R. Carpenter, ''Natural Gas Pipelines after Field Price Decontrol: A Study of Risk, Return and Regulation,'' MIT Energy Laboratory Report No. MIT-EL 84–004, MIT, Cambridge, Mass., March 1984, makes an analytical case for gas pipeline common carriage.

33. For a more detailed description see, for example, Wolbert, *U.S. Oil Pipe Lines*.

34. Recall that, in contrast, under a mandatory contract carriage system where allocation is based on a first-come, first-served basis, the burden of excess demand falls entirely on the last arrived (whose needs may well be greater than available capacity). Existing customers are not affected.

35. Readers familiar with the argument advanced by the Department of Justice that oil pipelines are apt to actually *undersize* their facilities (see Edward J. Mitchell, ed., *Oil Pipelines and Public Policy*, American Enterprise Institute for Public Policy Research, Washington, D.C., 1979) will note that the critical element in the argument—pervasive producer-pipeline integration—is (at least at the present time) not widespread in the gas industry. Although space does not permit analysis of the ''undersizing'' debate, it is worth noting that if the Averch-Johnson ''rate-base effect'' is operative at all, it would imply oversizing rather than undersizing. For an application of this effect to gas pipelines, see Stanislaw H. Wellisz, ''Regulation of Natural Gas Pipeline Companies: An Economic Analysis,'' *Journal of Political Economy*, February 1963, pp. 30–43.

36. There are other similarities that support (or at least do not damage) the argument for applying oil-pipeline common carriage obligations to gas pipelines. Both oil and gas demand are strongly seasonal, and as a result, both the oil- and gas-pipeline industries have extensively developed storage facilities. However, storage rates for gas are regulated, whereas those for oil are not, primarily because oil can be stored above ground in man-made units that are considerably less expensive than the natural underground facilities used for gas. Examination of the legislative history of gas-pipeline regulation reveals that arguments about the high costs of gas storage loomed large in Congress's decision not to impose the same carrier status on gas pipelines as that imposed on oil pipelines.

37. There are other differences, which generally derive from the nature of the two products. For example, (dry) natural gas is, for all practical purposes, a perfectly homogenous product, whereas oil is not. Therefore, gas common carriage tariff rates would not vary with product type as they sometimes do in oil.

38. As noted earlier, together with large economies of scale and sunk costs, the lack of intermodal competition in gas pipelining suggests that gas pipelines are prime candidates for ''essential facilities.'' On the other hand, the strength of intermodal competition in transporting oil (as well as other factors) raises doubts about the social desirability of common carriage regulation in oil pipelining. For discussion about regulatory reform in that industry, particularly along the lines of establishing ''competitive rules'' for joint

venture ownership of oil pipelines by shippers, see, among others, Mitchell, *Oil Pipelines and Public Policy*; U.S. Department of Justice, Antitrust Division, *Competition in the Oil Pipeline Industry: A Preliminary Report*, U.S. Government Printing Office, Washington, D.C., 1984.

39. However, as noted, some LDCs do perform contract carriage service, which could be compatible with pipeline pro rata allocation. But such service is only intermittent and not widespread. Moreover, even if the two systems could be harmonized, recontracting would be required of all customers in order to match contractual obligations with the new set of service obligations implied by pro rata allocation. A better allocation scheme that would be compatible with state regulation is one where recontracting would be required only of those customers who choose to alter their existing service agreements.

40. For recent developments in the theoretical literature on regulated pricing schemes, see John C. Panzar and David S. Silbey, ''Public Utility Pricing under Risk: The Case of Self-Rationing,'' *American Economic Review*, 68, December 1978, pp. 363–375; John Tschirhart and Frank Jen, ''Behavior of a Monopoly Offering Interruptible Service,'' *Bell Journal*, 10, October 1979, pp. 850–861. The potential application of such schemes to the gas industry is explored in Broadman and Montgomery, *Natural Gas Markets after Deregulation*.

41. For further discussion along these lines, see Broadman, ''Natural Gas Deregulation.''

Selected Bibliography

American Gas Association. ''Operating Problems under Mandatory Carriage.'' *Gas Energy Review*, 12, no. 4, April 1984, pp. 1–3.

ARTA Energy Insights. ''Carriage of Customer-Owned Gas.'' ARTA, Seattle, Wash., September 1984.

Broadman, Harry G. ''Competition in Natural Gas Pipeline Wellhead Supply Purchases.'' *RFF Discussion Paper EM–85–05*. Natural Gas Policy Series. Resources for the Future, Washington, D.C., November 1985, and forthcoming in *The Energy Journal*.

———. ''Elements of Market Power in the Natural Gas Pipeline Industry.'' *The Energy Journal*, 7, no. 1, January 1986, pp. 119–138.

———. ''Natural Gas Deregulation: The Need for Further Reform.'' *Journal of Policy Analysis and Management*, 5, no. 3, May 1986, pp. 496–516.

Broadman, Harry G., and W. David Montgomery. *Natural Gas Markets after Deregulation*. Resources for the Future/Johns Hopkins University Press, Washington, D.C., 1983.

Broadman, Harry G., W. David Montgomery, and Milton Russell. ''Field Price Deregulation and the Carrier Status of Natural Gas Pipelines.'' *The Energy Journal*, 6, no. 2, 1985, pp. 127–139.

Broadman, Harry G. and Michael A. Toman. ''Non-Price Provisions in Long-Term Natural Gas Contracts,'' *Land Economics*, May 1986, pp. 111–118.

Cambridge Energy Research Associates. ''Mandatory Carriage: Consequences for the Natural Gas Industry and for Consumers.'' Cambridge, Mass., 1984.

Carpenter, Paul R. ''Natural Gas Pipelines after Field Price Decontrol: A Study of Risk, Return and Regulation.'' MIT Energy Laboratory Report No. MIT-EL 84–004. MIT, Cambridge, Mass., March 1984.

Energy Planning. "The Texas Natural Gas Transmission Industry during the 1970s." Houston, Tex., October 1983.

Illinois Commerce Commission. "Analysis of the Cambridge Energy Research Associates Study of Mandatory Contract Carriage." Illinois Commerce Commission, Springfield, Ill., October 1984.

Interstate Natural Gas Association of America. "An INGAA Review of 'Mandatory Contract Carriage: An Essential Condition for Natural Gas Wellhead Competition and Least Consumer Cost' by Putnam, Hayes, and Bartlett, Inc." Background Memorandum. Interstate Natural Gas Association of America, Washington, D.C., November 1984.

———. "Voluntary Carriage through 1984." Issue Analysis. Interstate Natural Gas Association, Washington, D.C., May 1985.

Kahn, Alfred E. *The Economics of Regulation*. Wiley and Sons, New York, 1973.

Keeler, Theodore E. *Railroads, Freight, and Public Policy*. The Brookings Institution, Washington, D.C., 1983.

Lambert, Jeremiah D., and Nathalie P. Gilfoyle. "Reforming Natural Gas Markets: The Antitrust Alternative." *Public Utilities Fortnightly*, May 12, 1983.

Means, Robert C., and R. Angyal. "The Regulation and Future Role of Direct Producer Sales." *The Energy Law Journal*, 1984, pp. 1–25.

Means, Robert C., and Deborah A. Cohn. "Common Carriage of Natural Gas." *Tulane Law Review*, in press.

Mitchell, Edward J., ed. *The Deregulation of Natural Gas*. American Enterprise Institute for Public Policy Research, Washington, D.C., 1983.

———. *Oil Pipelines and Public Policy*. American Enterprise Institute for Public Policy Research, Washington, D.C., 1979.

Panzar, John C., and David S. Silbey. "Public Utility Pricing under Risk: The Case of Self-Rationing." *American Economic Review*, 68, December 1978, pp. 363–375.

Pierce, Richard J. "Reconsidering the Roles of Regulation and Competition in the Natural Gas Industry." *Harvard Law Review*, 97, December 1983, pp. 345–385.

Putnam, Hayes, and Bartlett. "Mandatory Contract Carriage: An Essential Condition for Natural Gas Wellhead Competition and Least Consumer Cost." Cambridge, Mass., September 1984.

Tschirhart, John, and Frank Jen. "Behavior of a Monopoly Offering Interruptible Service." *Bell Journal*, 10, October 1979, pp. 850–861.

U.S. Congress, House of Representatives. *Hearings of the Committee on Energy and Commerce*. 97th Cong. U.S. Government Printing Office, Washington, D.C., May 10 and September 23, 1982.

———. *Hearings of the Committee on Public Works and Transportation*. 98th Cong. U.S. Government Printing Office, Washington, D.C., November 9 and 19, 1983.

———. *Hearings of the Subcommittee on Fossil and Synthetic Fuels of the Committee on Energy and Commerce*. 98th Cong. U.S. Government Printing Office, Washington, D.C., April 7, 12, and 14, 1983.

U.S. Department of Energy, Office of the Assistant Secretary for Policy, Safety, and Environment. *Increasing Competition in the Natural Gas Market: The Second Report Required by Section 123 of the Natural Gas Policy Act of 1978*. U.S. Government Printing Office, Washington, D.C., January 1985.

U.S. Department of Justice, Antitrust Division. *Competition in the Oil Pipeline Industry:*

A Preliminary Report. U.S. Government Printing Office, Washington, D.C., 1984.

U.S. Federal Energy Regulatory Commission. *Order 436*. U.S. Government Printing Office, Washington, D.C., October 9, 1985.

Wellisz, Stanislaw H. "Regulation of Natural Gas Pipeline Companies: An Economic Analysis." *Journal of Political Economy*, February 1963, pp. 30–43.

Williams, Stephen F. "How to Spur Competition in the Natural Gas Market: Remedies Available to the Federal Energy Regulatory Commission." Unpublished manuscript. University of Colorado at Boulder School of Law, Boulder, Colo., 1985.

Wolbert, Jr., George S. *U.S. Oil Pipe Lines*. American Petroleum Institute, Washington, D.C., 1979.

Comments

CATHERINE G. ABBOTT
Vice President
Gas Supply and Marketing
Transwestern Pipeline Company

Harry Broadman's chapter combines a broad review of the literature on the economic structure of the natural gas pipeline industry with a carefully argued policy analysis of alternative solutions to the problems he defined. Unfortunately, rather than significantly advancing the current debate beyond its narrow confines, Broadman adopted the conventional wisdom that "open" access to interstate pipeline capacity is *the* critical problem in the natural gas industry today. His policy prescriptions flow directly from this key premise. In this regard, the chapter fails to achieve the goal set out by the Harvard Gas Study—to provide a new, dispassionate look at the key public policy problems currently facing the natural gas industry. Instead, the chapter provides a polished brief for one side of the current policy debate.

The argument for greater regulation of access to pipelines has two major foundations: first, that pipelines have the ability to exercise monopoly power in most markets and, second, that an economic loss is occurring today because willing buyers and willing sellers of gas cannot arrange for transportation from the wellhead to the burner-tip. The solution is to mandate transportation of gas by pipelines.

Broadman's view of competition in the pipeline sector relies on the kind of analysis presented in Chapter 5. This analysis focused on the number of markets that are concentrated, rather than the volume of gas that flows into these markets. As a general rule, large-volume markets have both multiple suppliers and potential entrants nearby. Small-volume markets, on the other hand, tend to have only one supplier. Yet Broadman chose to rely on analyses that examine only the number of markets, without regard to size.

The chapter presents no independent assessments of the social costs arising from lack of access to transportation. Nor did Broadman seek to verify the anecdotal evidence used in the public debate over the lack of access. Finally, he did not make the reader aware that the major benefits of carriage allegedly come from the additional impetus that mandatory carriage provides for producers to agree to lower their contractual prices and take requirements with pipelines.

Specifically, the chapter has four key flaws:

1. It ignores the fact that the vast majority of pipeline customers are either regulated local distribution companies, which effectively are granted monopoly franchises within their service territory, or other pipelines. The efficiency gains that Broadman alleged arise from his proposals depend on the implementation

of open access all the way to the end user. He never questioned whether the transfer of discretion over the use of ''essential'' pipeline facilities from the pipeline itself to an LDC customer (which has a monopoly franchise over gas distribution) in fact will increase significantly the likelihood that willing buyers and willing sellers will be able to obtain transportation for their gas. All that his proposals do is transfer the control of pipeline access from one regulated middleman to another. The record of LDC direct purchases of high-cost gas during the late 1970s and early 1980s suggests strongly that LDC purchase patterns are not likely to differ significantly from the pipelines' patterns. In addition, LDCs typically have unlimited statutory obligations to serve in their franchise areas and therefore may be very risk adverse with respect to contracting for gas.

2. The chapter never squarely addresses the argument that the root cause of today's market dislocations (the persisting gas ''bubble,'' the reports of lack of access, the complaints of ''shut-in'' producers) are above-market prices and high take requirements in pipeline/producer contracts. Broadman apparently believes that the key problem is pipeline exercise of monopoly power. But aside from some hotly contested allegations of excessive profits to pipeline producing affiliates, he produced no credible arguments as to why a pipeline would prefer to sell rather than transport gas. Absent the risk of increased take-or-pay exposure, an interstate pipeline will, given proper rate design, be indifferent between transportation and sales. (No markup is allowed on the resale service.) Thus the central argument of Broadman's thesis is, in my view, flawed. The key problems in today's gas market are being caused by inflexible provisions in pipeline/producer contracts—not lack of access to transportation facilities. In my view, these contracts are yet another legacy of price controls.[1]

3. The analysis explicitly disregards any transitional costs associated with Broadman's proposals to restructure pipeline regulation. First, pipelines and their customers would have to renegotiate their contracts; second, pipelines and producers would have to restructure their contractual relationships. The recontracting process is difficult and time consuming, and dislocations will persist in the market until the recontracting process has run its course. But the desirability of government intervention in this recontracting process is open to considerable debate. Good public policy analysis always includes an assessment of what it takes to get from here to there. Yet Broadman failed to recognize that market signals may be distorted during the recontracting period.

4. The chapter gives short shrift to the efforts of the FERC to increase competition in the industry through its voluntary open-access program. Broadman suggested that effort is doomed to failure because ''most major pipeline companies have yet to embrace the [FERC's] new program'' to encourage open access. Yet, as of June 1986, the FERC had recorded twenty-eight filings for their new program, six ongoing settlement negotiations, and three filings that lay the foundation for accepting open access.[2] These indications of intent to offer open access involve a majority of the major pipeline systems. Although this greater indication of pipeline willingness to offer open access on a voluntary

basis merely may reflect the change in industry attitudes, I believe it also shows that competitive pressures in the industry are much stronger than Broadman admits.

Interestingly, approval of some of the pipeline applications to offer open access has been delayed because producers are concerned that current pipeline customers can (and will) use the FERC's program to ''lock up'' capacity—and thereby deny producers the right to market gas directly to end users. Broadman's proposal appears to be open to the same critique.

Broadman has gone beyond the boundaries of the current debate to provide a useful insight in one significant area. His analysis of the role of entry and exit regulation of natural gas pipeline service and his call for relaxation of this regulation is a major advance. This aspect of his analysis displays the insightful analytic reasoning readers have come to expect from his work.

The question of which market problems are endemic and which problems are transitional is always challenging to the public policy analyst. It is not surprising in an industry as complex as this one, with a long history of market distortions caused by misguided regulation of wellhead prices, that parties differ over the root cause of current market problems. This chapter suffers precisely because it takes sides in the current debate, rather than facing the basic causal issues squarely and providing new insight into possible solutions to these problems.

Notes

1. Another major distortion in the industry today is that pipelines remain obligated to provide firm sales service to customers who have no obligation to either take the gas or pay the cost of reserving the supply.
2. Appendix B to Order No. 451, IV CCH *FERC Reporter* (1986), pp. 266–267.

PHILIP R. O'CONNOR
Chairman and Chief Executive Officer
Palmer Bellevue Corporation

Harry Broadman's history, analysis, and proposed alterations in the regulation of the natural gas pipeline industry leave little room for dissent. As recently as late 1982, the vigorous debate over natural gas policy focused on wellhead price decontrol. Throughout 1982, as the NGPA ground on, gradually decontrolling supplies of gas, the regulatory and statutory framework was producing a thoroughly perverse outcome. As a surplus of available gas supplies increased, consumption remained depressed, the prices of competing fuels stabilized or dropped, and gas prices continued to escalate, often dramatically. This counterintuitive and unintended result forced a reconsideration of what the focus of policy should be.

The key factor in the attractiveness of ''open access'' as the key to restructuring the natural gas market was both that it appeared to solve the problem of supply/demand signals easily moving back and forth between buyers and sellers, and it also cut the political Gordian knot. For a generation, natural gas policy battles were based on the perception that there was some primal conflict of interest between producing and consuming states. This regional warfare paralyzed the congressional decision-making process and cast natural gas policy into the often Byzantine regulatory process. The emergence of the "open-access" concept gave producers, consumers, and their respective political champions a common enemy who not only was big but seemed to play the role better each day. Ideology and blind regionalism began to give way to the notion that only if the market were allowed to operate free of the prescriptions of public and private government would a favorable result ensue.

Broadman's open-access plan is a welcome refinement of the currently imperfect regime of nondiscriminatory access to the pipeline system. Importantly, open access offers both the protective benefits of modest regulatory oversight and opportunities for pipelines to operate with greater freedom and flexibility as long as they do not abuse their market power. It is that abuse—the conscious effort by many pipelines to control the commodity market for natural gas in both production and consumption through control of transportation—that must be explicitly prohibited in the future. The only realistic instruments are the antitrust laws. In an era characterized by widespread acceptance of open access, pipelines that discriminate in allowing access to their facilities will face massive damage claims under the antitrust laws. Only an explicit and mandatory regime of regulated open access will protect pipelines from prosecution under these laws.

During the past three short years, interstate pipelines moved from an industry based on resale and private carriage to one characterized by a mix of resale and nondiscriminatory transportation for customer-owned gas. This may prove to be one of the more notable economic upheavals of modern times. It is this rapid, near revolutionary change that will permit a free market to set gas prices based on supply and demand factors. Since investors will make decisions conditioned by market forces rather than by regulatory distortions, it will also be more likely that an adequate supply of natural gas will be available at reasonable prices well into the twenty-first century.

One lesson the natural gas industry's experience provides for other industries facing deregulation is that the catalog of arguments against "ruinous competition" and "transference of fixed costs" should be viewed with healthy skepticism.

7

State Policies under Pressure

COLIN C. BLAYDON

One must show some compassion for the members of state Public Utility Commissions (PUCs) who regulate natural gas local distribution companies (LDCs). Federal changes in the wake of the Natural Gas Policy Act (NGPA) of 1978 have slammed into regulatory and business practices with the force of a hurricane. Although the eye of the debate over further regulatory reform has zeroed in on wellhead and pipeline issues, the force of the storm has reverberated downstream. The LDC segment is closest to the consumer, and as a result, the debate over downstream changes is contentious, and the political stakes are high.

Some argue that PUCs were shortsighted and should have anticipated these changes. Such assertions are unwarranted, for the virtual revolution in natural gas regulation came about faster and more extensively than anybody possibly could have foreseen. State PUCs, many with meager staffs, hardly could have steered an appropriate course amid the tempest. Although more sophisticated PUCs, such as those in California, Illinois, Wisconsin, and New York, have begun to take new initiatives, most are still attempting to determine how the storm will affect their jurisdictions. As demonstrated throughout this volume, the ultimate course of the natural gas producing and pipeline industries still remains to be charted. However, PUCs now can begin to assess the range of changes that plausibly might occur.

PUCs must address two fundamental changes. First, with decreased wellhead controls, natural gas will compete more directly with other fuels based on price. Second, with more open access to pipelines, once-captive LDC customers (such as electrical utilities and large industrial users) will purchase a large percentage of their gas directly at the wellhead. The debate in the 1970s and 1980s over natural gas regulatory reform largely has ignored the effects of change in other segments of the industry on LDCs. Yet many of the issues confronting LDCs are as important as those confronting producers and pipelines. LDC issues very well may spearhead the natural gas policy debate into the 1990s.

"Attempts at resolving the natural gas problem, solely at the wellhead and at the pipeline segments of the industry, are like carving a two-dimensional sculpture," a manager of regulatory affairs at an LDC explained. "The reforms will lack depth unless the LDCs' and PUCs' issues are also addressed. Solving the problems of the gas industry up to the 'city gate' does not help all that many consumers, whether they are residential, commercial, or industrial. Except for a few large industrial customers who can connect directly to pipelines or the fortunate town or city near a gas field, most everyone else who uses gas will be affected most directly by what LDCs and PUCs do."[1]

Indeed, it can be argued that refashioning wellhead and pipeline regulation will stumble at the city gate, unless the changes extend all the way to LDCs. State policies could thwart the federal goals of wellhead deregulation and open access to pipelines. For regulation that encourages competition to flow completely through the natural gas system, federal and state policies must be compatible, and PUC regulation of LDCs must complement regulation of producers and pipelines. In particular, LDCs must be permitted to pursue business strategies that stimulate competition among pipelines.

These are new issues for PUCs. Before the 1980s, LDCs sold gas essentially as an "administered commodity." Because of low prices and high demand, PUCs allocated gas to customers through a variety of administrative mechanisms. They included rules for new hookups, limitations on certain customer classes, and use of interruptible industrial loads. Price, as an allocation mechanism, had little part in the distribution of natural gas to end users.

With gas an administered commodity, its regulation focused on income redistribution issues. Nonprice and political issues rather than economics guided PUC policy. Rather than vigorous analysis, most PUCs relied on rules of thumb primarily designed to preserve existing arrangements among various classes of customers. This worked smoothly as long as interstate gas was relatively cheap and substantial shortages did not occur.[2]

After the NGPA, gas prices began to move to an equal footing with other fuels. But as gas prices actually surpassed market-clearing levels in the early 1980s, industrywide concern over pricing and allocation issues arose. Above-market prices for gas caused fuel switching among industrial users and protests from residential consumers, not to mention a sizeable surplus supply.

At the state level, the changes were often overwhelming. Price competition caught managers of LDCs and PUCs by surprise, and they were largely unprepared for the challenges of the marketplace. The managerial skills needed before the 1980s tended to be engineering and legal, rather than marketing or innovation oriented. Further complicating the issue is the fact that some LDCs are owned by municipalities and must be responsive to political interests; other LDCs are so small that they have only a few highly trained, professional managers.

PUC staffs are not much better off. Many PUCs, such as in Massachusetts, have assigned only one or two staff members to assess what the changes in federal policies will mean for downstream markets.

In the new gas market, both LDCs and PUCs must undergo a learning process. LDCs must devise more competitive business strategies, and PUCs must redesign regulations to be appropriate for LDCs and their customers.

LDC Market Structure

The twenty largest interstate pipelines sell approximately 95 percent of all natural gas consumed in the United States. Although their size and the customers they serve vary, these companies generally experience the same regulatory policies and similar financing and operating decisions as their much smaller brothers. Thus although a Tenneco is relatively large compared to a Texas Gas, both must purchase gas in the same markets, raise capital from the same sources, and operate under the same Federal Energy Regulatory Commission (FERC) regulations. Monitoring and preventing market abuses by twenty major pipelines is a substantial task but one that should be well within the capabilities of federal regulators.

The structure of the LDC industry is very different. More than fourteen hundred LDCs are scattered throughout the United States, and they vary greatly in terms of sales, assets, and service areas. Some LDCs, such as Blackstone Gas Company in Massachusetts, serve small communities that consume less than 40,000 thousand cubic feet (Mcf) per year; others, such as Pacific Gas and Electric (PGandE), SoCal, and Brooklyn Union, span thousands of square miles and serve millions of people. Unlike pipelines, most LDCs operate in very concentrated geographic areas. Moreover, the one hundred largest LDCs account for only 75 percent of total sales and the ten largest for only 25 percent.

Unlike interstate pipelines, which are regulated at the federal level, LDCs are regulated at the state level. Most states have different political, social, and economic objectives that dictate the actions and objectives of their respective PUCs. Thus LDCs face different regulations from state to state. PUCs may regulate as few as two or three large LDCs, as in California with PGandE, SoCal, and San Diego Gas, or as many as twenty, as in Illinois or Indiana.

The managerial capabilities and market opportunities of natural gas companies differ dramatically. Management in large LDCs can respond to competitive changes with greater ease and efficiency than in small LDCs. Although many smaller LDCs have flourished under the regulatory shield of administrative prices, momentous changes in the industry now leave many of these companies facing enormous difficulties. Regulators may find that defining policy for smaller LDCs is considerably more challenging than for large LDCs.

The difficulties of formulating policy at the state level are made even more daunting by the heterogeneity of LDCs. First, consider differences in ownership. Pipelines tend to be publicly owned entities operating in the private sector. But this is not uniformly true for all LDCs. As Table 7.1 indicates, local munici-

Table 7.1
Local Distribution Company Industry Characteristics

Company Type	Number of Companies	Share of Total Companies (%)	1983 Sales (Trillion Btu)	Share of Total Sales (%)
Municipally owned	750	55	636	5
Combination	75	6	3,269	26
Integrated into transmission	180	13	6,029	47
Distribution only	345	26	2,925	22
Total	1,350	100	12,859	100

Source: American Gas Association, *Gas Facts*, Arlington, Va., 1984; and unpublished data of the American Gas Association, 1984.

palities own seven hundred and fifty LDCs, slightly more than half of the total, and their managers must respond not only to economic pressures but to the political concerns of local governments as well.

Second, some LDCs are "combination companies." Of the total, seventy-five LDCs sell both electricity and gas, accounting for 26 percent of total U.S. gas sales. In theory, electricity and gas services fall under separate regulatory regimes, but electricity and gas compete for many of the same markets. Thus these LDCs have an opportunity to exercise considerable market power. Furthermore, the practice of selling both gas and electricity hinders the accurate reporting of the costs of selling each fuel. Both of these conditions considerably complicate PUC regulation of combination companies.

Although, in principle, regulating "single-purpose" LDCs is simpler than regulating combination companies, PUC policies benefiting the former may adversely affect the latter and vice versa. As a result, different LDCs in the same state often find themselves in conflict over public policy alternatives. For example, PGandE, which sells both gas and electricity in California, holds a different view of contract carriage than SoCal, which sells only gas.

Finally, LDCs differ in their level of vertical integration into pipeline activities. Over one hundred and eighty LDCs are integrated to varying degrees, accounting for approximately 47 percent of gas sold in the interstate market. These companies face a different set of issues than nonintegrated companies. Although integrated LDCs may enjoy greater security of supply, their gas costs are not always lower than those of independent LDCs who purchase from nonaffiliated pipelines, particularly when PUCs influence costs. Columbia Gas, for example, encountered resistance from PUCs when its LDC portion sought to include "high-cost" gas in its rates—costs that resulted from integrated sales by the pipeline portion and that reflected its high-priced purchase agreements at the wellhead.

Considering this heterogeneity among LDCs, it is not surprising that the regulatory standards of fifty-one state jurisdictions are so widely diverse. Nonetheless, from a political standpoint, PUCs in neighboring states are probably mindful of each other's policies; if there are vast differences, the public is sure to protest.

PUC Policy toward LDC Pricing

The dramatic changes of the past decade have negated conventional assumptions about the retail pricing of natural gas. LDCs and PUC regulators are recasting pricing policies in light of the turgidity of gas markets. The shortages of the 1970s first prompted a reconsideration of LDC pricing, particularly for industrial customers; PUCs began to focus on how prices rather than curtailment schedules might be used to reduce excess demand. The passage of the NGPA, with its incremental pricing provisions, consolidated changes in how prices were charged to industrial customers, the end result being higher prices. In both cases, federal and state regulators acted from a desire to shelter residential customers from sharp price escalations.

With the shift in relative prices across LDC customer classes, industrial rates became rigid and unresponsive to rapid changes in market conditions. The unanticipated break in oil prices, beginning in 1982 and accelerating thereafter, heightened the desire of industrial gas consumers to seek less expensive alternative fuels, particularly oil. At the same time, as a result of inflexible wellhead contracts, wholesale gas costs continued to rise. For a time, LDCs could pass higher costs on to industrial customers in an attempt to moderate residential prices. However, this did not succeed for long, and industrial loads began to drop, falling nearly 30 percent nationwide. Some LDCs experienced industrial load losses as great as 60 percent. As a result, LDC profit margins began to shrink significantly. Furthermore, from 1974 to 1984 operating expenses as a percentage of operating revenue increased from 90.2 to 94.8.[3]

In light of this increased uncertainty and risk, there are questions about whether traditional regulation can respond adequately. How can policymakers at PUCs devise new LDC pricing rules to accommodate a more competitive gas market? A number of refinements are needed; yet for regulated parts of their business the basic element underlying the setting of rates will remain unchanged: Prices must be set so as to provide LDCs revenue streams that allow them to remain in business. If an LDC fails to receive an adequate revenue stream to justify capital investments, maintenance deteriorates, service quality declines, and investments in new facilities falter. The current pricing issues facing LDCs highlight this problem. If LDCs reach the ceiling they can charge to industrial customers but cannot recoup their costs from other sources—whether from residential users or from transportation fees—their revenues may fail to meet fixed capital costs. Similarly, if LDCs are not free to lower prices to industrial users in response to interfuel competition and if prices to residential consumers remain unchanged, the resulting load losses could cause a prohibitive loss of revenue. Thus price rigidities in a dynamic market may result in unstable and inadequate revenues.

Against this backdrop, what rules might PUCs establish for setting prices? There are at least two approaches that can help: so-called Ramsey pricing and peak-load pricing. Both methods ultimately rely on how consumers value gas in determining price levels.[4]

Ramsey pricing is useful when prices set equal to marginal costs cannot provide the revenues required for a regulated utility. If, in order to achieve these required revenues, prices are adjusted relative to marginal costs, the PUC should do it in a way that distorts consumption patterns as little as possible. If price adjustments are done to minimize distortion in consumption, the least damage will be done to economic efficiency. This means that the largest price adjustments should be imposed on those customers who will change their consumption patterns the least, that is, on the least elastic customers. Adjusting prices in this manner, with adjustments inversely proportioned to price elasticities, is what is called Ramsey pricing.

In fact, LDCs have intuitively been using this approach to try to achieve their revenue requirements with their attempts to retain fuel-sensitive industrial loads. When LDC revenue requirements could not be met with prices at marginal costs, price increases were imposed on alternative fuel customers, but only up to the point where they would switch fuels. Up to that point, they were probably the least price-sensitive of the LDC customers. At that point, they became the LDCs' most price-sensitive customers, and any further price increases had to be imposed on other customers. This is a rough form of Ramsey pricing. But a rough approximation to Ramsey pricing is probably all that can reasonably be achieved given the difficulty of accurately estimating customer class price elasticities. Moreover this approach to pricing is discriminatory, relies on often unreliable estimates of customer class price elasticities, and can be controversial and divisive. Still, Ramsey pricing suggests the directions that LDC pricing adjustments probably should follow.

Peak-load pricing is another pricing innovation that certain LDCs should consider. This pricing approach simply recognizes that the marginal costs of providing gas service vary markedly over the year in some areas of the country. It is simply more costly to provide gas in most areas in the winter months when capacity may be strained and both storage gas and peaking supplies are required to meet demand. Most LDC pricing averages out these cost variations over the year, and thus customers are not given the incentives to take proper measures to reduce peak-period gas consumption.

Like Ramsey pricing, implementing peak pricing is difficult. Both LDCs and regulators lack accurate measures of cost variation with which to determine optimal peak and off-peak price levels in winter and summer months, respectively. More importantly, however, peak pricing is likely to raise social-equity concerns. Under peak pricing, less affluent consumers will suffer more during the winter months than will the more affluent. As a consequence, PUCs sensitive to social-equity issues are likely to find peak pricing unacceptable without generous provisions for low-income customers. The same holds for Ramsey pricing.

PUC Policy Regarding LDC Gas Procurement

Regardless of how rates are set, the ultimate price an LDC pays for its supply and hence charges to its customers will vary with the terms and duration of its supply contracts. Gas sold on a short-term basis is selling today at a lower price than gas sold under long-term contracts, which afford security of supply and a degree of price stability. With greater market risk and uncertainty in gas supply the practice of contracting and linking upstream gas costs with downstream retail prices is troublesome to LDC managers, who carefully must weigh price differences against degrees of supply and price security. The crux of their concern stems from their need both to be profitable and to meet their legal service obligations.

If spot prices remain lower than those of long-term contracts, the LDC will appear to have paid excessive prices for these contracts. If spot prices rise, the LDC will have saved consumers money by obtaining a "cheap" long-term contract. If regulators are lenient in granting cost passthroughs, LDCs may follow the safe course of securing largely long-term contracts. If this occurs, LDCs may pay a premium in excess of what consumers would prefer. However, if regulators encourage spot-market purchases, LDCs may forego the higher costs of long-term contracts in favor of spot transactions. Yet undue reliance on the spot market also could lead in the future to prices higher than what consumers would be willing to pay. The difficulty in quantifying the value of supply security and in predicting how PUCs will react to LDC purchasing practices leaves LDC managers in a quandary.

To be sure, in a dynamic gas market LDCs would not rely solely either on spot transactions or on long-term contracts. Instead, they would attempt to diversify risk by holding a portfolio of contracts at various prices and with different terms. In short, even if they devise new pricing methods, they must continue to ponder the appropriate method of ensuring supply security.

Many LDC managers recall with anxiety the chronic shortages of the 1970s when their pipeline suppliers were curtailed. The ensuing loss of jobs and plant closings provoked political outcries. LDCs felt the political repercussions perhaps more than any other segment of the gas industry. As a result, despite the current supply glut, risk-averse LDC managers are likely to be very concerned with maintaining supply security, perhaps more than with lowering costs. It can be argued that these supply shortages were caused by the failure of the regulated wellhead market and that, in today's largely unregulated market, supplies should always be available to those willing to pay the necessary price. Even so, the past history of shortages and fears of sudden large price increases lead LDCs to be greatly concerned about future patterns affecting gas supply and price.

LDCs may purchase gas in one or more of the following three ways: (1) directly from pipelines; (2) at the wellhead directly from producers or indirectly through brokers; and (3) through vertical integration into production activities. Most LDCs will continue to rely on pipelines for a major portion of their gas. In turn, pipelines will be responsible for securing gas at the wellhead and delivering it to LDCs. With the FERC Order 380, which eliminates minimum-bill requirements for LDCs (see Chapter 6), pipelines have an incentive to maintain the lowest possible gas cost if LDCs can shift their purchases to the pipeline offering the lowest prices.

Many LDCs, however, also will begin to purchase directly from producers. They then will attempt to buy only contract carriage transportation from pipelines. The prospects of success depend on the extent of regulatory reform in the pipeline sector (see Chapter 6). In any event, the pipeline may serve as the broker; otherwise, LDCs will rely on independent brokers or negotiate directly with producers. Still other LDCs, particularly larger ones, may increase their degree of vertical integration and thus increase their purchases from production affiliates.

Few LDCs will rely on any one of these three methods. Throughout the 1970s, LDCs relied heavily on pipelines to supply their gas. An LDC simply negotiated a contract with a pipeline for a fixed supply of gas at prices to be determined periodically. For the most part, the typical LDC took no additional measures. However, some large LDCs attempted to lessen their reliance on pipelines by engaging in the exploration and development of their own sources of gas. In addition, some LDCs embarked on LNG import projects. Still, the main source of gas remained the pipeline.

This pattern changed in the mid–1980s. Burdened because their pipeline suppliers had wellhead contracts with onerous take-or-pay clauses, LDCs, to obtain cheaper gas, began to purchase supplies from brokers and producers, thus reducing their reliance on pipelines' private carriage services. The implementation of the FERC's nondiscriminatory contract carriage rules in late 1985 fostered further LDC use of pipelines as contract carriage. Order 380 enhanced this shift.

Whether LDCs will rely increasingly on independent brokers and contract carriage arrangements depends not only on federal regulation of pipelines but also on the disposition of PUCs. If PUCs disapprove, widespread use of brokerage and contract carriage arrangements will not develop. There are many attractive arguments in favor of allowing LDCs to engage in such transactions. Perhaps the most compelling is that they allow LDCs in disparate regions to compete effectively with one another, which will ensure that consumers nationwide face minimum gas prices. They also establish necessary conditions for developing a bona fide spot market for gas sales and purchases.

Despite these advantages, PUCs foresee problems. For one, unlike pipelines, brokers are unregulated. If brokers fail to deliver gas, LDCs have little recourse. Although LDCs can file suit, the capital structure of brokers is likely to be such that LDCs will be unable to collect much in the way of damages. If pipelines fail to deliver gas, however, they will bear the brunt of the FERC's wrath.

Table 7.2
Flexible Rate and Carriage Options of Large Customers

Status	States	Share of Interstate Market (%)
Flexible rates and LDC carriage	MI OH NY PA NJ WI[a] MD	33
Flexible rates only	CA GA FL MS NC	22
LDC carriage only	IL IN KS MO IA MA CO KY	25
Other	MN[b] AR[c]	4
Total		84

[a]The flexible rate program in Wisconsin was tied to a pipeline program that is currently in abeyance because the FERC declined to extend the program.

[b]Minnesota allows confidential negotiated rates for two-year periods for a few large-volume, interruptible customers.

[c]An LDC's pipeline counterpart offers some large customer options. The commission staff was not aware of any LDC alternative fuel rates.

Source: Interstate Natural Gas Administration of America, "The Interplay of Federal and Consuming State Regulations," research report, Washington, D.C., March 1986. Note that 28 states representing 16 percent of the market were not surveyed.

PUCs may remedy the broker problem in several ways. They may establish general guidelines for LDC use of brokers. They may issue licenses that subject brokers who arrange for gas deliveries into a particular state to purchase performance bonds or to construct capital structures, which assure LDCs that a broker will provide gas on a long-term basis. The PUCs also might establish limits on quantities that LDCs could purchase from brokers.

LDC Contract Carriage, Service Obligations, and Bypass Restrictions

As interstate pipelines extend contract carriage access, pressure has mounted for LDCs to provide similar transportation to industrial users. A number of PUCs already have implemented transportation rates for their LDCs, as shown in Table 7.2. The California PUC established a transportation rate that allowed SoCal and PGandE to recoup all costs and revenues that they would have received through private carriage.

Such a pricing scheme, insofar as it encompasses both costs and a fair rate of return that otherwise would have been recovered under private carriage, should make LDCs indifferent between transportation and traditional sales arrangements.

Full-recovery LDC transportation tariffs offer an equitable tradeoff relative to current circumstances for captive consumers, industrial users, and LDCs. Under such tariffs, captive consumers (mainly residential users) avoid the burden of increased fixed costs. Industrial users who employ LDCs to transport gas purchased at the wellhead directly to their plants can lower their costs of production.

Without such tariffs, LDCs have been reluctant to play a contract carrier role. Their opposition to transportation schemes stems in part from their concern about service obligations. In most states, LDCs operate under statutory obligations to serve customers on a demand basis. As such, they are responsible for securing long-term supplies and maintaining the system to service customer needs. In general, LDCs have a legal responsibility to serve some retail customers on a "firm" basis (usually residential customers) and others on an "interruptible" basis (usually industrial users). Unlike pipelines, whose contracts specify the terms of sale for all of their transactions, LDCs depend only on "implicit contracts" with most of their firm customers. Such contracts implicitly confer on LDCs the obligation to provide service on demand, and in return residential users agree to pay their monthly bills in a timely fashion.

The LDC service obligation carries other requirements. PUCs often designate curtailment schedules that become effective under conditions of excess demand. Residences, schools, and hospitals typically fall into the category of high-priority users, whereas commercial establishments are usually designated low-priority users. In case of excess demand, high-priority users continue to receive gas, while low-priority users may be shunted from the system.

It is not surprising that there is little willingness on the part of LDC managers to grant transportation arrangements without a modification of their service obligations. Absent an alteration of its service obligations, an LDC would be compelled to maintain both the capital investment of its system and gas supplies for customers who may switch on and off the system. As a result, those captive customers with no alternative gas supplies would bear the additional cost. If PUCs allow LDCs to transport gas, they also must modify service obligations.

LDCs cannot easily diversify the risk from service obligations, but industrial and some commercial customers can—by fuel switching and by arranging direct gas transactions. On the other hand, residential consumers cannot easily switch fuels. To saddle LDCs with the entire responsibility for absorbing downstream market risk is inefficient and inequitable. Captive customers should share the risk to some degree. As a first step toward that goal, PUCs could encourage LDCs to offer a marketbasket of services to residential customers. Thus when residential customers seek a high degree of reliability and price stability of service, they may choose a package of services at a relatively high price. If residential customers prefer less supply security or price stability, they may choose another package that allows the price to fall in some periods but for which they may pay a very high price in other periods. Such an approach may be most practical in areas with temperate climates where consumers can rely on other heat sources for extremely cold days.

This modification in LDC service obligations applies only to demand-related service obligations. Other components would remain intact. PUCs would still grant franchises that entail the legal obligation to serve and to maintain a safe and reliable gas-supply system. This allows PUCs to minimize the hazards of explosions, leaks, and fires sometimes associated with the distribution of natural gas.

As pipelines enlarge their reliance on contract carriage, some industrial customers have been tempted to bypass LDCs entirely. Today, pipelines serve industrial customers directly for about 5 percent of total interstate gas volumes.[5] In California, some pipeline companies are proposing to serve the enhanced oil-recovery market. A consortium of companies is seeking to build an interstate pipeline—the only one in California—to ''heavy oil'' fields. Such a pipeline would eschew the jurisdiction of the California PUC. In other states which already contain interstate pipelines, many PUCs tightly constrain the ability of these pipelines to sell directly to industrial customers. In fact, state policies vary widely: Some impose few obstacles to bypassing LDCs, whereas others impose nearly insurmountable obstacles.

The principal concern of a PUC when making a decision about bypass is determining which party will bear the portion of the fixed costs that otherwise would be recovered from the customers leaving the system. This problem is solvable. For example, ''exit fees'' could eliminate lost revenues. In such a scheme, customers wishing to bypass the LDC would pay a fee equal to a portion of the uncovered fixed costs attributable to their historical use of the system. Since the customer may want to retain the option of tapping back into the LDC, it could also pay a ''reservation charge.'' Such a charge would reserve capacity in the system for possible use at a future date. These charges should reflect the portion of current and prospective fixed costs to the LDC of maintaining its capacity for future deliveries and storage of natural gas. In this way, the LDC will make efficient capital allocation decisions.

Concerns expressed over bypass are exaggerated. One purpose of franchises is to avoid the inefficiency of duplicating investments. Just as it is inefficient to have many LDCs serving the same residential households, it is likewise inefficient for many supply sources to serve one industrial customer. However, using alternative sources of supply that bypass LDCs is unlikely to be a widespread practice, and thus duplication of facilities is unlikely to be a major problem. Bypasses will be rare if LDCs have pricing flexibility. With flexible pricing, any potential threat of a bypass will compel LDC managers to price their gas at competitive levels to avoid loss of sales. Alternatively, an LDC burdened with high-cost gas could offer itself as a contract carrier, which would thwart bypass efforts as well. The attitudes of PUCs toward bypass in early 1986 have been mixed, as Table 7.3 illustrates.

Conclusions

Generally, LDCs display ''natural-monopoly'' characteristics in the distribution and sale of gas, although they face significant competition with other

Table 7.3
Public Utility Commissions' Attitudes toward Bypass

Attitude	**States**	**Share of Interstate Market (%)**
Neutral	IL MI FL *WI MA CO AR* KY *MS*	29
Against	CA OH *NY PA* IN *NJ* GA KS *MN MD NC*	49
No response	MO *IA*	5

Italics indicate states reporting no recent formal bypass proposals.

Source: Interstate Natural Gas Administration of America, "The Interplay of Federal and Consuming State Regulations," research report, Washington, D.C., March 1986. Note that 28 states representing 16 percent of the market were not surveyed.

fuels for some customers, particularly industrial users. PUCs and the LDCs they regulate generally are heterogeneous in terms of size and other characteristics. They are highly differentiated in their attempts to grapple with changes underway in the gas industry. In the new market environment, both LDC managers and PUC staff members must undergo a learning process. LDCs must devise more competitive business strategies, and PUCs must redesign regulations so that LDCs can accomplish this efficiently.

One area in need of regulatory reform is rate design. Apart from issues such as who bears the risk of a pricing mistake (e.g., ratepayers versus shareholders), LDC pricing needs to be made more flexible. Ramsey and peak-load pricing principles point to the direction that LDC rate patterns should follow. Sales adjustment and fuel passthrough mechanisms also need to be reevaluated both in light of these principles and in light of the financial health of utilities.

Procurement-policy reforms also are required. Approaches depend significantly on how far rate designs change. LDCs likely will turn more toward a mix of long- and short-term supply contracts for core markets and a greater reliance on short-term contracts and spot purchases for noncore markets. However, the contract mixes actually adopted will depend on the extent to which retail customers are willing and able to pay for service reliability and price stability.

The preceding discussion also sheds light on how service obligations of LDCs should change. Although there is still a strong need to require service obligations for firm customers, adjusting service obligations for a broader class of interruptible customers is likely to be useful. In general, the need for mechanisms that provide for mutual obligations between customers and LDCs, including the need for a greater degree of risk-sharing involving captive customers, necessitates PUC reform.

Finally, the need to harmonize federal and state initiatives should guide PUC policy-making. This is most important in terms of the interrelated issues of LDC bypass restrictions and LDC contract carriage. Attempts at bypassing LDCs are likely to be fewer than expected, given federal regulations governing pipeline entry, and will be fewer still if LDCs are able to price more competitively in industrial markets. Following regulatory reform of the pipeline sector, PUC policy should begin more directly to motivate LDCs to unbundle their service into two products, transportation and gas. For LDC transportation, there is significant natural monopoly, and thus LDC contract carriage tariffs should continue to be subject to regulation.

Notes

1. Interview with a manager of a major local distribution company.
2. Douglas D. Anderson, *Regulatory Politics and Electric Utilities*, Auburn House Publishing Company, Boston, 1981.
3. American Gas Association, *Gas Facts*, Arlington, Va., 1980, p. 176; idem, *Gas Facts*, Arlington, Va., 1984, p. 162.
4. Frank P. Ramsey, ''A Contribution to the Theory of Taxation,'' *Economic Journal*, 37, March 1927, pp. 47–61; William J. Baumol and David Bradforn, ''Optimal Departures from Marginal Cost Pricing,'' *American Economic Review*, 60, June 1970, pp. 265–273.
5. U.S. Department of Energy, Energy Information Administration, *Recent Market Activities of Major Interstate Pipeline Companies*, U.S. Government Printing Office, Washington, D.C., January 1984, pp. 14–15. This volume also disaggregates direct industrial sales for the twenty major interstate pipeline companies.

Selected Bibliography

American Gas Association. *Gas Facts*. Arlington, Va., 1980.

———. *Gas Facts*. Arlington, Va., 1984.

Anderson, Douglas D. *Regulatory Politics and Electric Utilities*. Auburn House Publishing Company, Boston, 1981.

Averch, Harvey, and Leland L. Johnson. ''Behavior of the Firm under Regulatory Constraint.'' *American Economic Review*, 52, December 1982, pp. 1052–1069.

Baumol, William J., and David Bradforn. ''Optimal Departures from Marginal Cost Pricing.'' *American Economic Review*, 60, June 1970, pp. 265–273.

Interstate Natural Gas Administration of America. ''The Interplay of Federal and Consuming State Regulations.'' Research Report. Washington, D.C., March 1986.

Ramsey, Frank P. ''A Contribution to the Theory of Taxation,'' *Economic Journal*, 37, March 1927, pp. 47–61.

U.S. Department of Energy, Energy Information Administration. *Recent Market Activities of Major Interstate Pipeline Companies*. U.S. Government Printing Office, Washington, D.C., January 1984.

Comments

DANIEL E. GIBSON
Vice President, Fuel Resources
Pacific Gas and Electric Company

Colin Blaydon's discussion focuses on the market forces that have been unleashed in the natural gas industry with profound consequences for LDCs and for the state policymakers and PUCs that regulate them. These market forces are challenging fundamentally the conventional regulatory wisdom that almost every segment of the gas industry and gas-utility business must be pervasively regulated. It is becoming clear that LDCs require a much more flexible regulatory environment if they are to deal successfully with competitive forces on both the supplier and customer sides while continuing to perform their basic role of serving "core" customers with reliable and affordable service. The real question arising from Blaydon's chapter is whether state policymakers and PUCs can meet this challenge.

State policymakers, like LDCs, face the inescapable fact that many large customers increasingly have other energy choices in addition to traditional utility service and will stay on the LDC's system only if they are offered competitive prices and service options such as transportation. Yet LDCs must continue to maintain their financial health and supply position to serve the needs of their core residential and small business customers who do not have a wide range of choices. PUCs must balance these sometimes conflicting interests in restructuring regulation for new market realities. LDCs will be in their strongest position to serve core customers reliably and at least cost if they have the marketing flexibility to continue to attract the highly competitive noncore market. Unfortunately, this point is not always well understood by regulators and by some customers. What is needed is regulation that encourages LDC flexibility in their gas purchases and in the rates and services they offer to customers, including services tailored to individual customers. This would best serve all customers and is necessary to give the LDC the opportunity (but not the assurance) to survive as a viable business entity in the new competitive marketplace.

In response to the new market realities, the California PUC is restructuring fundamentally the framework that regulates PGandE and other California LDCs. Since some of the elements in this restructuring are represented in the actions of other state PUCs and can be found in parts of Blaydon's chapter, a brief comment on their policy implications for the LDC provides insight to the market and regulatory challenges now confronting PUCs.

First, the California PUC is proposing a revision of the LDC's "obligation-to-serve" service obligation, which is the fundamental "social contract" between the LDC and its customers. Customers are separated into core and noncore classifications. *Core customers* are primarily residential and small business customers who are not large enough to qualify for gas transport and who likely will continue to be dependent on the utility for energy service. *Noncore customers*, on the other hand, are larger customers that do qualify for gas transport service and that, if only for that reason, would not necessarily continue to be dependent on the utility to arrange for their energy supply. The noncore market is where the California utilities face strong competition. Under the California PUC proposal, core customers will continue to enjoy the traditional "bundled" utility services, and noncore customers will have the responsibility to make their own supply arrangements, either using transportation or by specifically contracting for supply from the LDC. The LDC no longer will have the responsibility to incur supply-acquisition risks for noncore customers unless the customer obligates itself by contract to take gas-supply service.

Due to the highly seasonal nature of the core market, the ability of the LDC to serve core customers requires a strong supplier base. Loss of noncore customers erodes the market base that the LDC can offer to a supplier. This is not a new problem, but it now is a greater problem because of the dramatic increase in competition fostered by changes in gas transportation arrangements. Thus the service obligation to core customers requires that the LDC be a strong survivor in competitive marketing to noncore customers. This in turn will depend on the extent to which regulators provide the LDC with the ability to respond quickly to market forces. Since the degree of competition may differ among customers and alternative suppliers, the LDC will need to have the ability to tailor competitive options to individual customers.

Second, intrastate transportation of customer-owned gas has been authorized. This meets the desires of those customers, mainly large volume gas users, who desire the flexibility and diversity that is available through the transport option. It also places significant new competitive pressures on the LDC as a seller of gas. Accommodating customer desires for service options is only one element the PUC must address; the other is allowing the LDC broad marketing flexibility in the competitive market sector. Without this flexibility, the LDC could be overrun by the competition and be disabled from continuing to play a strong supply-acquisition role.

Finally, the California PUC is moving toward cost-based rate design. This will accomplish several goals. First, it will ensure that customers will pay for their fair share of system costs, whether they purchase from the utility or transport customer-owned gas. Second, it largely will eliminate subsidies between customer classes. This is essential. The LDC must have the ability to compete on a commodity-cost basis with alternative fuel suppliers for noncore customers. But this cannot happen without the LDC having the flexibility to adjust purchases and rates to meet the competition.

A new regulatory framework imposes significant challenges for LDCs. What are the new opportunities? What are the new risks? It also imposes new challenges on PUC staff. Defining new regulations is one matter; making them work is another.

For example, PGandE follows a gas-purchase strategy that allows it to foster competition among its gas suppliers. Spot gas purchases from domestic suppliers and discount purchases from Canadian suppliers have significantly lowered gas costs. This benefits core and noncore customers alike and places very effective price pressures on traditional suppliers. With lower gas costs, PGandE has undertaken new rate design and has been able to offer new competitive services to customers. But this is not a one-time fix. Market challenges will exist for a long time to come. Flexibility in every aspect of an LDC's business will be necessary if it is to survive in ever-changing supply and customer markets, and it should be an essential element in any new regulatory framework based on serving customers in a competitive market.

In the final analysis, market forces will prevail in the natural gas industry. The PUCs' success in continuing to advance the interests of consumers, especially the core residential and small business customers, will be heavily dependent upon how quickly and completely the PUCs recognize the strength and inevitability of those market forces and then free their LDCs to turn competitive challenges into opportunities for achieving lower costs and continued market strength.

ROBERT JOHNSTON
Chairman
Arkansas Public Service Commission

DAVID SULLINS
Arkansas Public Service Commission Staff

The following are thirteen comments on specific points made in Colin Braydon's chapter.

1. In his introduction, Blaydon stated that PUCs must address two fundamental changes in the natural gas market: interfuel competition based on price, absent wellhead controls; and, with open access to pipelines, the direct purchase of gas at wellhead by some large LDC customers. We suggest a third fundamental change that PUCs must address: the threat of bypass. Along with open access to pipelines, federal policy encourages, or at least removes obstacles to, competition among natural gas suppliers. This competition is likely to have significant ramifications for cost-allocation methodologies currently in place for many LDCs, similar to the cost shifting that recently has occurred in the telecommunications industry.

2. Blaydon's statement that "Because of low prices and high demand, PUCs allocated gas to customers through a variety of administrative mechanisms,"

while technically correct, might be more accurately expressed as, ''Due to artificially low interstate prices and demand that exceeded deliverability . . . ''

3. Some PUCs may regulate more than twenty LDCs, as in Illinois or Indiana; the Kentucky PUC regulates about forty.

4. After stating that ''Regulators may find that defining policy for smaller LDCs is considerably more challenging than for large LDCs,'' Blaydon might appropriately have pointed out that for some companies, the concept of a regulated monopoly may still be the most viable operating form. For instance, isolated, rural LDCs may not be threatened by competition to the extent that an urban LDC would be, and even though gas supply is unregulated with regard to price, nongas costs still can be allocated using traditional regulatory concepts. However, these situations will probably be the exception rather than the rule. For the most part, regardless of their size, customer mix, geographic location, and so on, LDCs will have to allocate costs according to the true cost of serving their customers, with some requirement that ''value of service'' be considered when costs are allocated, because the total cost of gas service will be close enough to alternative energy sources to invoke competition.

5. Blaydon's point that PUC regulations may affect some LDCs positively and others adversely in the same jurisdiction suggests that PUC policy on some issues ought to vary depending on what is in the public interest in a given situation.

6. In discussing the integration of LDCs into pipeline activities, it should be noted that many LDCs will be faced with customers who wish to bypass the LDC directly to its pipeline affiliate to avoid distribution costs.

7. Regarding the discussion of PUC policy toward LDC pricing, it may be that some distribution systems, or service to certain customers/customer classes on some distribution systems, was only economically feasible when natural gas was underpriced and in effect subsidized the nongas cost to customers. If so, when natural gas rises to market value, service provided at the fully allocated cost of service will be economically unfeasible, no matter what pricing mechanism is used. The resulting load loss will exacerbate further the problems of such systems. Under such circumstances, the LDC may have to recognize a loss, or institute an excess capacity adjustment, to remain as a viable operating entity.

8. Rather than Ramsey or peak-load pricing, perhaps a more practical approach for PUCs to take might be to start with the current, fully allocated cost of service and then shift costs only as competitive alternatives present the threat of bypass. (This assumes that customers are allowed access to the deregulated gas market and therefore that the threat of bypass due to differences in commodity cost is not a factor.) In effect, the price to customers having competitive alternatives (usually industrial customers) is based on the value of service in the particular instance, and the remaining customers are ''residualized.'' What may become evident is that historical cost allocation has overallocated costs to industrial users because the ''subsidy'' from an underpriced (that is, federally regulated natural gas, pre–1977) maintained the total price well below the value of service even

to industrials. Although the end result of such an approach probably will resemble the pricing mechanisms described by Blaydon, the phased-in approach will be more palatable for residential customers. A key factor in the move to shift cost to residential customers may be educating them about their alternative energy sources/costs, explaining the economic development benefits of allowing industrials to take natural gas at nationally competitive prices, and demonstrating the consequences of not pricing energy at competitive prices and, as a result, losing load from the system. Again, if residential prices exceed the value of service to residential customers (propane, heat pump, fuel oil, or a new technology), the company may be in a position of not recovering traditional costs of service, to keep things from getting any worse.

9. In Blaydon's discussion of PUC policy regarding LDC gas procurement, we suggest that it is likely that long-term gas-supply contract-pricing provisions will change relative to what we have seen in the past. As producers and LDCs begin to understand that neither can afford to assume the risks of what energy prices will be in the next ten to fifteen years, renegotiable price provisions in long-term contracts will appear. There still should be some differential between the long-term price and the short-term price, but the difference should be the insurance cost described by Blaydon, rather than reflective of energy price predictions gone sour. The difference between pre–1983 long-term contract prices and today's spot-market prices is an example of the mistaken belief that one can predict market prices for several years into the future, as also is the difference between some fixed-price old-gas contracts and the higher, regulated ceiling price for the old gas. Since both the producer and the LDC now have been "burned" by trying to predict future energy prices beyond two to three years, it would not be surprising to see long-term contract price provisions that negotiate prices more frequently.

10. Concerning Blaydon's discussion of PUC remedies of the broker problem, it should be emphasized that whatever course is chosen by the regulators, it will be important for the PUC to become involved in the decisions made by the LDC, instead of merely reviewing decisions after they are made. Although this exposes the PUC to increased exposure for its actions, such predecision review is important both to large and small LDCs.

11. In his section on LDC contract carriage, service obligations, and bypass restrictions, Blaydon ignored the impact of transportation rates on LDCs that depend primarily on wellhead supply. In large producing states, many LDCs rely on wellhead supply, which usually involves "take-or-pay" contracts. So, in addition to the service obligations discussed by Blaydon, these LDCs have significant financial obligations resulting from the obligation to serve. LDCs that are served by pipelines have not faced this dilemma since the FERC's minimum-bill order. These pipeline-supplied LDCs can choose among competing pipelines without having to pay for gas that they do not want to buy, paying only the demand costs of the pipeline. So not only do they have the ability to let customers transport customer-owned gas without incurring take-or-pay costs, they also can

cease to buy their own gas. Therefore, the cost of gas to the remaining ''system-supply'' customers is much less likely to be adversely affected. Conversely, wellhead-supplied LDCs not only may incur take-or-pay costs when customers cease to buy from system supply but also are constrained by further take-or-pay threats from choosing the least-expensive system supply gas to supply their remaining customers. Another of their fears is that, as demand for system supply declines, their buying power will be diminished, and future wellhead supplies will be more expensive because the LDCs have less to offer producers in terms of total volume of takes and percentage of deliverability taken.

12. In stating that concerns over bypass are exaggerated, Blaydon does not seem to understand the differences in the economics of serving industrial and residential customers. Industrial customers are a much more desirable load, especially when considered individually, than are residential customers. Industrial customers will be targets for competing suppliers, much as they are in the telecommunications industry. It is also important to remember that many LDCs do not have franchise areas and therefore are much more vulnerable to competition. Although it is true that appropriate rate design can prevent uneconomic bypass, the threat of economic bypass is much more difficult. Economic bypass occurs when a competing supplier can serve the customer at a lesser cost than the current supplier can; that is, the customer's value of service is less than the variable costs of the current supplier.

13. In Blaydon's concluding paragraph, it should be noted that the FERC's Order No. 436 makes significant changes to restrictions on pipeline entry, removing most barriers to pipeline entry as long as the pipeline assumes the risk of cost recovery.

PART III

DESIGNING STRATEGIES FOR COMPETITION

The current turbulence in natural gas markets may well represent the industry's future operating norm rather than a period of temporary adjustment. Policy changes now underway are bringing the U.S. natural gas sector into direct linkage with the world energy market—a market noted for its own turmoil and volatility. As with the domestic oil industry, the U.S. gas industry likely will be driven in large measure by events that are beyond national control or origin.

It is probably of little solace to gas industry regulators and managers—who have been accustomed to a relatively controlled and routinized environment—that the prospect of perpetual instability and unpredictability merely means that the natural gas industry is being put on the same footing with the bulk of American industries. Nevertheless those who control decisions in the natural gas industry will be forced to adapt. Successful adaptation will be defined by the ability to survive and prosper and likely will be guided best by coherent strategic planning.

In Chapter 8 Frank C. Schuller examines the generic components of successful business strategies that are called for in today's natural gas markets. Schuller argues that industry planners, now more than in the past, must focus on the demand side of their markets and seek out new ways to attract and keep customers. The key to this lies in firms' abilities adroitly to adjust levels and terms of purchases and sales in response to changing price, risk, and regulatory conditions and in their abilities to distinguish themselves from other energy suppliers. The ability to adjust to conditions is promoted by flexible contracting as well as geographic and product-line diversification. The latter strategy entails the matching of marketing and contract terms to customers' needs.

One function of contracts and trading relationships in the natural gas industry is to spread the risks attendant to unanticipated changes in economic circumstances among various industry participants. Unless allocated to those parties best able to adjust to uncertainty, risk will deter investment both in gas-producing and in gas-using assets. Carmen D. Legato takes up the complex problem of risk allocation and contract design in Chapter 9. He argues that if regulation increases competition in the pipeline sector the industry will move toward greater reliance on short-term contracts and spot markets for gas supply. Independent marketers and futures markets, in turn, will contribute to improved flexibility and more efficient allocations of risk. Even with such changes in industry practices, long-term contracts will continue to be employed. Legato argues that the challenge to regulators will be to ensure that these contracts allocate more of the industry's risks to pipelines and LDCs—in exchange for higher potential returns.

The current state of the natural gas industry not only demands the redesign of business strategies and practices but also requires that *policymakers* focus upon strategies for accomplishing regulatory reform. In Chapter 10 George R. Hall addresses the task of matching changes in the specifics of gas industry regulation to the outlines of an overall package of improved policy. The challenge of ''getting from here to there'' lies in following a path of reforms that minimizes disruptions and transition costs while remaining alert and responsive to the ultimate objectives of a more flexible, responsive, and competitive industry.

8

The Roles of Differentiation and Regulation

FRANK C. SCHULLER

In competitive industries, companies differentiate themselves by offering different products or services to specific markets. In doing so, they attempt to match their internal resources—such as lower costs or innovative skills—with markets in which they have a unique competitive advantage.[1]

Thus firms compete only with those companies who are competing for a particular market segment, not necessarily with all companies within an industry. In essence, differentiating firms are trying to create a minuscule monopoly based on their unique skills, by segmenting the market and pursuing selective strategies.

Examples abound.[2] Two currently prominent illustrations are airlines and telecommunications. In the airline industry, People Express appeals to travelers who seek low prices, without luxuries, whereas Eastern attracts travelers who value fast and free baggage handling, in-flight comfort, and reliability of scheduling. Similarly, in the telecommunications industry, some companies offer lower prices, whereas AT&T offers audio quality, credit for misdialed numbers, and reliability of service based on decades of performance.

As deregulation of the natural gas industry increases, it will also begin to differentiate. Indeed, the process is already under way. Producers are becoming gas marketers; pipelines are competing over prices; local distribution companies (LDCs) are arranging transportation of gas for industrial users. As the effects of competition begin to show, firms from all sectors—producers, pipelines, and LDCs—will position themselves to limit the effects of price declines, conservation, and loss of industrial markets to alternative fuels. This move by the natural gas industry toward differentiation will test the skill of policymakers who must formulate responsive and responsible regulation. A new era of competition in the gas industry has some favorable results: Increased competition eliminates some of the need to balance economic efficiency and social-equity concerns, since prices will adjust quickly to market demand, instead of lethargically to outmoded regulatory processes; supply levels will reflect real-world market prices instead of artificially regulated wellhead rates; and consumer well-being will be satisfied by the natural effects of competition, instead of being mandated by regulation. The challenge for policymakers is how to devise regulation that promotes public welfare through competition without permitting abuses of market power.

Despite the welter of changes that have already occurred, regulators have not yet felt the total impact of deregulation on competition in the natural gas industry. There are few precedents to offer guidelines. For instance, what are the responsibilities of pipelines and LDCs to maintain service obligations if voluntary or mandatory contract carriage flourishes? Should policymakers rely on a spot market to ensure secure supplies? These questions do not have antecedents in the gas industry. Many decisions will be made through trial and error. Others will result from political and economic compromises or the imperatives of expediency. Furthermore, once made, most public policy decisions will need to be revamped after real-world experience brings their inefficiencies and flaws to the forefront.[3]

Differentiation: Strategic Choices in Competitive Markets

Sources of Differentiation

Differentiation is thriving in many industries.[4] Firms differentiate to serve specific market segments to gain competitive advantage. Competitive advantage can arise from two sources. One is through technological changes that alter products or their manufacturing processes; the other is through responding to changes in a given market.

The computer industry is an archetypical example of segmentation through technological changes. Apple specializes exclusively in small personal computers, and DEC produces computers for large industrial and scientific applications; IBM produces both small personal and large mainframe computers. In each case, the technology defines which market segment a firm targets.

In other industries the technology remains constant while the market changes. Overnight package delivery is a good example. For decades, the U.S. Postal Service held a virtual monopoly on mail and package delivery. But in the late 1970s, Federal Express, recognizing the colossal need for overnight package and mail delivery, began to provide this specialized service. Similarly, following airline deregulation, commuter airlines arose to serve geographic locations not served by large carriers. In both industries, the recognition of specialized market needs produced differentiation.

One conventional approach to securing a market segment is to reduce costs in order to lower prices. Once a firm becomes a low-cost competitor—whether by accelerating up the learning curve, by securing low-cost inputs, or by increasing productivity through capital, equipment, and process innovations—it gains a competitive advantage that competitors cannot duplicate without enormous capital expense and risk. For example, the U.S. Postal Service can still deliver mail to individual homes at less expense than can Federal Express, due to its established infrastructure and expansive network. Although Federal Express has steadily increased its volume of deliveries, the U.S. Postal Service still processes millions of pieces of mail every day. Thus one very effective means of differentiation is through price, based on lowering costs.

Other forms of differentiation involve nonprice issues. Commuter airlines, for example, may be more expensive than transportation by bus, rail, or automobile, but they save time by conveying passengers faster than the alternatives. This illustrates how consumers, when choosing companies to provide goods or services, weigh low prices against other attributes.

Stages of Evolving Segmentation

Before segmentation occurs (as, for example, between Federal Express and Purolator Courier), markets often appear monolithic. The U.S. Postal Service blanketed the entire nation with mail and package delivery. The need for commuter airlines remained obscure when major carriers operated in small towns. Similarly, with AT&T intact, telephone customers seemed satisfied. In all of these cases, segmentation happened only after managers, motivated by competition or deregulation, began to seek specific markets in which their firms could gain a competitive advantage.

Markets often seem fixed in size, as if any segmentation will only divide the market into a variety of submarkets whose sum will equal the whole. Recent history has proved this perception false. Segmentation may expand or create entirely new markets by inducing demand where previously there was none. There is perhaps no better illustration of this than the revolution in the computer industry, where miniaturization has brought millions of new users and applications into the market.

Incipient Movements toward Differentiation: Responses to Competition

The natural gas industry is moving toward differentiation in all sectors: producers, pipelines, and LDCs. In years past, although producers displayed some differentiation, interstate pipelines and LDCs more or less pursued remarkably similar strategies: regulation of prices and transmission ensured excess demand along with uniform guidelines under which firms could operate. Regulation ensured a high degree of uniformity among firms; differences tended to result from firms' absolute sizes. But this is changing as competition enters the industry. The extent of differentiation, however, varies by sector, each of which has different ranges of opportunity to differentiate.

Producers

Differentiation among natural gas producers has been common for years. Both major oil companies and independents approach exploration for gas in different ways. Although both majors and independents share common exploration strategies, the independents use differences in their exploration strategies as their selling point.[5] Some producers concentrate on drilling for decontrolled gas, and others focus on less productive but less risky development wells.

Recently, producers have begun to differentiate significantly in their selling practices. Before the turmoil of the early 1980s, producers sold gas under long-term contracts with pipelines. These contracts detailed the terms of price, quantity, and the revision of terms. After wellhead decontrol, exclusive reliance on long-term contracts began to wane.

Several reasons contributed to this change. With declining demand and surplus supply, shut-in producers, particularly those requiring improved cash flow, began to cut prices to meet internal financing needs. Pipelines (through special marketing programs [SMPs]) created temporary sales on a spot-market basis to relieve take-or-pay penalties. Overall, however, pipelines bore enormous losses from take-or-pay contracts, estimated to be as much as $7 billion in the aggregate. As a result, they shied away from entering into irrevocable and inflexible long-term contracts.

Many producers, witnessing and experiencing contract renegotiating, recognized the need to develop a means of marketing gas directly to end users, not just to pipelines. The contracts that resulted mark one of the most significant new developments in the gas industry. These contracts are short term, often less than thirty days. At the expiration of the contract, producers and purchasers may terminate or renegotiate the contract.

Large producers exercise relatively strong bargaining positions with pipelines. Since large producers supply up to 30 percent of a pipeline's supply, they have the power to secure favorable contracts with a pipeline. They can negotiate adjustable pricing provisions and "market-out" clauses to be exercised if terms become untenable. Through financial stamina and myriad contracts, large producers can reserve the option to sell in the spot market, thus ensuring that they receive market prices at all times. Although in principle a producer has an equal chance of gaining or losing under a fixed-price contract, larger producers frequently view pipelines' contracting practices as one-sided: If the fixed price remains above market-clearing prices, the pipelines abrogate their contracts (as occurred in 1982–1983). Yet if prices increase, pipelines enforce the contractual agreement. By using short-term contracts that reflect spot-market prices, producers' gains are greater than they would be under fixed contracts.

Small, independent producers are more at the mercy of pipelines than are larger producers. Without the financial resources to hold back production, independents lack the capability to await price rises if their purchasers are paying below-market prices. Needing a secure cash flow to obtain as well as maintain bank financing, independent producers frequently yield to pipeline preferences. Although they could attempt to market gas directly to industrial users, the transaction costs are prohibitive. These costs arise for several reasons.

First, the direct costs of locating buyers are high. A small producer with twenty wells spread across Texas, for example, could spend thousands of dollars annually in travel, legal, and other expenses to find direct buyers and to arrange transport with various pipelines. Second, with only a handful of managers in a small firm—primarily geologists and engineers—the firm would incur high costs in switching its expertise from discovering to selling gas.

Third, the costs of capital for independents depends upon the security of their purchaser contracts. Without long-term contracts that specify quantity and price, banks and venture capitalists may charge independents prohibitively high rates. Higher capital costs reduce the amount of debt and equity capital the small firm can raise.

An efficient brokerage system could eliminate some of these difficulties. Brokers could establish an active market, matching up buyers and sellers and thus economizing on transaction costs and reducing uncertainty in selling. A network linking producers to multiple purchasers would develop. This would dissipate the potential for opportunistic behavior by either pipelines or producers. However, a brokerage system would not remove all of the difficulties of financing, particularly the risk of price instability.

Pipelines

Integration

Since passage of the Natural Gas Policy Act (NGPA) of 1978, pipelines have accelerated integration upstream into the producing sector. Before the NGPA, pipelines were required to include all of their costs in their rate base: Any exploration activity that the pipelines pursued would reap the same rate of return on investment. Allowable costs, however, were limited to out-of-pocket expenses and did not include the "user cost" of reserve depletion. As a result, pipelines saw little incentive for integrating backward, except to gain supply security.

After the NGPA, pipelines could reap the wellhead profits from exploration. With this change in regulation, many pipelines integrated into the production sector. Table 8.1 illustrates the degree of backward integration of the twenty largest pipelines.[6]

Pipeline/producer integration offers certain benefits. Owning production adds security to supply. Instead of waiting for exploration and development by producers, pipelines, through their producer affiliates, can plan exploration schedules to correspond with their demand needs and transportation availability. By exploring for gas themselves, they gain an opportunity of becoming a low-cost supplier if finding costs are relatively low. For example, when a producing

Table 8.1
Percentage of Total Production of Post–Natural Gas Policy Act Wells by Pipeline Affiliates by Inter- and Intrastate Market and Year

Interstate

Year	Total Production (Tcf)	Share of Production by Pipeline Affiliates (%)	Total Pipeline Affiliate Production (Tcf)[a]
1978	1.6	3.0	0.06
1979	3.8	4.0	0.15
1980	6.2	5.0	0.31
1981	9.0	5.0	0.45
1982	10.5	5.0	0.53

Intrastate

Year	Total Production (Tcf)	Share of Production by Pipeline Affiliates (%)	Total Pipeline Affiliate Production (Tcf)[a]
1978	1.6	1.0	0.02
1979	3.8	1.0	0.04
1980	6.2	1.0	0.06
1981	9.0	1.0	0.09
1982	10.5	1.0	0.11

[a]Numbers are rounded to the nearest hundredth.

Source: U.S. Department of Energy, *Drilling and Production Under Title I of the Natural Gas Policy Act*, U.S. Government Printing Office, Washington, D.C., June 1984, Figure 32.

company finds a field offshore, bidding by other pipelines will raise the price. But in the case of an integrated pipeline/producer (although in principle it will charge market prices), the pipeline can use its affiliate to attain flexibility with prices and volumes at the wellhead. In short, pipelines may use their producer affiliates to overcome contractual rigidities of price and volume that they bear under nonaffiliated producers.[7]

Few pipelines have integrated forward.[8] The exceptions include Internorth and Columbia Gas, which, during their formative years, acquired a number of LDCs. With the appearance of SMPs and the Natural Gas Clearinghouse, pipelines have inaugurated programs that bypass LDCs and sell gas directly to industrial users.

Marketing Innovations and Skills

When gas prices were regulated below market prices, marketing consisted simply of order taking and informing interruptible customers when they could expect gas to be turned on or off.[9] In fact, some pipelines abolished their marketing departments altogether. But when fierce competition with oil demanded an aggressive marketing policy, pipelines hastily resurrected their defunct sales departments and adopted new marketing strategies.

For instance, in 1984 Transco introduced the first SMP in the United States, hoping to relieve its take-or-pay contract problems and to prevent loss of industrial customers.[10] This program sparked similar innovations throughout the industry, as shown in Table 8.2. Yet some pipelines have been reluctant to implement SMPs. Those that did tended to be relatively high-cost producers with a pressing need to innovate.

Some pipelines, with low-cost, old-gas contracts, used them to gain competitive advantage. Texas Eastern, for example, had a historically low cost of gas that permitted it to sustain its market share of industrial sales while other pipelines were losing sales or struggling to hold customers with SMPs. In general, pipelines with a shortage of reserves pursued completely different strategies than those with relatively abundant supplies. Pipelines with the least reserves of gas aggressively bought high-cost gas to restock their dedicated reserves, as shown by Table 8.3. Those with ample cushions of controlled gas tended to refrain from contracting for relatively high-cost gas.

Field Purchase

Pipelines have begun to differentiate themselves through purchasing policies. Some pipelines offer lenient terms for installing systems and compressors. In general, these companies attempt to honor all of the terms of their purchase contracts. When terms cannot be upheld, pipelines attempt to negotiate with producers to overcome difficulties. Other pipelines have unilaterally abrogated some or all of the terms in contracts with producers—an action that has frequently triggered a deluge of litigation.[11]

A pipeline's reputation in part determines its range of strategic options. For instance, if a producer considers one pipeline fair and another troublesome, the producer is likely to contract with the pipeline with the better reputation, even if the troublesome pipeline offers slightly more generous terms. In such a case, the producer views the costs of litigation, production delays, and managerial time spent in lengthy negotiations as outweighing the price incentives offered by the unreliable pipeline.

Consolidation

Other forms of differentiation occur through consolidation of pipelines. Consolidation can lower costs through increased economies of scale and a diversified consumer mix. Houston Natural, for example, purchased TransWestern (which

Table 8.2
FERC-Approved Special Marketing Programs (SMPs) as of December 27, 1984

Approved SMPs	
Company	*Dates Authorized to Run*
Transcontinental Gas Pipeline	6/29/84-10/31/85
Tennessee Gas Pipeline Co. (a division of Tenneco)	12/10/83-10/31/85
Columbia Gas Transmission Co.	11/10/83-10/31/85
Panhandle Eastern Pipe Line Co. and Trunkline Gas Co.	3/19/84-10/31/85
Texas Eastern Transmission Co.	6/29/84-10/31/85
El Paso Natural Gas Company	8/24/84-10/31/85
Producer-Oriented SMPs	
Company	*Dates Authorized to Run*
Tenneco Oil Company, Inc.	11/10/83-10/31/85
Cities Service Oil & Gas Co.	6/29/84-10/31/85
TXP Operating Company	7/24/84-10/31/85
Amoco Production Company	8/20/84-10/31/85
Sun Exploration & Production Co.	10/9/84-10/31/85
ARCO Oil & Gas Company	10/9/84-10/31/85
Shell Offshore, Inc. and Shell Western E&P, Inc.	11/20/84-10/31/85
Champlain Petroleum Company	12/17/84-10/31/85
ANR Production Company	12/17/84-10/31/85
Cenergy Exploration Company	12/17/84-10/31/85
Odeco Oil & Gas Company	Pending
Texas Gas Exploration Company	Pending
Pending SMP Proposals	
Company	*Date Filed*
Southern Natural Gas Company	4/9/84
Yankee Resources[a]	8/24/84
Mesa Petroleum	10/24/84
American Petrofina Company of Texas	11/13/84
Diamond Shamrock Exploration Co.	11/20/84
Union Texas Petroleum Company	11/28/84
Exxon Corporation	11/21/84

[a]Yankee Resources is the first nonpipeline or producer to file for a Special Marketing Program with FERC.

Source: Federal Energy Regulatory Commission, *Federal Energy Regulatory Commission Monitor*, Washington, D.C., January 10, 1985, p. 4.

Table 8.3
Purchasing Behavior of the Twenty Largest Pipelines

Pipeline	1983 R/P Ratios (Years)	Volume 1983 (%)		
		Old Gas	*New Gas*	*High Gas*
ANR	6.26	59	29	15
Colorado Interstate	14.06	52	32	16
Columbia Gas	9.18	29	49	22
Consolidated	11.21	23	77	0
El Paso	16.90	43	47	10
Florida Gas	5.19	58	38	10
K N Energy	17.37	70	27	4
Natural Gas Pipeline	6.62	60	38	2
Northern Natural	11.86	55	43	2
NW Central	27.25	55	33	12
NW Pipeline	29.97	46	45	9
Panhandle Eastern	13.31	53	43	4
Southern Natural	5.67	42	51	7
Tennessee Gas	8.55	51	37	12
Texas Eastern	5.88	60	27	14
Texas Gas Transmission	6.15	56	31	14
Transcontinental	6.97	32	55	12
Transwestern	5.63	38	41	21
Trunkline	9.02	63	30	7
United	6.56	38	50	12

Source: U.S. Department of Energy, *Gas Supplies of Interstate Natural Pipeline Companies 1983*, U.S. Government Printing Office, Washington, D.C., 1984, Tables 5 and 11; and U.S. Department of Energy, *Preliminary PGA Filings* and *Preliminary PGA Filings*, U.S. Government Printing Office, Washington, D.C., February 1985.

serves California) and Florida Gas (which serves the U.S. Southeast). As a result, it now serves residential heating markets on both coasts during winter months when demand is high and the intrastate (Texas) market for industrial users in the summer months when residential demand is lower. Other pipeline mergers, such as Mid-Con with United and ANR with Coastal States, indicate that consolidation is successful in bringing about increased economies of scale and geographic diversification.

Summary

Pipelines have embraced differentiation in a number of ways. Some attempts—such as experimentation with SMPs—were undertaken to resolve short-term problems. Other changes in strategy—geographic diversification and the use of brokers and networks—have the markings of long-term strategic behavior. Further experimentation will identify opportunities that pipelines can forge into cohesive strategies.

Local Distribution Companies

Interim differentiation is a means of competing for business. LDCs, however, typically are legal monopolies, suggesting an absence of competition. But LDCs must compete with oil in the industrial sector and with conservation initiatives in both the residential and industrial sectors. This has forced them to engage in strategic behavior to differentiate sales in ways attractive to customers. This differentiation has involved methods of guaranteeing supply security, rate (price) flexibility, and aggressive marketing.

Supply Security

During the shortages of the late 1960s and early 1970s, many LDCs began seeking more reliable ways to ensure secure supplies. Utilities, such as Bay State and Brooklyn Union, funded their own drilling programs; Brooklyn Union now operates its own oil and gas operations in twenty-five states. Union and Public Service Gas and Electric installed technologies for extracting gas from landfills.[12] In some cases, the pressure to find secure sources of gas led LDCs to bypass pipelines and to contract directly with suppliers. Boston Gas and Southern California Gas launched liquefied natural gas (LNG) projects. Through such strategies, LDCs seek to provide customers with reliable gas supplies. The demand for such assurances is unlikely to diminish.

PUC Regulation

With rising gas prices, LDCs have sought flexible rates to maintain industrial sales against residual fuel oil. Most also have petitioned PUCs to abolish moratoriums on hookups and curtailments. One company even petitioned its Public Utility Commission (PUC) to install conversion units for households at no cost in order to induce switching from oil to gas.[13]

Marketing and Related Diversification

Some LDCs have implemented conservation programs and arranged financing for homeowners to install energy-saving equipment, often gas fired. Many LDCs still sell gas-fueled hot water heaters and furnaces. Others have begun to work with industrial users to address those demands that otherwise would be lost to fuel oil or coal. Smaller LDCs are consolidating or sharing common functions to gain economies of scale.

Strategies for the Future

The degrees of differentiation now exhibited in the natural gas industry suggest some likely future strategies, although in an uncertain world they are far from definite. Many depend on further regulatory reform. New market opportunities in service areas, pipeline behavior, and exogenous changes in the world energy market will also influence strategies. Ultimately, success will depend on the ingenuity and creativity of managers in identifying market segments and seizing competitive advantages.

Producers

Producers, which are already extremely differentiated, are likely to pursue strategies similar to ones currently under way. If regulatory reform expands buyers' access to wellhead markets, a major shift in producer strategy might follow.

As end-user access to pipelines increases, some producers, particularly major oil companies that already have sharp marketing skills, are negotiating gas sales directly with large users. As shown in Table 8.2, some are using SMPs. Independent producers, discontent with their treatment from pipelines, also might seek to market gas directly, either through brokers or through user cooperatives set up to facilitate gas sales.

Regulation that permits producers to bypass pipelines and sell directly to end users creates opportunities to differentiate. Many producers still will be likely to favor long-term contracts, although with more flexible pricing terms than in past contracts. However, other producers, who may have obtained marketing strength with pipelines and other purchasers, might opt for much shorter contracts or participate solely in a spot market. A variation might arise in which producers would commit a certain daily portion of reserves to a pipeline but would sell excess supply on the spot market.

The ability of a producer to differentiate by type of sale will depend upon the types of customers. For example, a producer in New Mexico attempting to sell gas directly to a New England utility will be offered a lower price than a producer in West Virginia, for the West Virginian's gas has a lower transportation cost. By contrast, a New England utility whose customers highly value security of supply might pay a premium to a Texas producer who has ample supply from one field despite the relatively high transportation fee. Thus both the distance of the market and the needs of customers will determine producers' ability to differentiate through sales mechanisms.

Interstate Pipelines

Pipelines have numerous opportunities for differentiation. Each pipeline serves a different market area with different characteristics. Similarly, each pipeline has a logistics configuration that determines its market area. For example, Tenneco serves many rural areas and rural utilities, while Transco tends to serve more densely populated areas, such as Philadelphia and New York. The differences in these markets and customers, especially differences in the needs of the LDCs, influence how pipelines define their market share and their competitive advantages.

Not all pipelines have similar competitive advantages. Pipelines that serve numerous industrial users but that hold only short-term supplies may find that a contract carriage arrangement best suits their circumstances. Other pipelines that serve residential users with inelastic demand but that hold abundant supplies may find that long-term contracts with producers and LDCs best suit their strengths.

The low-cost pipeline obviously has a competitive advantage over a higher-cost pipeline. Thus for the higher-cost pipeline to serve the same market, it must satisfy market needs that compensate for its higher cost. This might involve providing more personalized service in identifying industrial customers' or LDCs' needs. It might also provide storage facilities or guarantee a level of supply security that the low-cost pipeline cannot. Finally, the high-cost pipeline might serve as a swing supplier, selling only supplemental volumes at premium prices.

Pipelines' strategic choices are circumscribed by their service area and the resulting customer base. Most have a mix of customers. Most pipelines sell directly to industrial users connected to their systems and are monopolists or duopolists in serving LDCs. In turn, each LDC linked to the pipeline supplies gas to industrial, commercial, and residential customers. In other words, along its system a pipeline may serve a multiplicity of users, each having different demands.

How a pipeline competes in any given region will depend on its total logistical configuration. For example, New York is served by Transco, Tenneco, and Texas Eastern. The different logistical configurations of each pipeline might lead to their adopting completely different strategies for serving the New York area, which is the terminal point of each of their systems. Transco might act predominantly as a contract carrier, Texas Eastern might act as the secure low-cost private carrier, and Tenneco might act as the standby swing supplier.[14]

As consolidation increases, pipelines may become so diverse that their logistic systems might be partitioned into separate divisions, operating independently and autonomously. Such multiple divisions frequently appear in manufacturing plants and are termed ''a factory within a factory.'' A pipeline could organize in a similar way. For example, it might create two divisions: one specializing in industrial sales and one specializing in residential sales through LDCs.[15]

Local Distribution Companies

LDCs differentiate to guard against incursions on their markets by fuel-oil distributors, independent marketers, and pipelines. As with pipelines, LDCs will develop their strategies based on the characteristics of the market and on price and supply conditions.

Industrial Users

LDCs serving large industrial users will continue to try to prevent fuel switching. As competition increases, LDCs may seek to reduce costs by purchasing gas directly at the wellhead or through brokers. They might also engage in various types of carriage activities to ensure reliable supplies.

Contract carriage would not require LDCs to abandon completely the business of supplying gas to industrial users. An LDC might agree to transport a certain amount of gas to an industrial user through contract carriage, and the industrial user may agree to contract for a steady volume of gas from the LDC. In fact, to ensure supply, the industrial user might be willing to pay a premium for a secure supply at some predetermined price.

Commercial/Residential Users

Most LDCs serve a multitude of residential customers. State PUCs, which regulate those LDCs, often stress security of supply over lower prices. Furthermore, PUCs may use an LDC as an instrument for social policies such as providing energy for low-income users. LDCs whose PUCs emphasize nonprice issues such as security of supply and income redistribution may seek regulatory protection from competition on the grounds that it is needed to finance PUC-mandated objectives. PUC attitudes on various economic and social issues vary from state to state. For example, the Illinois Commerce Commission may offer LDCs little regulatory protection against competition. The priorities of state PUCs will determine LDC strategies.[16]

Brokers, Marketers, and Gatherers

Differentiation has led to the rise of brokers/special marketers.[17] Brokers are completely new entrants into the market, sometimes taking the form of subsidiaries of pipelines, producers, or even LDCs. Regardless of origin, they herald a new type of marketing and purchasing procedure.

Brokers/special marketers provide additional flexibility to the market. By reducing transaction costs and quickly matching up buyers and sellers, they allow producers to sell gas at posted prices and under short-term contracts. They also expedite flexible pricing procedures that clear the market of supply/demand imbalances.

Closely related to brokers/special marketers are independent gas gatherers, who enhance a service often provided by pipelines. By offering producers take-or-pay contracts and then brokering the gas on the spot market or reselling it to pipelines or end users under long-term contracts, they expand the number of options under which producers sell gas.

Alternatively, gatherers may simply transport gas, allowing producers either to negotiate their own contracts or to decide whether to sell gas on the spot market or under a long-term contract. Texas Gas receives about 25 percent of its gas supply from one gatherer in Louisiana. In this case, the gatherer earns a profit by transporting gas from the wellhead to the trunk line.[18]

Many types of companies may enter the brokerage business. The barriers to entry are neglible. Quoting one broker: "All you really need is a telephone, a copy of the *Yellow Pages*, and a few connections in the oil patch. With that, you can become a gas broker. Of course, you have to know something about buying and selling gas, but there's so much gas being shut-in, you have producers willing to make a deal for you."[19] In 1982–1983 one industrial user in Houston was contacted by more than a dozen independent brokers. Approximately seven of them had recently resigned from major interstate pipelines where they had been employed in gas-purchasing departments. Others had simply worked in some oil- or gas-related activity.

To the extent that they can retain crucial personnel, pipelines have a distinctive advantage as brokers. Several pipelines have already established brokerage and marketing divisions that link buyers and sellers. Two prominent examples are Internorth-Houston Natural Gas and Tenneco, and others are forming.

What endows pipelines with an unparalleled competitive advantage over other brokers is their accumulated knowledge both of purchasing practices at the wellhead and of the demand characteristics of end users. Pipeline managers have advanced up the learning curve so far that new entrants have difficulty replicating their experience. For example, pipeline managers have substantial and intimate knowledge of producers' production estimates and the reliability of producers' wells. In addition, they are familiar with the geologic formations upon which to base their evaluations of production volumes, and have an understanding of the logistics and operational issues of the pipeline, such as line pressures and load balancing.

At the consumer end, pipeline managers understand market demands, having amassed information on demand patterns and the special needs of individual industrial users and LDCs. Except for major industrial users such as GM and large LDCs such as Brooklyn Union Gas, whose organizations possess the skill and size to bargain directly for gas as efficiently as pipelines, pipelines' knowledge of consumer needs allows them effectively to coordinate buyers and sellers at minimal costs. Unless pipelines decline to enter the brokerage business, they clearly hold a competitive edge over new entrants.

Private Carriage

Despite the advantages of brokers, the spot market, and freer access to pipelines, private carriage is likely to remain the predominant method of gas transportation for some 75 percent of gas consumed in the United States. But if private carriage is to remain the primary form of gas transportation, it will be shaped by the strategic choices of pipelines.

What is the importance of these changes? Their importance is one of discipline—not of overhauling the gas industry. They offer a type of measuring stick by which to determine the economic efficiency of the pipeline industry. Most consumers couldn't care less how gas is purchased and transported, as long as it is the least expensive and conforms to their specific needs. In fact, most consumers would prefer to eliminate the related transaction costs, if they could acquire the same gas and associated services at the same price. Increased access to pipelines and direct wellhead purchases provide the assurances.

A spot market and open access to pipelines provide the standard for comparisons of price and service. The use of spot markets is not unambiguously detrimental to pipelines. First, pipelines can tie their gas purchased for private carriage to the spot market to avoid signing contracts that are uneconomic, as they did in the early 1980s. Second, LDCs and their PUCs can establish prudency tests based on spot-market prices and published transportation tariffs. Thus a state PUC can determine objectively if LDCs are paying the appropriate price for gas by comparing their purchases with prices paid on the spot market and in verifiable transportation tariffs.

Public Policy: A Framework for Regulatory Design

Despite recent moves toward a competitive gas market, regulation will continue. However, it will not be as simple as it was in the past. It must be redesigned to be responsive both to the policy objectives of flexible and competitive gas markets and to the strategic behavior of firms. This task is complicated by several important factors.

First, state and federal regulators sometimes work at cross-purposes. For example, state PUC prudency reviews effectively mandate long-term contracts at the same time as the Federal Energy Regulatory Commission (FERC) prompts transportation access, spot markets, and independent brokerage. The two approaches are in fundamental conflict.

Second, competitive markets are dynamic. Regulation is likely to become obsolete with rapid changes in markets. Even with an extremely responsive agency, the lag between reality and regulatory response will distort both the intended efficiency and equity of the regulation. Meanwhile, distortions could expand as participants in a quasi-competitive market find opportunities to exploit the inefficiencies of regulation.

Third, uniform regulations are often poorly matched to individual markets. Although each market exhibits different demand, supply, and logistical characteristics, federal and state policies typically apply uniformly. The application of a single uniform code across highly diverse markets is likely to make regulation counterproductive. Uniform and strict service obligations, for example, may be a reasonable mechanism to police abuses of market power in monopoly distribution markets, but they are harmful in markets with multiple competitive firms.

Fourth, inflexible regulation will worsen gas industry performance. In years past, regulation allowed pipelines and LDCs to earn acceptable rates of return and serve customers at prices below market levels. These low prices, which created excess demand, allowed regulators to pursue social equity and political goals. This system provided a rate of return for pipelines that covered their capital costs, while certain customers benefited from stable, below-market prices. All actors benefited except producers (who provided artificially cheap gas to pipelines, LDCs, and customers), curtailed users, and other potential customers (particularly those on the East Coast who, denied service, purchased higher-cost fuel). Competitive pressures have made simple, stable rate regulation and priority rationing infeasible. With wellhead prices of gas equal to those of oil, excess demand disappeared. Pipelines and LDCs can earn only their fixed rate of return by marketing gas against fuel oil, coal, and, to a lesser extent, electricity. In an environment in which the prices of these alternative fuels are highly volatile, rate flexibility is crucial. For example, gas prices that are artificially high due to regulation can induce loss of industrial markets, particularly when oil prices are falling.

Fifth, pipelines and LDCs have vastly different cost structures. These differences arose long before competitive pressures in the gas industry reached the level of those that developed after the NGPA, for several reasons.[20] First, prices in different contracts were negotiated at different times under different market and regulatory conditions.[21] Second, the different operating efficiencies of different pipelines and LDCs created different costs. Third, transportation distances between the wellhead and end markets varied from pipeline to pipeline. Fourth, the time required to construct a pipeline and the associated capital cost both influenced cost structure (for example, pipelines built after 1955 cost more than pipelines built immediately after World War II).[22] Fifth, these cost differences became even more exaggerated after the passage of the NGPA.[23] As indicated in Table 8.2, the cost structure of pipelines (and their respective customers) now differ sharply. A regulatory policy of uniformly forcing renegotiation of high-cost gas contracts, for example, would have a widely disparate impact on the financial and strategic options of different firms. Sixth, the market areas and customer mixes of pipelines and LDCs differ markedly.

Regulation that fails to account for these differences will discourage innovative approaches to the selling of gas. If, for example, regulation terminated all private carriage by pipelines by relying on independent brokers to arrange supply scheduling, small and rural LDCs and end users would be forced to turn to less-preferred and more costly alternatives.

Segmenting Regulatory Practices

Much of the difficulty in enacting effective public policy on federal and state levels arises from differentiation in the natural gas industry. Uniform regulation will worsen rather than improve performance; yet it is impossible to regulate each individual pipeline company and LDC. Perhaps policymakers can learn from those they regulate.[24] Some firms will pursue strategies aimed primarily at residential users, while others will concentrate on industrial sales. The two markets are distinct, with different needs and expectations. They could be regulated in different ways, as they are in Texas and other gas-producing states.

In industrial markets, policymakers could experiment with different levels of regulation. There is no doubt that suppliers can exercise market power over some industries. But pipelines and LDCs compete for industrial markets with firms that supply fuel oil, coal, and electricity. When there are easily substitutable fuels, being a monopolist does not ensure significant monopoly power. Moreover, the cost of imposing regulation, both in administrative burden and in inhibiting competition, may be greater than the cost of some suppliers exercising undue market power. Since most pipelines compete with other fuels, it is likely that they will be able to serve the industrial market more efficiently with less regulation than with more.

The residential sector is different. Residential consumers cannot switch to oil or electricity without expensive capital outlays. None requires special services. Their consumption is too small and uniform to expect that they will seek out brokers. Thus in the residential markets, continuing existing regulations is preferable to many of the proposed regulatory reforms, since the potential for market abuse in this segment is larger. The exception is regulation that reduces wasteful overhead costs or that encourages gas to displace more expensive energy sources in the residential market.

Separating regulatory practices by market segments would lessen the difficulty of regulating differentiated firms without jeopardizing public welfare. In the case of pipelines, the procedure might work as follows. If residential and industrial users each consumed equal shares of a pipeline's capacity, the FERC might apply rate-of-return calculations for the residential sector, while effectively deregulating the remaining 50 percent for industrial users. Under this method, the pipeline would earn its allowed rate of return only on that half sold to residential customers, while having the opportunity to earn a greater rate of return from industrial sales. This system would both ensure a fair allocation of fixed costs to residential users and prevent pipelines from abusing market power. State regulators could adopt similar proposals and additionally could establish industrial zones based on geographic markets in which LDCs could compete without regulation.

Federal and state policymakers can devise a variety of ways to segment the gas market. The strategies they use in fitting regulation to specific markets should be dictated by the characteristics of the market and the ways in which regulated firms are differentiating.

Conclusions

During the last decade, a number of industries in the United States have weathered the move from regulation to deregulation. Trucking, telecommunications, railroads, airlines, banking, financial services—all have survived the stresses and challenges of deregulation. Even firms not directly regulated by federal or state governments have felt the tugs of the trend toward deregulation. The relaxation of trade barriers, for instance, has incited increased competition in the automobile industry. Some companies have not survived: Braniff capsized, Pan Am and Eastern are bailing fervently to avoid being swamped, and many small banks and trucking companies have gone under. Despite the casualties, deregulation has worked. For the most part, prices have fallen and service has improved.

Yet policymakers must be cautious about using these deregulated industries as models for the natural gas industry. Unlike the other industries, the natural gas industry cannot be completely deregulated, in part because pipelines tend to be natural monopolies. Policymakers must achieve a level of deregulation that optimally balances costs and benefits—no easy task. Although there is no blanket prescription for formulating policy, there are some guidelines.

First, policymakers must understand that natural gas firms will evolve as they adjust to a newly competitive world. Second, they must evaluate market demands and anticipate how firms will develop in response to them. Third, they must formulate a sector-sensitive regulatory strategy. Separate policies for industrial and residential user must be set in a way that leaves pipelines and LDCs with incentives to serve both markets.

These guidelines are not definitive, but they underscore the need for regulatory policies that respond sympathetically to the needs and realities of the diverse, differentiating, and newly competitive natural gas industry.

Notes

1. This chapter owes a great debt to Michael E. Porter's books: *Competitive Strategy: Techniques for Analyzing Industries and Competitors*, The Free Press, New York, 1980; and *Competitive Advantage: Creating and Sustaining Superior Performance*, The Free Press, New York, 1985.

2. John R. Meyer, "Toward a Better Understanding of Deregulation: Some Hypotheses and Observations," *International Journal of Transport Economics*, 10, April-August 1983, pp. 35–53.

3. Good examples of various public policy questions can be found in Milton Russell, "Overview of Policy Issues: A Preliminary Assessment," in *The Deregulation of Natural Gas*, ed. Edward J. Mitchell, American Enterprise Institute for Public Policy Research, Washington, D.C., 1983; Thomas K. McCraw, ed., *Regulation in Perspective: Historical Essays*, Harvard University Press, Cambridge, Mass., 1981; U.S. House of Representatives, Committee on Energy and Commerce, Subcommittee on Fossil and Synthetic Fuels, *Hearings on Proposed Changes to Natural Gas Laws*, 98th Cong., 1st sess., Washington, D.C., Serial No. 98–30, pt. 3, 1983.

4. Much of the following section is based on Porter, *Competitive Strategy*; idem, *Competitive Advantage*.

5. Bernard J. Picchi and Caren E. Winnall, "Proved Petroleum Reserves of 30 Large Energy Companies, 1978–83: Data and Analysis," Report prepared for Salomon Brothers, New York, August 1984.

6. U.S. Department of Energy, *Drilling and Production under Title I of the Natural Gas Policy Act*, U.S. Government Printing Office, Washington, D.C., June 1984, fig. 32.

7. J. S. Graves, W. W. Hogan, and R. T. McWhinney, "Mandatory Contract Carriage: An Essential Condition for Natural Gas Wellhead Competition and Least Consumer Cost," Report prepared for Putnam, Hayes & Bartlett, Cambridge, Mass., September 1984.

8. Harry G. Broadman and W. David Montgomery, *Natural Gas Markets after Deregulation*, Resources for the Future/The Johns Hopkins University Press, Washington, D.C., 1983, Report prepared for Resources for the Future, Washington, D.C., 1983.

9. U.S. Department of Energy, *The Current State of the Natural Gas Market*, U.S. Government Printing Office, Washington, D.C., December 1981.

10. U.S. Department of Energy, *The First Report Required by Section 123 of the Natural Gas Policy Act of 1978*, U.S. Government Printing Office, Washington, D.C., July 1984.

11. Thomas E. Kennedy, "Analysis of the Cambridge Energy Research Associates Study of Mandatory Contract Carriage," Monograph No. 282, Illinois Commerce Commission, Springfield, Ill., November 1984.

12. See annual reports of these companies for details.

13. Examples are found in the annual reports of Southern California Gas and Public Service Gas & Electric of New Jersey. See also U.S. Department of Energy, *Increasing Competition in the Natural Gas Market: The Second Report Required by Section 123 of the Natural Gas Policy Act of 1978*, U.S. Government Printing Office, Washington, D.C., January 1985, Table A–5.

14. U.S. Department of Energy, *Underground Natural Gas Storage in the United States, 1981–1982 Heating Year [April 1981-May 1982]*, U.S. Government Printing Office, Washington, D.C., August 1982.

15. At present, Houston Natural and Tenneco are experimenting in this way. The national potential for this can be seen in U.S. Department of Energy, Energy Information Administration, *Natural Gas Monthly*, U.S. Government Printing Office, Washington, D.C., December 1984, Table 14.

16. U.S. Department of Energy, *The Current State of the Natural Gas Market*, pp. 83–100.

17. See U.S. Department of Energy, *Increasing Competition*, pp. 88–89.

18. In the Texas Gas Company example, the gatherer receives payment for transpor-

tation from the proceeds from the sale of natural gas liquids, which are stripped from wellhead production.

19. Interview with William N. Carl, oil and gas investor, Houston, Texas, March 1985.

20. American Gas Association, *Gas Facts: 1984 Data*, Section V, "Transmission and Distribution," Arlington Va., 1985.

21. U.S. Department of Energy, *Structure and Trends in Natural Gas Wellhead Contracts*, U.S. Government Printing Office, Washington, D.C., November 1983.

22. American Gas Association, *Gas Facts: 1984 Data*.

23. See U.S. Department of Energy, *Structure and Trends in Natural Gas Wellhead Contracts*.

24. For a view of the latitude regulatory commissions have and how this latitude changes, see Douglas D. Anderson, *Regulatory Politics and Electric Utilities*, Auburn House Publishing Company, Boston, 1981.

Selected Bibliography

Abbott, Catherine Good, and Stephen A. Watson. "Pitfalls on the Road to Decontrol: Lessons from the Natural Gas Policy Act of 1978." In *The Deregulation of Natural Gas*. Edited by Edward J. Mitchell. The American Enterprise Institute, Washington, D.C., 1983.

American Gas Association. *Gas Facts: 1984 Data*. Section V, "Transmission and Distribution." Arlington, Va., 1985.

———. "Gas Industry Actions by Field Purchasers to Reduce Gas Costs." Mimeograph Report. Arlington, Va., February 1984.

Anderson, A. Scott. "The Texas Approach to Gas Proration and Ratable Take." *University of Colorado Law Review*, 57, Issue 2, Winter 1986.

Anderson, Douglas D. *Regulatory Politics and Electric Utilities*. Auburn House Publishing Company, Boston, 1981.

Arrow, Kenneth J. "Vertical Integration and Communication." *The Bell Journal*, 6, Spring 1985.

Broadman, Harry G., and W. David Montgomery. *Natural Gas Markets after Deregulation*. Resources for the Future/The Johns Hopkins University Press, Washington, D.C., 1983. Report prepared for Resources for the Future, Washington, D.C., 1983.

Bryant, Patricia A. Gregory G. Nikel, and Jeff D. Sandefer. "The Future of the Independent: A Study of the Challenges and Opportunities Facing the Independent Oil and Gas Operator." Mimeograph Report. Harvard Graduate School of Business, Boston, April 1986.

Federal Energy Regulatory Commission. *Federal Energy Regulatory Commission Monitor*. Washington, D.C., May 3, 1984.

———. *Federal Energy Regulatory Commission Monitor*. Washington, D.C., January 10, 1985.

Flaherty, M. Therese. "Prices versus Quantities and Vertical Financial Integration." *The Bell Journal*, 12, Autumn 1981.

Graves, J. S., W. W. Hogan, and R. T. McWhinney. "Mandatory Contract Carriage: An Essential Condition for Natural Gas Wellhead Competition and Least Consumer

Cost.'' Report prepared for Putnam, Hayes & Bartlett. Cambridge, Mass., September 1984.

Jacoby, Henry D., and Arthur W. Wright. ''The Gordian Knot of Natural Gas Prices.'' *The Deregulation of Natural Gas*. Edited by Edward J. Mitchell. American Enterprise Institute, Washington, D.C., 1983.

Kennedy, Thomas E. ''Analysis of the Cambridge Energy Research Associates Study of Mandatory Contract Carriage.'' Monograph No. 282. Illinois Commerce Commission, Springfield, Ill., November 1984.

Leibenstein, Harvey. ''Allocative Efficiency versus 'X-Efficiency.' '' *Microeconomics: Selected Readings*. 4th ed. Edited by Edwin Mansfield. W. W. Norton Company, New York, 1982.

———. *Beyond Economic Man*. Harvard University Press, Cambridge, Mass., 1976.

McCraw, Thomas K., ed. *Regulation in Perspective: Historical Essays*. Harvard University Press, Cambridge, Mass., 1981.

Meyer, John R. ''Toward a Better Understanding of Deregulation: Some Hypotheses and Observations.'' *International Journal of Transport Economics*. April-August 1983, pp. 35–53.

Picchi, Bernard J., and Caren E. Winnall. ''Proved Petroleum Reserves of 30 Large Energy Companies, 1978–83: Data and Analysis.'' Report prepared for Salomon Brothers. New York, August 1984.

Porter, Michael, E. *Competitive Advantage: Creating and Sustaining Superior Performance*. The Free Press, New York, 1985.

———. *Competitive Strategy: Techniques for Analyzing Industries and Competitors*. The Free Press, New York, 1980.

Rossbach, Peter. ''Policy Analysis of a Natural Gas Clearinghouse.'' Mimeograph Report. John F. Kennedy School of Government, Harvard University, Cambridge, Mass., May 1984.

Russell, Milton. ''Overview of Policy Issues: A Preliminary Assessment.'' *The Deregulation of Natural Gas*. Edited by Edward J. Mitchell. American Enterprise Institute for Public Policy Research, Washington, D.C., 1983.

U.S. Department of Energy. *The Current State of the Natural Gas Market*. U.S. Government Printing Office, Washington, D.C., December 1981.

———. *Drilling and Production under Title I of the Natural Gas Policy Act*. U.S. Government Printing Office, Washington, D.C., June 1984.

———. *The First Report Required by Section 123 of the Natural Gas Policy Act of 1978*. U.S. Government Printing Office, Washington, D.C., July 1984.

———. *Gas Supplies of Interstate Natural Gas Pipeline Companies, 1983*. U.S. Government Printing Office, Washington, D.C., December 1984.

———. *Increasing Competition in the Natural Gas Market: The Second Report Required by Section 123 of the Natural Gas Policy Act of 1978*. U.S. Government Printing Office, Washington, D.C., January 1985.

———. *Natural Gas Monthly*. U.S. Government Printing Office, Washington, D.C., December 1984.

———. *Structures and Trends in Natural Gas Wellhead Contracts*. U.S. Government Printing Office, Washington, D.C., November 1983.

———. *Underground Natural Gas Storage in the United States, 1981–1982 Heating Year [April 1981-May 1982]*. U.S. Government Printing Office, Washington, D.C., August 1982.

U.S. House of Representatives, Committee on Energy and Commerce, Subcommittee on Fossil and Synthetic Fuels. *Hearings on Proposed Changes to Natural Gas Laws*. 98th Cong., 1st sess. Washington, D.C., Serial No. 98–30, pt. 3, 1983.

Wheelwright, Steven. ''Factory within a Factory.'' *Harvard Business Review*, 1982.

Comments

WAYNE D. JOHNSON
President
Entex, Inc.

This chapter takes dead aim at one of the key strategies that must be employed by natural gas marketers in a deregulating environment. Although most of us with day-to-day contact with the problem are unfamiliar with the term *differentiation* and would probably avoid the phrase as an essentially bloodless description of a life-and-death struggle, Frank Schuller used it to provide an apt description of a successful competitive technique that the regulated must quickly learn to exploit and whose dynamics regulators must learn to understand.

The dominant force in the gas industry today is competition. The development of competition can be traced to: (1) the decontrol of crude oil prices in 1981; (2) the supply-demand imbalances that materialized at the wellhead in 1982–1983; (3) the pipeline load loss that made pipelines willing to transport for others on a broad scale; (4) the political alliance between some producers and end users that led to pressure for mandatory carriage; and (5) to the FERC's recent Notice of Proposed Rulemaking. Competition is the irresistible force that has, at least in this decade, not met an immovable object.

One cannot understand competition and the need for differentiation without analyzing two variables that determine one's ability to compete: (1) gas cost and (2) margin above gas cost, or "spread." If either is out of sync, a firm cannot successfully compete.

It is important to note that since the beginnings of the industry, the gas cost for a particular pipeline or LDC has been set on a "rolled-in," or average cost, basis. That is, a weighted average cost of gas was computed by dividing the total dollars spent for all gas purchased by the total units sold. Schuller might describe such pricing as "undifferentiated." This system worked well from 1930 to 1980, when prices steadily moved upward. In general, producers of newly discovered gas received prices higher than the average of all purchases; this encouraged exploration at the margin. End users benefited because they paid average prices representing gas purchased at lower price levels over the years. The producers of older vintages of gas (which were subject to price and other controls) suffered in comparison.

The collapse of wellhead prices between 1983 and the present rendered the rolled-in pricing system obsolete. Newly discovered gas became available at prices well below the average gas cost of most pipelines. Because of take-or-pay obligations, many pipelines were unable to purchase significant volumes of new gas. In any event, they would not have been able to purchase a sufficient volume of new, cheap gas to reduce their weighted average cost of gas to the prices at which newly discovered gas was available. As a result, new entrants, such as brokers, mythical Hinshawed intrastate pipelines, and paper LDCs, were able to offer gas at prices far lower than their established competitors.

Pipelines quickly discovered that differentiation was the key to survival. A great variety of competitive techniques resulted from the need to compete with these new actors in the marketplace. All are designed to avoid noncompetitive weighted average cost of gas schemes by isolating a competitive source of gas in order to hold a competitive load. It is sometimes said that gas is marketed to such customers on a ''source specific'' basis, that is, that gas is priced at the cost of the specific source of gas for such customers, rather than on a rolled-in, weighted average-cost basis.

Among the early techniques used by pipelines to avoid their own weighted average costs were SMPs, under which lower-cost gas was made available by a pipeline to an LDC for resale to an end user who could shift to other energy sources. The D.C. Circuit Court, studiously ignorant of the irresistible forces of competition, struck down this highly useful tool for differentiation.

Notwithstanding this momentary setback, pipelines continue to develop other techniques for differentiation, some of which fit into the ''rose-by-any-other-name'' category. Discount gas, ''shadow pipeline'' gas, marketing-program gas, and transportation deals are all techniques designed to allow pipelines and LDCs to remain competitive with new entrants into the marketplace. These entrants enjoy a principal competitive advantage because they are not obligated to buy, either directly or through pipeline suppliers, any of the high-cost gas contracted during the period 1978–1983.

Pipelines and LDCs must also differentiate in terms of their margins, or spreads, above gas cost (whether gas cost is based on weighted average cost or is ''source specific''). Typically, utilities set rates for sales for resale and for sales to end users based on broad principles of utility law. Hundreds of thousands of pages of testimony at the FERC and its predecessor analyze the merits of various forms of demand-commodity rates, such as the Seaboard formula, the United method, and fixed-variable approaches. Although the desire for a low commodity cost was frequently a motivating factor in these debates as early as the late 1950s, primary emphasis in earlier times involved concerns about cost responsibility, equity, and like issues. The primary consideration in rate design is now competition, for it is the irresistible force. Demand-commodity rate schemes, however derived, may fail to permit the differentiation that a truly competitive marketplace requires. Pipeline rates may well be headed toward the flat, one-part rates that have long prevailed in the intrastate market.

LDCs, who traditionally have priced gas on a flat rate markup (somewhat complicated by blocking), increasingly will be required to differentiate in establishing their margins. Rate design for LDCs is dictated by the desire of regulators to maximize industrial margins in the interest of cross-subsidizing domestic rates. LDCs share this objective, provided that regulators grant them the flexibility both to make the rapid price adjustments necessary to maximize available margins and to adjust rates to remain competitive.

In the past, broad rate classifications were established under which many disparate customers were treated equally (except to the extent of any blocking contained in the rate schedule). This approach is totally inappropriate in today's highly competitive environment. It is obvious that there is no competition for some loads, that competition varies from area to area, and that competition varies in one area at different points in time. It is necessary that utilities be permitted to differentiate, or "discriminate," among customers who, although appearing similarly situated, are in fact distinguished by competitive circumstances. In this connection it should be noted that regulation does not prohibit "discrimination," only "*undue* discrimination." Competition has always been one of the factors that converts otherwise discriminatory conduct into action that is not unduly discriminatory. It is critical that regulators apply this concept to the present environment. If it is not, distribution utility loads will be lost to the brokers, the phony LDCs, the shadow pipelines, and other entities whose margins play no role in holding down the cost of service to consumers.

FRANK M. WEISSER
Principal
Morgan Stanley and Company, Inc.

As an investment banker for energy companies and a cofounder of Morgan Stanley's Natural Gas Clearinghouse, my comments on the responses of industry participants to deregulation in an environment of surplus supplies are based on observations as an outsider and financial consultant rather than as a day-to-day participant.

Current Natural Gas Environment

In the current political environment, the federal government and most regulatory bodies have acknowledged that free, competitive markets offer the best value for all consumers because of the rational allocation of resources and superior decision making that occur in the absence of distortive regulation. Policymakers who endorse these fundamental economic principles appear less concerned with devising regulation to promote public welfare than with providing a regulatory environment that allows the natural gas industry to enter free markets without chaos caused by distortive regulation from prior eras.

All market participants in the natural gas industry are currently grappling with far-reaching issues: the last stages of a natural gas surplus artificially induced by the Organization of Petroleum Exporting Countries (OPEC)-established world energy prices, the subsequent plummeting of world oil prices as OPEC lost control, the evolution of a Reagan era-inspired deregulation of the industry most recently manifested in the FERC Order 436 and effective decontrol of natural gas prices, and a new Canadian government's commitment to increase gas exports. Normal market reactions to these events have been exacerbated by the overreaction to regulation-induced shortages in the lower price era of the recent past. Examples of this distortion include uneconomic long-term take-or-pay gas contracts entered into by pipelines that feared they might run out of gas and excessively leveraged producers seeking to develop gas reserves, including deep gas priced arbitrarily high by NGPA regulation.

Producer/Pipeline Reactions

Selling practices were changed less by producers than by pipelines, which altered their purchasing practices in response to this environment. Producers generally did not initiate price cuts or seek to avoid long-term contracts by selling into a developing spot market. Instead, these changes were induced by the pipeline industry reacting to its surplus contract position and painfully learning the wisdom of seeking to retain market share originally through SMPs, which have been struck down by the courts as discriminatory, and now through transportation of spot gas for others and formation of their own unregulated brokerage subsidiaries.

Most pipelines have escaped from potential take-or-pay losses relatively cheaply, generally at around ten cents on the dollar. This can be attributed at least partially to the independent nature of a fragmented producer industry that chose not to pool individual limited financial resources to pursue legal remedies aggressively as a group. Even large producers, who set the pattern for take-or-pay settlements, have exercised their somewhat better bargaining position independently.

Crude oil and natural gas liquid product markets offer evidence that a more open, unregulated market can restore financing availability without fixed price contracts, provided some minimum-take assurances can be restored into long-term contracts. Oil markets benefit more from being world commodities with visible market prices than they do from being more freely marketable than natural gas. A deregulated, relatively open market for North American natural gas should mirror world oil markets more closely both in relative price (adjusted for transportation differentials), as well as in other functional characteristics.

New Entrants and New Strategies

Pipelines are entering a post-Order 436 era by tying acceptance of nondiscriminatory transport provisions to the FERC approval of contract settlements negotiated between the pipelines and their customers or producers. Because the FERC instituted contract demand reductions without decreasing take-or-pay obligations, the post–436 environment will be somewhat of a hybrid versus the open environment envisioned by the order, as each pipeline electing open carriage chooses to interpret and apply 436 differently. Astute producers and pipelines are embracing aggressively a marketing mentality that places great emphasis on maintaining markets by keeping "customers" on both ends of the pipeline happy through creative rate design, unbundling services, and expanded knowledge of the ultimate consumer on the part of both pipelines and producers.

The most dramatic changes are occurring through mergers and acquisitions in both the pipeline and the producer sectors. Pipelines have been consolidating in order to reach new markets and new supply areas and hope to justify premiums paid through enhanced operating flexibility and reduced overhead. Producers are realizing that there is no economic justification to assume exploration risks for gas at costs in excess of $1.50 per million Btu when it can be acquired for less than $0.75 per million Btu in a market environment in which spot gas sells below $1.50 at the wellhead. The damage to the industry's infrastructure caused by a sustained halt to drilling activities in an environment where world oil surpluses will last longer than the domestic gas bubble may actually shrink the natural gas markets in favor of fuel oil in the balance of the 1980s.

The creation of brokers and marketing companies, both affiliated and unaffiliated with pipelines, serves to enhance the open-market environment and utilizes the capacity of unaffiliated pipelines better. Pipelines traditionally knew very little about their ultimate customers beyond the local distribution companies, but they are learning fast. The unaffiliated entities, such as the Natural Gas Clearinghouse (a wholly owned subsidiary of Morgan Stanley no longer affiliated with any of its original six pipeline partners), rely for their competitive edge on their ability to attract aggressive and experienced personnel from the industry rather than on physical ownership of pipeline facilities. These organizations approach the market without the constraint of a priority to fill their own pipelines but with a national market mentality. These new entrants and the response of traditional participants have increased the nontraditional, or spot, market to 30–40 percent of all gas flowing in the United States.

Regulatory Response

A casual look at a natural gas pipeline map of the United States would lead one quickly to conclude that the long-haul gas pipelines have no more of a natural monopoly than do oil or product pipelines. The extent of possible fuel substitution likely will provide assurance that the few apparent monopolies cannot operate as such in a deregulated environment.

The only regulatory bodies directly concerned with residential consumers are the state PUCs. These customers, who have limited short-term alternatives to natural gas, exercise their collective market power through regulated public utilities. This is probably the only area in which continued regulation is justified, and it should become even simpler after a transition period. Complex regulation is unresponsive to the dynamics of competitive markets. Since the primary form of regulation is based on rates of return, PUC focus should be on both facilitating the proper reallocation of costs in rates to different customer groups based on the value of added investment and promoting consolidation where utility enterprises are too fragmented to serve their customers efficiently in a free market environment.

Ultimately, the concern of regulators should be to accelerate the removal of constraints that inhibit market forces and to help the natural gas industry reestablish normal activity. If this is not done, sustained regulatory-induced demand dislocations may damage the industry's infrastructure and create future environments of shortage that may tempt regulators to reimpose dislocating regulation and price controls.

9

The Role of Regulation in Risk Allocation

CARMEN D. LEGATO

The concept of ''risk'' is most often thought of as a danger or hazard that accompanies a gamble or speculative investment. In fact, however, risk is a basic and unavoidable component in every economic transaction. In the gas industry, risk to a buyer means either: (1) having to pay a price that proves to be higher or lower than available alternatives or (2) agreeing to buy a quantity that proves to be more or less than the buyer requires. Risk to a seller means either: (1) having to make sales at prices that turn out to be lower or higher than were anticipated or (2) being unable to sell or produce the quantities that were developed and into which costs are sunk.

Consider, for example, a local distribution company (LDC) that would like to obtain supplies at the lowest price possible and in sufficient quantities to meet all demands it faces. To achieve the latter objective, the LDC quite reasonably could seek out opportunities to tie up long-term guarantees of gas. In so doing, however, the LDC has to make commitments of its own to the sellers of gas; in particular, the LDC may have to offer to pay certain prices or to guarantee that it will purchase a specified minimum level of the contracted volumes of gas. Once contracts with these characteristics are signed, and the LDC is locked in, the marketplace may take unexpected turns. Consequently, the LDC may have to buy gas under long-term contracts at prices considerably above contemporaneous market prices. The results are real and sometimes painful monetary losses for either the LDC or its customers. The consequences of these losses are some combination of diminished earnings for the affected LDC, angry ratepayers, loss of market share, and charges of imprudence before the company's Public Utility Commission (PUC). At the extreme, contracts that turn out to be out of line with market conditions may force contract renegotiation, contract abrogation, and bankruptcy. In short, one aspect of bearing risk is the possibility of losing money—or at least of not making as much money as investors had hoped.

Another aspect of bearing risk is the possibility of making more money than investors had expected. In the case of the LDC with a fixed-cost contract, if the market prices exceed the contract price, those bearing the risk of the fluctuation (in this instance the ratepayers) are enriched by acquiring the product at a price below its current production cost.

Now consider a producer trying to decide where and how to sell its gas. It may be facing anxious LDCs or pipelines who expect shortages and are willing to pay what appear to be premiums above current and expected market prices or who may be willing to commit to taking guaranteed volumes of gas over extended periods. This producer nevertheless is at risk because, for example, if a long-term contract is accepted, it may turn out that what appear to be premiums at the time of negotiation are in fact far below the market prices that later develop. The producer then finds itself forced to sell gas at less than the prevailing market price. Alternatively, the producer who eschews a long-term contract may encounter prices that turn out to be much lower than the premiums that might have been offered by buyers. The consequence of the fluctuations in price levels is that revenues may be either insufficient or much more than sufficient to cover investments that have been made and that were expected by investors.

Investments in all segments of the natural gas industry—extraction, transmission, and distribution—carry substantial risk. They are long lived, capital intensive, and, once in place, sunk and cannot be redeployed elsewhere. Investors must earn their return over a long period during which unforeseen events may produce wide fluctuations in returns. Regulation and private contracts allocate these risks.

Aspects of risk allocation in contracts include price-change clauses (indefinite escalators, market-outs) and supply/purchase requirements (e.g., take-or-pay terms). Aspects of risk allocation in regulation include minimum bills, demand charge tariffs, and, at the extreme, laws govering reorganization and bankruptcy.

The risks encountered in gas markets are not totally avoidable. They reflect in part the fact that it is not possible to foresee how much gas the market will demand and at what prices, or how much supply will be produced and at what prices. To the extent that contract, regulation, or industry structure do not allocate risks to those parties that are best able to avoid, minimize, or otherwise dampen their blow or to diversify unavoidable risks at least cost, economic efficiency will be impaired. To the extent that this objective is not met, cases will arise in which gas is transacted at prices and in quantities that are out of balance with underlying supply and demand conditions, investors will shy away from the gas market, and customers will be less willing to install gas-using equipment.

In theory, a competitive market allocates risk efficiently because competition prompts purchasers and sellers to negotiate the least-cost distribution of risk. However, ideal circumstances do not exist in the natural gas industry. Since LDCs and pipelines possess market power, they require continued regulation. But regulation has reduced efficiency by imposing or permitting inefficient distribution of risk and by creating incentives that caused regulated companies to negotiate inefficient allocations of risk. The task of public policy is to ensure that the gas market's institutions and practices do not misallocate risk. This chapter examines existing distributions of risk in the natural gas industry and appropriate public policy responses to it.

Existing patterns of risk allocation in natural gas production and marketing are outdated and inefficient and largely reflect conditions existing before the Natural Gas Policy Act of 1978 (NGPA). After the NGPA, which deregulated prices for gas developed after 1977, pipelines signed many contracts that placed on them the risks that natural gas might decline in value or markets shrink, while producers stood to gain should prices increase above their current investment costs. Regulation, in turn, allowed pipelines to transfer these risks, together with the risk that pipeline facilities would be underutilized, to LDCs. The LDCs also were allowed to shift their business risks to captive consumers. One result among many was that regulation stifled competition in the pipeline and producer markets and impaired the free flow of price signals.

With the elimination of ''wellhead'' price controls for half of the current gas supply, the industry now faces a new, more competitive, and more volatile market. Gas prices must be able to fluctuate rapidly to respond to competition from other fuels. Many large consumers can switch between gas and fuel oil in as little as thirty minutes. These customers will not absorb the risk that production properties or pipeline facilities might not earn expected returns. They will simply leave the gas market if the price becomes too high. But such risks can be shifted to the majority of end-use markets (some 70 percent) that cannot switch fuels without expensive equipment changes. This fact poses important policy questions of fairness and economic efficiency.

This analysis concludes that the new competitive market demands new methods of risk allocation. Three principal regulatory changes would improve efficiency in risk allocation:

1. Regulation should permit broader participation in short-term contracts and futures markets for gas supplies.
2. Regulations that artificially encourage or require long-term contracts for dedicated reserves of gas should be revised.
3. Regulation should allocate more of the risk of loss and opportunity for gain on transmission and distribution investments to investors in pipelines and LDCs and away from consumers, who are the least efficient bearers of risk.

Existing Patterns of Risk Allocation

The Period 1978 to 1985

The natural gas industry historically has had a tripartite structure: producers, pipelines, and distributors. Producers explored for and developed gas, which was sold to pipeline companies under long-term contracts lasting from seven to twenty-five years. Pipelines sold and delivered gas to LDCs under long-term agreements, generally lasting for twenty-five years. LDCs did not have long-term contracts with consumers but, like pipelines, sold and delivered gas on a bundled basis.

The producer/pipeline relationship was rigidly defined by the terms of their contracts. Most contracts contained ''dedicated-reserve'' provisions, under which all gas developed from particular wells had to be sold to the pipeline. Take-or-pay clauses and minimum-take requirements established the pipeline's obligations to accept or pay for available supply, usually defined as a percentage of ''deliverability.''

Prices that initially were fixed but were subject to escalation under two types of indefinite escalators were prevalent: (1) oil-parity clauses, which established the escalated price by reference to the price of an alternative fuel; and (2) most-favored-nation (MFN) clauses of various types. A *two-party MFN* gives the producer the right to take the highest price paid by the purchaser, either under other contracts in the same producing area, in one or more producing states, or in the continental United States. A *three-party MFN* gives the producer the right to take the highest price paid by any purchaser in defined areas as large as three states.

Most contracts in this period provided for escalation but not deescalation, and few had market-out or similar price-adjustment provisions. Thus all of the risk that the commodity value of gas would decline was borne by pipelines.

The pipelines, in turn, had nearly total freedom to transfer this risk to LDCs. Due to the lack of alternative means of transporting gas, LDCs generally could not obtain gas from other sources. In addition, under some regulated service agreements between pipelines and LDCs, ''sole-source clauses'' prohibited LDCs from purchasing from other pipelines. In any case, minimum-bill or demand-charge tariffs made switching suppliers prohibitively costly.

As is true today, the prices interstate pipelines paid for gas were automatically passed through to LDCs by the Federal Energy Regulatory Commission (FERC) without regard to the prudence of the pipeline's purchasing practices. The NGPA gave pipelines a ''guaranteed passthrough,'' without regulatory lag, ''absent fraud or abuse.'' The FERC construed the fraud and abuse standard of the NGPA to apply only in cases of ''serious impropriety.''

Risks associated with pipelines were also passed downstream with little scrutiny by the FERC. If a pipeline's traffic and hence revenues declined for reasons other than weather, such as conservation or fuel switching, the pipeline simply filed a new rate case, declared a lower sales volume, and collected higher rates per unit of sales.

LDCs enjoyed a similar freedom to transfer risks. Higher gas and pipeline costs typically were passed on to customers by adjustment clauses.[1] When an LDC's throughput declined for reasons other than weather, it, too, could file new higher rates to recover fixed costs. The net effect of these rules was to shift all of the upward price risk to consumers.

These risk-allocation measures have had severe social-equity and allocative-efficiency consequences. Apparently, the measures apply only when prices are rising. When fuel-oil prices fell relative to gas prices, the one-way ratchet escalators described above did not allow gas prices to fall. Instead, a number of pipelines and LDCs automatically passed on prices to consumers in excess of the commodity value of gas. Consumers reacted by conserving gas, and many who could switch to oil did so. This confronted pipelines with declining markets; furthermore, because many had seriously overestimated demand, their exposure to take-or-pay obligations was increased.

Pipelines initially reacted by cutting back on the contracts with the greatest take-or-pay flexibility. Unfortunately, those contracts were also the lowest-price contracts. As a result, average costs increased further and prices eligible for automatic passthrough jumped again. The spiral continued as pipelines filed higher rates to recover fixed costs lost by reduced throughput volumes, thus driving up rates to consumers and inducing still greater throughput losses. The same process happened at the LDC level.

Producers responded by demanding that pipelines buy at the volumes and prices for which they had contracted. Average-cost pricing blunted the effect of diminished throughput on price signals; indeed, producers selling the lowest cost gas often were those most shut in. Newly developed gas priced at market levels was shut in, and consumers willing to use gas at a market price pursued less satisfying alternatives. Due to the lagged response of residential and commercial demand to price increases, the above-market prices have the effect of depressing demand artificially and reducing allocative efficiency for years into the future.

Responding to these circumstances, the FERC in July 1983 created experimental "special marketing programs" (SMPs) that authorized pipelines for a two-year trial period to transport market-priced gas sold directly by producers to end users on a flexible basis. These experimental programs and above-market prices led to the rise of the so-called spot market. But the FERC allowed pipelines to operate these programs on a discriminatory basis, excluding customers that lacked fuel-switching ability and hence were otherwise captive to the pipeline's sales, even at above-market prices.

These programs partially improved economic efficiency by stemming the loss of fuel-switchable loads. But the discriminatory eligibility rules created an escape valve through which accumulated competitive pressures were bled off without transmitting market signals to producers that the prices to the captive market (some 70 percent) were too high; the discriminatory program thereby forestalled the broader realignment of contracts with lower priced market conditions.

It is clear that the producer/pipeline contracts and the FERC regulation failed both to allocate supply to its highest uses or to send accurate quantity and price signals to producing and consuming markets. Pipelines, perceiving the additional supply security associated with high levels of reserve additions, negotiated for reserve cushions with the expectation that the cost would be borne by producers. Producers, perceiving an opportunity to increase profits by accelerating production, increased current deliverability at the expense of future deliverability, despite the unavailability of current demand sufficient to meet those production levels.

Dedicated reserve provisions also constrained the realignment of contracts with market conditions. Shut-in producers sought to sell their shut-in production elsewhere at a lower price but often were unable to do so because pipelines refused to release the gas from their contracts. When they did, only current deliverability for a short period was released.

Regulatory Developments Affecting Risk Allocation in the Post–1985 Period

In October 1985 the FERC issued comprehensive new regulations governing the transportation of gas by pipelines. Participating pipeline companies are now authorized to transport gas for LDCs and end users on a nondiscriminatory basis. The new rules proscribe tariff conditions permissible under the experimental programs, by which transportation of lower-priced gas can be withheld to preclude displacing a pipeline's own sales of higher-priced gas. The new rules are intended to promote competition. However, an important limitation is that the entire program is voluntary: A pipeline can avoid competition if it provides no transportation to end users or no new transportation to LDCs after October 1985. The voluntary nature of the program stems from the FERC's perceived lack of authority to impose a comprehensive carriage requirement on pipelines. Its statutory authority is limited to proscribing discrimination in carriage voluntarily undertaken by pipelines.

The FERC also introduced "optional-expedited" certificate authority to construct new facilities and provide new services if a pipeline accepts the risks and rewards of fluctuations in throughput; again, this program is optional. However, here the FERC has authority to compel all pipeline services to be regulated on that basis.

In 1984 the FERC issued rules prohibiting pipelines from collecting gas costs as part of the minimum bills often charged to LDCs. This change will have the effect of promoting competition for wholesale sales to LDCs served by more than one pipeline.

Principles of Risk Allocation

The risks associated with an investment relate to variations in potential returns. The greater the range of potential rewards, the greater the risk. Firms generally prefer steady, predictable returns over broadly dispersed returns having the same average value. This explains the prevalence of transactions in which one party incurs real costs to diversify or ensure against risk. Acceptance of the administrative costs of insurance coverage illustrates this willingness to incur added costs to ensure more regular outcomes.

Under ideal competitive conditions, voluntary contracts distribute risks and compensation in a socially efficient manner. The less efficient bearer of a particular risk shifts compensation to the more efficient bearer of risk. By doing so, the contract increases the value to both parties.

Where market imperfections exist, however, this process may be socially inefficient. As discussed above, this was the case when producers, pipelines, and LDCs shifted production risks to consumers. Rate regulation of pipelines and LDCs can improve allocative efficiency by preventing the charging of monopoly prices for transmission and distribution services, but regulation will not completely achieve efficiency unless it also encourages efficient allocations of risk.

Specifically, regulation should create incentives to allocate risks that mimic the results of an efficiently operating market:

1. Regulatory policies should encourage the development of market institutions and ratemaking procedures that will induce participants in each sector (producer, pipeline, LDC) to bear the risks of financial losses over which they can exert control.
2. Risks that are beyond practical control should be allocated to the party that can bear or diversify those risks at the lowest cost.
3. Specific risks that are partially in the control of both parties should be divided among the parties.[2]

Analysis of Risk Allocation in the Natural Gas Industry

This section analyzes the sources of potential variations in returns associated with fixed investments in extraction, transmission, and distribution and determines which of the four sectors—producers, pipelines, LDCs, or consumers—can bear at the least cost the risks of these fluctuations.

Investments in Production

Sources of Risk

Investment risk in the exploration and development of natural gas relates principally to the relationship of the market value of gas to the initial investment cost over the life of the well.

The principal components of the initial investment are: the ''finding cost'' of locating successful wells and the cost of developing proven reserves. These costs must be recovered over the life of the well, usually five to fifteen years. Once these costs are sunk, the return on investment will fluctuate with unforseeable changes in market prices.

Another risk is the potential of opportunistic behavior by monopsonistic pipelines.[3] After investments have been sunk, a pipeline with monopsony power can appropriate some of the returns the producer otherwise would earn on its investment (unless prevented from doing so by contract or by regulation). Fixed-price contracts and most-favored-nation and take-or-pay clauses are intended in part to prevent opportunism under a regulatory regime in which a producer cannot be assured of obtaining transportation over monopsony facilities.

Comparative Cost to Minimize and Diversify Risk

Some of these risks can be controlled and some cannot. Producers, pipelines, LDCs, and consumers all lack control over cyclical conditions, the actions of foreign governments, weather, and other such factors affecting the demand for gas. There are classes of risk, however, that can be managed by producers, although not by pipelines, LDCs, or consumers.[4] The skillful exploration, development, and operation of gas fields will permit individual producers to enjoy favorable levels of cost relative to industry averages. Placing the risk of performance on producers for the risks associated with fluctuations of these returns serves the crucial economic function of rewarding only those with the greatest skills, thus encouraging them to remain in the gas-producing business.

Producers can spread the risk of fluctuations less expensively than can regulated pipelines and LDCs. Theoretically, a pipeline or LDC could charge sufficiently high prices for gas when demand is robust to offset their financial exposure when end-use market prices drop below wholesale cost. But these levels would have to be established in regulatory proceedings, thereby adding significant expense.

Consumers are the least able to spread and diversify risks. If consumers were to bear production investment risks, there would be wide fluctuations in the value of their gas-burning appliances within several years. Consumers change residences infrequently enough that these fluctuations would not even out. Because they engage in fewer transactions, consumers cannot spread the risks over the business cycle as inexpensively as can the producer. For these reasons, the risk of fluctuations in the value of production investments should be borne by producers, provided a mechanism can be established by which such fluctuations can occur without opportunism risk.

However, producers are not necessarily the most efficient bearers of supply risks. The take-or-pay level establishes permissible limits of fluctuations in cash flow to the producer. Economic efficiency is furthered by take-or-pay clauses, since without them, the primary factor affecting the level of takes would be the actions of another party—the pipeline company—that may regulate takes for its own reasons. For example, absent take-or-pay clauses, one would expect a pipeline to contract for volumes much greater than their expected demand, since the added supply security would have no costs to the pipeline, even though removing that supply from the market is costly to society.

The supply risks to pipelines arising from take-or-pay clauses will be reduced if prices to producers are allowed to fluctuate with supply and demand conditions.

Prices would reflect any discount below the long-run equilibrium price that producers as a whole offer in view of surplus conditions. Thus a producer with a high take-or-pay variable-price contract might achieve a greater ratio of deliveries to deliverability than one without such a contract, although the price risk the producer bore would insulate the pipeline from significant overall exposure. In contrast, under fixed-price contracts, take-or-pay clauses impose substantial risks on pipelines. These risks cannot be borne efficiently by producers, distributors, or consumers; only the pipeline or other seller of gas can determine the optimal ratio of supply to expected demand. For efficiency reasons, regulation should not insulate pipelines from the consequences of imprudent purchasing decisions.

To summarize, fixed-price contracts are inefficient because they shift production risks from producers, the most efficient risk bearers, to pipelines and ultimately to consumers, the least efficient risk bearers. The monopsony power of pipelines underscores the need for a contractual price floor and take-or-pay protection for producers against opportunistic behavior by pipelines. Regulation that dissipates this monopsony power (such as open access to pipeline transportation) would eliminate the need for contractual price floors and reduce the need for and risks of take-or-pay provisions.

Investments in Pipelines and Distribution Facilities

Sources of Risk

The value of pipeline and LDC investments fluctuates with conditions that affect capacity utilization. When pipelines or distribution facilities are used to a high percentage of their capacity, the returns on investment will be the greatest, decreasing continuously with declining use.

Throughput will be affected by both changes in supply and in demand. For example, if finding costs for new gas supplies increase, gas prices would increase, reducing demand and hence throughput. Throughput also will be affected by the prices of competing fuels and the efficiencies of gas-burning appliances relative to other appliances. The depressing effect of higher prices on demand may be offset by greater efficiency in gas appliances and economic growth. Other factors affecting throughput include technological developments and cyclical conditions.

The value of investments in pipelines is more significantly affected by changes in regional economic conditions than is the value of investments in production. Pipelines serving regional markets therefore face greater risk from regional changes than production companies whose gas flows to numerous regions of the country. LDC investments are subject to the same fluctuations as pipeline investments but are more sensitive to shifts in regional economic performance.

Comparative Cost to Minimize and Diversify Risks

Risks affecting pipeline and LDC investments include those that are controllable and those that are not. Some of these risks can be affected by the investors and owners of pipelines and LDCs, and these risks cannot be affected by the actions of any other sector of the gas industry. For example, those who supply capital are in the best position to investigate the likelihood that the proposed investment in facilities will earn expected returns over the life of the investment, skillfully channeling investment to areas with the best prospects for growth. Managers also can maximize returns through aggressive marketing efforts and cost cutting.

Consumers and producers are in a poor position to do this. The transactions costs for consumers and producers are higher than for pipelines and LDCs, as are the costs for consumers and producers to ensure (through contracts) that the facilities are operated in a manner that maximizes throughput.

Similarly, regulation is a poor surrogate for the self-interest of pipeline and LDC managers that would exist if pipeline and LDC investors bore the risk of fluctuations in performance. Self-interest would induce prudent investment and operating decisions. Suppliers of equity and debt capital are better equipped than regulators to determine whether the potential returns justify the risks.

The idea that regulation is inferior to capital markets in assessing potential returns cuts against the grain of conventional wisdom. Entry and exit regulation of pipelines, for example, in part reflects the view that regulation can and should seek to provide stable returns to investors and screen and preclude investments that are likely to cause ''losses'' to consumers. But even accepting for sake of argument the traditional view that regulation can perform the screening function as well as or better than capital markets, this does not take into account that investors can spread and diversify risk at lower costs than can consumers.

Pipelines and LDCs can spread risks better than can consumers because, for example, periods of economic recession may be balanced by periods of economic growth that help to balance returns over a period of years. In contrast, the individual consumer who must bear the lower returns on investments when throughput is diminished may live elsewhere when throughput is increased and the value of investments increases.

As was the case with the comparative advantages of diversification between producers and consumers, investors in utilities can also diversify risks at lower costs than can consumers. Regionally focused companies can diversify geographically through merger or acquisition. There is little cost for investors in utilities to diversify risks through portfolio management of publicly traded securities. Even investors in companies not publicly traded can diversify at little cost by making investments in publicly traded companies with offsetting risks.

It should be noted, however, that although there is little cost to the investor to diversify risks through portfolio management, there is a cost associated with bearing the risk of wider fluctuations. An investment subject to broad fluctuations will require a higher return than one that offers the same average earnings with less dispersion in the returns. Pipelines that diversify geographically, therefore, may achieve a lower cost of capital than more regionally focused companies.

Similarly, capital costs in industries with similar levels of risk will be lower for companies that are diversified in industries in which the risks are somewhat offsetting.[5] Regardless of whether a utility is geographically diversified or diversified in different lines of business or whether its shareholders diversify risk through portfolio management, it will be less expensive for the utility investors to spread and diversify risks than it will be for consumers.

Conclusions

Consumers are the least efficient bearers of risks associated with fluctuations in investments in production, transmission, and distribution. Therefore, in addition to the traditional goal of preventing pipelines and LDCs from exercising market power by charging monopoly prices to consumers, regulation also should prevent them from shifting risk to the consumer. Conversely, regulation should not seek to protect consumers or producers from changes in market prices. Fluctuations in market prices are necessary to equilibrate markets to achieve efficient levels of investment.

New Marketing Institutions Are Essential to Achieve Efficiency

This section argues that reliance on long-term contracts between producers and pipelines increases risks and costs and impedes development of more efficient market mechanisms (like spot and futures markets). If greater competition were introduced, the development of large-volume, short-term contract and futures markets would establish reliable market prices to which longer-term contracts could be referenced. This would permit a more efficient allocation of production risks to producers while protecting them from the monopsony power of pipelines—the principal, original impetus for long-term contracts.

Exclusive Reliance on Long-Term Contracts Is No Longer Efficient[6]

An enterprise that requires large investments in specialized capital gives rise to the potential for opportunistic behavior after the capital is invested. This in turn encourages the use of long-term contracts to protect the agreed-upon allocation of risks. The length of the contract is related to the useful life of the specialized capital. When there is significant potential for opportunistic behavior, long-term contracts reduce risks to an acceptable level, permitting investments to be made.[7]

However, long-term contracts can involve substantial costs. As the length of a contract increases, so does the difficulty of specifying the possible changes in economic circumstances that could affect the willingness of each party to perform as promised. Thus negotiation of long-term contracts imposes higher information, transaction, and enforcement costs than is the case with shorter-term contracts.

If buyers and sellers were able to contract for gas deliveries under short-term contracts, rather than for dedicated reserves, the supply risk to purchasers would be reduced, since they could contract for a more predictable quantity of gas. A shorter period (e.g., two to four years) also would allow producers to alter production rates and shift sales among purchasers to meet market demands. Because the purchaser would not have a call on reserves, producers could determine the rate of current production based on market supply, demand, and price. By controlling the disposition of deliveries without the restrictions of dedicated reserve contracts, they could also meet peak demand more efficiently. A significant market for short-term deliverability also would permit gas to flow more easily to its highest valued uses.

The development of a more significant short-term contract market has been frustrated, in part, by the refusal of pipelines to release gas under dedicated reserve contracts for resale to others. If dedicated reserve contracts were replaced with contracts for gas deliveries, spot-market prices could efficiently allocate supplies. Producers could decide how much gas to bring to market and how fast to develop and market reserves in accordance with economic conditions, including the cost of developing underground storage.

Another inefficiency of long-term dedicated reserve contracts is their contribution to the high costs associated with delays in passing through price signals. Because market prices are not published, other mechanisms are necessary to ensure that producers receive reliable information on market prices. The MFN and indefinite escalator clauses used to achieve this goal are cumbersome to monitor and difficult to enforce.

The MFN clauses require pipelines to pay the same price other producers are receiving in specified producing regions. Determining whether a new contract contains the same nonprice terms as existing contracts must be done on a contract-by-contract basis.[8] When new contracts continually and frequently are being negotiated, efforts to comply with MFN strictures are complicated by the overlapping of MFN areas and by the fact that in any given MFN area there are any number of producers and pipelines, resulting in multiple rounds of reoffers. Because the pipeline has most of the information, the opportunities for cheating are rife and have led to elaborate efforts by producers to exchange information to protect their rights under the agreement.

Indefinite escalator clauses also are inefficient; they attempt to approximate the long-run equilibrium price but ignore short-run market conditions. Oil-parity clauses in effect between 1978 and 1983 failed to achieve equilibrium, a defect pipelines recently sought to ameliorate by renegotiating periodically the oil-parity benchmark in light of changed market conditions. However, these clauses cannot facilitate adjustments to short-run conditions in gas markets. Prices that reflect short-run fluctuations in supply and demand for gas are essential to achieve efficient market clearing. Oil-parity clauses are ill suited to this purpose.

Alternative Market Structures

Allowing alternatives to the principal reliance on rigid contract terms will lead to new, more efficient market developments. Essential for these developments is open access to pipeline transportation and competition in the marketing of gas. *Open access* refers to a regulatory regime under which pipelines are required to provide transportation services and to do so on a nondiscriminatory basis (based on available capacity); pipelines would be permitted to compete in the marketing of gas on an equal basis with nonregulated marketers. Open access would eliminate monopsony power of pipelines and allow (but not require) producers and consumers to rely on short-term markets to satisfy a substantial portion of their requirements to market and buy gas. Under open access, new market mechanisms could flourish.

Short-Term Contract Markets

Short-term markets are essential to establish published prices that can be used in formulating long-term contracts. Price discovery is essential to equilibrate markets efficiently, and extensive, freely accessible short-term markets allow relatively low-cost and high-quality price discovery to replace the cumbersome oil parity and MFN mechanisms. Given open transportation, producers would not need to establish price floors to protect against opportunism, thereby allowing the allocation of price risks to producers, who are the most efficient bearers of such risks.

A sizeable and reliable short-term contract market will also help to shift supply to where it is most needed. This will ensure both that no higher-valued users are deprived of gas and that producers receive true market value for their supply.

Futures Markets

Futures markets provide an additional and superior price-discovery mechanism to complement short-term markets, because of greater participation: Futures markets, unlike short-term contract markets, attract investors not directly engaged in production or marketing. In addition, futures markets operate as centralized exchanges, which, like securities markets, make the market more accessible and participation less costly. A commodity futures market also permits producers and product handlers to shift risks to speculators through "hedging" (an investment strategy aimed at minimizing risk that involves an investor holding equal but opposite positions in both a spot and a futures market). Efficiency is furthered because the price the speculator demands for bearing the risk will be less than the risk premium that would be demanded by the hedger. A futures market in natural gas—one is pending approval by the Commodity

Futures Trading Commission (CFTC)—would contribute to more efficient risk allocation.[9]

Independent Resellers and Brokers

In the oil industry, approximately five hundred independent brokers buy and resell oil and serve a market-making function. The current number of brokers in the gas industry is much smaller, but given more open transportation policies, many more may arise. This additional competition should improve performance and reduce costs.

Long-Term Contracts

Two- to five-year contracts for gas deliveries will become much more prevalent with pricing terms tied to published benchmarks of short-term contract or futures-market prices. Longer-term contracts for dedicated reserves also may retain a significant role. The principal advantage of such contracts would be to reduce transaction costs. But in a market in which supply and demand conditions rapidly change, marketeers may view the rigidity of such contracts as a serious offsetting disadvantage and hence limit the extent to which they rely on them in a portfolio of contracts.

Principal Reliance on Long-Term Contracts to Allocate Production Risks Is Outmoded

Long-term contracts arose from regulatory and industry conditions that no longer exist in the industry. The potential for gas to be traded as a commodity is supported by comparing the gas industry to other industries in which short-term contracts and organized markets are prevalent and those in which private long-term output or requirement contracts are prevalent.

The principal impetus for long-term output contracts was that the producer's investments were inextricably tied to a long-term agreement with a particular pipeline, because of monopsony power and lack of an open transportation requirement. However, because "pipeline quality" gas is a fungible commodity and the transportation system is now adequately developed for gas to be sold interchangeably in numerous city-gate markets, an open transportation regulatory regime can eliminate this market constraint.

First, natural gas is a commercially homogeneous and fungible commodity. This distinguishes it from commodities such as coal. Coal is principally traded under long-term contracts because its myriad variations in quality and application (for example, heat content, ash content, sulfur content, and so forth) require investment in specialized capital. Thus long-term contracts are necessary to prevent opportunistic behavior once power plants are constructed to use a particular type of coal purchased from a particular source.

Second, most natural gas is located in areas with access to trunklines that serve multiple major consuming markets. For example, much of the Southwest is served by pipelines that also serve a majority of the major consuming states.

Vast Canadian reserves are accessible through pipelines to many of the same market areas in the Midwest and Northwest, and New England is not far behind in gaining such access. This national pipeline network provides the potential to trade gas as a commodity, rather than on a dedicated reserve basis.

The rapid development of short-term contract markets from 1983–1985 is strong evidence of this potential. Transaction costs for these sales were reasonable, usually 1 to 2 percent of the commodity value (delivered). This experience supports the conclusion that the transportation network—even constrained by pipelines' refusal to transport gas that would displace their own sales—can support a significant amount of short-term trading.[10]

The next consideration is whether long-term output contracts are required by features endemic to consumers. One such feature is the security requirements of "high-priority" uses: to heat homes, hospitals, and schools. In markets for necessities such as fuel oil, food, housing, and critical medical supplies, public policy has not interfered with reliance on short-term contracts. There is no reason to believe that in industries not characterized by relation-specific capital investments, long-term contracts could equilibrate markets more efficiently than shorter-term contracts. Concerns about major supply shortages are understandable under rigid wellhead price controls but less so under wellhead price deregulation.

The natural gas industry can weather supply shortages without adversely affecting human health, safety, and welfare. In the late 1970s, an era marked by oil-market imbalances caused by a half-regulated, half-free market, an oil embargo, and the absence of a strategic petroleum reserve, the interstate gas market witnessed only spotty and brief shortages to the highest priority consumers. In fact, about 34 perecent of the total gas-consuming market could switch to residual fuel oil before commercial and residential markets were affected.[11] This buffer will allow for price efficiently to bid gas away from fuel-switchable boilers to nonswitchable users without affecting service to high-priority users. Even assuming a failure of the market to allocate supplies efficiently, there is stand-by regulatory authority under federal and state law to allocate gas based on health and safety criteria.

The "security" rationale assumes that long-term contracts protect against any price run-ups that may occur during shortages. But recent history shows this to be false. For example, the oil-parity and MFN clauses under long-term contracts for deregulated gas permitted rapid, quantum price increases from 1978 to 1983 for gas committed to the interstate market. Only fixed-price contracts can prevent the contract price from reflecting the market value of gas. But fixed-price contracts impose a corresponding risk that under surplus conditions prices will exceed market value, creating the same "harm" to consumers as if they were exposed to price increases during shortages.

A related misconception is that prices "spike" (move rapidly up and down) more under short-term than under long-term contracts. The opposite is true. "Spiking" is associated with small markets that magnify shifts in supply and demand, causing prices well above the new equilibrium price. Thus when a Texas intrastate pipeline company needed more gas to serve high-priority markets than was available from new wells, its bidding had the effect of driving up the contract price to all other pipelines in Texas, due to MFN clauses. When the lower-valued users shift off gas, shutting in gas supplies to all other pipelines, the shut-in gas is not available for sale to that pipeline because it is dedicated to other pipelines. Only more development or conservation could equilibrate the market (which could take three or more years). This could only occur because (1) the long-term dedicated reserve contracts prevented the higher-valued uses of the pipeline from bidding away gas supply from lower-valued uses of all other pipelines; and (2) the prevalence of MFN contracts.

Under short-term contracts, the spike would not occur. There would always be sufficient gas available in the market to supply higher-valued uses. An open-carriage system allows the higher valued markets to be served promptly at a price closer to the long-run equilibrium price. In summary, greater reliance on shorter-term contracts will keep price fluctuations closer to long-run equilibrium values than the ''boom-and-bust'' pricing experienced under long-term contracts.

Another characteristic supposedly requiring long-term contracts is the capital-intensive investment in pipelines and LDCs. It is argued that because transmission lines are capital intensive, market specific, and immovable (economically), long-term reserves are necessary to protect equity capital and to attract debt capital. From the 1930s to the 1950s this probably was true. Relatively little was known of the extent and nature of gas formations. Gas often was produced as an accidental by-product of oil exploration and development. Consumer acceptance of gas had not been demonstrated. Pipelines were heavily leveraged with debt/equity ratios, as high as 90:10. Debt capital markets sometimes insisted on bond indentures requiring a specified reserve life index.

All of these conditions have changed. Geotechnical advances and consumer acceptance of gas have combined to promote the development of a large, sophisticated, and competitive gas-exploration industry. Although there is still considerable uncertainty surrounding projections of discoverable reserves, there is little doubt that major producing formations will be adequate for decades to come. Trunklines are largely amortized and pipeline-company debt/equity ratios are typically 50:50. Furthermore, the lead time from a decision to invest in exploration and development to commercial production is typically three to five years; thus the production market can respond to price signals that demand is increasing by developing more supplies in time to avoid significant shortages, even if most of the contracts are no longer than three to five years. Under these conditions, the argument that pipeline investment is specifically related to production from particular wells no longer holds.

Another justification for long-term contracts is that the FERC, and its predecessor, the Federal Power Commission (FPC), requires them before it will approve construction of pipelines. True, the FPC initially required pipelines to demonstrate a significant reserve-life index in certificate applications for new construction, and the production sector uncertainties of that era may have justified such a requirement to protect consumers' and LDCs' investments. As geotechnical and market developments improved, however, the FPC gradually reduced the reserve-life indices required to support pipeline construction and by 1976 had eliminated any specific requirement of a reserve-life index. Furthermore, the FERC more recently adopted new regulatory mechanisms to protect consumers without requiring long-term contracts. Under these regulatory changes, a pipeline company can opt to modify its business practice in order to assume the risk of diminished throughput.

Finally, long-term contracts are supposedly justified because they reduce the costs of negotiation. There is some validity to this argument. Given a significant short-term market to reference a market price under long-term agreements, price risks could be dealt with efficiently and the remaining risks of longer-term contracts might not be so great as to offset reduced transaction costs. Under these conditions, it would be reasonable to expect that a significant, but much reduced, share of gas would continue to be marketed under longer-term contracts.

But in the absence of a short-term market, the inefficiencies of the existing system of rigid contracts are likely to outweigh any savings in transaction costs. This is demonstrated by the fact that pipelines and producers have begun to negotiate price-redetermination, market-out, and other clauses that essentially reopen negotiations at intervals as frequent as every six months. These provisions effectively defeat most of the savings in transaction costs supposedly gained by long-term contracts.

In summary, long-term contracts for dedicated reserves are unnecessarily inefficient. Their prevalence derives from historical conditions, outmoded regulation, and industry tradition. Gas is a fungible commodity that can be traded under shorter-term contracts provided that regulation requires nondiscriminatory access to pipelines.

New Regulatory Policies Are Needed to Make Risk Allocations More Efficient

The Allocation of Risk through Direct Regulation Should Be Avoided

New market conditions create new opportunities for efficient risk allocation. In the absence of effective regulation, however, the ability of utilities to transfer risk to captive consumers creates an artificial incentive that ultimately forces captive customers to accept risks that would be borne more efficiently by producers. The effect of such action dampens incentives necessary for efficient purchasing and operating practices. Hence risk will not be allocated efficiently by private contractual arrangements absent effective regulatory intervention.

Public policy debate has focused appropriately on rules specifying risk allocations under contracts between pipelines and producers, such as limiting take-or-pay levels or placing limitations on the use of indefinite escalator clauses.

These efforts move in the wrong direction. They would introduce new rigidities that would interfere with efforts to allocate risk at the least cost to the superior risk bearer. Establishing a rule that take-or-pay levels should not exceed 50 percent, for example, would preclude different allocations for particular markets or would block the effects of individual attitudes toward risk, that, with the correct incentives, could establish a lower-risk premium and lower cost to consumers.

Even if regulators were able to develop contract risk-allocation rules more efficient than those established by an imperfect market, they could not respond dynamically to changed market conditions. Regulation directed to specifying take-or-pay levels and other purchasing practices is aimed at treating the symptoms of market disorders. This section advocates regulatory changes that overcome the rigidities caused by existing regulation by establishing incentives for the industry to use new market mechanisms to improve efficiency.

Regulation of Gas Marketing

Improving Risk Allocation by Controlling Monopsony Power

Current regulation attempts to control monopsony power only by preventing pipelines from charging more than they paid for gas. This dampens the incentive to drive down prices to producers, but not completely. The MFN and oil-parity clauses reflect the need for producers contractually to guard against opportunism. The best way to ensure efficient pipeline purchasing decisions without imposing regulatory distortions is to substitute competition for regulation of the purchasing-reselling or ''marketing'' function. At the pipeline level, marketing is potentially competitive because it lacks elements of a natural monopoly. But marketing can be monopolized if pipelines tie that service to transmission. Open-carriage regulation would eliminate the ability to link the sale and transmission of gas. All marketers—pipelines, independent resellers, LDCs, and end users—would compete in the marketing of gas; they would be forced by competition to offer terms that reflect the real risk preferences of their customers. By introducing such competition, regulation of pipeline purchasing practices could be minimized. Rate regulation of pipelines would be confined to transmission and storage, activities over which pipelines possess market power.

Such a strategy does not resolve the difficulty of how to regulate purchasing decisions effectively; rather, it transfers those difficulties downstream. Small consumers probably will have no choice but to rely on LDCs, which also possess market power, to perform the marketing function. This will necessitate the regulation of LDCs' purchasing decisions.[12] Nevertheless, this can be accomplished more effectively at the distribution level, for several reasons.

Under open carriage, large end-use markets could directly access the wellhead market and competitively bid against established marketers. This would contribute to the efficient ordering of the production market. The larger number of participants would lessen the distorting effects of inefficient purchasing practices and significantly reduce the potential for firms with affiliated production interests to distort the market. Open carriage also would make possible the development of significant spot and futures markets.

Strategies to Control LDCs' Allocations of Risk

There are further challenges in preventing local utilities from shifting to consumers risks more efficiently borne by producers. The best approach is for PUCs to control LDCs' purchasing practices by applying the prudence standard customarily applied to local utilities' purchases of unregulated commodities such as coal, fuel oil, or uranium. The prudence standard disallows passthrough of an operating expense if, considering all circumstances that prevailed when the costs were incurred that were known or capable of being known, the cost was unnecessary or extravagant. In applying this standard, regulators must be sensitive to market conditions; they would be assisted in this regard by market-generated data furnished by contemporaneous end-user transactions and by short-term contract and futures markets.[13]

The prudence standard is the regulatory tool that best approximates the dynamics of a competitive marketplace. Under competition, firms strive to improve net revenue and market penetration. A firm selling a product identical to that of a competitor but purchasing inputs at higher cost will face declining revenues. A utility marketing to a captive market is not self-regulating; the prudence standard provides the same incentives as would competition, since regulators can measure performance by the competitive yardstick.

An important feature of the prudence standard is that it looks back at completed transactions. Managers recognize that relaxing control over costs now may result in reduced earnings at the end of the next rate case, without knowing whether a specific transaction subsequently will be found imprudent. Under these circumstances, a manager's most efficient course is to be aggressive and vigilant in bargaining with suppliers for fear that the ''yardstick market'' may outperform him.[14] Yet because the standard does not specify which purchasing practices are prudent and which are not, managers would be free to exercise creativity and skill to develop purchasing practices that achieve optimal results.[15]

Despite the general recommendations above that public policy should not specify risk allocations, regulation should directly proscribe contractual allocations of risk that tamper with the incentive mechanism described above. An example of this is commonly called the ''FERC-out'' clause.[16] This clause provides that if the pipeline is denied passthrough of costs paid to the producer because the FERC deems them imprudent, the producer shall refund to the pipeline any amounts denied passthrough to consumers. In the absence of competition, this type of clause is objectionable because it ensures that the marketer will never incur a loss as a result of its contracting practices, regardless of prudence. It therefore defeats the positive incentives of a prudence review. If a prudence review is conducted, it shifts all of the risk of imprudent purchasing from the utility to producers and, if the imprudent purchases are not detected, to consumers.[17] As a result, consumers would pay more for gas than they would absent such a clause. Under a regime of open carriage, this should not be a problem at the pipeline level, since competitive pressures will force pipelines to purchase prudently. The "FERC-out" clause should be prohibited if LDCs adapt it to their purposes when they play the marketer role filled by pipelines (in which case the clauses will become known as "PUC-out" clauses).

Regulatory Strategies to Induce Efficient Transmission and Distribution

Currently, pipelines and LDCs are free to vary their target throughput level, which determines rate levels, by filing a new rate case, and at least until the case is decided, they may unilaterally establish higher rates based on lower throughput. In ruling on such adjustments, regulatory agencies typically permit adjustments to the throughput level based on factors affecting throughput, other than weather.

When throughput falls below previous levels, rates are increased. Consumers bear this risk. This is not unfair because when throughput is increased above expected levels, utilities must file rate reductions (spreading fixed costs over the greater throughput). This practice makes utility earnings more predictable than they would be if utilities bore the risks of diminished throughput. Presumably, the rate of return needed to compensate for investment capital would be higher if utilities rather than consumers bore risks associated with throughput fluctuations, because the expected range of returns would be greater even if the average expected return were the same. Thus under current practice, utilities bear the risk of earnings loss due to catastrophic events such as wars and a substantial market loss, but consumers bear most risks associated with returns on the utility investment that are affected by throughput.

One consequence of consumers bearing risks associated with returns on investment capital is the perverse price signals sent to consuming markets. When pipeline and LDC facilities are underutilized, the price of transportation increases, although economic theory holds that the utility would decrease prices to attract more business. Conversely, when utility facilities are used to their maximum or are oversubscribed, prices to consumers *decrease*, sending a false signal that the cost of using those facilities is lower than it is in actuality.

Signals to capital markets are similarly confused. Returns to two pipelines with throughput-to-capacity ratios of 50 and 100 percent, respectively, would be identical. Clearer signals would be sent about the value to investors of expanding capacity if returns to pipelines varied with capacity use. These higher returns would attract the capital needed to finance new construction or efficiency improvements.

The current method of allocating risks associated with the fluctuating value of investments in pipeline and LDC facilities is inefficient. Economic efficiency would be improved by placing these risks on utilities, the superior bearers of such risks, for several reasons.

First, because utilities would have significant incentives to maximize throughput, performance would be improved; it would therefore cost society less to transport and distribute gas if consumers directly compensated utilities for the added uncertainty of returns by paying higher prices than it would cost if consumers bore the risks and rewards of fluctuations. Second, because utilities can diversify risks at less cost, the price paid by consumers for investors to bear these risks will be less than the value to the consumer of not being subjected to such risks. Third, efficiency is furthered by improved price signals about the value of utility facilities. When throughput is low, rates will be the same as when throughput is high. Prices would not vary with changes in throughput. This is not the best signal to consuming markets because, ideally, prices should vary directly with throughput. It is the second best alternative, however, and a decided improvement over the current system in which price varies inversely with throughput. Finally, this alternative provides the correct signals to capital markets since net revenues to the utility will vary directly with capacity utilization.

A Regulatory Strategy to Shift Throughput Risk/Reward to Investors

An improved allocation of risk could be achieved by establishing the throughput capacity of a pipeline for rate purposes over a five to ten-year period. In rate hearings, the utility's rates would be calculated by dividing the revenue requirement by the previously established design throughput level. All else being equal, when actual throughput exceeded the design target, profits would increase above the authorized fair return, and when actual throughput fell short of it, profits would decrease below the authorized level. By freezing throughput levels for five to ten years, the utility would bear the losses and reap the rewards of diminished or greater revenues due to fluctuating capacity utilization of its facilities and would be induced to maximize throughput by minimizing costs and by aggressive marketing.

By placing all risks of changes in throughput on utilities, financial risks and rewards also would increase. Profits may decline due to secular and cyclical changes beyond a utility's control; conversely, they may increase due to changes in the opposite direction.

It is important to note here that the objective of regulatory change is not necessarily to balance returns over five to ten years. Due to unforeseeable changes, a utility may do very poorly or very well, just as a producer investing in development today may do very poorly or very well depending upon the relationship of market prices to fixed costs over the life of the investment. The current return allowed to the utility would be higher to compensate for the additional risk. Nevertheless allocative efficiency is improved because consumers are likely to pay less for gas and are relieved of fluctuations in prices due to business risks.

The purpose of limiting the period to five to ten years is to bracket the extent of risk borne by the utility, since at the end of the period, the utility could change the throughput level to reflect a persistent downward performance based on secular changes. Conversely, in a period of sustained economic growth, regulators could increase the throughput level. At the same time, five to ten years probably is long enough to ease concern that the utility is pursuing uneconomic long-run goals, such as inflating the rate base or mismanaging operating costs and marketing strategies.

During the five- to ten-year freeze period, the utility could file for and obtain rate increases due to changes in operating expenses or due to a general increase in returns to equity. But it could not increase or decrease the rate of return based on increased risks since the throughput freeze period began.

Contrary to the above conclusions, it has been argued that the essential nature of natural gas service to residential consumers requires that regulation provide stable earnings to investors to ensure continuity of essential services; it also has been argued that existing regulation promotes stable rates to consumers. This argument is not applicable to allocating risks of investments in production since producers do not have market power and are not regulated. Therefore, there is no need for regulation to set a floor price or otherwise interfere with the operation of the production market. As applied to pipelines and LDCs, the argument is premised on conditions no longer extant—that is, the extremely risky investments that characterize a new industry with an uncertain future. The natural gas industry is now mature: The expectation of substantial future supply and demand ensure its continued attractiveness to investors.

Conclusions

A change in regulation is needed to prevent utilities from inefficiently shifting to consumers risks that are more efficiently borne by utilities and by producers. This end must not be achieved by imposing rigid rules that will impair the flexibility that markets need to adapt to the complex and changing realities facing the gas industry; instead, regulation of pipelines and LDCs should be adapted to shift greater financial risks to the regulated portion of the industry, thereby inducing marketlike incentives that will unleash in regulated firms a spirit of creative enterprise. Only if this approach is pursued will the competitive production industry achieve its potential to maximize social welfare.

Notes

1. Technically, under state law an LDC's transmission and gas costs are subject to a prudence review, but federal constitutional principles prohibit the states from disallowing recovery of any expense approved by the FERC, which, in the interstate market, typically includes all of the LDC's gas and transmission costs, for example: *Nantahala Power and Light Co. v. Thornburg*, 106 S. Ct. 2349, 2354–57 (1986); *Narranganset Electric Co. v. Burke*, 119 R.I. 559, 381 A.2d 1358 (1977), *cert. denied*, 435 U.S. 972 (1978). This rule limits prudence reviews to choice among competing suppliers, which, absent open

transportation, has not been a significant factor. *Pike County Light and Power Co. v. Pa. Public Utility Comm.*, 165 A.2d 735 (1983).

2. In some circumstances, these criteria will be difficult to apply. Of the two parties to a given transaction, one may be the superior averter of risk, the other the superior diversifier or insurer. As between a driver and an auto insurer, for example, the driver is clearly the superior averter of risk, and the insurer is clearly the better diversifier. Allocating all of the risk to the driver would encourage maximum safety precautions but would sacrifice the welfare improvements that the insurer's diversifying abilities can provide. Conversely, allocating all of the risk to the insurer would provide maximum diversification but would eliminate some financial incentives for the driver to avoid accidents. Theoretically, under these circumstances the most efficient contract would isolate the sources of risk over which the driver could exercise control (e.g., alcohol intake and driving speed) and provide financial incentives, such as premium reductions, for risk avoidance in these areas. Risks deriving from sources outside the driver's control (recklessness of other drivers) would be borne solely by the insurer.

In practice, however, it is frequently impossible to determine at reasonable cost the extent of one party's control over a particular source of risk or to attribute a particular outcome to a specific cause. Tradeoffs between the utility gains associated with incentives to avert risks and utility gains associated with allocation of risk to superior diversifiers and insurers, therefore, are unavoidable. Under these circumstances the best attainable result divides between the parties those risks that can be efficiently reduced through behavior.

Economists investigating the welfare consequences of divided risk-allocation strategies have described the circumstances in which shared risk is appropriate as a "principal/agent" relationship. The "principal" shares in the risks associated with outcomes determined by both chance variables and the actions of a second party, the "agent." The principal/agent literature focuses mainly on the value of direct information (apart from information inferred from outcomes) about the level of effort expended by the agent (see, for example, Shavell "Risk Sharing Incentives in the Principal and Agent Relationship," *Bell Journal of Economics*, 10, no. 1, 1979, pp. 55–73; A. M. Spence and R. Zeckhauser "Insurance, Information, and Individual Action," *American Economic Review*, 61, no. 2, 1971, pp. 380–391). It has been suggested that the applicability of principal/agent theory to risk allocation in the natural gas industry warrants investigation (see H. G. Broadman, *Natural Gas after Deregulation*, Resources for the Future, Washington, D.C., 1983). As shown later in the text, the principal risks inherent in gas production, pipelining, and distribution are not risks that can be shared efficiently. The principal/agent literature is not applicable to the extent that it focuses on the optimal distribution of risks between parties, each of which is a superior bearer of components of a risk.

3. Opportunism or opportunistic behavior refers to extraction of rents from another person. A person is subject to opportunism risk when, for example, in the absence of effective contractual protection he commits significant *specialized* capital that is tied to trade with another person, for example, a producer who sinks 90 percent of the value of a well into development where the gas would have a below-market value unless a particular pipeline buys the gas or agrees to transport it to market.

4. For purposes of this analysis, the term *producers* includes exploration and development companies, operators and service companies, and royalty owners and mineral rights lessees. Although these categories are economically distinct in function and perhaps also in risk-bearing characteristics, and in some cases are not vertically integrated, they

are treated here as a single unit because they are part of a market segment subject to effective competition. Therefore, public policy safely may rely on competition to allocate efficiently among producers any risk associated with the economic interests of this group.

5. Many interstate pipeline companies are diversified into industries such as oil pipelining, gas production, barge operation, railroads, and farm equipment. Most finance capital requirements for all such ventures are on a consolidated basis through a parent holding company. The FERC thus far has used the cost of capital to the holding company as a proxy for the cost of capital of the regulated pipeline without adjusting for potential variations in risk levels of components of the unregulated enterprises.

State commissions or state statutes often prohibit the diversification by local utilities into unrelated businesses or sometimes into any unregulated venture. If state regulators were to adopt the principle espoused here of placing greater risk on local utilities of fluctuations in the value of investments in distribution, utility diversification might offer an attractive means to reduce rates to consumers through the lower cost of capital that may be obtained by diversified companies.

6. Here we are concerned only with contracts governing risks of production investment, as between producers, pipelines, and LDCs. Long-term contracts for the transmission of gas may be required between pipelines and LDCs to encourage investments in pipeline and distribution facilities, but these contracts need not (and for the sake of efficiency, should not) entail bundled commitments that coercively tie the contract length for transmission or distribution services to gas purchases.

7. Vertical integration is an alternative means for markets to overcome opportunism risk. Here are evaluated only the relative efficiencies of short- versus long-term supply contracts and the institutional and regulatory barriers to the use of shorter-term contracts. If the policies recommended here did not create the necessary efficiencies, the market might tend toward greater vertical integration as an alternative to long-term contracts (see Chapter 5).

8. If the older contracts subject to an MFN clause had nonprice terms that were more favorable to the producer, the producers under the old contracts would not be entitled to the higher price offered under the new contract. The MFN clause usually requires that the pipeline offer the combination of price and nonprice terms under the new contract to the existing contract holders.

9. A futures market would not allocate all of the risks of natural gas production and marketing. The longest period of trading authorized in a futures market is five years. Moreover, as the period established for future delivery increases, so does the risk premium. Thus a futures market would not be a mechanism for reallocating long-term price risks for gas supply.

10. Transportation has been available only on a limited basis, principally to serve end-use markets that have alternatives cheaper than the pipeline's supply. The blanket certificate regulations, under which 38 percent of interstate spot gas was transported in 1984, limited contract carriage to a two-year term ending June 30, 1985, for producer direct sales to fuel-switchable end users. Five- and ten-year terms were authorized for certain "high-priority uses." However, the high-priority uses are largely those that would displace a pipeline company's sales, and pipeline companies generally refused to transport under blanket certificate authorizations for producer direct sales that encroached on the pipelines' resale markets. Core-market restrictions under SMP orders, which limited competition for a pipeline's captive or nonswitchable markets, have had the same effect. In addition, much transportation has been available only for gas released from a pipeline's supply.

Such releases have been made for limited periods (one to two years) and are subject to recall by the pipeline if they are no longer deemed surplus. In addition, until 1986 transportation was also nearly always interruptible, which limited the reliability of the markets that could be served. Finally, because the transportation was made available during a glut market when new drilling fell off, almost all of the gas available to be transported was gas under contract to pipelines, which, as noted above, was released for limited terms and subject to recall.

11. See Chapter 2, Figure 2.1. Nearly 50 percent of industrial customers in 1983 were capable of switching from gas to fuel oil in the very short run, and 20 percent were capable of using three or more fuels.

12. Although the transaction costs of direct purchasing by small consumers on an individual basis are prohibitive, the possibility remains that a cooperative of small consumers or an independent marketer may be able to merchant gas to small consumers at reasonable cost. On the other hand, the transaction costs for purchasing on a household scale may be so significant that in many cities substantially all of a local distribution market would have to be served by a single marketer for the necessary economies of scale to be achieved, thereby precluding competition in marketing to this market segment.

13. Theoretically, a prudence standard could be applied to pipelines in lieu of an open-carriage policy, but this would be inferior to the arrangements proposed in the text because the end-user access and substantial spot and futures markets that depend on open-pipeline carriage would not be available to order the market and to generate market data for use in administering a prudence standard. Without open carriage, spot and futures markets could not develop adequately to promote price discovery and flexibility.

14. Another advantage of the retrospective prudency review is that it is seldom employed. The knowledge that it may be employed at any time in the future generally is enough to induce care on the part of managers. There are relatively few rate cases in which commission staff and intervenors challenge recovery of expenses on grounds of imprudence.

15. It is argued that the prudence standard unfairly exposes local utilities to unfair, politically biased, or negligent decisions by state regulators as to which costs may be recovered by ratepayers. Two observations are pertinent to this objection. First, it is much more valid when applied to a regulator's decisions concerning the inclusion of costs in the rate base of custom-built power plants, gas transmission lines, and so on, where the absence of a market price for the investment and the question of need for a long-term investment can make effective judicial control of unfair regulatory decisions a real problem. The problem of controlling unfair regulatory decisions is least when shorter-term purchases of commodities with competitive market prices are involved. Second, to the extent that some unfair or inefficient decisions are not judicially controlled, it is true that the system is inefficient. The question is what is the least inefficient means of regulating. (It is because regulation is far from perfect that it generally is reserved for industries with significant market imperfections.)

One fair argument posing this issue is whether federal regulation of pipeline purchasing decisions under a prudence standard (but automatic passthrough of amounts LDCs pay to pipelines) is a more efficient alternative. Those who argue that it is regard federal regulators as fairer or better qualified than state regulators. Against any greater efficiency on such account must be offset the inefficiency to the market when a single agency affecting the entire market errs occasionally but with nationwide effect compared with somewhat more frequent errors among some thirty state agencies, each of which affects a much smaller part of the market. Even if a strong case were made for federal standards, it would be better to allow LDCs to purchase gas directly and to subject LDCs' purchasing decisions to federal standards or regulation than to lose the competitive gains associated with LDCs' purchasing gas.

16. The ''FERC-out'' clause principally was used by the FERC-regulated pipelines in gas purchase contracts before the NGPA, which the FERC construed to require guaranteed passthrough of purchased gas costs regardless of prudence.

17. The device is objectionable for reasons other than its effect on incentives. The price paid to the producer implicitly includes a premium to compensate the producer for bearing the risk that the utility might get ''caught'' in a prudence review, triggering a refund by the producer. To begin with, the local utility already has been compensated for this risk in its overall return, so consumers probably are being charged twice for the same risk: once in the return on the utility's rate base and once as a hidden component of the purchased gas costs, which is passed through as an operating expense. Even assuming that an adjustment is made to the utility's return to reflect the reduced risk to it arising from the use of a ''PUC-out'' clause, allocative efficiency will be impaired because aggregate welfare would be improved if the utility rather than the producer bore the risk. The producer is the inferior bearer of this risk, since it does not have the same knowledge that the utility does of all of the surrounding circumstances of the utility's purchases, to determine whether in their light this purchase would be prudent. Therefore, the producer must charge more to bear the risk that the utility's contract is imprudent than the fair return to the utility for bearing that risk.

Selected Bibliography

Alchian, Armen A., Robert C. Crawford, and Benjamin Klein. ''Vertical Integration, Appropriable Rents, and the Competitive Contracting Process.'' *Journal of Law and Economics*, 21, 1978, pp. 297–326.

American Gas Association. ''The Changing Nature of Investment Risk for the Natural Gas Industry.'' Publication Number FA 83–3. Arlington, Va., 1983.

———, ed. *Regulation of the Natural Gas Industry*. Vol. 1, Matthew Bender and Company, New York, 1984.

Barlow, Connie C., and Arlon R. Tussing. *The Natural Gas Industry: Evolution, Structure, and Economics*. Ballinger Publishing Company, Cambridge, Mass., 1983.

Broadman, H. G. *Natural Gas Markets after Deregulation*. Resources for the Future, Washington, D.C., 1983.

''Columbia Gas Costs Exposure to Some Pacts.'' *Wall Street Journal*, November 13, 1984, p. 4, c. 1.

Interstate Natural Gas Association of America. ''1985 Effects of Decontrol: An Update on the Interstate Market.'' Report No. 85–2, Washington, D.C., 1985.

MacNeil, Ian R. ''Contracts: Adjustment of Long-Term Economic Relations under Classical, Neoclassical, and Relational Contract Law.'' *Northwestern University Law Review*, 72, 1978, pp. 854–901.

Means, Robert C., and Robert S. Angyal. ''The Regulation and Future Role of Direct Producer Sales.'' *Energy Law Journal*. 5, 1984, pp. 1–45.

Posner, R. A., and A. Rosenfeld. ''Impossibility and Related Doctrines in Contract Law: An Economic Analysis.'' *Journal of Legal Studies*, 6, 1977, pp. 83–118.

Shavell, S. "Risk Sharing Incentives in the Principal and Agent Relationship." *Bell Journal of Economics*, 10, no. 1, 1979, pp. 55–73.

Spence, A. M., and R. Zeckhauser. "Insurance, Information, and Individual Action." *American Economic Review*, 61, no. 2, 1971, pp. 380–391.

Sykes, A. O. "The Economics of Vicarious Liability." *Yale Law Journal*, 93, 1984, pp. 1231–1280.

Tussing Associates, Arlon R. "The Price Elasticity of Residential Gas Demand (The Dangers of a 'Death Spiral' for Gas Distributors)." *ARTA Energy Insights*, no. 4, Seattle, Wash., 1983.

U.S. Department of Energy, Assistant Secretary for Policy, Safety and Environment. *The First Report Required by Section 123 of the Natural Gas Policy Act of 1978*. Report No. DOE/PE–0054. U.S. Government Printing Office, Washington, D.C., 1984.

U.S. Department of Energy, Energy Information Administration. *Natural Gas Producer/Purchaser Contracts and Their Potential Impacts on the Natural Gas Market*. Report No. DOE/EIA–0330. U.S. Government Printing Office, Washington, D.C., 1983.

———. *Structure and Trends in Natural Gas Wellhead Contracts*. Report No. DOE/EIA–0419. U.S. Government Printing Office, Washington, D.C., 1983.

Williamson, Oliver E. "Transaction-Cost Economics: The Governance of Contractual Relations." *Journal of Law and Economics*, 22, 1979, pp. 233–261.

Comments

JOSHUA BAR-LEV
Attorney
Pacific Gas and Electric Company

Carmen Legato's description of the severe economic distortions in the natural gas industry during the 1978–1985 period is certainly accurate for the Northern California area served by the Pacific Gas and Electric Company (PGandE). There has indeed been a mismatch between the pre–1978 risk-allocation mechanisms in contracts and regulations governing production and marketing of natural gas and market conditions that developed after the Natural Gas Policy Act of 1978.

The mismatch has imposed high costs on all sectors of the industry. Legato assumed that producers and captive consumers with weak take-or-pay protections have primarily borne these costs. Yet no empirical evidence is presented to demonstrate how the costs of these distortions have been distributed in the industry, sector by sector. Shareholders in LDCs like PGandE have absorbed a substantial portion of the distortionary impacts through write-offs of prudent investments in abandoned projects, lower authorized rates of return, bond-rate reductions, and reduced revenues reflecting loss of markets due to high prices. Reduced revenues from loss of markets cannot simply be made up among remaining customers, since that would cause further loss of markets. A shrinking customer load due to increasing prices reduces LDCs' bargaining leverage with pipeline suppliers, brings about intense political criticism, and even threatens municipalization and annexation of portions of the service area. For example, during 1979 through 1984, PGandE's average price to customers rose 118 percent, and direct sales to customers declined from 600 to 431 billion cubic feet (Bcf), a 28 percent decrease.

PGandE has been more fortunate than most LDCs in realigning supply contracts to reflect current market conditions. Due to multiple supply sources (Canada, California, and the Southwest), PGandE has been able to renegotiate lower prices with pipeline suppliers. Thus between 1982 and 1986 it reduced its average purchase cost from $3.91 to $2.48 per million Btu. In 1985 alone, PGandE reduced gas rates by $502 million and increased gas sales for the first time since 1979, led by a 30 percent increase in industrial sales.

The severe economic distortions described by Legato are being corrected through a combination of federal and state regulatory initiatives and aggressive renegotiation of supplier contracts by pipelines and LDCs. For the future, Legato advocated a more passive role for PUCs; they should remain on the sidelines while earnings for LDCs and market prices for the consumer fluctuate widely in response to market conditions. Except through retrospective prudence reviews, he advocated that PUCs exercise no authority over LDC investment and operating decisions, on the premise that the cost to consumers and investors will be less in the long run than the present system. Finally, long-term contracts with LDCs' traditional pipeline suppliers should be replaced by short-term contracts with myriad producers and pipelines.

For sound public policy and political reasons, the present system of regulation of LDCs by PUCs is not likely to be modified as Legato advocated. There is reason to believe, however, that the "regulatory contract" will become considerably more maleable to accommodate near-term changes in the market. Adaptation is necessary for the traditional regulatory contract to survive the pressure from off-system market forces (see Figure 9.1).

Traditional regulation obliges an LDC to provide an adequate and reliable supply of natural gas at the lowest cost possible. Large investments must be planned and implemented by the LDC to serve its customers long before the actual supply and demand patterns are apparent. In return, its customers must pay for the costs the utility prudently incurs in planning and meeting such obligations.

A utility that turns out ex post to have made an unusually good investment will return most of the financial reward of that investment to the consumers, not its stockholders. In return, if an investment turns out ex post to have been prudent but unprofitable, the utility expects to be compensated for the cost of planning and constructing for the future needs of its customers. Without this basic understanding that the utility will be adequately compensated in return for making prudent investment and operating decisions, the utility would not be willing to plan and provide service on such a long-term, obligatory basis.

Contrary to Legato's assertions, LDCs are not riskless enterprises. In practice, the intended mutuality of obligation poses too many asymmetrical risks associated with the leaden and politicized regulatory process. For example, LDCs face lengthy, costly regulatory lags because the regulatory process does not match revenues with costs at the same point in time, as would occur in an unregulated enterprise. Recovery of long-term investments and the costs of short-term purchases of natural gas are subject to long procedural delays and disallowance of admittedly prudent costs. Often the critical issue in the proceedings, prudence, is subsumed by pressures on regulators to disallow costs to satisfy legislators or consumer groups. Utilities uniformly cannot recover the admittedly prudent and real carrying costs of abandoned plants (allowance for funds used during construction, for example) or a return on such amounts during their amortization period. Finally, regulatory agencies typically respond to "rate-shock" problems of new plants by reducing the return on utility investments. LDCs seem to earn higher returns when costs are stable or falling and demand is growing rapidly than when costs are rising rapidly and there is a perception of excess capacity.

In short, given the political and social objectives regulators superimpose over the long-term obligations of the utility, traditional regulation does not simulate well-functioning, short-term competitive markets. To achieve this, regulation must provide better financial incentives to induce cost-minimizing and short-

Figure 9.1
Forces Driving Industry Competition in Northern California Natural Gas Markets

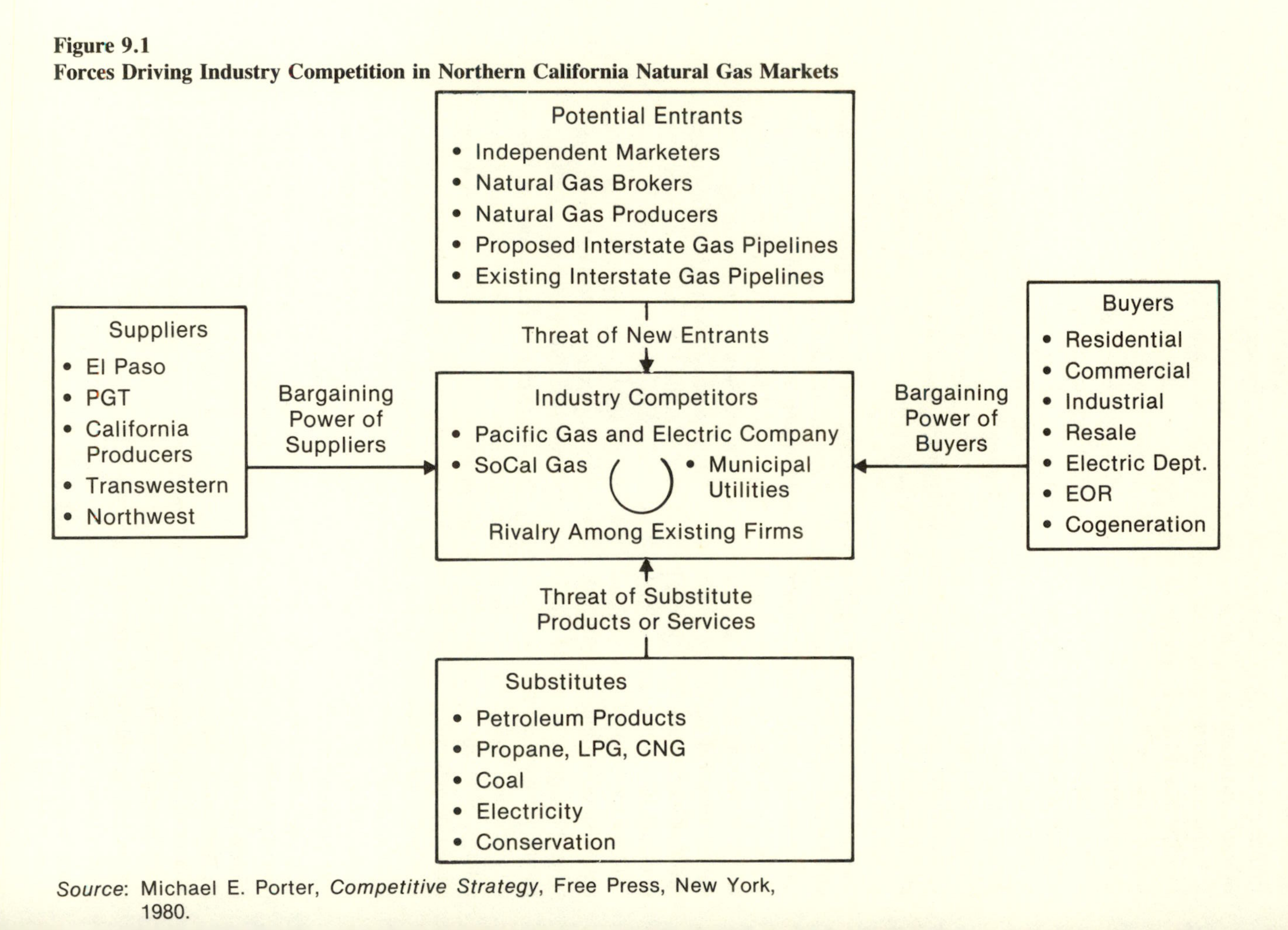

Source: Michael E. Porter, *Competitive Strategy*, Free Press, New York, 1980.

term and long-term investments. Such incentives can be effective only if they reflect the empirical evidence of competitive markets. Hence utilities must participate, and regulators must encourage them to participate in short-term markets. Second, customers who do not want to rely on and pay for the traditional long-term obligation to serve should be given an opportunity to exit the system in a manner that does not hurt the customers who remain. Increased freedom of exit can enhance efficiency in the regulated market and act as a barometer of competitiveness.

The effectiveness of these reforms depends largely on whether the private carriage regime continues on interstate pipelines or whether open carriage (as provided under the FERC's Order 436) is implemented on a long-term basis. If private carriage continues, significant pipeline power in LDC markets (even when more than one pipeline serves the market) will expose LDCs to greater opportunistic risk and more relationship-specific investment. When combined with the regulatory obligation of the LDC, longer-term reliance on spot purchases would be risky. Under an Order 436 regime, however, LDCs would be less exposed to opportunistic risk from pipelines, and long-term obligations could be met through diversifying short-term supply contracts.

However, all parties—producers, pipelines, LDCs, and consumers—continue to have a primary interest in preserving regulation (albeit more flexible regulation), because it ensures long-term reliability of service, stability of price, recovery of fixed costs, and operating efficiency. A continuation of long-term contract requirements is probably critical to ensure new investments in production to replace depleting reserves and major new investments in distribution facilities. Spot trading will be perceived as a less reliable source of revenue for suppliers, and will therefore not encourage the investment needed to satisfy LDCs' long-term obligations to retail customers. Furthermore, because of the politicized nature of PUCs, short-term transactions expose LDCs to more frequent prudence reviews and thus greater financial risk from hindsight judgments about proper conduct. The risk aversion of the various sectors of the industry means that long-term arrangements are likely to continue to dominate LDCs' supply portfolios. It is not clear, however, that regulators recognize the value of such long-term stability; nor have regulators adequately defined the future regulatory obligation of the LDC in this changing market. The California PUC exemplifies this ambiguity.

In December 1985 the California PUC issued Decision No. 85–12–102, which required the three LDCs to file tariffs providing for long-term (at least five years) intrastate transportation of customer-owned gas on a nondiscriminatory basis to all wholesale and retail utility customers who meet a minimum transportation volume of 25 thousand cubic feet (Mcf) per year. The Commission acknowledged that prevailing market forces had made intrastate gas transportation an attractive option for certain gas consumers for at least two years before the issuance of the decision. The FERC's Order 436 ensured that LDCs could purchase gas in the interstate market on a least-cost basis, with no minimum-bill costs. LDCs could thus participate in the burgeoning spot market alongside end-use customers, and they therefore would not be competitively disadvantaged by this intrastate transportation decision. Significantly, the Commission acknowledged that transportation for off-system customers could produce system efficiencies to benefit all gas ratepayers, such as direct transmission of price signals from the burner-tip to the wellhead, increased utilization of in- and out-of-state pipelines, and establishment of a competitive benchmark to evaluate the utility's own gas-purchasing practices.

The Commission set forth three guiding principles. The first is ratepayer indifference. Transportation rates should leave all gas ratepayers at least indifferent to whether any particular customer transports its own gas or purchases gas from the utility. That is achieved by setting the transportation rate at the equivalent margin existing in the current sales rate for that class. The Commission specifically rejected a cost-based transportation rate because it would have induced off-system customers to purchase gas supplies, even if they were more expensive than the utility's incremental supply. Second, the program was made comprehensive and available to both existing and incremental gas consumers. Finally, the program required long-term transportation agreements of five years or longer.

Three months later the California PUC issued Decision No. 86–03–057, which acknowledged that the natural gas market was changing so rapidly that its previous decision no longer enabled LDCs, such as PGandE, to be competitive. It recognized that a vigorously competitive commodity market was forming that would avoid the kinds of shortages that emerged in the 1970s under price controls, although at the risk of volatile price fluctuations. The Commission concluded that the changes in the market warranted a fundamental reevaluation of its regulatory policies. Indeed, with gas sales becoming increasingly competitive, the portion of the gas industry that remains a natural monopoly is transportation. Transportation is perhaps the essential business of the gas companies that the California PUC regulates. For customers who could participate in such commodity markets, the Commission concluded that the utility should separate its transportation service from its sales service; furthermore, even its sales service should be made flexible to accommodate the "firmness" of service desired by different customers.

Thus to meet such changes in the market, the Commission ordered utilities to file short-term transportation tariffs. It also rescinded its policy of obligating utilities to purchase sufficient supplies to serve most of the retail market. Instead, it divided all utility ratepayers into core and noncore segments. *Noncore customers* were defined as customers with access to other gas supplies through transportation. The LDCs were still obliged to buy gas supplies only for the core market and were still obliged to serve noncore customers only to the extent that they signed long-term sales contracts with the utililty. The Commission also proposed to "unbundle" gas rates to noncore customers and to use marginal costs to allocate fixed costs to the various customer classes. "Bundled" rates would be retained for core customers. The utility should offer gas to such noncore customers only at current prices for short-term supply. Indeed, the Commission anticipated that the price could be very high during periods of supply shortage and could even be unavailable; the utility would be subject only to a best-efforts obligation to serve such noncore customers.

A second reform advocated above is the accommodation of the remaining regulatory contract to current market conditions while preserving the long-term stable relationship between the LDC and its core customers. In California, both the PUC and PGandE recognize the need to balance short- and long-term objectives in making spot gas-purchase decisions in an uncertain gas market. In Decision No. 85–08–007, issued in August 1985, the Commission stated:

> In today's gas market, purchases of relatively low-cost spot gas provide short-term economic benefits to ratepayers and help minimize purchased gas costs. On the other hand, spot gas purchases may adversely affect the reliability and costs of long-term gas supplies. Like minimizing purchased gas costs, ensuring long-term supply reliability is an important goal that must be considered in any gas sequencing policy. We believe that the economic benefits from spot purchases must be carefully balanced against the long-term effect such purchases may have on the cost and reliability of more traditional gas supplies. At the present time, it is difficult to determine where the optimal balance lies because of the uncertainty and volatility in today's gas market.[1]

The search for the right balance is left to the discretion of utility management and is subject to Commission prudence review.

In its March 1986 decision (Decision No. 86–03–057), the Commission elaborated on the purchasing standards expected from the utility on behalf of its core customers. Utilities should adopt a "portfolio strategy . . . utilizing a mixture of short- and long-term contracts."[2] Utilities would have to justify their purchase strategy and demonstrate that a particular portfolio minimizes gas acquisition costs over the long term. The Commission acknowledged that long-term price stability benefits core customers, and this could only be accomplished through long-term contracts. However, it stated that utilities would have to carefully document ratepayer benefits associated with such long-term pipeline purchases: "Until we see substantial evidence that the pipeline's gas supply contract will actually guarantee future price moderation for core ratepayers when spot prices inevitably turn upward, we will remain skeptical of the reasonableness of utility reliance on higher priced pipeline supplies for service to the core market."[3]

Such reforms in the traditional regulatory contract between the LDC and the PUC are one means of adjusting to current market conditions. The lesson of the period 1978 to 1985 is that traditional regulation was too rigid. Nevertheless, regulatory reform will not, and should not, match the price terms and conditions of a perfectly competitive market. The purpose of regulation is not to simulate competitive markets perfectly but to pursue public policy objectives as consistently as possible with economic efficiency objectives. Thus in the post-Order

436 period, local regulators and LDCs will search for the new regulatory contract that integrates both the obligation to core customers and market risk.

Notes

1. Federal Energy Regulatory Commission, Decision No. 85–08–007, August 1985.
2. Federal Energy Regulatory Commission, Decision No. 86–03–057, March 1986.
3. Federal Energy Regulatory Commission, Decision No. 86–03–057, March 1986.

10

Getting Regulation from "Here" to "There"

GEORGE R. HALL

Introduction

In the future, the natural gas industry will be far more competitive than it has been in the past. This increase in the role of competition is in the public interest, and a major thrust of public policy should be to encourage further substitution of free-market forces for public intervention and regulation. However, government regulation and intervention will not disappear. Ironically, not less but more regulation may result from the increase in competition.

This increase in regulation does not imply that competition in the natural gas industry is a problem. To the contrary, more competition is part of the solution to the current ills of the industry. Dramatic changes are occurring, changes that will provide benefits but that will also create new and different challenges for state and federal regulators. Two immediate problems are galvanizing the industry and its regulators.

Out-of-Date Contracts and Prices at the Wellhead

Many contracts between pipelines and wellhead suppliers are out of line with current consumption and market realities. "Old gas" is priced far below "new gas" and far below the average, marginal, or replacement costs of gas. Contracts not only require pipelines to pay prices far out of line with current prices but include economically hazardous "take-or-pay" clauses that require pipelines to accept deliveries of gas or incur liabilities equal to the price of gas not taken. How can we move to more rational pricing arrangements in an equitable and lawful manner?

Out-of-Date Contracts at the City Gate

Many contracts and tariffs at the city gate were predicated on expectations of consumption levels higher than have been realized or are likely to be realized in the future. These contracts were also predicated on a regulated-monopoly type of industry rather than the emerging mixture of a part-competitive and part-regulated industry. How can new contracts and tariffs be designed so that they are more pertinent, while still providing appropriate levels of protection to consumers and investors?

In addition to these two immediate problems, two longer-term policy issues must be addressed before the industry will have completed satisfactorily the transition from the old regime to a new regime that better serves the needs of consumers.

Harmonizing Contract Carriage and Sales for Resale

The natural gas industry developed on the basis of private carriage. Today contract carriage plays a major and growing role. How can we move to a new mode of operation that encourages competition in the pipeline industry but still provides the requisite level of consumer protection?

Replacement of Long-Term Relationships with Short-Term Flexibility

Until recently, contracting and regulatory practices in the natural gas industry were predicated on long-term relationships. These relationships are now out of harmony with present and expected future market conditions. How can we equitably move from an industry and regulatory system based on long-term relationships to one based more on short-term relationships? How can we do this and still preserve the necessary protections to consumers provided by long-term contracts and certificates?

Fundamental Changes in the Natural Gas Industry

The natural gas industry is relatively young. The pipeline network developed in the late 1930s and 1940s; then, with the national pipeline network essentially completed after World War II, the industry grew rapidly in the following two decades, reaching its peak in 1973. This dramatic growth was followed by a sharp decline, a leveling-off period, another sharp decline, and recent sharp fluctuations. Figure 10.1 shows the annual production of natural gas from 1925 to 1985. The industry enjoyed high growth in demand, due to both low prices and the desirable characteristics of natural gas, until the regulation-induced shortages of the 1970s. Despite the curtailment problems of the 1970s, natural gas prices were held below those of competing fuels. This ensured that interstate

Figure 10.1
U.S. Marketed Production of Natural Gas: 1925–1985

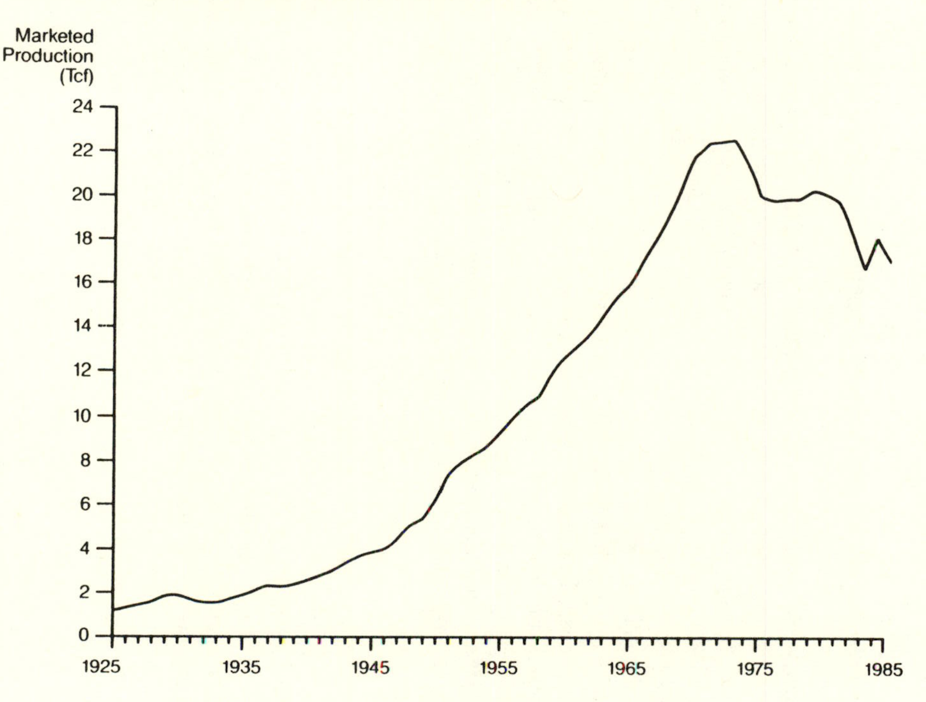

Source: Based on data obtained from: 1925-1948, U.S. Department of Commerce, *Statistical Abstract of the United States*, 1933, 1941, 1949, 1950; 1949-1972, U.S. Department of Energy, Energy Information Administration, *Annual Report to Congress, 1978*, 2 1978; 1973-1985, U.S. Department of Energy, Energy Information Administration, *Monthly Energy Review*, January 1986.

pipelines and the local distribution companies (LDCs) to which they sold gas could easily market whatever supplies they were able to obtain. This situation ended in the 1980s. The shift from an industry in which it was easy to market gas to one with slowly growing demand and intense competition is the most fundamental change that has taken place in the natural gas industry.

The low growth in demand and intense price competition prevailing since 1980 likely will continue through the next decade. The premium markets served by gas probably will demonstrate little or no significant growth, because of fuel conservation and other factors. Although there is the potential to expand applications for industrial uses of gas, interfuel competition is fierce and profit potential is limited.

In the early 1980s another important change took place. In prior decades, the industry was shaped by federal regulation at the wellhead and by an "add-on" pricing system; since the early 1980s, the industry has been governed by competition at the burner-tip and "netback" pricing. Figure 10.2 illustrates the differences between the two systems.

Under the add-on pricing system, the burner-tip price for natural gas was determined by taking federally regulated wellhead prices and "adding on" allowances to cover the costs of transmission and distribution. Under the netback system, prices are determined by competition at the burner-tip and the costs of transmission and distribution are subtracted to derive the wellhead price. The need to clear end-user demand markets by equating gas supply with gas demand (one margin) with supply and demand for alternative fuels (another margin) determines gas prices at the burner-tip.

The scheduled price deregulations mandated by the Natural Gas Policy Act (NGPA) of 1978 suggested that the switch from add-on to netback pricing would take place by 1985, but the change occurred sooner than anticipated. Many of the current problems faced by the natural gas industry represent its attempts to adapt to, or resist, this fundamental change in price determination.

The third important change followed the sudden and dramatic rise in energy prices during the 1970s. Before this, 70 to 85 percent of the costs charged to natural gas consumers went to cover payments for services rendered by pipelines and LDCs; today, about 50 percent of a customer's final bill goes to cover the cost of gas itself.

Regulation and the Natural Gas Industry

The natural gas industry comprises three basic sectors—producers, LDCs, and end users—linked by a fourth, the pipeline sector. Figure 10.3 illustrates these sectors and their integration.

Producers sell gas in the wellhead market, usually to pipelines. In recent years, however, direct sales associated with transportation for others (contract carriage) have increased the importance of brokers, LDCs, and large end users in the

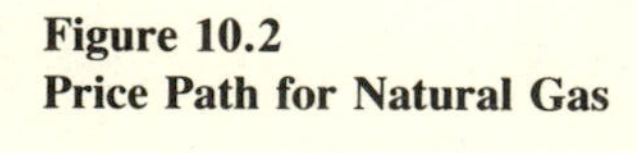

Figure 10.2
Price Path for Natural Gas

Add-on System (Regulated Field Prices)

+

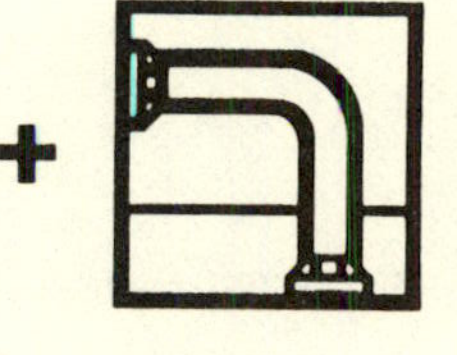

+

=

Consumer "Burner Tip" Price

Net-Back System (Unregulated Field Prices)

–

–

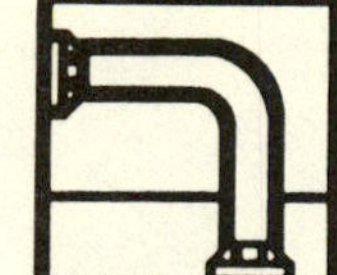

=

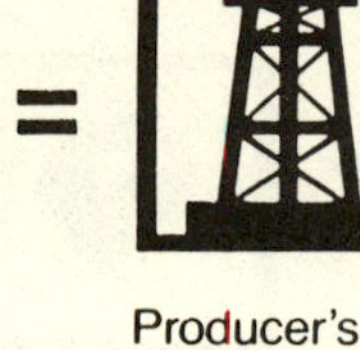

Figure 10.3
Natural Gas Markets

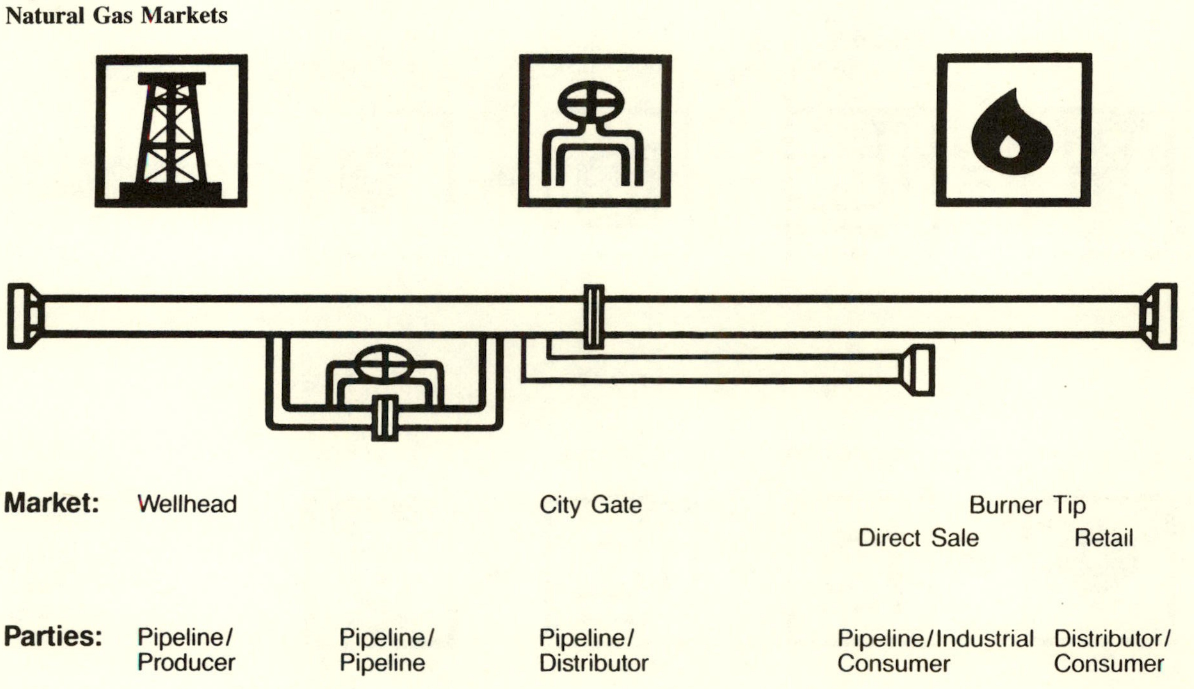

wellhead market. This change accounts for much of the increased competition in the natural gas industry since 1980.

LDCs purchase gas from pipelines in the city-gate markets and retail it to end users in the burner-tip market. LDC sales to end users account for most retail sales, although a small amount—about 15 percent—are made directly from pipelines to end users. The possibility that such sales will increase as a result of "bypass" and the regulatory response to bypass is an increasingly contentious issue and is addressed below. Pipelines may also sell natural gas to other pipelines. These sales are important in the integration of the natural gas industry.

Two features of the pipeline system should be noted. The first is that the interstate pipeline system (in contrast to the intrastate system, which is prevalent in states such as Texas) developed on the basis of long-term relationships. Regulators and investors wanted assurances that sufficient gas would be committed to a proposed system to justify investments, and producers wanted assurances of purchasing markets before committing future production.

The second feature is that pipelines developed as private carriers, rather than as common or contract carriers. This resulted from historical conditions, not from economic imperatives. The pipelines performed the long-term planning function for the industry and generally served as the balancer of supply and demand and as the seller of last resort.

Since January 1, 1985, the wellhead market has been partially deregulated. Remaining regulation of wellhead prices has been administered by the Federal Energy Regulatory Commission (FERC) pursuant to the Natural Gas Act (NGA) of 1938 and the NGPA of 1978. The FERC also regulates pipeline sales for resale and transportation for others pursuant to the same authority.

Pipelines are required by the NGA to file rates with the FERC, which determines whether they are "just and reasonable." Significant investments and initiation of new services require receipt of a FERC certificate of public convenience and necessity; abandonment of facilities and services also must be FERC-approved. The statutory standard is demonstration of public convenience and need.

The end-user market is regulated by state Public Utility Commissions (PUCs), which have authority over the margins of LDCs. In the past, PUCs have had little ability to control the cost of the gas sold by LDCs, because prices charged by pipelines were under the jurisdiction of the FERC. However, as wellhead deregulation and changes in FERC regulations reduce federal control, PUC review of how LDCs purchase gas will become a more significant state regulatory function.

The goals of pipeline regulation by the FERC—as they were for its predecessor, the Federal Power Commission (FPC)—are efficiency, equity, and competition. PUC emphasis on competition has varied. Many states grant exclusive franchises to LDCs; others allow competition. Interfuel competition has long been a factor in regulating LDCs, and in the 1980s PUCs adapted their regulations to allow LDCs to compete more effectively with sellers of other fuels.

With respect to efficiency, the major regulatory challenge is to set rates so that the regulated entity has a fair chance to recover the prudent and reasonable cost of providing service, including a fair rate of return on capital investments. Such cost-based rates are often referred to as ''just and reasonable'' (J&R) rates.

Once a rate is established, if the pipeline or LDC can increase throughput above the level used to establish the rates, it can obtain an actual return on equity greater than that allowed by the regulators in the determination of the rate. Alternatively, throughput lower than that estimated when the rate was set will have a negative impact on stockholders. As a result, regulation provides powerful incentives to maximize the amount of gas moving through a pipeline.

Competition is a priority public policy goal embodied in the requirement that the rates approved by the FERC serve the public interest. This fact has long been emphasized by the FERC and the FPC. Competition and regulation are two different ways to serve the same economic and social ends.[1] The courts have emphasized the importance of competition in the regulatory scheme for natural gas and its compatibility with the FERC's regulatory responsibilities.[2]

Regulatory commissions also determine rate designs—that is, how the recovery of the costs of providing service, particularly the fixed costs, will be apportioned among customers. Equity considerations play a major role in such decisions.

The earliest pipeline rates were based on the two-part demand/commodity concept, common in public utility regulation. The commodity component included the cost of the gas and the compressor fuel consumed to move gas through the pipeline. The demand component covered all other costs, mostly fixed costs.

In 1952 the FPC introduced the Seaboard rate design.[3] Fixed costs were divided equally between demand and commodity components. Put differently, 50 percent of a pipeline's fixed costs were allocated to customers on the basis of annual deliveries (commodity) and 50 percent on the basis of peak deliveries (demand). The concept motivating Seaboard was that all consuming sectors should bear some responsibility for fixed costs.

In 1973 the FERC switched to the United policy, in which 75 percent of fixed costs are allocated to the commodity component.[4] The concept motivating United was that, by increasing the commodity rate relative to the demand change, conservation of gas supply would be encouraged. The lack of supply rather than the lack of pipeline capacity was viewed as the factor limiting the availability of gas for consumption.

Recently, the FERC has moved away from using United and Seaboard rates to using modified fixed-variable rates. These are similar to the conventional two-part rates discussed earlier, but some fixed costs are left in the commodity charge as an incentive to maximize throughput.

In contrast to pipeline rates, two-part rates have been extremely rare at the burner-tip. The standard LDC rate has been a one-part volumetric rate. However, as end users take advantage of alternatives to purchasing gas from the LDC serving its applicable geographic area, the need for demand charges has become a pertinent issue. We may expect to see the development of two-part or even more complex rate designs on the local level during the next few years. An associated and major emerging policy issue is how to determine demand or standby charges at the retail level.

In recent years, interfuel competition for the price-sensitive boiler-fuel load has led many PUCs to allow LDCs to quote flexible rates to industrial and electric utility customers. In some jurisdictions, PUCs have permitted the indexing of gas prices with oil prices. One way of interpreting this development is that the deregulation of retail gas prices to industrial customers has begun. An equally plausible interpretation is that public utility regulation of industrial gas sales is shifting from control of prices to control of profits (or contribution to overhead). Either way, this marks a major transformation in the regulation of industrial gas pricing.

If LDCs are to compete effectively with fuel oil and coal, pricing flexibility is essential. On the other hand, this creates obvious ancillary difficulties for LDCs and PUCs. For example, residential and commercial customers (and their PUCs) will have concerns about cross-subsidization that favors industrial users. Yet for years local rates have favored residential and commercial customers.

LDC and pipeline regulation usually has been based on "rolled-in," or average-cost pricing. Until recently, wellhead prices under both the NGA and NGPA used a vintage pricing system in which the lawful price in part was determined by when a well had been drilled. The FERC has decided to "devintage" some gas, but there still will be differences in prices among wells. Usually, the prices of gas from different wells are averaged and the buyer pays the weighted average cost of gas (WACOG). Cost-of-service calculations and rate designs for pipelines and LDCs generally have resulted in prices based on average costs rather than marginal or incremental costs. Increasingly, at both the local and state level, competitive forces will place pressure on the tradition of average cost pricing.

The FERC's Reformulation of the Regulatory Scheme

In recent years, the FERC has emphasized the importance of competition in natural gas markets. Recent FERC actions to increase competition culminated in Order 436.[5] On May 30, 1985, the FERC issued a 195-page Notice of Proposed Rulemaking (NOPR). The NOPR outlined a comprehensive plan by the FERC to restructure natural gas regulation in light of the partial deregulation of wellhead prices. The Final Rule was issued October 9, 1985, and the program commenced November 1, 1985.

In most industries, a fundamental restructuring of regulation such as that proposed in the NOPR would be legislated by Congress. Since 1954, however, natural gas regulation has been an exceptionally contentious public policy issue, which Congress has been extremely reluctant to address. This perceived reluctance prompted the FERC to take the initiative in restructuring natural gas regulation.

The NOPR proposed a comprehensive reform package consisting of four basic changes:

1. A simplified program allowing transportation (contract carriage) by interstate pipelines of gas owned by others on an "open-access," voluntary basis and an associated reduction in LDC contract demand levels
2. A "buy-out" program for wellhead contracts to respond to take-or-pay liabilities of pipelines to producers
3. A program to expedite the process by which pipelines obtained certificates of public commerce to build new facilities
4. A new design for pipeline rates consisting of a "block billing" scheme for gas costs

The FERC does not have authority to require interstate pipelines to transport gas for others, so the major aspects of the NOPR program had to be voluntary. However, the FERC's ability to decline to issue alternative "blanket" certificates for transportation in today's competitive environment calls into question the label of "voluntary."

A pipeline volunteering for the Order 436 program is relieved of various regulatory requirements. In exchange, it has to provide nondiscriminatory access to its transportation facilities and set maximum and minimum rates for both firm and interruptible service during peak and off-peak periods. These latter rates must be on a one-part volumetric basis.

A participating pipeline also has to agree to permit any LDC it serves to reduce its contract demand (CD) level—the maximum amount of gas the pipeline is obligated to provide—by 100 percent over five years. If an LDC exercises this option, the pipeline is allowed to abandon service to that LDC to the extent of the reduction. Many pipelines argue that if the pipeline participates in the Order 436 program, current customers will exit the system, although the pipelines still would have contractual take-or-pay obligations to suppliers. To address this take-or-pay problem, the NOPR proposed a "safe-harbor" arrangement in which a pipeline would be encouraged to "buy out" uneconomic producer contracts; the NOPR provided a relatively high assurance that these costs could be passed through to consumers.

Order 436 did not comprehensively and simultaneously address all of the problems addressed in the NOPR. It withheld the FERC intervention in several key areas. For example, Order 436 dropped the "safe-harbor" proposal with respect to take-or-pay buy-outs. Pipelines protested this action, arguing that they had no assurance that they could negotiate their way from under the burden of their take-or-pay obligations to producers, which would be increased if LDCs reduced CD levels.

The block-billing provisions contained in the NOPR were not implemented but were renoticed for further comments. Opposition was substantial, and block billing is unlikely to be implemented.

Order 436 promulgated most of the NOPR's proposals for expediting the awarding of certificates to build new facilities. Fears were expressed that this would be used by pipelines to "bypass" LDCs and take away customers. The FERC responded by stating that it would not protect LDCs from competition by pipelines.

The NOPR clearly was envisioned by the FERC as initiating a new regulatory era predicated on extensive competition. The first reaction of pipelines was to reject it, arguing that Order 436 made the four industry problems listed earlier worse rather than better. Only one pipeline announced participation soon after the promulgation of Order 436. A few others joined several months later. As time passes, however, more and more pipelines either are accepting the Order 436 program or developing broad open-carriage programs "in the spirit of Order 436."

It seems likely that by end of 1986, either the Order 436 program will attract widespread participation or, alternatively, the FERC will allow "do-it-yourself programs"—"Order 436-like" programs developed as a result of settlements among pipelines and their customers. In any event, it is certain that a new mode of operation is emerging, based on greater competition and greater reliance on contract carriage.

Problems in Getting from "Here" to "There"

Contract Adjustment in Wellhead Markets

Wellhead prices reflect, on the one hand, the below-market prices of vintage price regulation and, on the other hand, the above-market prices and high deliverability obligations pursuant to contracts entered into when expectations about energy were far different from the present. Order 436 did nothing about regulated below-market prices and backed off from the NOPR's proposal of federal intervention in the take-or-pay problem.

Take-or-pay clauses require either that a pipeline accept deliveries of some defined amount of gas or pay if it does not. Under the latter option, a pipeline has make-up rights; during some defined period it can still take delivery. Because of this right, take-or-pay payments are treated as prepayments (investments) for gas to be delivered later, and they are placed in the rate base. Carrying charges on such costs are allowed to be passed through to customers.

There are two disparate viewpoints, both valid, about the seriousness of the take-or-pay liabilities pipelines face. The first is predicated on the fact that producers and pipelines generally have been able to reach adequate agreements about past liabilities, so that the costs of prepayments now included in the rates on most pipelines are manageable. The second viewpoint is predicated on the fact that producers generally have been unwilling to waive take-or-pay rights for the future.

Thus if one looks at current rates, only a few pipelines are in serious gas-marketability difficulty as a consequence of take-or-pay payments to producers. However, if one looks at the potential contract liabilities of pipelines as regards future payments, particularly if demand does not permit make-up of past deficiencies, the potential liabilities are a nightmare.

The ultimate solution is recontracting to bring future liabilities into line with present and future competitive conditions. A high degree of risk is inherent in the natural gas industry's operating with a netback pricing system driven by competition in end-user markets where there is substantial gas-on-gas and interfuel competition and where consumption is affected by weather and business cycles. Most of this risk ultimately will have to be borne by unregulated entities—producers, buyers, and end users—rather than by the regulated pipelines and LDCs, because the unregulated entities have opportunities to make large "windfall" profits. In contrast, the "upside" profit potentials of regulated entities are constrained.

Low-growth, competitive end-use markets will not support all of the existing legal claims on pipelines by producers. Thus renegotiation of both price and future take-or-pay liabilities is an economic imperative. The NOPR safe-harbor arrangement, which assured pipelines that payments made to extinguish take-or-pay provisions would flow through to end users, was flawed in that it obscured the fact that many current contracts are out of line with competition in end-use markets, a netback pricing system, and the inherent pressure for risk and rewards to move to the wellhead. Thus the FERC's abandonment of the safe-harbor provision was understandable. Less understandable was the FERC's failure to implement some of the alternative proposals, such as that requiring producers participating in open-carriage programs to renegotiate contracts. Such a requirement would have produced significant leverage to obtain renegotiation of future claims. In the absence of such leverage the contract adjustment process is exceedingly slow.

The basic economic argument for the FERC intervention in the renegotiation process is that take-or-pay liabilities create such constraints that pipelines cannot react to the emerging competitive market. Moreover, in a low-growth, price-competitive environment, pipelines are in a poor position to offer quid pro quos when they renegotiate contracts. The recent FERC decision to devintage wellhead prices reduces the ability of pipelines to "roll in " high-priced gas with low-priced gas and further reduces pipelines' negotiating positions. Pipelines point out that in a world of netback pricing, there is no assurance that feasible end-user prices will permit recovery of the carrying costs on prepayments. Also, the ability of a number of pipelines to take the prepayed gas within the allowed period becomes increasingly questionable as each day passes.

The basic argument against federal intervention is a pragmatic one. Renegotiation is done on a contract-by-contract basis. This requires patience, individual attention, and an abundance of "hands-on" experience. The process is one of hard, behind-closed-doors negotiations and compromises. These are tasks for which federal agencies are singularly unsuited because of their organization, lack of ''hands-on'' expertise, and procedural requirements. Administration of any regulatory involvement in the take-or-pay adjustment process would be extremely difficult. Pragmatically, the FERC intervention would permit pipelines and producers to look to a third party—the government—to solve their problems. In sum, the cast against federal intervention is the more persuasive. The FERC reluctance to intervene is understandable. If the policy of relying on the self-interest of the industry to resolve the contract-renegotiation problem is not successful, however, some FERC action restricting open access to pipeline services to those producers that have granted future take-or-pay relief to their pipeline purchases seems an indicated federal response.

Looking beyond the immediate take-or-pay problem, a portfolio approach toward gas-supply acquisition by pipelines is required to balance price against take-or-pay liabilities. Pipelines should be willing to provide the cash-flow protection that take-or-pay contracts guarantee if they are associated with price concessions or price advantages granted by producers. Alternatively, producers desiring ''top'' prices should be willing to allow pipelines to ''swing'' on their gas production. In the future, producers and pipelines likely will spend considerable effort designing contract portfolios that will balance cost-flow-production desires and risk-exposure preferences.

Long-term contracts will be rare, if not extinct, in the future. The only certainty about the future of the natural gas industry is that it will be uncertain. This perception has motivated the building of considerable flexibility into contracts executed in recent years through devices such as market-out clauses and renegotiation arrangements that essentially convert long-term contracts into short-term relationships.

Turning to the problem of below-market prices, for almost four decades vintage-price regulation has been the crux of the natural gas problem. A vintage-price scheme for wellhead regulation was adopted by the FPC following the Supreme Court's decision in *Phillips Petroleum Company v. Wisconsin* and retained by Congress when it legislated the NGPA. Vintage pricing means that current transactions reflect prices and costs that prevailed in prior years, not current prices and costs. The vintage-price regulation built into the current regulatory system by the NGPA has created a ''gas cushion,'' consisting of the difference between average gas prices and the price of ''old gas.''

The cushion is unevenly distributed.[6] A pipeline that is abundantly endowed, and that was motivated by strategic considerations, might use this cushion to increase market share. This fact greatly complicates the problem of implementing ''fair competition'' on a ''level playing field.'' More fundamentally, the diversity of prices at the wellhead, many of which are below the replacement cost of gas, leads to inefficient decision making.

There are three basic policy options for dealing with the below-market price aspect of the wellhead contracts problem: (1) continuing the current practice of one-block rolled-in prices, (2) adopting the block billing plan proposed by the FERC Docket RM85–1, and (3) deregulating old gas.

The option of continuing the present practice of single-block rolled-in pricing is essentially a choice to live with the status quo. Each pipeline would have a cushion available to use as best fits its strategy in dealing with past customers on-system, new customers off-system, or with producers. In particular, each pipeline would have the widest possible ability to offset or cross-subsidize high-priced gas sources. The main appeal of this option is that it does not require regulatory changes that would be difficult or impossible to implement.

The second option was proposed by the FERC in the NOPR and would have involved implementing two pricing blocks for gas. Block 1 would have consisted of purchases of ''old'' gas, and Block 2 of ''new gas.'' Existing LDC customers of each pipeline would have received an entitlement of Block 1. Block 2 prices would, in effect, have been deregulated and priced at the pipeline's discretion.

The block-billing concept was an attempt to distinguish between gas priced at or near replacement cost and gas priced far below current market levels or costs. The rents and quasi-rents associated with the old gas would have flowed through to consumers in order to provide a ''level playing field'' for competition. When Order 436 was promulgated, block billing was not included due to the extreme opposition it engendered when proposed in the NOPR. Although a new round of comments was requested, no one expects that the FERC will implement the proposal. Thus block billing is more a historical curiosity than a meaningful policy choice.

The third option is to eliminate the cushion by deregulating old gas. The Reagan administration has consistently supported total natural gas decontrol and in the spring of 1986 proposed a decontrol bill, but congressional action is unlikely. Congress still remembers the pain involved in producing the NGPA. At that time the industry and gas consumers were in such dire straits that something had to be done regardless of the pain. Current problems, difficult as they are, do not reach that level of misery. Congress sees the natural gas industry as ''working'' in that gas supplies are abundant and prices are falling. Today, to reproduce the agony and error that characterized the process of producing the NGPA in order to create a ''level playing field'' for fair competition or to improve economic efficiency is not an enticing prospect to legislators.

There is no way ''merely'' to decontrol old gas. Any legislation changing the NGPA will bring up for possible legislative enactment the entire agenda of disparate actions that the various entities in the industry desire. The lack of an industry consensus on legislative change means that action is unlikely. Nor is there a way to control the legislative process when natural gas is involved, as the NGPA proved. The result of an old gas decontrol bill is impossible to predict. Finally, in an era when gas priced on a rolled-in basis is at the market-clearing level or above it in burner-tip markets, it is hard to generate much congressional enthusiasm for raising the price of some sources of gas at the wellhead. Either prices to consumers will increase, making marketability harder, or, the much more likely scenario, some wellhead prices will have to decrease to allow the prices of below-market gas to increase. Certainly, the owners of the gas whose price will have to decline will not be pleased with that result. All of the economists in the world lecturing on allocative efficiency are not likely to generate much congressional enthusiasm for taking money from some gas producers to give to other gas producers, when it is likely that some money will slip out of the pockets of ultimate consumers in the process.

The Secretary of Energy and the Department of Justice have asked the FERC to take administrative action that would have many of the same pricing consequences as legislative deregulation of all gas production. The basic concept would be for the FERC to set just and reasonable rates for regulated new gas equal to deregulated or market-clearing rates and to devintage old gas prices.

The difficulty with setting regulated prices equal to market-clearing prices is that J&R is a "term of art." "Just and reasonable" refers to cost-based rates, and the costs are the average, historical costs that created so many problems before the NGPA substituted congressional incentive rates for J&R rates based on average historical costs. Rates can be adjusted by the FERC from an average historical basis to account for noncost factors. Nonetheless, J&R rates cannot be, as the Department of Energy argues, simply equated with market-clearing rates. There is too much legislative, judicial, and regulatory history on the point to permit the FERC to take the action that the Reagan administration desires and deregulate old gas by rule making.

Also, it is dubious that a FERC decision could appear soon enough to help the industry deal with its problems. A full-blown econometric discounted cash flow study has become the standard for establishing J&R rates for old gas. Such a study takes years to conduct. The Reagan administration suggests such that an analysis can be side-stepped, but would the courts agree?

Judicial review is a certainty. Until the full rate-development and judicial-review processes were completed, there would be considerable, counterproductive uncertainty about future wellhead prices. Such a cure for the industry's pricing problems likely would be worse than the disease.

Devintaging old gas is a separate issue. The FERC has decided to change the long-standing policy of regulating wellhead prices on a vintage basis. The argument is that vintage price regulation is not required by statute or the J&R concept but is a "policy decision" that can be changed by the FERC. Devintaging lessens the disparities among pipelines in the old-gas cushion and reprices much old gas now selling below market levels. In effect, instead of passing the old-gas cushion through to end users as block billing would do, some of the cushion will accrue to old-gas owners, largely at the expense of new-gas owners. Devintaging does not address the basic economic concerns of those who have advocated complete wellhead price deregulation. Devintaging also will have the side effect of placing more pressure on gas selling at high prices, and, therefore, it will exacerbate take-or-pay problems.

In short, the old-gas cushion produces efficiency and competition problems. History suggests that congressional decontrol is unlikely, though not beyond possibility. Block billing is highly improbable. The most likely course of action is continuation of the present system with or without devintaging, depending on whether the FERC's recent action passes judicial review. In time, old gas will disappear. Until then we likely will have to live with the problems created by past wellhead regulation.

Contract and Tariff Adjustments in City-Gate Markets

Most contracts between pipelines and LDCs were formulated during periods of rapid growth in demand or during supply shortages. When they were entered into, LDC purchases from pipelines and LDC sales to end users were almost the exclusive mode of business. These conditions no longer apply and relationships between LDCs and pipelines need to be redefined.

This process is already underway. In Order 380, the FERC eliminated minimum bills for the commodity cost of gas. The Order 436 changes—particularly the ability of LDCs to reduce CD obligations and to substitute transportation—represent a further, basic restructuring of the relationships between pipelines and LDCs.

The FERC does not have the option of merely exercising a general oversight role for contract adjustments at the city gate. Many of the problem arrangements are embodied in the FERC tariffs or certificates. The NGA rate case system of regulation creates a forum, as well as requiring that the FERC address the public-interest effects of the relationship between pipelines and LDCs. Competition is a major aspect of the public-interest standard and one that is particularly important today.

It is doubtful that many LDCs will seek to eliminate entirely their contract obligations. We almost certainly will see CD reductions to reflect current economic conditions and demand expectations and, possibly, some further reductions to permit a mix of pipeline purchases and transportation. It seems unlikely, however, that LDCs will choose to rely exclusively on the direct-sale market or that PUCs would allow LDCs to do so even if they wished.

Reducing contract demands frees pipeline capacity, which pipelines then can use to make firm transportation agreements with end users. Thus reductions in CD levels make it easier for end users to compete directly with LDCs. LDCs are not likely to reduce their contract demand levels and encourage their competitors. Instead, LDCs probably will push their supplying pipeline for rights to transport gas on favorable terms within CD levels. Thus as can be seen from these incentives, Order 436 does not end the arguments over transportation policy.

One problem of the relationship between pipelines and LDCs is bypass of LDC facilities by pipelines that choose to serve large end users directly. Order 436's streamlined certification procedures and the FERC's announced unwillingness to protect LDCs from competition beyond the city gate creates tempting opportunities for pipelines to "cherry pick" attractive industrial customers away from LDCs. This process has already begun.

Bypass serves competitive efficiency if a pipeline can service a large customer directly while using fewer resources than would be required if the consumer were served by the pipeline and the LDC in combination. However, if the pipeline, by virtue of having its fixed costs covered by CD obligations, has a competitive advantage over the LDC or if the LDC is unable to compete effectively because of PUC-required rolled-in pricing, bypass will be attractive to the pipeline and end user but will be uneconomic from a social point of view. Neither Order 436 nor the other procompetitive actions to date answer the question how to distinguish desirable from undesirable bypass.

From 1980 to the present, intense controversy has revolved around access to the interstate pipeline system. Order 436 and follow-on measures currently under consideration are bringing this dispute to a much lower level of intensity and importance. A host of vital questions remain to be resolved in pipeline rate cases, but public policy issues now are shifting to the burner-tip market, where new competition implies new relationships and new rates. The relationship between pipelines and LDCs can no longer be described as exclusively vertical; instead, it involves horizontal competition, so new regulatory and contracting forms will be required. Fixed-cost minimum bills and demand charges may not be compatible with the new competitive relationship and with actual or potential bypass. Also, the new relationship must accommodate the economic and regulatory changes that have taken place in recent years. Order 436 should be seen as the prelude to this process of adjusting LDC and pipeline relationships, not the finale.

Harmonizing Contract Carriage with Private Carriage

The interstate pipeline industry will provide more transportation for others than in the past. Order 436 provides a general outline of the new regulatory regime, leaving the details to be worked out by the FERC in individual rate cases. These details will determine the nature and extent of competition, as well as the relationship between transportation for others and sales for resale. Moreover, resolving these issues will require the FERC and PUC intervention into new areas of pipeline and LDC activities.

To illustrate, consider an issue that arose when Columbia Gas Transmission Corporation and Columbia Gulf Transmission Corporation joined the Order 436 program. Order 436 requires access on a "first-come, first-served" basis. But how is "first come" measured? If it is measured on the basis of who was using the Columbia system in the past, only LDCs will have rights to most of Columbia's pipeline capacity. If it is defined as "first come" at some post-Order 436 point in time, end users have equal rights with LDCs. Resolving this and similar operational issues will require increased regulatory attention by the FERC to details of pipeline management.

This example also shows that the future is likely to see increased conflict between end users and LDCs over pipeline rate matters. End users are interpreting

Order 436 as a charter to allow them all of the rights of access to interstate pipeline systems presently enjoyed by LDCs. LDCs, in contrast, believe their past support of the pipeline network, their general obligation to serve retail customers including "captive customers," their long-run commitments both to pipelines and to end-use markets, and their rights under contracts should give them priority over end users. LDCs are not likely to surrender their rights of access to pipeline capacity, even if it means paying sizable CD or capacity-reserve charges.

Pipelines will continue to provide a substantial amount of gas to LDCs through conventional sale-for-resale transactions. The natural gas industry developed on a private carriage basis. LDCs and end users have depended on "merchant" pipelines both to balance long-term reserve needs with short-term supply requirements and to meet surges in demand, to offset unexpected supply problems, and to serve as "sellers of last resort."

Pipelines are the entities best suited to act as wholesalers. They are large enough to capture economies of scale and scope, and they have the advantage of decades of experience. Most LDCs and large end users still look to their traditional suppliers—the interstate pipelines—to be long-term, viable, healthy, and efficient and to perform their traditional merchant role.

In Order 436 the FERC responded to the need for harmonizing contract carriage and sale-for-resale business by permitting LDCs unilaterally to reduce contract demand levels to zero and by mandating guaranteed transportation services. Contract demand levels are out of line with current economic conditions, but it is very unlikely that LDCs totally will eliminate CDs. The pipeline system is not going to shift from one in which sales for resale are dominant to one in which open access to transportation services is the standard mode of operation. Rather, pipelines will provide a mix of both types of services. Therefore, the issue is how can sale-for-resale transactions and transportation-for-others services be harmonized?

The key is rate reform. The contract carriage issue is rapidly changing from one of access to one of transportation rates. The basic issue for the FERC and the PUCs is the following: Should the rates for transportation services be based on some marginal-cost calculation of transportation services, or should they recover the same margin to the LDC that comparable sales rates provide? If the answer is a marginal-cost calculation, what costs should apply?

In proceedings in which only transportation rates apply and sale-for-resale rates are in effect, the transportation rate should consist of the fixed charges contained in the commodity rate and any pertinent compressor-fuel allowances. That is, it should be a simple margin rate. The transportation rate should be structured to be as similar as possible to the implicit transportation rate embodied in the sale-for-resale rate. If the transportation and sales rates are not the same, customers will play "rate-arbitrage" games. They will decide to use the transportation tariff or the sales tariff when, due to vagaries of regulation, the price is cheaper under one tariff than under another, although the identical gas is moving through the same compressors and pipes under both tariffs.

When a regulatory commission considers all of a pipeline's rates, the problem is more difficult. The fundamental concern should be to structure, simultaneously, transportation and sales rates that will stimulate the maximum efficient use of the pipelines. Modified fixed/variable rates for sales have significant advantages in this regard. However, if pipelines are competing with their LDCs, it is hard to see the justification for one competitor paying another a demand charge or fixed-cost minimum bill. Volumetric rates may be required to provide a fair basis for competition between pipeline and LDC.

A major issue in setting transportation and sale-for-resale rates simultaneously is which costs should apply to which customers. End users that directly access pipelines are likely to argue that they are marginal users of the system and should pay only incremental costs, which are small, but if transportation is available to all, it is hard to justify such a viewpoint. Traditional rolled-in pricing is implied.

In contrast to the likely movement from two-part to one-part pipeline rates due to competition between pipelines and LDCs, in burner-tip markets a movement is likely from one-part volumetric rates to two-part demand/commodity rates. LDCs that face competition as a result of bypass will seek some standby charge to reflect the likelihood of end users turning back to sales from LDCs if economic conditions change. This raises the issue of long-term obligations in dynamic markets, to which we now turn.

Long-Term Obligations in Dynamic Markets

The end-use natural gas market is now a short-term market characterized by price and volume variability. Yet LDCs and pipelines have contracts that bind them to long-term, stable commitments. Any business that "sells short" and "buys long" in today's environment is in an untenable situation. This brings us back to the need to revise contracts. The need for wellhead contracts to reflect the inherent risk of the new competitive environment facing the natural gas industry has been discussed earlier. This section concentrates on the contractual relationship of pipelines and LDCs.

The variability in prices and volumes in the end-use sector and increasing competition for industrial fuel markets have increased risks in the retail gas market.[7] Regardless of regulatory authorization granted by PUCs to LDCs to quote flexible prices at the burner-tip, reasonable rates of return on capital will not be achieved by LDCs and pipelines if end-user prices are out of line with final demand realities. Therefore, rates of return allowed by regulators for pipelines and LDCs will have to reflect their risk exposure, which is greater than it has been in the past.

Beyond rate of return, there is the broader issue of long-term obligations between LDCs and pipelines. The intensive gas-on-gas competition in gas markets suggests that obligations to serve will have to be replaced by more explicit contract, tariff, or service agreements defining the gas supply obligations of pipelines. A vital aspect of the new obligation-to-serve scheme must be a more explicit understanding with respect to pipeline pricing policies. It is unrealistic in a competitive market to believe economic efficiency will be served by allowing pipelines to pass forward the cost of gas that is priced out of line with the cost of gas from alternative sources. In turn, pipelines and the producers from which they buy will have to rely on price competitiveness rather than the obligation-to-serve commitment and contract demand obligations on the part of LDCs to ensure recovery of the pipelines' fixed obligations to producers.

PUCs are becoming more involved in LDC pipeline purchasing and pricing decisions.[8] In the past, PUCs generally deferred to the FERC regulation with respect to prices of gas purchased by LDCs. Deregulation of wellhead prices, changes in pipeline regulations, and the increased mix of LDC supply options have changed this. PUCs must confront such issues as whether LDCs are assuming an inappropriate amount of risk or are being sufficiently aggressive in seeking bargains. This new regulatory challenge has serious risks. If PUC oversight becomes ''heads-you-loose/tails-you-also-loose,'' or ''Monday-morning quarterbacking,'' the ability of LDCs to use competition to benefit consumers will be deterred. At worst, there could be counterproductive conflict between federal and state officials over regulation of gas prices.

LDCs looking to pipelines to provide guaranteed long-term supplies must be willing to obligate themselves to cover a fair share of pipelines' fixed costs. This implies an obligation to pay demand charges, not only now but in the future, regardless of the gas an LDC actually takes from a pipeline. It is the future commitment that distinguishes long-term transactions from spot transactions. Pipelines that have future assurance that all or most of their fixed costs will be covered are more likely to provide economical and assured sources of gas supplies and transportation over the long term. Conversely, pipelines that seek to compete with their LDC customers by bypass cannot reasonably expect to enjoy the competitive benefits of having fixed costs assured by demand charges and minimum bills. Moreover, LDCs face difficult problems in relying on a competitor for long-term ''merchant'' gas supplies. Pipelines soon will face hard choices about the tradeoff between these competitive and merchant roles in the overall gas industry.

In sum, relationships between pipelines and LDCs based on the old concept of a long-term obligation to serve are incompatible with present market realities. The new relationship must be based more on explicit pricing understandings, and those understandings will be of much shorter duration. Also, if pipelines decide to compete with LDCs for customers, the advantage of obligations by customers to cover pipeline fixed costs may have to be foregone. Finally, federal and state regulation increasingly will be focused on the supply acquisition policies of pipelines and LDCs, including risk exposure and competitive relationships.

Conclusions

The fundamental economic and regulatory changes taking place in the natural gas industry have greatly increased competition. These changes have benefited the consumer. Nonetheless, the changes do not solve all of the problems faced by natural gas markets, nor do they eliminate the need for regulation. Indeed, further regulatory reform is needed, especially reform of pipeline rates to ensure harmony between transportation-for-others and sales for resale. Equally important is the renegotiation of contracts at both the city-gate and wellhead ends of the pipeline. A framework for the former exists. The latter problem remains a critical concern. Government intervention would probably exacerbate the problem rather than aid in its resolution, but intervention may come if all else fails. In any event, with or without governmental assistance, pipelines, producers, and LDCs must reach accommodation soon if the transition from "here" to "there" is to be accomplished effectively.

Notes

1. *Northern Natural Gas Co. v. FPC*, 399 F.2d 953; *City of Florence v. Alabama-Tennessee Gas Pipeline Co.*, 24 FERC 61, 395.

2. *Northern Natural Gas Co. v. FPC*, 399 F.2d 953; *Maryland Peoples Counsel v. FERC*, 761 F.2d 780.

3. This rate design takes its name from an FPC decision in *Atlantic Seaboard Corporation*, 11 FPC 43 (1952).

4. This rate design takes its name from an FPC decision in *United Gas Pipe Line Corporation*, 50 FPC 1348 (1973).

5. FERC, *Regulation of Natural Gas Pipelines After Partial Wellhead Decontrol, Final Rule and Notice Requesting Supplemental Comments*, Order No. 436, Docket No. RM85–1–000 (1985).

6. See the comments of the Natural Gas Supply Association filed in the FERC Docket No. RM85–1–000 (1985).

7. Charles D. Stalon, "Distribution Utilities after Wellhead Deregulation: Pricing and Regulatory Problems," Unpublished paper, February 1983; idem, "Adjusting to the Economics of Natural Gas: A Statement of Issues," Address to Center for Energy and Environmental Management, Washington, D.C. October, 1983; Milton Russell, "Adjusting the Gas Industry to Fluctuations in Burner Tip Demand," *Public Utilities' Fortnightly*, October 27, 1983.

8. Carmel Carrington Marr, "On the Spot in the Spot Market," New York State Public Service Commission Speech to Twelfth Annual Rate Symposium, Arlington, Va., February 18, 1986.

Index

Contributors

JOSEPH P. KALT, a coordinator of the Natural Gas Project at Harvard, is a professor at the John F. Kennedy School of Government.

FRANK C. SCHULLER, a coordinator of the Natural Gas Project at Harvard, is currently a professor at the Amos Tuck School of Business at Dartmouth College.

COLIN C. BLAYDON is Dean of the Amos Tuck School of Business at Dartmouth College.

HARRY G. BROADMAN is a lecturer in the Department of Economics at Harvard and an adjunct lecturer at the John F. Kennedy School of Government. He is also a research fellow at the Energy and Environment Policy Center at Harvard.

GEORGE R. HALL is Vice President of Charles River Associates.

WILLIAM W. HOGAN is the director of the Energy and Environmental Policy Center at Harvard and a professor at the John F. Kennedy School of Government.

HENRY LEE is the executive director of the Energy and Environmental Policy Center at Harvard.

CARMEN D. LEGATO is a partner in the law firm of Swidler, Berlin & Strelow in Washington, D.C.

JOHN C. SAWHILL is a director in the international management consulting firm of McKinsey & Company.